MANAGEMENT CONTROL

Theories, Issues and Practices

Edited by

Anthony J. Berry, Jane Broadbent and
David Otley

MACMILLAN

First published 1995 by
MACMILLAN PRESS LTD
Houndmills, Basingstoke, Hampshire RD21 2XS
and London
Companies and representatives
throughout the world

ISBN 0–333–57242–4 hardcover
ISBN 0–333–57243–2 paperback

A catalogue record for this book is available
from the British Library.

10   9   8   7   6   5   4   3   2   1
04   03   32   31   00   99   98   97   96   95

Printed and bound in Great Britain by
Antony Rowe Ltd
Chippenham, Wiltshire

MANAGEMENT CONTROL

Theories, Issues and Practices

To those who have supported us throughout the project and
continue to give us their support

Contents

Preface

Following the publication of two monographs, *New Perspectives in Management Control* (Lowe and Machin, 1983) and *Critical Perspectives in Management Control*, (Chua, Lowe and Puxty, 1989), members of the Management Control Association conceived the idea of collaborating to produce a textbook. The book was intended to provide a broader and more flexible text on management control that those which were available at the time. The book which we have produced reflects this original aim, along with the interests and idiosyncracies of the various contributors. As such it should not be seen as providing the last or the definitive word on management control, but instead as a starting-point. The book does accept that managers are central in the process of managing, but it does not accept the concept of 'managerialism' uncritically. It seeks to provide ideas which will stimulate a wider search for knowledge, rather than close down possibilities.

The book is aimed at those attending both MBA and specialist masters courses as well as advanced undergraduate courses. It should also provide food for thought for practising managers. We do not aim to provide a prescriptive and structured course outline, but to provide a resource which can be 'dipped into' on a flexible basis. The volume falls into three parts, each with a rather different focus and each of the chapters is self-standing and can be amalgamated into courses to suit individual preferences.

In Part I, the aim is to extend the boundaries of management control and it therefore explores the various approaches to control which have been adopted by those writing on the subject. In Chapter 1 we examine the domain of organisational control, focusing on systems approaches. Chapter 2 reviews some of the approaches to control which have their roots in organisational literature. In Chapter 3 the way in which organisations and tasks are structured in order to achieve control is discussed, while Chapter 4 looks at the more detailed procedures which can be used. Finally in this Part, chapter 5 explores the context in which control exists. It discusses the extent to which organisations are constrained by external forces yet are able to reject or buffer the effect of unwanted changes.

It should be stressed that Part I does not seek to prescribe the 'one best way'. We do not believe that this is possible. Thus the material merely seeks to show the various dimensions of control which need to be considered by the practising manager as well as the different ways in which control can be conceived. Our hope is that a greater set of possible solutions can be generated as wider understandings are achieved.

In Part II we narrow the focus rather more and examine particular issues of control which may be encountered in various different types of organisation. Again we do not pretend that the list is exhaustive of the issues which could be raised, but we do feel a range of topical and relevant areas have been addressed. Chapter 6 examines the general use of one of the most pervasive tools of control, accounting. Chapter 7 reviews the issue of how to control in divisionalised companies and Chapter 8 examines issues of strategy. In Chapter 9 the issues of controlling companies which exist in close relationships with others, those which are embedded in production chains, is addressed. The contribution that economics can make to control is examined in Chapter 10. In Chapter 11 the use of performance indicators as a means of control in the public sector is the area for discussion. Chapter 12 reviews the literature which has seen culture as either a means to control or an element which impinges on the possibilities of achieving control. Following on from this are two chapters which consider the impact of another culture, the Japanese, on controls in particular situations. Chapter 13 looks at the way Japanese subsidiaries operating in Europe are controlled and Chapter 14 takes a broader look at the extent to which it is possible to speak of a 'Japanese approach' to control.

Part III is more specific again, this time focusing on control in particular organisational settings. The settings chosen represent a variety of contexts and the different authors have taken a variety of approaches. Some chapters are stand-alone case studies whilst others combine case material with more theoretical reflection. The five chapters cover the airline industry, the NHS, schools, financial services and manufacturing. Finally, Chapter 20 reflects on the book as a whole.

There are other issues which the book has not been able to cover. Issues of gender and power are ones which we have not addressed directly and no doubt many other aspects could be listed. The two monographs mentioned earlier cover important areas and readers are recommended to explore these books to fill in some of the omissions or to delve more deeply into other topics of interest. We have also sought to provide a comprehensive bibliography to enable deeper study of particular areas. Let us stress once more that this book is merely a starting point, offering some ideas about organisational control, but never pretending to have all the answers. The sheer complexity of human society and the creativity of individuals suggests we never will have all the answers to achieving total control. Our belief is that this is probably a good thing.

In writing this book we have had the support of a great number of people. Direct contributors are listed separately and our debt to them is obvious, but there are others who have given background support and assistance without which we could not have completed this project. Mandy Lowndes has provided secretarial support cheerfully and efficiently and David Simon has patiently read and commented on early drafts of some chapters. Members of the Management Control Association have commented on other chapters which have been presented at some of our regular workshop meetings. Our thanks go to everyone concerned.

ANTHONY J. BERRY
JANE BROADBENT
DAVID OTLEY

Notes on the contributors

Makoto Abe is Associate Professor in the Economics Department of the University of Oita in the South of Japan. By training and background, he is a specialist on labour and employment relations in Japanese manufacturing. His interest in comparative studies was stimulated by a year's sabbatical in Britain.

Toshio Aida is Professor in the Sociology Department at Hosei University in Tokyo. His activities and publications span a broad range in the social sciences. At present, he is particularly interested in Japanese overseas manufacturing and the changing balance between Japanese direct investment in Western market access and in Asian low wage production.

Anthony J. Berry is Senior Lecturer in Management Development in the Manchester Business School, which he joined after some years in the British and the American aircraft industries. His research interests are management development, consultancy and management control.

Jane Broadbent is a lecturer at the Sheffield University Management School, where she teachers Management Accounting and Management Control. Jane is a member of the Chartered Association of Certified Accountants, a qualification gained whilst working as an accountant in the National Health Service. Her research interests focus on the reforms in the public sector and the role of accounting in promoting change.

M. Broadbent holds the post of Head of Department of Accounting and Finance at Manchester Metropolitan University. He is a Fellow of the Chartered Association of Certified Accountants. He has written texts in managing financial resources and cost and management accounting. His research interests focus on the interface between accounting mechanisms and management control systems in large organisations.

Alan Coad is a Principal Lecturer at Sheffield Hallam University. Formerly a management accountant in both private and public sector organisations, his main research interests lie in exploring the interrelationship of strategy and management accounting.

J. Cullen is Principal Lecturer in Management Accounting at Sheffield Hallam University. He joined the university in 1983 after working in several line management and senior management posts in industry. He is the co-author of a book called *Managing Financial Resources* and has written numerous case studies, articles and chapters with other colleagues. His current research interest include the impact of environmental uncertainty on management control systems, the links between management control systems and strategy, management control systems in multinationals, management control systems in small businesses and issues surrounding business failure situations.

Istemi S. Demirag is Lecturer and Grant Thornton Fellow in Accounting and Financial Management at the Sheffield University Management School. His current research interests include financial aspects of innovative management, strategy and performance evaluation and management in multinational companies. He lectures in financial accounting and management of international business.

David Dugdale holds the post of Associate Dean in the Bristol Business School, a faculty of the University of the West of England, Bristol. He spent sixteen years in industry before joining Bristol Polytechnic in 1987. CIMA-qualified, Dr Dugdale has worked as a management accountant in industry and has developed several research interests in the field of management accounting. Working with Colwyn Jones he has published a number of papers in the professional and academic press. Together with Colwyn Jones he Ras a current research project on 'Throughput Accounting'.

T. Colwyn Jones is Principal Lecturer in the School of Sociology, and Research Fellow in the Centre for Social and Economic Research (CESER) at the University of the West of England, Bristol. Since 1975 he has been teaching sociology to accounting undergraduates. He is the author of an undergraduate text, *Accounting and the Enterprise: A Social Analysis* (1995) and a number of papers (many with David Dugdale) on accounting rationality, accounting and technology, investment appraisal, and change in costing systems. His current research focuses on the role of management accounting in changing manufacturing organisations, especially the development of 'Throughput Accounting'.

Colin Haslam is Reader in the Business School at East London University. Before studying under John Williams at Aberystwyth, he worked for British

Nuclear Fuels and has published on nuclear waste. He leads the statistical work for team research with John and Karel Williams which benefits hugely from his unequalled grasp of official sources.

Kim Langfield-Smith is a Senior Lecturer in the Department of Accounting and Finance at Monash University, Clayton, Australia, with main teaching interests in management accounting and control systems. Prior appointments were at the Universities of Melbourne and Tasmania. Before entering academic life she worked as an accountant in several commercial organisations. Her research interests are in the area of management control systems. Current topics include studying the interface between business strategy and management control systems, and investigating new developments in performance measures. She has publications in journals in both the accounting and management fields.

Itsutomo Mitsui is Professor in the Economics Department at Komazawa University in Tokyo. He has mainly researched the problems of small and medium enterprises and the organisation of supplier networks. As well as writing for an academic audience, he has acted as consultant and adviser to Western organisations such as the European Community. This is the second project on which he has collaborated with Colin Haslam and Karel Williams.

David Otley is KPMG Peat Marwick Professor of Accounting at the Lancaster University Management School, and General Editor of the *British Journal of Management*. He has taught and researched management control for many years and is joint author (with Clive Emmanuel and Ken Merchant) of the text *Accounting for Management Control* (1990). His current interests are in the use of performance-related pay, and in the impact of corporate strategy on management control systems design and use.

Derek Purdy is Reader in Accounting at the University of Reading. His work has been published in a wide variety of journals which relate accounting and management issues. He has published extensively about accounting for convertible debt. His main research interest lies in the effects of financial management accounting data upon people, their organisations and control issues, generally construed from a psychological perspective.

Willie Seal graduated in economics from the University of Reading and worked for Touche Ross as an articled clerk. He has lectured at Bath, Nottingham Trent and Sheffield Hallam Universities. He is now Research Leader in Management Accounting and Corporate Finance in the School of Financial Studies and Law at Sheffield Hallam University. One of his main research interests has been the application of institutional economics to accounting and management control (which was the subject of his doctoral thesis). More recently he has led a research project on accounting in the Czech Republic and the relationship between management control and professionalisation in UK banking.

Peter Smith is Senior Lecturer in Economics, Finance and Accountancy at the University of York. He has worked in local government and at the University of Cambridge medical school. His research interests are public sector efficiency and public finance, topics on which he has published extensively.

Kim Soin is a researcher in management accounting at Sheffield Hallam University. Her primary research interest is activity based costing in the UK financial services sector.

C. Wilkinson is the Deputy Director (Academic Affairs) of Southampton University Management School. Prior to this appointment in 1993, he was a Lecturer in Accounting and Finance at Lancaster University for seven years. His role at Southampton University Management School is the organisation and management of the full-time and part-time MBA programmes and teaching courses in the areas of accounting and finance, control and strategic planning systems. His research interests are focused upon the design of control systems, particularly the development of organisational and managerial performance measures and reward systems.

Karel Williams is a Reader in the Department of Accounting and Finance at the University of Manchester. He studied nineteenth-century history and published *Pauperism to Poverty* (1981) before being radicalised by British deindustrialisation and taking up contemporary issues through team work with Colin Haslam and John Williams.

John Williams has recently retired from a chair at the University of Wales, Aberystwyth, after some thirty years as historian of industrial South Wales. He has published extensively on South Wales coal-mining and edited the standard collection of Welsh historical statistics. Since *Why are the British Bad at Manufacturing?* (1983) he has worked mainly on more current issues with Karel Williams and Colin Haslam.

Acknowledgements

The editors and publishers wish to thank the following for permission to reproduce copyright material:

Harvard Business School Case Services, for Figure 7.1, from B.R. Scott, *Four Stages of Corporate Development – Part I* (1971); Basil Blackwell, for Figure 7.3, from M. Goold and A. Campbell, *Strategies and Style: The Role of the Centre in Managing Diversified Corporations* (1987); *Harvard Business Review*, for Figure 7.2, from R.S. Kaplan and D.P. Norton, 'The balanced scorecard – measures that drive performance' (1992), © the President and Fellows of Harvard College, all rights reserved; Pitman, for Figure 8.1. from R.D. Stacey, *Strategic Management and Organisational Dynamics* (1993); *Accounting, Organizations, and Society*, for Figure 12.1, from E.G. Flamholtz, T.K. Das and A.S. Tsui, 'Toward an integrative framework of organisational control' (1985), for Figure 12.2, from J.G. Birnberg and C. Snodgrass, 'Culture and control: a field study' (1988), and for Figure 12.3, from R. Simon, 'The role of management control systems in creating competitive advantage: new perspectives' (1990); Sage, for Box 12.1, from G. Morgan, *Image of Organisation* (1986). Simon & Schuster, for Box 12.4, from R.T. Pascale and A.G. Athos, *The Art of Japanese Management* (1981); Melbourne Case Study Services, for Box 12.6, from A. Sinclair and J. Baird, *SPC: New Deal* (n.d.); Prentice-Hall, for Box 19.2, from A.G. Hopwood, *Accounting and Human Behaviour* (1974); Penguin Books Ltd for an extract from *The Art Japanese Managment* by Richard Tanner Pascale and Anthony G. Athos (Allen Lane, 1982); Elsevier Science Ltd for an article from Long Range Planning, vol. 20, no. 5, pp. 42–52: 'Managing diversity: strategy and control in diversified British companies's by M Goold and A. Campbell (1987) and extracts from Accounting Organizations and Society, vol. 10, no. 1; vol. 13, no. 5; and vol. 5, no. 2; An earlier version of Chapter 9 was published in the Leadership and Organisational Development Journal, 15 July, 1994, with permission.

Every effort has been made to trace all copyright-holders but, if any have been inadvertently overlooked the publishers will be pleased to make the necessary arrangement at the first opportunity.

PART I

Theories of Control

CHAPTER 1

The domain of organisational control

Anthony J. Berry, Jane Broadbent and David Otley

Introduction

Organisational control concerns everyone. Whether you are a manager attempting to run a department, a politician trying to frame legislation to control multinational corporations, or just an individual affected by the activities of the many organisations that have an impact on you, organisational control is a fundamental issue of modern life. In what ways are organisations controlled? By whom and how? And how can we influence what they do? These are some of the questions that this book tries to answer.

We shall approach the topic in a questioning and critical fashion, although primarily from the point of view of a manager who has a role in an organisational hierarchy. What control mechanisms are available to managers and how may they best operate the levers of power? But in trying to answer these questions we shall also need to adopt the points of view of other organisational participants and ask how controls affect what they do. Indeed control systems often take on a different complexion when viewed from the perspective of those being controlled rather than that of those doing the controlling. In addition, we will sometimes step outside the organisation and address the issue of corporate governance, or how organisations themselves are controlled by external interest groups. But our discussion will centre on the use of controls by managers within organisations, a topic which has become known as management control.

Many people have attempted to define the term 'management control' and we shall examine some of the alternative definitions that have been proposed in this and subsequent chapters. But for the moment let us begin with a simple but widely applicable definition: 'Management control is the process of guiding organisations into viable patterns of activity in a changing environment.' Thus managers are concerned to influence the behaviour of other organizational participants so that some overall organisational goals are achieved. Of course, this does not preclude managers from taking other actions that advance only their own personal self-interest, and which may even detract from overall goal achievement. Nor does it imply that organisational goals are fixed or even well understood by most participants. But, without some control mechanisms, organisational behaviour would degenerate into a composite of unco-ordinated activities that are unlikely to possess the cohesion necessary to allow continued organisational survival.

As can already be seen, discussion of organisational control raises fundamental issues concerning the nature of human organisations and the activities that occur within them. These issues cannot be avoided, although it is all too easy to let such debate prevent discussion of the more practical issues of control systems design and implementation. We shall attempt to steer a middle course by pointing out issues and problems as they arise, yet continually keeping in mind the central aim of this book, namely, to set down some of the principles governing the design and use of managerial control techniques within managed organisations in both the public and private sectors.

The domain of control

In analysing a controlled system, it is first necessary to define the boundaries of that system. These boundaries are not laid down by some external agency, but are open to definition by the analyst. Thus we may choose to consider the control of an individual, either by themselves or by some external agent, the control of a group of people, the control of an organisation or the control of a whole society. Secondly, it is necessary to consider who is exercising control. Again this may be an individual or an organisation; or it may even be an organisation apparently exercising self-control through a set of designed control mechanisms that relate to no easily defined individual or group. The boundaries of the controlled system and those between controller and controlled are thus essentially arbitrary, but they are not unimportant. Some ways of looking at a system may be more helpful than others, so it is up to the analyst to make an appropriate choice.

In general we will draw our systems boundary around an organisation as a legal entity, but there will be occasions when we wish to include within our boundaries groups such as customers or creditors who would usually be considered as external to the organisation. We will also generally consider the controller to be a manager or a group of managers, such as a board of directors. But we would wish to emphasise that these are arbitrary choices which can be varied if a more fruitful analysis can be obtained thereby.

There is also the question of what the system's goals are. In what sense do organisations have goals and how can we establish what they are? This has been an issue of considerable interest to organisation theorists, but no conclusive answer has been reached. In a well-known article, Cyert and March (1963) assert: 'Individuals have goals; organisations do not', although the remainder of that article is devoted to discussing how the concept of an organisational objective can be made meaningful. Certainly there is great difficulty in coming to any conclusion on the issue. Whose goals are we considering and how stable are they over time? What agreement is necessary between participants before we can accept a goal as belonging to the organisation rather than to a group of individuals within it? Indeed who should be regarded as participants and who are external parties?

One solution was provided by Barnard, in his construct of the purposive organisation. Another answer was provided by Cyert and March themselves, who spoke of the goals of the 'dominant coalition' as being essentially the goals of the organisation. While it would be too limiting to believe that any organisation had only one purpose or, indeed, that the only purposes of members of organisations were those of the dominant coalition, it is a helpful notion to regard organisations as purposive. In that sense, control includes both problems of regulating the process of the formulation of purpose, and of regulating the processes of purpose achievement. The schools of managerial thought which would claim some of this territory would include corporate strategy and policy formulation.

J.D. Thompson (1967) suggested these problems could be further understood through three major themes; firstly, the establishment of purpose; secondly, the pursuit of effectiveness; and thirdly, the struggle for efficiency. By the establishment of purpose is meant the general problem of giving shape and meaning to the patterns of activity and resource allocation within the organisation. It is not necessary to claim that purposes are stable over long periods of time, for they may be formulated in ways which are contingent upon changes, both within and outside an organisation.

If we are to define effectiveness as a measure of the achievement of purpose, then without some notion of purpose it is impossible to conceive of any notion of effectiveness. Usually an effective organisation is one which achieves a substantial number of its purposes in any given time period. Of course it is possible that an organisation's effectiveness could be weaker in the long run than in the short run or, indeed, vice versa. It would appear, then, that the notion of effectiveness may be rather inexact, in that some measure of the achievement of a set of fuzzy purposes may itself be 'fuzzy'. Figure 1.1 illustrates this point.

Given that one might locate a boundary for an organisation and test, at that boundary, whether purpose had been achieved to establish the notion of effectiveness, we might also create a boundary around the notion of effectiveness, and only within that boundary may we discuss the questions of efficiency. Here efficiency is the relationship of outputs to given sets of inputs. These relationships can be expressed in many ways. Often accountants, for example, find themselves relating the value of outputs in the market-place to the value of inputs in the factor market-place, and concluding that efficiency gains might occur if either the value of the outputs rises per unit of input, or the cost of the inputs fall per unit of output. It is helpful to notice that even these technical efficiency gains measured in this way might be a confusion of relative price changes and gains in the technical efficiency in the transformation process. Thompson has argued, and the present authors agree with him, that technical efficiency can only be discussed in a bounded system, where the boundaries are closed for analysis, and that effectiveness can only be discussed in an equally, but differently bounded, system (Figure 1.1). Purpose, however, by its very nature, will tend to be unbounded and to be the product of social interaction.

FIGURE 1.1   Bounding domains, for purpose, effectiveness and efficiency

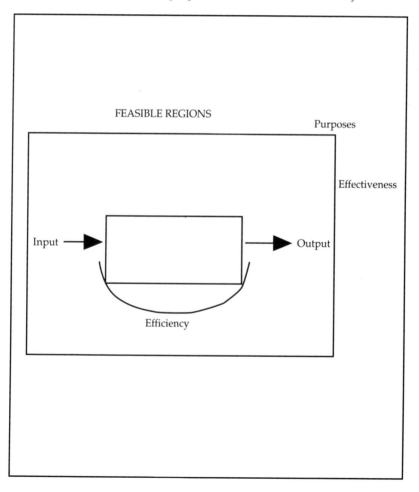

These notions, then, of purpose, effectiveness and efficiency, lie at the heart of the task of control in an organisation. The regulation of the processes for formulating purposes becomes an arena of considerable interest, as indeed does the regulation of the processes of the achievement of effectiveness. It is a commonplace observation that most accounting control has tended to focus on the processes of attaining efficiency. However recent developments in, for example, strategic accounting, have begun to move the focus of this work to the more general problems of organisational management. In this sense the control model of Robert Anthony (which we shall discuss in Chapter 2 in some depth) which talks of strategic control, managerial control and operational control, is clearly a mirror of the layering of purpose, effectiveness and efficiency. These three problems, then, will be with us as we pursue the general puzzles of control, especially that of goals and their achievement.

However we can for the moment sidestep the complexities arising from the problem of defining goals in a precise manner. For our present purposes we can substitute 'accepted plan of action' for 'goal' in most control applications. For example, many organisations seem to move between periods of relative stability, while agreed plans of action are pursued, and more turbulent periods when various interest groups engage in processes of negotiation and bargaining to establish new agreements. Perhaps the minimum overall goal we need to consider is that of survival. This goal is less problematic in that most organisations seem to exhibit a fundamental commitment to remaining in existence (Lowe and Chua, 1983). Beyond that, the importance assigned to various subsidiary goals appears to be largely a function of the relative power of the interest groups espousing particular concerns.

We are thus taking a stakeholder view of an organisation where various interested parties exert their influence to ensure that the programmes of action undertaken reflect their individual concerns to the greatest extent possible. The overall plan of action finally settled upon will depend upon the relative power and influence of the groups involved. Yet it is usually still in the interest of most groups that the organisation continue to survive. From this perspective, it is the feasibility of a plan (that is, its acceptability to disparate groups of interested parties, given their respective bargaining power) that is the fundamental guiding principle on which subsequent control actions will be based. Ideas of optimality are very much the icing on the cake, for identifying and operating within such a feasible region is difficult enough. We are therefore adopting a 'satisficing' (Simon, 1957) point of view where the attainment of satisfactory results is regarded as adequate, rather than pursuing some concept of the best possible result. However this is not to understate the importance of goals as having a cultural and symbolic significance. Individuals may feel commitment to an organisation because of its espoused goals, even when these goals do not necessarily guide many of its actions. Indeed it is probably more helpful to think of goals in this symbolic manner, rather than as their being the guiding feature of a control process.

However different organisations exhibit significant differences in the nature and the use made of their goals. Etzioni (1961) developed a useful typology. He distinguished between three ideal types of organisation; normative, utilitarian and coercive. Normative organisations exist where most participants share the same goals; here the concept of an overall organisational goal is helpful and can be considered as the aggregate of those goals held in common. Utilitarian organisations exist where the goals of participants are irrelevant to the activities of the organisation; participants' involvement is on a contractual or instrumental basis. Here some form of inducement/contribution analysis (Barnard, 1938) is appropriate, but the derivation of overall organisational goals is not possible or helpful. It can be argued that most business organisations are predominantly of this type. Finally, there are coercive organisations, where the values of participants are opposed to those of the organisation (or perhaps, more precisely, to those of the ruling coalition within it). Here it is only the power of this coalition that enables it to impose its values upon unwilling participants.

Mechanisms of control differ significantly in each of these different sets of circumstances. Thus the relationship that exists between individual and organisational goals can be seen as one determinant of the processes of control that will be used rather than the definition of the object of control. One task of the management control system of an organisation may be seen as assisting the organisation to identify a feasible set of activities that will provide acceptable inducements to all participants to carry them out. In such a way, the organisation will continue to exist as a viable entity.

But in practice the issue is considerably more complicated than the preceding ideas might suggest. Not only do different organisations exhibit different characteristics, but different parts of the same organisation may also behave differently. The norms and values prevalent in one part are often quite dissimilar to those found in another. Different forms of involvement also occur at different hierarchical levels, with senior managers exhibiting (or being expected to exhibit!) normative involvement, and lower level workers exhibiting instrumental or coercive involvement.

The study of organisational control therefore involves considerable complexity and is subject to the vagaries of human behaviour. Nevertheless it is open to analysis and has been approached in a number of different ways. In Chapter 2 we will take up the approaches of organisation theorists. Here we turn to a discussion of the approaches to organisation and control in the literature of cybernetics and systems theory.

Cybernetic and systems approaches to control

The purpose of this section is to outline and examine the concept of control from the perspective of cybernetics and general systems theory. The term 'cybernetics' was coined by Norbert Weiner in 1947 and was intended to denote an area of study which covered 'the entire field of control and communication theory, whether in the machine or the animal' (Weiner, 1948). A more modern definition, given by Pask (1961), extends it to the study of 'how systems regulate themselves, reproduce themselves, evolve and learn'. Thus cybernetics merges into the wider field of General Systems Theory (GST) and no attempt is made here to limit the scope of the term; the aim is to draw out those concepts which are useful in understanding the process of management control in organisations.

The cybernetic paradigm has underlain much work in management control. Hofstede (1978) reports that 'a review of nearly 100 books and articles on management control theory issued between 1900 and 1972 reflects entirely the cybernetic paradigm'. From the beginning, cyberneticians have been concerned with the common processes of communication and control in people and machines that were used in attempting to attain desirable objectives, and have attempted to map the self-regulating principles found in human biological systems onto systems of machines. Others have attempted to adapt the self-regulating principles found in the human brain to organisations. Most notable in this area is the work of Stafford Beer, in books such as *Decision and Control* (1966) and *Brain of the Firm* (1972). Finally systems theorists have attempted to develop approaches to the study of systems as wholes, rather than merely as the sum of their parts. Such approaches have not always been well-fitted to organisational systems, leading to the development of 'soft systems' approaches, pioneered by researchers such as Checkland and expounded in his *Systems Thinking, Systems Practice* (1981).

We will begin by outlining the cybernetic approach to the study of controlled systems and then extend it by considering the contribution of GST in general and the 'soft systems' theorists in particular. This section will conclude with an evaluation of the contribution that these approaches can make to the study of management control.

The cybernetic concept of control

Cybernetics is intentionally non-specific about the nature of the process being controlled; in this way it hopes to derive general principles of control that can be applied in different situations. The basis of controlled activity is seen as reducing deviations between actual process outputs and those which are desired; that is, it focuses on negative feedback. Although this may seem to be a very restricted point of view, part of the contribution of the cybernetic framework lies in its contention that this negative feedback mechanism is able to explain much apparently purposive and adaptive behaviour.

This basic process of error reduction can be elaborated following the general definition of control put forward by Tocher (1970,1976). From his work, a basic model of a cybernetic control process can be derived which indicates four necessary conditions which must be satisfied before control can be said to exist.

1. the existence of an objective which is desired;
2. a means of measuring process outputs in terms of this objective;
3. the ability to predict the effect of potential control actions;
4. the ability to take actions to reduce deviations from the objective.

These conditions are schematically represented in Figure 1.2, taken from Otley and Berry (1980). The contribution of this particular scheme over and above similar models, often presented in the early pages of management control texts in terms of a detector, a comparator and an effector, is that it emphasises the central role of the predictive model. The role of this model is reinforced when anticipatory (or feedforward) control is considered in addition to reactive (or feedback) control. Whereas reactive control waits for the occurrence of an error and then takes action to counteract it, anticipatory control predicts the likely occurrence of an error and takes action to prevent it occurring. Thus control is most effective when the process never deviates from its desired state. In the context of business enterprises, anticipatory controls essentially reflect the operation of planning systems. The more complex the system, the more likely it is that reliance will be placed on anticipatory controls as opposed to reactive controls. Ashby (1956) notes that a lesson that can be drawn from biological systems is that it is advantageous to control not by error but by what gives rise to that error.

FIGURE 1.2   Outline scheme of necessary conditions for a controlled process

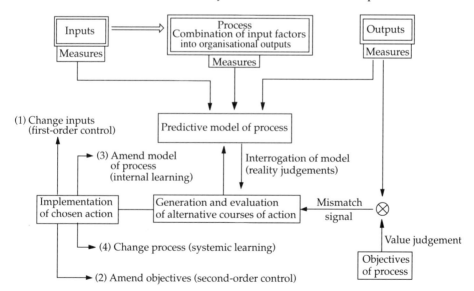

Unfortunately these concepts of control do not apply in any straightforward manner to the analysis of organisational control, an issue explored in some depth by Otley and Berry (1980). Nevertheless the contribution of cybernetics may well lie most importantly in the idea that error avoidance can explain much apparently goal-seeking behaviour. This point of view is put forward most strongly by Morgan (1979) when he states that: 'Organisms in nature do not orient themselves towards the achievement of given purposes or ends; they do not orient themselves towards the goal of survival. Rather they adopt modes of behaviour and organizational forms which help them avoid certain undesirable states.' Such an approach certainly seems applicable in explaining much organisational and economic behaviour, but it must be recognized that the feedback process is often highly imperfect. As one of the most cogent administrative writers informed by a cybernetic perspective, Geoffrey Vickers (1967) writes: 'In the management of human organizations, feedback is often absent, ambiguous or uninformative and [the cybernetic concept of control] points to the complementary process of mental simulation which enables management to function in such conditions.'

This process of mental simulation is essentially that of attempting to predict the possible outcomes of alternative courses of action. In this context it should be noted that the cybernetic control model presented here allows the possibility of adaptation and learning. Indeed this is one of the most important features of a viable control system operating in an open system, and will be explored further when GST is considered. It is this cybernetic perspective that informs Lowe (1971) when he defines a management control system as:

A system of organizational information seeking and gathering, accountability and feedback designed to ensure that the enterprise adapts to changes in its substantive environment and that the work behaviour of its employees is measured by reference to a set of operational sub-goals (which conform to overall objectives) so that the discrepancy between the two can be reconciled and corrected for.

The cybernetic approach thus represents a logical and abstract approach to the study of management control systems. It can give some powerful insights into the operation of control systems, but its very power means that it lacks specificity. It also tends to assume that control is exercised from outside the system; self-controlled systems may be better approached from the GST framework.

The General Systems Theory Approach

The central concept of systems thinking is that of a system itself. That is, the systems approach stresses the point of view that seeks to explain behaviour by means of studying the interrelationship of parts rather than the nature of the parts themselves. It is thus essentially holistic in nature, in contrast to the reductionist stance of much scientific activity. This approach to systems analysis stresses the importance of emergent properties, that is to say, properties which are characteristic of the level of complexity being studied and which may not have meaning at lower levels of analysis. (An example from a physical system is the concept of temperature which is a property of an assembly of molecules but which has no meaning in relation to a single molecule). Systems may be arranged in a hierarchy, derived from an inherent distinction of complexity (Boulding (1956):

1. static frameworks,
2. dynamic systems with predetermined motions,
3. closed loop control or cybernetic systems,
4. homeostatic systems, such as biological cells,
5. the living plant,
6. animals,
7. man,
8. organisations,
9. transcendental systems.

Most control systems theory is derived at a relatively low level of analysis, and the attempt is then made to transfer it to a much higher level of analysis, with probable adverse consequences in terms of applicability.

A major contributor to the application of cybernetics and GST to the management of organisations has been Stafford Beer. In his *Brain of the Firm* (1972) he takes the human brain and nervous system as a model for organisational control. Using this, he identifies five levels of control or systems, labelled Systems 1 to 5. The lower levels are concerned with the transformation processes required by the whole system and the maintenance of internal stability. The penultimate level is concerned with the maintenance of dynamic equilibrium with the external world, and the final, fifth level, with the self-conscious determination of goals. The interactions between these systems are modelled directly from the neurophysiological analogy and are interpreted in terms of managerial situations. The presentation of Beer's work is intuitive rather than carefully argued, but, while it contains much stimulating material, it is difficult to assess how much derives from the models propounded and therefore its validity is *not* demonstrable.

GST is primarily a tool for dealing with very high levels of complexity, particularly with reference to systems which display adaptive and apparently goal-seeking behaviour. That this approach to complexity can be of value to the study of management control can perhaps best be illustrated by a definition of accounting put forward by Weick (1979): 'Accounting is the attempt to wrest coherence and meaning out of more reality than we ordinarily deal with.' Although borrowed from a definition of art, it is a graphic portrayal of the central problem faced by accounting, and by management control more generally. Indeed the approach to management control via accounting, as exemplified by Anthony (1965), can be seen as an attempt to deal with the control of a complex, interconnected human activity system by a *systematic* approach. The problems in such an approach, summarised in Weick's definition, can perhaps be best appreciated when one adopts a *systemic* viewpoint. Thus accounting controls are the result of a great deal of effort being put into the development of organisational controls by being systematic; it remains to be seen what will be the result of a similar amount of effort being applied to being systemic.

An important distinction has been made between 'hard' and 'soft' systems approaches. The former tend to relate to physical systems having relatively clear objectives and decision processes, with quantitative measures of performance. The latter tend to relate to systems which include human beings, where objectives are vague and ambiguous, decision processes that are ill-defined and possibly irrational, and where, at best, only qualitative measures of performance exist. From this distinction it appears that the 'soft' systems approaches will have most to offer the study of management control. The leading proponent of soft systems approaches (Peter Checkland) claims that systems ideas are used primarily in a process of inquiry, an exploration of the meanings which actors attribute to that which they observe. Thus the soft systems methodology copes with the central problem of objectives in a subjective manner (Checkland, 1981). First, there is a stage of analysis, deliberately undertaken in non-systemic terms where the analyst becomes familiar with the rich complexity of the system being studied. Second, a root definition–that is a fundamental statement of purpose from first principles–of the basic nature of the system thought to be relevant to the problem situation is sought. Third, a conceptual model of the system is constructed using the minimum necessary system that can achieve the root definition; this is validated by the data gathered at the analysis stage. The crucial step in this process is the construction of the root definition, and this is evidently the most subjective part of the process. Smyth and Checkland (1976) have attempted to build some safeguards into the process of root definition formulation, using checklists and suggesting that definitions are exposed to participants in the situation. Both these safeguards are designed to facilitate what Vickers (1965) would term the process of appreciation, that is, the development of a rich and insightful way of viewing a real-world situation. Such an appreciative judgement requires both factual (reality) and value judgements, and therefore any assessment of its validity is itself an appreciative judgement.

Despite such safeguards it is inescapable that the application of systems methodology to organisations is dependent upon the subjective judgement of the analyst. Whether this is considered to be a strength or a weakness depends upon your point of view; however it signals a substantial shift from the methodologies of the physical and biological sciences. The model of scientific activity used by this type of systems approach is quite distinct from that used in the natural sciences.

It may therefore be argued that a systems approach carries within it a conservative ideology (Lilienfeld, 1978) as the analyst works within a framework of co-operative people who co-operate with the ends of the system. It has also been suggested that systems analysis is in the same philosophical tradition as sociological structural functionalism. Although this is clearly true of cybernetics and hard systems approaches, it is less true of soft systems approaches which may be seen as lying more within the *verstehen* tradition of thought. This tradition takes its name from the German verb 'to understand' and seeks through detailed knowledge of the system to understand how the participants within a system understand it. As Berry (1983) observes, in this school great stress is laid upon the accuracy and honesty of observation, the sensitivity and perception of the observer and on imaginative interpretations of observations.

Although there has been much academic criticism of the functionalist approach, it is important to recognise that it is less limiting than is often supposed. Burrell and Morgan (1979) point out that organisation theorists have often mistakenly equated open systems theory with the use of an organismic analogy. There are also wider perspectives available that have been much less fully explored. These involve either taking a more subjective stance (moving to an interpretive position) or being more concerned with radical change than with regulation (regulation refers to the maintenance and continuity of the system relationships which have been established or have emerged over time). From the perspective of the study of control systems, the subjectivist position poses no particular problems; however regulation is evidently of central importance, although the study of regulatory processes does not necessarily preclude the use of more radical perspectives.

The contribution of systems thinking and cybernetics

GST and cybernetics can contribute to the study of management control systems (MCS) in various ways. First, a systems point of view can be adopted in (MCS) analysis. This is the least controversial approach and may represent little more than the adoption of an organisational level of analysis and a conscious attempt to be holistic rather than reductionist in approach. The most insightful use of this approach is that of Vickers (1965,1967) who, as a practising administrator, has attempted to codify his experience in more general terms by adopting a systems point of view and using cybernetic terms. In particular he argues for a systemic point of view which explains organizational behaviour in terms of ongoing relationships rather than by the imputation of objectives.

Second, there is the use of systems approaches to handling real-world MC problems, perhaps best exemplified by the Checkland methodology. But although such an approach may provide a means by which real-world problems can be dealt with, it does not provide any theoretical basis for the study of management control. Indeed it discounts the possibility of any such general theories, arguing that each problem is unique and must be dealt with on its own merits.

Third, there is the use of concepts developed in cybernetics and GST to study MCSs and to develop a theory of management control. However there seems to be a gulf between the available concepts and their application to the study of management control. For example, the introductory text by Schoderbek *et al.* (1975) presents the basic concepts of systems theory and their application to management systems in a particularly lucid manner, but immediately runs into difficulty when applying these concepts to any particular topic. Admittedly this is partly because of a hard systems orientation, but the conclusions seem disappointingly diffuse and vague after the initial excitement offered by the original concepts. Similarly Amey's (1979) analysis of budgetary planning and control systems misses out on the behavioural, organisational, forensic, strategic and political elements of control, according to one reviewer (McCosh, 1990). Perhaps most successful in this area is the text by Maciariello (1984) who makes a consistent attempt to apply the cybernetic paradigm to management control systems, but even so achieves only mixed results. Perhaps we shall do no better; the reader is the best judge of that.

Finally, systems ideas have been used in other disciplines related to the study of MCSs, such as the open systems and sociotechnical systems movements in organisation theory. It is notable that all the open systems theories considered here adopt, explicitly or implicity, an organismic analogy, utilising concepts such as survival and functional attributes related to this end, such as differentiation and integration, and purposive rationality.

In summary, the application of systems thinking and cybernetics to the study of management control raises more questions than it answers. Yet the very fact that these approaches raise questions may be valuable in a field that is pre-paradigmatic in its development. In the West the discipline which has probably had the greatest influence on management control to date has been accounting, which is a clear application of a systematic approach. The systemic approach of systems theorists may provide a useful countervailing force in developing more comprehensive theories of management control.

A social system contains components, each of which is self-controlling, and which contain models of the behaviour of the whole. Further, in the study of organisational control, the system's environment is itself complex, as noted by Buckley (1968): 'The environment of the enterprise is largely composed of other equally groping, loose-limbed, more or less flexible, illusion ridden, adaptive organizations.' If management is an activity which involves an attempt to control situations involving greater amounts of complexity and uncertainty than we have techniques adequately to cope with, then the systems approach offers a method of studying management control that has the potential to at least recognize some of the fundamental problems. For example, it may indicate areas in which the wrong questions are being asked and in which inappropriate concepts are being adopted. It is in no sense a complete theory, but it is the nearest to a method of developing a theory that we currently have, and it deserves serious consideration for that reason alone.

Summary

In this chapter we have introduced the idea of organisational control and some definitions of management control. We discussed the idea of the domain in which control might be exercised, raising the interesting questions of purposes and goals, using them, following J.D. Thompson, to connect organisational control to the ideas of purpose, effectiveness and efficiency. From a review of the cybernetic and systems approaches to organisational control we have argued that these approaches are not limited to mere description, but offer a systemic frame of thought through which ongoing relationships become foci of analysis. Further, as Checkland has demonstrated, there is value in these approaches for the understanding of real-world problems. While the step from the abstract idea to the concrete event is not trivial, these approaches do offer both possible routes to practical and intelligent theory development and also to helpful problem solving.

Far from replacing managers with general system theories, we argue that the role of the manager is still central to the notion of organisational control. Also it is possible, we saw, to relate theories of learning to the cybernetic concepts of control to show that these approaches are not static.

CHAPTER 2

Approaches to control in the organisational literature

Anthony J. Berry, Jane Broadbent and David Otley

As we noted in Chapter 1, not all aproaches to control have adopted a systems perspective. The aim of this chapter is to provide a broad outline of the work of some of the authors and researchers who have considered the problem of control using various social and organisational frameworks. Social and organisational approaches seek to locate control in their context and, therefore, in various different ways take into account the structures, the people connected to them and the environment of the organisation. The approaches give differential emphasis to the various elements. Subsequent chapters will seek to look in more depth at the impact on control of the structures of organisations and the contexts in which they exist, as well as the roles of people within them. The intention in this chapter is not to provide any prescription as to a 'best' way to operate systems of control, but to continue the task we began in Chapter 1, of sketching an outline of the huge diversity of approaches which have been adopted in seeking to theorise control in organisations.

The 'mainstream' approach is perhaps best represented by the work of Anthony *et al.* who can perhaps be credited with the first contemporary attempts to formalise the subject area of management control (MC), through the management control systems textbook which is now in its sixth edition (Anthony *et al.*, 1992). Working from an accounting base they claim to have sought to broaden accounting's interest and to link it to other disciplines to provide the frame of interest of MC. In so doing they seek to consider the structure and design of relationships in the organisational system, as well as the process – the set of activities that the system does.

More specifically Anthony *et al.* (1989) provide a framework of control *processes* within the organisation in order to try to bound the notion of management control *systems*. The management control processes that they define are threefold: strategic planning and control, task control and management control. Strategic planning and control is concerned with the longer-term goals and objectives, deciding what these are and evaluating the means by which they are to be achieved. It is seen as oriented to the external environmental issues. Task control is the more routine process of ensuring that tasks in the organisation are carried out, in the terminology of Anthony *et al.* (1989, p. 11) 'effectively and efficiently'. Management control is the link between these two elements; it is seen as the process that makes sure that the strategy of the organisation is reflected in the tasks which are carried out.

The relationship between these three processes is claimed to be distinct and hierarchical (with strategy setting the agenda of management control, which in turn sets the agenda for task control) yet the boundaries are seen as overlapping. By bounding the interest of MC in this fashion the authors arrive at their definition of the subject:

> Management control is primarily a process for motivating and inspiring people to perform organization activities that will further the organization's goal. It is also a process for detecting and correcting unintentional performance errors and intentional irregularities, such as theft or misuse of resources.

The process they describe is one which includes organisational responsibilities and authorities. It is a tool for *managers* and is argued to have psychological considerations, needing the ability to communicate and inspire other employees. It is taken for granted that the process is goal-oriented, and efficient and effective performance is also related to the organisation's goals. Management control is argued by these authors to be built around a financial control system and, as such, the budgetary control cycle is seen as central.

The inclusion of financial systems is important enough for the authors to highlight the distinctions between management, task and accounting control. Amongst these the authors highlight the people primarily involved in the different functions, and their source disciplines. Thus management control is the domain of managers and has a source discipline of psychology, accountants deal with accounting control using the source discipline of economics, while supervisors control tasks, using engineering as their source discipline. Accounting control, however, as articulated by these authors is seen as very much akin to the stewardship function of accounting and is not proactive (this latter feature being seen as attributable to management control). When consideration is given, however, to the descriptions of management control systems elaborated by the authors, its structures are ones which relate to what are usually seen as accounting based – a responsibility centre based model – and the process is one of budgetary control. Thus, although formally the authors distinguish between accounting and management control, this rests on what might be argued to be a very limiting view of accounting. Given the more usual view of accounting, which includes more managerial accounting such as budgeting, it is hard to see a distinction between accounting and management control.

Thus the exposition of management control that is provided does not do much to broaden the interest of the topic. Psychology, the source discipline of management control, does not form a substantive part of the thesis offered. The actuality is that management control is located very firmly in the domain of accounting, albeit more managerially based than that rather restricted stewardship function described by the authors. This observation is one which has been made elsewhere (Lowe and Puxty, 1989) in their critique of this approach and it is to a critical evaluation of the classical model that we shall now turn.

Lowe and Puxty (1989) provide a critique of what they call the 'prevailing orthodoxy in management control' and in so doing provide a recognition of the influence and importance of the 'Anthony' approach. Specifically this approach reflects a very narrow view of MC, despite its early promise to broaden the subject. Other of the organisational approaches will show how the boundaries of the domain can be usefully extended. Lowe and Puxty point to other problems. The three-tier approach offered by Anthony *et al.* does mean that the possibility of offering a holistic view of the organisation is lost. This means that interlinkages between the different levels, which are interdependent, are not shown, also the environment in which the organisation exists is omitted from consideration. It is this concern with the internal processes which leads to a tendency to see control as simply a feedback process, and to a decoupling of planning and control, such that planning takes place, action follows and finally there is feedback on that action. This may be contrasted with a situation in which there is a more dynamic interplay between the planning and control processes, such that feedforward as well as feedback control is possible.

Another crucial issue which Anthony *et al.* do not consider is the issue of organisational goals. They assume their existence and the possibility of their existence as completely unproblematic. In so doing, they reify the organisation; that is, they treat it as an unambiguous, concretely existing object, and forget the debate as to whether it is organisations or the people within the organisations which have goals (Cyert and March, 1963; Pfeffer and Salanick, 1977; Lowe and Chua, 1983). Along with this is the issue of whether stated goals can be used as an indicator of actual behaviour (Perrow, 1961). This issue is well debated elsewhere (Lowe and Chua, 1983) but it is essential to realise that the stated goals of an organisation may not be unproblematically accepted as the actuality towards which organisational members strive.

These weaknesses can be seen in some of the more specific techniques of MC which are widely used and can be seen as elements illustrative of this classical approach. Thus accounting-based controls such as budgeting, standard costing and variance analysis are typical of the 'classical' controls which are used in organisations. These approaches are ones which are geared to the role of management controls which is concerned to operationalise the strategy of the organisation. They assume organisational goals and indeed institutionalise them in 'the budget'. The extent to which the environment of the organisation is considered will depend on individual circumstances, but there may well be a tendency to promote an inward-looking attitude and one in which the means to control becomes more important than the control which is desired (Drucker, 1964).

Moving towards different approaches to control

Hopwood (1974) focused on the notion of control, pointing out that control of the enterprise involves administrative, social and self controls. The accounting-type controls of the 'classical' model are ones which fit into the administrative category, but now different dimensions are being added. In defining three elements of control Hopwood's work provides a bridge between the 'classical' approach and the ideas in the anthropological literature. He also provides the linkage to self controls, which will be discussed below.

Social controls are those which are reflected in the 'social perspectives and the patterns of social interactions' (Hopwood, 1974, p. 26). In essence they are the elements which define 'the way we do things here'. Hopwood points to the fact that these factors are likely to intervene in the implementation of the administrative controls and therefore organisational control cannot be achieved without reference to these patterns of social interaction and norms.

In a similar vein, Merchant (1985) is concerned to emphasise the social or behavioural side of control: 'Control is seen as having one basic function: to help ensure the proper behaviours of people in the organisation.... Control, as the word applies to the function of management, involves influencing human behaviour' (p. 4). This he calls 'personnel control' and it includes both social and self control; it is also linked to what he calls 'action controls' and 'results controls'. Results control refers to an approach which holds individuals accountable for achieving particular results, and then rewards them for their achievement. In so doing it allows the possibility of managers having autonomy for detailed action, provided that they produce the desired outcomes. The outcomes must therefore be quantifiable, and when this criterion is not available action control might be used. In this situation the outcome might be difficult to define, but the actions which are required can be specified, and so the control process is geared towards seeing that the correct actions are carried out. Neither of these is geared to the social aspects of control with which this chapter is concerned, but they help to define the domain which Merchant sees as being the area in which social controls are useful. Thus, in areas where it is difficult to define and measure outputs and in areas where it is not entirely clear what actions are required, social controls are seen as important.

Social controls, for Merchant, include such items as 'getting the right person for the job' or training and culture. The latter two items may well be linked, as periods of training may be seen as socialisation processes instilling into a new recruit the culture of the organisation, 'the way we do things round here'. Merchant provides a 'broad conceptualization of control' (p. 4) which he focuses upon the control of behaviour, he also provides some discussion of the implementation of the systems. While he sees control of behaviour as important, he sees this as coming, not just from personnel control, but from its combination with action and results controls. This leads to his conclusion that multiple forms of control are desirable. However the drawbacks of this (cost and the increased possibility of dysfunctional side effects, p. 131) are glossed over by the author. Also, while some consideration of the advantages and disadvantages of the different approaches is given, the choice between them is left to the individual in their particular circumstances, and as such is underconceptualised. The conflict between the different elements is not, therefore, considered and developed. Moreover the 'broad' conceptualisation which Merchant provides is one which is very inward-looking, and which does tend to neglect the influence of the wider environment on the behaviour of people in organisations.

The 'social' theme is also developed in the work of Etzioni and of Ouchi, who also provides a three-part analysis of the approaches to control, again linking the social and classical aspects, but providing a rather different emphasis. Etzioni (as mentioned in Chapter 1) bases his work on the assumption that there are three major sources of control: coercion, economic assets and normative values. All would exist in organisations but some might predominate at different times or in different locations. He is centrally concerned with the notion of power, and power is the means to make subjects comply. This, if we see control as influencing others to carry out your intentions, is therefore a control mechanism. Coercive power relies on the physical threat of pain, or restriction of movement, and might be found in prisons. Remunerative power is founded on the ability to provide material reward, salaries and wages for example, and this can be seen to provide the main element of the control which an employer has over the employee. Normative power rests on the ability of an organisation to provide symbolic reward to its members, in a 'pure' form it might be a religious organisation such as a monastery.

The involvement that individuals have with organisations will then rest on different bases, and the way in which control is exercised will depend on the type of involvement. For example, if coercion was the influential mechanism it would be pointless expecting an individual to act on the norms of the organisation in a voluntary fashion. In most organisations there may well be different combinations of all these types of power, those who work in the 'caring services' might well forgo a larger remunerative reward for the normative reward of 'doing a worthwhile job', but would still require a salary. This signals the pluralistic nature of control and it raises the possibility that different people may well respond differently to various approaches.

The attention to the role of power and the use of the pluralist framework is to be applauded, but the work does have its problems. While the different notions of power are highlighted the implications of its existence are not dealt with rigorously. Power is not a zero-sum issue and thus conflict is always a possibility and this needs to be considered. The extent to which power is legitimate or illegitimate can be closely linked to this issue of conflict, as can the question of positive and negative power (the ability to get things done or not get things done). Thus the theory does not give much indication of the extent to which its insights might be operationalised to achieve control in different circumstances.

Contingency approaches

The different approaches considered above can be seen to provide a link between the 'mainstream' approaches and those which take a rather broader view of control. As well as dealing with internal matters such as the social and self controls, acknowledgement is also given to the structures and the environment and the technologies of the organisations and the tasks performed in them. In that respect a link to the area of contingency theory, which has developed in the organisational literature, can be made. Contingency theory argues that there is no one 'best' way to approach organisations, but that the organisational design should reflect the environment in which it is found. There is much work in this area, one well-known study being that of Burns and Stalker (1961) which differentiated between the 'mechanistic' organisation, operating in stable conditions and with a known task technology, and the 'organic' organisation operating in a more uncertain environment, with less defined technologies. In the former a bureaucratic structure is seen as appropriate; in the latter situation the laying down of such tight rules is seen as inappropriate and impossible and thus a more flexible structure is required.

The more recent organisational work of Hannan and Freeman (1977) and Aldrich (1979) sees the environment as more active in shaping the organisation. In the population–ecology approach the environment is seen as providing a 'natural' selection process for firms, those which survive being ones which are suitable for the given environment. Thus the organisation is seen as less able to adapt to the environment, survival depends upon fitness for the changing environment.

There is, then, some tension between the notion that by adopting the 'right' structure and control system an organisation can survive, and the notion that the organisation has only a limited space within which to operate in a given environment. This tension raises questions as to the ability of contingency theory to provide a satisfactory basis for action. There is also a problem of specifying the environment. Typically the environment is seen as one or two specific issues, and there is a danger that it is underspecified in many contingency approaches. Nevertheless contingency theory does signal that managers and controllers should give consideration to variables in the environment of the organisation. Consequently it alerts us to a wider set of issues than does the classical approach.

This rather broader approach can be illustrated by the work of Emmanuel *et al.* (1990) which shows how this approach can be used, in the form of accounting techniques, as a way to achieve management control. Unlike the classical approach it signals the different approaches which need to be adopted in various circumstances. One particular difference which is highlighted is that between programmed and non-programmed decisions: in programmed decisions there is a clear and predictable link between action and outcome and the outcome can be planned for; in non-programmed decisions there is a greater degree of uncertainty making the potential outcome less predictable, and planning correspondingly more problematic.

Anthropological approaches

Some writers, in moving away from the classical approach, focus exclusively on the social domain. This type of work can take many guises, but has been popularised by the work of Peters and Waterman (1982), which has brought the notion of 'culture' to the fore in management thought. Culture is not easy to define closely, but may be seen broadly as the norms, values and symbols which enable members of a society or an organisation to make sense of what happens in similar ways.

The reviews of Allaire and Firsirotu (1984) and Smircich (1983) both showed that there are many different ways to approach the study of culture in organisations. A broad difference emerges between the view that culture is a variable which can be manipulated in order to achieve the 'correct' outcome for the organisation, and the view that culture is a dynamic and symbolic element which needs to be taken account of but which cannot be determined externally. The former situation is that portrayed by the Peters and Waterman (1982) approach. Here the thesis is put forward that the role of management is to promote the appropriate culture from which control will 'naturally' flow. The implicit idea is that control will thereby come from internal self-control, rather than being externally imposed by bureaucratic rules and regulations. This assumes that it is possible to impose a culture, and this may not necessarily be the case. Socialisation, through an apprenticeship period, staff training and selection, may well promote this 'cultural' control, but it is likely that such a process will be tenuous.

While being helpful in bringing the 'softer' cultural aspects to the fore, this work has been criticised for its thesis that certain 'excellent' companies achieve their position because of their culture. The categorisation of excellence has been questioned, and the companies 'excellent' position has not always been sustained, throwing some doubt on the thesis. If a more symbolic view of culture is adopted then the use of culture as a tool of control must also be questioned. In this view culture is not an independent variable which can be adopted or imposed at will; it is constructed by social actors in their daily lives. The Peters and Waterman approach takes a position which suggests that cultures are things which are imposed or encouraged by managers, and does not seem to position the ability of other groups to develop their own culture or to resist cultural imposition.

Brunsson (1985) considers what is required to promote action and differentiates between weak and strong ideologies. Action, he argues, is often promoted by the ability to act according to predetermined ideas of what is appropriate – ideologies. Strong ideologies avoid the need to follow long decision processes, making action and reaction more a pre-programmed issue. Strong ideologies mean that there is greater agreement about the way action should proceed, weak ideologies make action less likely as there is room for dissent. It is easier to promote action through strong ideologies, thus control via a strong ideology is relatively easy. However by its very nature a strong ideology is difficult to change and, should the ideology not be that which is needed (say in a changing environment) then promoting new patterns of action will be very difficult. While this provides an interesting insight into the possibility of change, there is little here that provides guidance as to how a strong or weak ideology might be recognised. Control in this schema is not so much proactive, as reactive, depending on the strength of the ideology of the organisation and the extent to which this ideology is aligned to that of the would-be controller. It is, therefore, not an insight which gives an easy route to help to operationalise a control system.

Pettigrew (1979) in a processual study looked at the emergence of an organisational culture, the way that reality was constructed within a developing organisation. This study considers culture much more as a symbolic artefact, acknowledging its emergence and relating it to its context and history. In a later study based on the NHS (Pettigrew, McKee and Ferlie, 1989), the implications of this emergent view of culture are examined. The view put forward here sees the cultural dimension as fundamental to change, but is much more tentative and sensitive to the possibilities of promoting change. They point out that a universal recipe for change is not possible. Highlighting local history politics and people, they are sceptical about the role of rational design, and point to the paradox that stability may be necessary to promote effective change at a later stage. Control in this context is therefore much more of a political balancing act. It involves working within the cultural system and moulding it rather than seeking to 'knock it into shape'. While again helping to sensitise us to the role of cultural issues, this type of study does not provide any overall answer to the issue of control, and neither does it seek to. This type of approach is useful in that it highlights the process which must be adopted in seeking to develop control systems, but it does not specify the content.

This approach is one which has been adopted by Bourn and Ezzamel (1986) who also consider the NHS and the role of culture in a situation of change. This work uses that of Ouchi (1980), previously mentioned, and the notion of clan control: that is, the social control exerted on individual members because they are part of a group and identify with the group and the common values of the group. It suggests that new moves for change in the NHS (intended to change the control of the service) may not have the intended effect as they promote a culture which is not in line with that which already exists in the service. This study therefore underlines yet again the importance of considering culture when control within an organisation is desired. It also highlights the difficulty of achieving a desired outcome by imposition.

That is not to say that change cannot be achieved. Dent in a study based on the railway industry, shows a situation where a change has taken place in the culture of an organisation. This study provides no generalisable conclusions: again it is an interpretive piece of research and sees situations as uniquely contextualised. Laughlin (1991), however, uses the case to provide a rather more structured argument about the role of the symbolic elements of an organisation in the process of change. Using a theoretical framework developed from the Critical Theory of Jurgen Habermas, Laughlin emphasises the symbolic elements, the interpretive schemes, suggesting possibilities which will help to understand the processes of change in organisations. This theory is meant to provide a framework of possibilities which will have to be fleshed out in the context of particular situations. The point is that it holds as central the role of the interpretive schemes in determining the pathway of change. This points to the notion of the interpretive scheme in defining the level of control that is possible in a situation where control is deemed to be reliant on changing organisational practices and the organisational cultures which produce them.

The anthropological literature which is relevant to control is therefore somewhat diverse. While all those who have used the construct are equally convinced about its importance, there are those who see it as a possible tool of the controller, and those who see it instead as a constraining influence, particularly in a changing situation. To this extent it can be implied that an existing culture can be a useful control in a situation in which there is no change. When change is needed this is only unproblematic when it does not seek to alter the culture which already exists. The main problem with these types of approaches is that they offer no guidance as to the problem of recognising cultures, although in the case of those who see culture as a concrete entity their manipulation is a substantive control tool. If the more symbolic approach to culture is adopted then the possibility of controlling cultures disappears. In different ways both these approaches fail to give direction as to the content of control systems; they do, however, provide good advice as to the process which needs to be followed to identify particular controls in particular situations. A further problem which is posed by critics of the approach is the lack of consideration of the element of power.

Summary

In these first two chapters we have attempted to give a broad outline of the various approaches to control which have been suggested by a number of authors. In Chapter 2 we have been specifically concerned with sketching the mainstream accounting-based approach to control and considering various approaches which have sought to broaden the focus. In so doing we have used as illustration the work of authors such as Hopwood and Merchant who have introduced the idea that there are multiple dimensions to the controls in organisations, some which are administrative and based on organisational structures and procedures, others being based on social relationships and self controls. Contingency theorists have suggested that different contexts require different approaches to control and have sought to identify frameworks for 'matching' control approach to context. Anthropological approaches have emphasised the importance of the values, ideologies and cultures of those who are the subject of attempts to control (or who are controlling).

We have sought to explain, briefly, the strengths of the different approaches as well as the weaknesses in order that managers may be aware, not only of the diversity of possibilities, but also of their potential in different circumstances. We may seem to be somewhat pessimistic in our approach, as every method we suggest appears to have weaknesses. This is not meant to be discouraging, but is based on our belief that there are no clear indications of the 'right' or the 'best' way to achieve control. We are simply seeking to be honest about our view that there are no perfect solutions. This does not mean to say that we can ignore the problems and forget any attempt to control. The rest of the book will move on to consider, in more depth, different issues of control and some of the solutions which are offered.

Structures of control

Anthony J. Berry, Jane Broadbent and David Otley

As Chapters 1 and 2 have shown, there are lots of different approaches to considering control. Different approaches lead to the creation of diverse structures within organisations. When we come to consider the structures of control then, once more, we can look at the creation of these structures through a number of different 'lenses'. The approaches adopted by organisational theorists and by economists are the two with which we shall be concerned in this chapter. The approaches adopted by organisational theorists are important because they have provided ways of structuring organisations and the processes within them. The approaches of economists are included because they provide a framework for discussion of the question as to whether large organisations are the best way of structuring industries and services. This then provides a framework for the chapter. First, consideration will be given to the question of structuring large organisations and the tasks within them. This will be done through a reflection of the influence of classical management theorists, as well as by giving some attention to more recent attempts to structure through divisions or matrices. Next the contribution of the economists will be presented, in particular the debate as to the reasons for the formation of markets or hierarchies in particular circumstances. Finally the debate as to the superiority of either markets or hierarchies as a structure for organising the supply of goods and services in contemporary society will be raised.

Organisational theorists and approaches to structures of control

The classical management theorists provide a useful starting-point to begin a consideration of control structures. The work of F.W. Taylor provides an important, and, even today, influential account of the way *tasks* can be controlled in organisations. After studying the process of manual labour in a particular task (shovelling pig iron) he defined the way in which the task should be done most efficiently, thus increasing productivity. This definition of the 'one best way' to do a job, coupled with the choice of 'the best man' is called 'scientific management'. The focus for control was in the separation of conception and execution of the tasks within a workplace. Managers had to plan and then workers carried out their behest. This may seem unsurprising to those of us born into present society, but in an era of craft control of the work task this was a revolutionary idea. In craft control the task was under the control of the craftsman who held the knowledge and expertise needed to carry out the task. Taylor wished to minimise 'soldiering', the restriction of work from both natural laziness and the restriction of workloads to group norms. He also wished to make management more effective. He saw the task of management as being to gain the knowledge of the task skills from the workers and then to organise those skills in a 'scientific' fashion to ensure maximum efficiency. Managers had to ensure that the 'best man' for the job was hired and that the tools required were available. There was also an element of payment by results, although this was designed to ensure that the working man could not earn sufficient to engage in drunkenness!

Taylor's work was oriented to the problem of task control. Working in a similar vein, but looking at the overall management of the firm, was Henri Fayol, who has also been seen as highly influential. He provides a model which structures the whole organisation as a unified hierarchy, with control and authority coming from the highest level and filtering down the organisation. This familiar structure is illustrated in Figure 3.1.

Fayol, like Taylor, distinguished the role of managers from other functions in the organisation. This was in line with his overall ideas of division of labour and specialisation. Part of the manager's role was that of providing discipline and being responsible for actions of subordinates. For this to happen there has to be a structure which provided 'unity of command' – workers being responsible to just one superior. The model supplied by Fayol has a conception of the organisation as having a unified set of purposes (indi-

FIGURE 3.1   The functional hierarchy

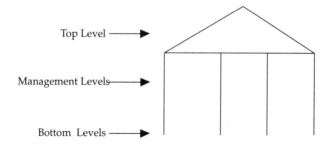

vidual interests being subordinated to these). Communication, through which instructions to enable control are passed, basically follows the hierarchical 'up and down' structure, although for efficiency horizontal communication is enabled.

The structures of control which are typified in the work of Taylor and Fayol are formally described by Weber. Weber was not an organisational theorist as such. He did not seek to promote particular ways of organising, but he was interested in understanding the society in which he lived and how it was developing. He saw the ways of organising as typical of approaches in a society in general, in which authority is given by the acceptance of rational–legal principles. This can be contrasted with other societies in which authority comes from either tradition (direct rule by elders or by the monarchy as a matter of tradition and by reason of their *position*) or charisma (the acceptance of control by those perceived to have special *personal* qualities, for example a religious leader or a strong political leader).

Rational–legal authority is that which comes from following a set of rules underpinned by rational calculation. Authority is given to people because they have particular abilities and knowledge and the whole structure is based on predetermined roles and impersonalised relationships. The aim is to provide efficiency. In providing this description Weber formalised his model of a bureaucratic structure. We sometimes use the term 'bureaucracy' in a pejorative fashion, as a way of condemning 'red tape', but the term was originally used positively as a means of improving efficiency. While we might sometimes be dismissive of the elements of bureaucracy, we might also do well to consider the proposition that the bureaucratic structures of control contained in the model are routinely employed in almost all organisations in our society, be they large or small. The reader might also try to imagine an organisation which does not use bureaucratic controls and what it might be like. This can be a difficult task!

We cannot consider classical management approaches to the structure of control without some mention of the Hawthorne experiments, which were argued to show the importance of the social relations of the work group. These experiments were carried out in the Hawthorne works of the Western Electrical Company from 1924 for the next 20 years or so. Many experiments were undertaken, but they included the study of changing physical conditions on output. The 'Hawthorne Effect' was that changes in conditions, whether making them 'worse' or 'better', all produced increased output. This was argued to be as a result of the increased interest in the work group as a result of the research. There has been some debate about the interpretation of the data collected in this huge project (Rose, 1975) but the results are conventionally argued to show that the social composition of the work group is as important as physical aspects of the working environment. Thus the psychological effect of increased interest was argued to be as important as physical issues and issues of 'human relations' became the concern of organisational theorists.

While the organisational structures of the whole organisation are not affected by the adoption of Hawthorne-type approaches, the organisation of task control is somewhat different. The human relations approach does move away from the underlying assumption of bureaucratic ones, in which the employee is seen as little more than a cog in a machine. It accepts that humans are not just motivated by money. Control of the work process is undertaken with more emphasis both on the creation of group solidarity and on the social needs of the workers. One technique which has been influenced by this type of approach to control is budgeting, where the use of participation is advocated in setting targets.

The classical management theorists have, therefore, considered the structures of both organisation and of task control. The structure of task control suggested is 'nested' in organisational structures which emphasise hierarchical and centralised structures, and in which authority lies with top management. However, as organisations have increased in size, problems of a centralised and unitary control structure have materialised. Thus divisionalised structures were developed to deal with the problems of allowing sufficient specialisation and yet provide an integration of the tasks carried out.

Divisionalisation allows for a large organisation to be structured in a series of smaller units which organise their own activities to an agreed extent, but which are still accountable to the parent organisation. The amount of decentralisation, that is the extent to which decisions are made at lower levels of management, can differ between divisionalised organisations and even within divisions of the same organisation. The divisionalised structure came into prominence through its use in the General Motors Corporation, by A.P. Sloan, and provides various advantages. Using this structure, decisions can be delegated to be made at or near its environment where there is argued to be better knowledge of environmental conditions. The structure also provides the possibility to give training and responsibility to a wider range of employees. This, it is argued, will not only motivate them but also provide a pool of workers from which to recruit top managers in the future. The structure is also claimed to provide a means of filtering information flows to top management so that they do not suffer overload. This is said to make it easier for top management to identify strategic issues. The careful allocation of responsibility for decision making can also ensure that decisions can be made faster, as they do not all have to be made at one central point. The main disadvantage and a crucial problem for an organisation which has adopted a divisionalised structure is that decisions which are suboptimal for the organisation *as a whole* may be adopted because they are optimal for a particular division.

Divisionalisation can be organised in a number of ways, but popular bases are product differentiation or geographic location. Whatever the basis, the extent of decentralisation of decision making can differ depending on company policy, thus, while control structures of divisions may be similar, the operation of control within them may differ. (Similarly, within centrally managed or unitary organisations there can be differences in the levels and extent of decentralisation.) The operation of control within the divisionalised company may still operate on the basis of bureaucratic form. To that extent divisionalisation breaks down the unitary bureaucratic structure but does not replace it completely.

The decision as to the formal structure of the organisation, be it unitary or multidivisional, and the decision as to how much to centralise or decentralise have to be taken and organisational theorists have also considered the extent to which it is possible provide general rules about the applicability of different structures to different circumstances. This has led to the contingency theories of organisations which imply that there are 'best structures' but that these best structures are associated with (or are contingent on) other factors in the organisation and its environment.

Burns and Stalker (1961) studied the structures of firms and suggested that those which existed in a stable environment with well-recognised technologies (mechanistic systems) should be structured in the sort of way suggested by the classical theorists. In more uncertain environments, where there is rapid change and a need to respond to this change, organismic structures are more appropriate. Organismic structures are much more fluid and dynamic, adapting to their environment in order to survive, as do living organisms. Here lateral communications are encouraged, roles may change and consultation rather than command is more appropriate.

Other contingent variables have been suggested; for example, Woodward (1958) suggested the type of technology of the production process was important, resulting in different spans of control. Where the technology is not complex, the span of control can be wider. Hence the organisation structure must reflect the need for diverse spans of control. Company size has also been claimed to be important. Whatever the contingency, the claim is that once the important contingent factors have been identified then an appropriate control structure can be identified and used in order to provide the most efficient operation.

We shall finally consider the matrix structure which has been suggested by organisational theorists to offer another approach to structure. Matrix management is that which provides leadership on a functional basis and also on a product basis. For example, in the educational world it is common to find a structure which gives subject leadership (function) and also course leadership (product). Thus a member of staff may be responsible to two different people for different aspects of their work. This approach allows for development and control of expertise within the function, but also allows some integration of the different functions in the development of different products. In the latter case faster responses to customers can be given. In this way matrix management structures come nearer to meeting the needs of the organismic organisation than do bureaucratic structures. The problem of having 'two bosses' can be a significant disadvantage, and if the product teams are working on short term projects then the frequent need to build new teams can also cause difficulties.

Organisational theory has thus provided a series of suggested structures which can be used in organisations. All these structures provide different solutions to control problems and in real-life situations are no doubt adapted to deal with specific problems which arise. On the whole the solutions offered by the organisational theorists we have considered are based on an a priori view of a legal–rational system and on the nature of control resting on internal organisational relationships.

In many ways economists have a similar view of the structures available for control. However their existence is justified by a very different view of why the firm exists. Also more consideration is given to the interrelationships of different organisations within the economic environment. It is to these views that we shall now turn.

Markets or hierarchies?

Economists have taken a rather different view of organisations from that discussed above; they have focused on the exchange relationships which are an essential part of social life. In particular they have used ideas of *economic* rationality as a basis to guide the decision as to how to structure exchange activities. Their basic premise is that division of labour and specialisation which characterises modern production leads to a need to exchange goods and services. These exchanges or transactions must be co-ordinated and it is the cost of co-ordination which leads to the decision as to the best structure in which to organise them. The determining factor will be the cost of the information.

The line of argument can be traced back to the work of Coase (1937). The starting-point of the discussion relates to the notion of ideal markets. It is through the medium of the market that exchanges or transactions are supposed to take place. Here is the platform where co-ordination of the transactions takes place, buyers and sellers can be introduced, and allocation takes place through the price system which balances supply and demand. The ideal market is one in which this allocation process is efficiently carried out because of the costless availability of perfect information to all those who might wish to engage in the market-place. Coase pointed out that the allocation process is not cost-free, and that the market is therefore not perfect. Therefore exchange relationships may be better organised through the medium of an agreed contract, especially where the conditions of the exchange are complex. The developing and agreeing of a contract has the possibility of incurring significant costs. When these contractual arrangements are of a longer-term nature the development of an organisational context in which to operate becomes an alternative and possibly cheaper way of operating. Thus the cost of information on which to co-ordinate the allocation process becomes a key variable in the decision as to whether transactions are best organised through the market or in a hierarchical organisation. The issue is to decide whether the exchanges are such that transaction cost can be minimised best by entering into the longer-term contractual relationship of an organisation, or whether a market relationship is appropriate.

Williamson (1975) has developed these ideas in the context of what is referred to as 'transaction cost economics'. In doing so he is more specific about both the nature of transaction costs and what gives rise to them. First, he raises the issue of bounded rationality. Bounded rationality accepts that human beings do not necessarily act to maximise the outcomes of a set of actions. Because of the complexity of decisions and the limits of people to process information, people will seek outcomes which are sufficient to satisfy. March and Simon give the example of the difference between searching a haystack for the sharpest needle (maximising) and searching for a needle sharp enough to sew with (satisficing) (March and Simon, 1958, p. 141). Thus, we have the person who intends to be rational but can only be rational within the limits of his or her own capacity to process the information available in a complex world. The consequences, in transaction cost terms, of bounded rationality are increased by complexity.

A second element giving rise to transaction cost is opportunism. This arises from the information asymmetry which might exist. Here one person will have better access to information than the other and this allows a person to act in their own interest. If this can happen, then the allocations in the market will be affected and the exchanges in the market-place will not seem to be fair or effective. This is enabled, in particular, when there are few transactions and few trading partners. If there are large numbers involved in the market, then a customer finding him or herself compromised by a supplier can move to another trading partner; this is not as easily available in a limited market.

It is the bounded rationality implicit in a situation, along with the issue of the possibility of opportunistic behaviour, which are seen as producing transaction costs. To these is added the issue of 'atmosphere'. This relates to the preferences that individuals have for working in different types of organisation, and with groups who hold to different value sets. Thus human attributes are considered along with economic transaction costs, and so different structures can be seen to be the result. In a situation where there is great uncertainty, Williamson argues that the desire to minimise the costs resulting from bounded rationality will lead to keeping the transactions within the organisation, thus favouring the organisational form over the market form of exchange. Market exchange is seen to be favoured in the situation where there are large numbers of trading partners, minimising the cost of opportunistic behaviour.

In relation to a consideration of the issue of opportunistic behaviour, the cost of obtaining information is also significant. Agency theorists (see Baiman, 1982 and 1990, for a thorough overview of the area) who focus on the contractual relationship between the superior (manager) and subordinate are particularly interested in the cost of the information needed by the superior to monitor performance of the contract. This can be seen as complementary or related to the markets and hierarchies approach. Spicer and Ballew (1983) argue that agency theory is a special case of organisation failure. Organisation failure (Williamson, 1975) is said to occur when the cost of organising in a particular fashion is greater than moving to another structure.

The two extremes of market and hierarchy of organisation can be argued to be best seen as ends of a continuum, and various levels of combination of the two extremes may be the best way to achieve efficiency. Thus structures may be designed in such a fashion as to mix hierarchy and market in the form of a divisional structure. Williamson discusses several forms of organisation operating at different levels of complexity and relating in different ways to co-operating. Peer groups are seen as a simple non-hierarchical way of co-operating in which economies of scale in the use of expertise, information and physical assets may be achieved. As the groups get bigger the problem of avoiding 'free-riders' means that more formal organisation is required and simple hierarchies will be preferred. Here there is a recognised superior to co-ordinate, make decisions and inform.

Because of the impact of bounded rationality and because the impetus to specialise as a firm grows, the co-ordination problem increases; Williamson posits a structure called the unitary or U-form organisation in which the co-ordination process is such that several managers are needed. These managers will be in control of functional areas, such as production or marketing, and there will be at least two management layers. The need to communicate up and down the hierarchy will lead to loss of information and of control. This is exacerbated by the problem of bounded rationality in a situation which requires the summarising of increasing amounts of information. Bounded rationality also means that, as only limited amounts of information can be considered, some decisions may be unattended. Given the pressing needs of day-to-day activities, the danger is that longer-term strategic activities may be neglected.

Because of the growing complexity in larger organisations, and particularly those which have moved into diverse product markets, Williamson suggests that a multidivisional (or M-form) organisational structure would be advantageous. This type of organisational structure is one in which there is a specialisation of managerial decision making and a splitting of responsibility for strategic and day-to-day decisions. In an M-form structure the day-to-day operations are carried out in divisions which are quasi-autonomous, allowing the division to be committed to its own operations. The group is controlled in a strategic sense from a centre, which is committed to the future of the organisation as a whole, and which has a monitoring role in relation to the performance of the divisions. Organising in this fashion is seen to be reduce information loss due to bounded rationality. This is the result of the divisions having responsibility for their day-to-day decisions; this in turn reduces the need to communicate information about these activities to so many people.

The M-form of organisation can be seen to provide a mixture of markets and hierarchical organisation. The M-form organisation allows the mixing of the hierarchy, which controls the strategic issues, and the market, in which the day-to-day activities are placed. Thus at divisional level some competition takes place, not just between the divisions and their external competitors, but also between the divisions for internal allocations of resources. This latter type of competition may be for intermediate goods to be transferred between the divisions (producing transfer pricing problems) or for basic resources such as capital or human resources. It is the possibility of achieving the advantages of the market alongside the strategic direction of the hierarchy which has perhaps led to the movement towards the implementation of internal markets in some of the bureaucratically and hierarchically organised public services. This phenomenon will be examined in more detail later, in conjunction with considerations of more recent developments. First, in order to finish the overview of the basic theoretical work, consideration will be given to the work of Ouchi (1979, 1980), who used the transaction cost approach to examine organisational control.

Ouchi alerted us to the fact that transaction costs are linked to the equity or reciprocity in the terms of any exchange. Where it is difficult to value the goods or services which are exchanged, transaction costs will be increased as valuations need to be made and uncertainty must be borne. Ouchi is also concerned with the ability to measure output and the understanding of the way in which inputs are transformed into outputs. Where it is possible to measure outputs easily, but the transformation process is not well understood, it makes sense to use a control system which is concerned with output measurement, and this Ouchi sees as being most economically dealt with in a market. This is because there will be little need for internal mediation of the exchange – all can be measured by the output. Thus the transaction does not need to be organised through extensive contracts.

In the case where outputs are not easily measured but the transaction process is well understood, the key element to control is the behaviour of those involved in the transformation process. In this case the most economical form of control is argued to be through the organisational structure of a hierarchy. This is the result of the ongoing employment relationship, which does not require constant renegotiation and which engenders a sense of belonging and commitment to the organisation. The costs of monitoring employee behaviour are therefore seen as less than those of monitoring them through the market. Figure 3.2 illustrates these relationships.

Where it is possible to measure the outputs easily, and where transformation is well understood, either markets or hierarchies offer possibilities for control. Where the opposite scenario exists and it is not easy to measure outputs and the transformation process is not well understood, then neither markets nor hierarchies are seen as offering a way of controlling. It is in this situation that Ouchi posits the usefulness of the self and social controls of the 'clan'. Clan control offers a mutual monitoring through the norms and values

FIGURE 3.2   Approach to control of organisations

OUTPUTS	Easily measurable	Not easily measurable
TRANSFORMATION PROCESS		
Well understood	Market/hierarchies	Hierarchies
Not well understood	Markets	Social control of the 'clan'

Source: W.G. Ouchi (1979) (adapted).

of the group. This type of control is more part of the process of action within the organisations concerned than structure. In evaluating the market-structured approach to control it is important to remember the existence of approaches such as clan control. Often markets and hierarchies are considered but the issue of clan control is not discussed.

The use of different structural configurations

The debate as to what structure is most appropriate is not just an academic question, but relates to issues which are affecting most our lives in the 1990s. The economists' approach to organisational structure has been adopted as a frame of reference, and there is a distinct movement towards the adoption of 'market'-type answers to the economic problems of societies as different as the UK and the 'emergent' economies of the countries of Eastern Europe.

Having reviewed the main background literature in the area, the next aim will be to examine an example of the most recent attempts to approach control issues through the market structure. The overriding strength of this approach is illustrated by the fact that it can be found in relation to both the public and the private sectors. We shall first consider the use of this logic in the public sector. The belief of the market approach is summed up by Enthoven (1985): 'When all alternatives have been considered, it becomes apparent that there is nothing like a competitive market to motivate quality and economy of service.' (p. 42). This belief has been the basis for much of the recent legislation in respect of the UK public sector. First implementation of these principles in organisations such as the National Health Service (NHS) was in their peripheral activities. It was required that services such as catering, cleaning and laundry be put out to competitive tender to test the efficiency of the internally organised services. Similar local government services have also been required to submit to competitive tendering processes. Having attempted to impose market discipline on these services, legislation has now gone on to require that professional services be subject to market discipline. Therefore in local authorities, for example, services such as the legal department are planning for the introduction of competitive tendering for some of their services and the provision of service level agreements in others. In the latter case a quasi-market discipline is being attempted, in which local government departments act as purchasers and providers of each other's services, rather than as different functional parts of the same organisation. This requires the formalisation of the requirements of the purchaser and the agreement of the standards of service. In essence exchange relationships are being created within the organisation, and a type of M-form logic is being used.

This type of logic is being explicitly used to guide changes in the structure of the UK health and education services. Delegation of responsibility to units directly concerned with the service provision is being introduced. Thus those who previously had responsibility for managing the service through direction of the service units are now the delegated purchasers of the service. The management of the service provision is in the hands of the units themselves. In the case of the NHS the units are, for example, hospitals and the creation of self-governing trusts has given greater autonomy to some units. The intention is that units must now compete to offer their services to the purchasers and that, in this competition, efficiency gains will obtain. In the case of education, delegation for service provision has been to school level and, given that funding is largely related to pupil numbers and freer choice is available in school enrollment, competition between schools is being promoted. There are other issues, such as the publication of league tables of school examination and test results, designed to promote this competition.

The question is whether the imposition of market-type controls is effective in these situations. One of the problems which is being encountered in the NHS is the provision of sufficient information to allow the market to carry on transactions efficiently (Purdy, 1993a,1993b). Another problem is the lack of use of the information that has been provided (Purdy, 1991, 1993a) Transaction costs must be increasing, at least in the short term, in relation to this provision of basic information. This seems on the face of things to be against to the logic of transaction cost economics. Using Ouchi's (1979, 1980) framework, it could be argued that, as the process of transformation of inputs to outputs is not well understood, and as there is no easy measure of output, neither market nor hierarchical control is appropriate, but clan control is needed.

In terms of the private sector, the need for flexibility in response to change has led to an interest in and use of the market structure (Starkey *et al.*, 1991). Flexibility is seen as an important issue in the context of a rapidly changing environment and in terms of strategic management. The new manufacturing technologies and the approaches to management promoted by responses to Japanese success have promoted flexibility at many different levels. Popular management texts (for example, Peters and Waterman, 1982) have stressed the need for flexibility in order to achieve excellence in a firm. The economic and political failure of the bureaucratically organised regimes in Eastern Europe has given impetus to the belief that the flexibility promoted by the market is the key to economic success.

In this context, the organisation of exchanges within and between firms has been examined. In the case of internal organisation, firms have been advised to ensure that there is flexibility to cope with rapidly changing environments. Perhaps the greatest effect of this has been in the way in which the boundaries of firms have been redrawn in order that activities which were once internally performed are now contracted out. Management buy-outs of sectors of firms and the contracting out of peripheral activities are consistent with the advice of Peters and Waterman (1982) to go back to basics and to divest other areas. Joint ventures provide another means of co-operating in a shorter-term time horizon. This approach can be seen as an attempt to negotiate and control a complex environment through the use of contracts. This allows greater flexibility to change the contract mix and also the activity mix of the firm. The increased cost of renewing and renegotiating contracts may be offset by the benefits of being able to react to change much more quickly. Yet in some situations, such as 'just-in-time' systems, the whole approach relies on very close relationships organised through specific contracts. In this type of relationship the extent of flexibility is questionable. The extent to which this kind of relationship is more aligned to market or to hierarchy can also be debated!

The ultimate question to be answered is whether this 'economic' approach can help us to define the best structure for control in a given set of circumstances. The economic or market model is certainly achieving a good level of support at present, hence its adoption in current thinking about the public and private sector. However some questions need to be asked, based on the insights of Ouchi's approach to the area. His model provides an indication that in some circumstances it is not appropriate to adopt market-type controls, and the key issue is the ability to measure outputs. There is some evidence that the current legislation in the public sector is seeking to impose ways of defining and measuring outputs as this is a fundamental requirement of the market model. This is fine on one level, but if the situation is such that inadequate or inappropriate output controls are being developed, then problems are likely to occur. There is some evidence (for example in the area of education: Broadbent *et al.*, 1992, 1993) of grave doubt about the ability of the output measures being developed to measure the activity of the organisation in a meaningful manner. This fear is most pronounced in the public sector in services which are geared towards care and service to individuals, such as the aforementioned case of education, or in health and welfare services. If this is the case then the market cannot control effectively. What is more, the increased transaction costs expended to provide the increased information for the market to develop cannot therefore be set off against any benefit.

The situation in the private sector also needs to be considered. Although the divestment of activities and the downsizing of operations may be a good way of achieving short-term flexibility, there is still a need for co-operation between producers. The relationships between suppliers and producers in the 'just-in-time' system must be close if the system is to work well. If contracts are intermittent and all that happens is that the risks of a changing environment are passed down to suppliers, the costs of the contract may increase. This would be the result of producers seeing their risk profile increase and therefore increasing prices accordingly.

It needs to be recognised that the decision as to an appropriate structure is not merely a question contingent on factors such as addressing complexity. It must also attend to the need for long-term stability and investment (in people as well as financial resources). This needs a consideration of the patterns of working, the identity that employees have with their firms, and the scale of operations, together with patterns of uncertainty and ambiguity. Unless these things are taken into consideration the danger is that the decision to adopt a particular control structure will be an ideological one. At the moment evidence as to the success or otherwise of the implementation of the market based approach in both the public and private sector is not yet available. More research and exploration need to be carried out in order to inform an ongoing discussion. This will enable us to broach the question as to whether the decision between markets and hierarchies is one which can be based on objective assessment, or whether it is more an ideological choice. Indeed the issue as to whether the choice between markets and hierarchies is culturally or ideologically based, rather than objectively directed, is an intriguing one. It is not, perhaps, possible to give an answer, but it might provide a useful consideration to bring into play in deliberations about the structures in given situations.

Some final comments: do not forget the organisational theorists

The latter part of this chapter has considered the current debate as to whether markets or hierarchies provide the better way of structuring the organisations which provide the goods and services we need in our economy. The reader might be forgiven for thinking that the suggestions of the organisational theorists are forgotten and part of some intellectual history. This is far from the case. The explication of the idea of a bureaucracy is one which is still extremely influential and indeed is reflected in the whole idea of a hierarchy. The two approaches are not mutually exclusive but provide many overlaps. Structure is indeed an important element in providing control in organisations. Whether the structure adopted is theorised through organisational or economic theory is perhaps less important than recognising that we have no perfect structures of control available to us yet. It should also be recognised that in the context of the contemporary debate as to whether markets or bureaucracies provide the 'best' organisational structure the issue of clan control has become somewhat forgotten. It should be remembered that clan control is useful in situations where it is difficult to measure the outputs and, indeed, where the process of achieving those outputs is difficult to define.

The issue of clan control can be explored in the context of a short consideration of the work of Merchant (1985) who categorises three approaches to control: action control, results control and personnel control. Action control involves supervision which ensures that the correct processes are followed. To use this approach those who seek to control must know the process required. Results control requires that the outputs be measurable and monitored to ensure they are as required. Where neither of these two possibilities exists then personnel controls have to be used. This is comparable to clan control and involves appointing those who can be *trusted* to do what the controller would wish to do in the same situation.

Much of the recent legislation in respect of the public sector in the UK has sought to adopt behaviour or results control and personnel controls have not been pre-eminent. For example, medical practitioners are encouraged to practise particular approaches to medicine by linking actions such as immunization programmes to pay. This is an approach based on ideas of action control. In schools, examination results tables have been published as a way of measuring outputs. Hence an output control has been developed and adopted. In both these examples, assumptions have been made about the relevant processes and outputs. Previously the professionals who undertake these tasks would have been controlled by personnel controls. Professionals would have been trusted and subject to much less scrutiny in the day-to-day operation of their tasks. Now the tasks have been redefined in such a way as to minimise the need for personnel control, and to allow the control process to operate through preferred structures, in the case of the UK public sector by the introduction of the market.

The issue of structure, it must be recognised, is not the only issue for consideration when control is considered. It is, however, in the context of contemporary debates, a central consideration. The aim of this chapter has not, therefore, been to present a picture of what control structure *should* be. It has been to present an overview of the ideas available from the organisational and the economic field. It has aimed to show the diversity of approaches available and to present an overview of where they are suggested to be of most use. The strengths and weaknesses of the different approaches have been considered. Finally some illustration of the current issues and debates of control has been provided. The fact that structures of control are a current and controversial element in the world in which we live has been highlighted, and some doubt about the solution of markets as a universal panacea has been voiced.

Notes

1. The gender of the 'best man' is that which was used by Taylor, not our own! We retain this original gender throughout our discussion of Taylor's work

CHAPTER 4

Procedures for control

Anthony J. Berry, Jane Broadbent and David Otley

In previous chapters we have addressed the issues of control and of control structures. In this chapter we address the question of procedures for control primarily through consideration of planning. We work from the idea that a plan constitutes a model of the expected or intended future activities of the organisation and can be a basis for control actions; however we will also argue that the procedure of planning contains within it more of the requisite variety for control than is contained in the plan itself.

We can commonly talk of planning as consisting of different elements in the simple control loop. First, there is a process of establishing the pattern of activities to be undertaken in the future; it is the representation of that pattern of activities in physical or financial terms, or perhaps both, that constitutes the plan. The second part of the cycle is undertaking the work that is contained in the activity programme and measuring the work that is done. The third part of the cycle is constructing reports and statements about the work done in relation to the plan. The fourth element in the cycle is reviewing the relationship between the expected pattern of activities and the actual pattern of activities and deciding what, if anything, should be done about it. This is, of course, the simple control or planning cycle which is best described as a first-order feedback.

In the simple feedback control loop (see Chapter 2) there is a requirement for a controller or decision maker to make decisions that would change either the input mix or the transformation process to achieve the desired ends. The desired ends are usually expressed in the plan which an organisation may have created. The plan is not the control model; for that, the controller needs models of the 'transformation process in their environmental context' to enable him or her to establish a plan or a modification to that plan. Hence there is a need to consider the control models in use; that is, we must consider the kind of planning processes which an organisation might create. In this chapter we set out to discuss, first, planning; second, managing complexity;

third, managing with uncertainty and the question of whether it is possible to conceive of some overall way of fitting these issues together, and what problems emerge.

Planning

At the heart of a great deal of the literature on planning lie the structural functional ideas of Talcott Parsons (1964). Planning may be seen as a process of choosing and setting in train patterns of activities in order to achieve certain *goals*. The pattern of activities in any sizeable organisation is a matter of establishing activities and differentiating them into sub-activities. This differentiation necessarily leads to the need for processes of *integration*. As all of these activities take place in a changing world, there is a need for *adaptation* and change in the pattern of activities and, indeed, the goals. All of this takes place in the context of a *social structure*; that is, in a human organisation where people may or may not share values, histories, traditions, languages, skills, or knowledge. These four ideas from the structural functional literature, that is of goal attainment, integration, adaptation and the social structure, underlie a great deal of what is actually written about planning and budgeting.

Note that we are distinguishing between the concepts of organisation structure (see Chapter 3) and social structure. By the latter we mean the patterns of emergent values, and beliefs, identity and identification, of persons within the organisation. By the former we mean the pattern of roles, authority, responsibility and accountabilities formally established. Hence, it will be noted, our interest, in most parts of this text, in the interplay of social structure and organisational structures and procedures.

In the example of the vehicle rebuild (Box 4.1), drawn from the real experience of one of the authors, we see how the imperatives of the social structure can dominate the apparent rationality of an accounting system which was reflecting the goals differentiation and integration procedures of this part of the enterprise. In effect the managers were being highly intelligent. They were more prepared to set aside an accounting system which did not reflect the full circumstances and they were not prepared to force unnecessary changes on the patterns of work, effort and use of skill of their labour force. Here we see that task activities in human organisations, whether they are of the physical work or the accounting representation or payment, take place within social structures. While these social structures may exhibit multiple values and multiple characteristics and may rarely operate with any kind of unitary consensus or, indeed, unitary authority, it is visible from this example that the social structure enabled managers to pursue organisational goals when the organisation procedures of accounting would cause dysfunctional behaviour.

Box 4.1   Accounting costs and social structures

A company owned a fleet of vehicles, and the life of each vehicle, with regular maintenance and irregular but well-programmed major rebuilding, was about 30 years. The company knew, five years ahead, which vehicles would appear when for the rebuild programme. In this programme they had organised a system of budgeting and were attempting to move to a system of flexible budgeting in relation to the work to be done. Clearly, the work was actually very predictable and was very well predicted. The company was puzzled because it had apparently lost control of the cost of the rebuild.

Upon examination it was clear that the standard costs which had been developed for the rebuild were being largely abused. The company faced problems in its local labour market in recruiting skilled manpower without apparently changing the pay rates that it was prepared to offer. It was necessary then to use the bonus and incentive system as a vehicle for increasing the take-home pay of the skilled workers without changing the daily and hourly rate. The method chosen for this purpose was to book some of the skilled workers' time to a category called 'idle time'. This then shortened the amount of time booked to do the specific pieces of work, and this in turn increased the bonus payable on each job. As booked idle time was held to be the responsibility of the management and not of the workers, it was paid at the rate of the average bonus earned that week in the whole of the rebuild system. So the allocation of time to booked idle time meant that there was a ratchet effect in increasing the bonus and thereby increasing the take-home pay. Further it was difficult to find the original standards that had been set up by work study engineers for the maintenance task.

It is sometimes assumed that there is an unequivocally determined time horizon for organisation plans. In the early days of corporate planning, as in national planning, it was common to find injunctions to have five-year plans. However the parts of real organisations work with very varied time horizons – from a few days or months to many years. So different parts of complex organisations plan over different time horizons, with the financial plan horizon being a compromise. For example, in the electricity supply industry the time span of decision making, implementation and consequences for a nuclear power station total some 45 years (and perhaps much longer). For a fossil power station they span anything between 20 and 40 years. Laying a new power supply to your house (a supply which perhaps lasts 30 years) may only require a few weeks. The very long time scales of implementation and consequences, characteristic of major projects like roads, tunnels, very large bridges and so on, seem to create problems all of their own, in that it is very difficult to predict either accurately or with any degree of confidence costs and revenues over such extended periods. Even in businesses with much shorter time horizons it is fairly clear that the time span of thinking and the time span of control vary considerably in different parts of complicated organisations. The following example illustrates this point. In an organisation which was supplying a commodity product, the accuracy of estimates or the accuracy of plans that was established by the organisations was as represented in Table 4.1.

Now it may be seen from the table that the senior managers could claim to be more effective managers than their subordinates in that they were able to have a more accurate short-term forecast of revenues and costs at their level of the organisation than the subordinate managers were able to attain at theirs. However we might note that the senior managers' major focus of concern was not on short-term control but on longer-term issues of effectiveness. It can be seen from the table that there was a curious similarity between some admittedly imprecise notion of time span of control and the error level which was apparently tolerable or, indeed, merely existing within this organisation (see Berry and Otley,1986, for a further examination of these issues). Senior managers, though, were not above using their better short term performance as a means of exerting claims of the greater competence in relation to their subordinates. In addition to the issue of time there are the problems of complexity and uncertainty, and we will take these up in the following sections.

Managing complexity

There are many studies and approaches to the structures which modern organisations have developed in order to manage their inherent complexity. In Chapter 3 we saw that Williamson discusses the difference between unitary and multidivisional forms of organisation. Another writer, Harrison, has suggested that there are four basic forms of managing complexity: the first of

TABLE 4.1   **Estimation accuracy of plans at different managerial levels**

Management levels	Planning years horizon		
	1	2	3
Top	0.5	0.11	0.15
Middle	0.11	0.15	
Lower	0.15		

these is organisational bureaucracy; the second is the organisational matrix; the third form is a person-centred organisation; and the fourth is a power-centred organisation. Obviously Williamson and Harrison (1972) and other authors (for example, Morgan 1986) have different pictures in their minds and different ways of thinking about organisations. If we take the first model of the functional bureaucracy, represented in Figure 4.1, it is fairly clear that this is a model of an organisation with a head office function, where each of the organisational arms represents some major activity of the organisation; for example, purchasing, personnel, manufacturing, marketing, finance, and so on. The character of this sort of organisation, as in all bureaucracies, is that it will operate with rules, structures and procedures, and certainly its planning and budgeting will be clearly structured via established organisational procedures. The principal criticism of functional bureaucracies is that, while in stable states they produce efficient goal attainment, in changing worlds they tend to be maladaptive. Clearly it is the functional model of Parsons being replayed here: the bureaucracy is essentially an organisation dedicated to the pursuit of goals through structures of integration to cope with its internal differentiation. It has the control modes of hierarchies and rules, from which are derived the processes of planning and plans to ensure compliance and goal attainment.

The next step in organisational form is to move to the horizontal linkages, shown in Figure 4.2, of the matrix organisation, where it is necessary to cope with adaptation by linking across the functions because of the interdependence of the operations. This linking via plans produces the capacity to relate the inner interdependent parts to the outside world; that is, it creates the capacity to think about and create adaptive processes. In the person-centred world, the third type suggested by Harrison, we have an organisation which is essentially rooted in its social rather than organisational structure, and the

FIGURE 4.1   The Organisational Bureaucracy

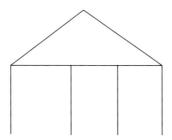

1. Funtions such as production, marketing, etc the.
2. Work is delegated from the top.
3. Co-ordination is by rules and procedures, up and down the hierarchy.

FIGURE 4.2   The Organisational Matrix

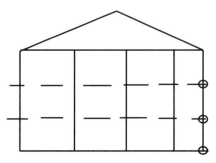

Horizontial linkages across functions modifies the process
of co-ordination via hierarchy to include co-ordination
across the functions, providing scope for faster
adaptive behaviours.

notion of goals and differentiation, integration and adaptation flow from the interests of the individuals as they go about their work. Some professional partnerships are like this.

The fourth kind of organisation which Harrison addresses, the power-centred organisation, is a kind of despotism where all power flows from the one central figure. It is a picture of monarchy, and it describes quite nicely some kinds of entrepreneur-created organisations, where the entrepreneur cannot delegate and cannot trust anybody to undertake work on his behalf or, indeed, on their own behalf. Most of the rest of this chapter will consider primarily the organisational forms of functional bureaucracy and of the matrix, as these are the most common core forms of managerial organisations.

Financial planning is, then, a control procedure in most organisations. A financial plan is usually represented by the four key financial statements; that is, the profit and loss account, which expresses the expected patterns of activity and the consequential revenues and costs; the balance sheet, which represents the pattern of asset structure to support those activities; sources and application of funds statements, which show the patterning in the way revenues and asset use are intermingled; and the cash flow, which is a simplified representation of money movements in and out of the organisation. Probably the most useful of these four for financial planning and control would be a sophisticated sources and application of funds statement, because that statement encapsulates the changing patterns of financial flows in relation to activity through time. Overall these four statements, taken together, are observations of resource flow and the consequences of activities.

The financial plan so created becomes a model for control. However, as it has been socially constructed and is used in the context of both an organisational structure and a social structure, it would be unwise to assume (see Chapter 3) that the 'plan' is uncritically accepted as the basis for all future actions. This idea of a financial plan fits well with the bureaucratic form of organisation, expressing integration of the programmes of activity in financial terms.

One critique arises from consideration of the source or the rationales underlying the plan. In earlier chapters we referred to the work of Etzioni and his typology of normative, instrumental and coercive organisations. If, for example, an organisation has a normative form, then clearly the question of goal differences does not arise, even though, of course, there are other problems. If it is a coercive organisation, the goals of those being coerced do not matter. If it is an instrumental organisation (as most commercial organisations appear to be) then there must be some mediation of the differences of values and goals, and so on, within an organisation. Organisations, in pursuit of economic rationality, use their need to satisfy capital markets, to justify entering into varieties of control processes of either motivation or manipulation to try to align organisation members to such institutional goals in a process of goal congruence. Otley has commented that it might be easier to recognise and work with behavioural congruence; that is, people can actually work together while having disparate views on why it is they are working together. The response of the authoritarian is, in the face of apparent deviance from institutional rationality, to propose more controls. It is also evident that the greater the control, or the number of controls that are invented, then the greater the deviance that apparently takes place. This endless game was charted elegantly by Hofstede (1967) and more sharply and more clearly by Van Gunsteren (1976) who pointed out the infinite regress of rule-based control (if there is a rule A, then we need a rule B, to define when A shall be applied. If there is now a rule B, we need a rule C, and so on). It seems that we cannot solve the issues in the social structure by creating additional control procedures in the organisation structure.

Simon (1957) and other researchers noted that managers in organisations behave as though they are not pursuing the same goals; as though the organisational plan and control mode did not wholly provide the criteria for their actions. He offered the following explanation. Given that large organisations deal with complexity via differentiated structures and procedures, they create the existence of sub-goals (and a need for integration). As the differentiation is not a simple decomposition of the work of the board, but is an elaboration of it – in products, technologies, markets and so on – then local rationalities are created, in relation to which local goals emerge. Hence managers working on such local goals are constrained by corporate goals rather than merely subordinated to them.

This brings us to what we might term the complexity critique in financial planning and control. Given the nature of complexity in organisations and the nature of differentiation, we clearly create a need for integration (a need that is powerfully served by accounting processes) and this is integration both of thought and action. In the Anglo-Saxon cultures, great store is set by a notion of autonomy and autonomous, personally responsible action. In the Asian cultures, a greater store is set by the notion of dependence and joint action. It would seem that, as in so many things, the truth of managing complex organisations lies between these two polar positions of autonomy and dependence. We find ourselves struggling to handle the interdependence between the internal and external worlds of organisations, meeting highly varied environmental demands, opportunities and constraints, while trying to hold to the stability of a transformation process and deliver goods and services into the product market-place. Given that statement, the question arises as to what can be differentiated. It would appear that the simple notion of the institutional goal and the institutional decision maker merely delegating different parts of the tasks is too simple. It would appear that, as organisations grow in size and complexity, it becomes logically necessary to differentiate work and the decision authority about what that work actually is. Having had that level of differentiation it would seem that we must rethink our notion of financial planning to create a control model, because it becomes impossible to see this merely as a process of disaggregation and aggregation of well understood and completely rational processes.

In more formal terms, we are arguing that the financial plan – because it is created in a complex organisation through highly differentiated procedures – is a variety-reduced descriptive model of the future activities of the organisation. Such a plan as model will lack the requisite variety for control which Ashby (1956) demonstrated was necessary for determining the state of the system. However it is the case that the model/plan and the processes which create it would contain substantially more variety and might approach the requisite variety for control.

Jalland (1989) introduced an elegant notion of plans between parts of organisations forming contracts or compacts, multidimensioned in nature, rooted in patterns of history and notions of incomplete understanding. These compacts, then, were spaces or domains within which there was an agreement to work, an agreement to behave in a certain way, through which skill, experience, knowledge and competence were mobilised at, for example, lower levels, as part of a bargaining process for resources to enable the organisation to function (with variety in the compact and in the process). It is a way of construing organisation as a rather late-twentieth-century form of Rousseau's social contract, that the planner's compact creates sufficiently common frames of understanding through which people will have the confidence to allocate major amounts of resource and to enable managers of differentiated units to handle both the differentiated tasks and the differentiated decision authorities that, perforce, must go with them. Through this process, then, the problem of adaptation can be handled, for it follows that adaptation must also be handled as a differentiated process. Here we see adaptation taking place on two levels: firstly, the macro-institutional level, which concerns the basic configuration of enterprise, and secondly, at a micro level, which concerns specific elements of the environment to the organisation and finding the appropriate configuration of the internal micro world for effective relationship with these specific elements.

Clearly one response to the problem of complexity is to seek control through vertical co-ordination. This process of establishing goal programmes and sub-goals and so on is characteristic of the functional bureaucracy which presupposes that decomposition is an appropriate algorithm for its internal world. To some degree the technique of management by objectives follows that particular approach. We suppose that in some limited circumstances that might work. More likely, though, is that the debate about goals would be on something of a dialectic or a process of negotiation between institutional and internal sub-systems. The dialectic would have to recognise the location of knowledge and expertise and competence to undertake work in the complex organisation. Depending upon the nature of work, complexity may be severe at 12 or more people, and almost certainly becomes so at numbers from 20 to 40 people. It is actually impossible for one person to know everything, therefore the contributions of others are required, and these contributions are unique. So we see again that the procedures of creating a plan or control model are richer and probably more important than the plan itself. In the dialogue about the creation of the plan we would expect to find the explanatory and predictive models from which managers argue their case for the plan itself.

What seems to arise here is the principle of subsidiarity, by which is meant that, as a means of coping with complexity, tasks and decision authority should be delegated as close to the point of enactment as one could possibly get. This principle of subsidiarity, which is a part of the evolution of the European Economic Community and its relations with its member states and the regions and local structures of those member states, constitutes a very interesting model for commercial organisations. The principle of subsidiarity is a response to the problem of complexity and internal differentiation which would appear to be appropriate if the differentiated units could effectively work for the most part separately from each other; for example, where the interdependence between the units is low we can create the classic multidivisional form of organisation. Where the interdependence between parts is very high, one has to find a means of managing that interdependence. It is clear that major problems arise at this point for goals, co-ordination and control. An extreme notion of subsidiarity essentially says that an institution is an aggregation of parts; in this sense the differentiated parts may negotiate between themselves as to what form of institution is actually needed. In the reverse of the case of an institution dominating its differentiated parts, co-ordination procedures would emerge to constrain the managers' actions. Those of our readers with a sense of history will recognise very nicely the conflict between the king and the barons which led the barons to force the king to sign the Magna Carta. This problem has also been played out in the evolution of the political structures of the United States of America and is unlikely to rest easily in the emerging structures of the European Economic Community. It is also a problem that emerges time and time again in the debates about the nature of multidivisional organisations. It is possible to see a rather simple-minded dynamic between integration and adaptation when problems arise in a highly complex multidivisional organisation, for if problems emerge about managing interdependence hierarchically and between the divisions, then the solution proposed is almost inevitably in forms of centralisation. If problems arise in centralised or unitary organisations as a product of complexity and ambiguity, the solution normally proposed is to decentralise or divisionalise. Of course these are polarities and, as Peters and Waterman (1982) found, there is much scope for acknowledging the paradox when they observed organisations with what they termed tight or loose control structures, by which they meant that decision authority on some matters was held centrally (tight co-ordination) while on other matters it was delegated (loose co-ordination to permit adaptation).

Perhaps more formally it is possible to argue that the principle of subsidiarity does not imply either a multidivisional form or a unitary form. What the principle of subsidiarity might lead us to in the design of organisation control structures is discerning the relevant and appropriate location of task and decision authority. Note, though, that these are all processes of control through vertical co-ordination, where the task is to hold the integrity of the institution together in the interests of the owners, or other principal stakeholders, such as the managers. The problems that arise here are the problems of aggregation across complex differentiated units which insist on working with different technologies and different time horizons. In the face of such complexity there is much sense in central or institutional control structures being construed with minimum variety. Hence financial models and financial targets, using the four financial statements, constitute one reduction of the complexity, delegating the processes of interpretation (or holding uncertainty) to unit managers.

Programme planning and budgeting systems and zero-based budgeting

In this section we turn to a discussion of two approaches to managing complexity through financial planning procedures: the first, programme planning and budgetary systems (PPBS), refers to the continuing integration of programmes with plans and budgets; the second purports to be more radical, zero-based budgeting, which is control through a process of requiring future rejustifying of all actions.

Where there was high complexity and interdependence in organisations, it became important to try to create some institutional means of handling it. The story is often told of how Robert McNamara used his industrial experience as a basis for his attempt to manage complexities and interdependence in the US Department of Defense (see Box 4.2) by the introduction of programme planning and budgeting systems. The essential point of programme planning and budgeting systems may be seen by referring to the models of organisation as functional bureaucracy and as a matrix. In a government there may be activities which contribute to some overarching policy; for example, the departments concerned with education, health, industry, welfare and housing may all be contributing to a policy of raising the level of social and economic well-being of a section of the community. Should the government organise its work only on a functional basis then the recipients of these efforts may experience a measure of discontinuity of policy and a lack of effectiveness. Further,

---

Box 4.2   An example of changes in the distribution of power through a change from a functional to a matrix organisation

It is said that in the bad old days there were four armed forces in the United States, each of which contributed one member to the Joint Chiefs of Staff Committee which reported to the Secretary of State for Defense. These four units were the Navy, the Air Force, the Army and the Marines. It was observed that in any serious fighting these four units mostly had to co-operate in a highly interdependent way to provide an effective military force in any given theatre of operations. It was also observable to the public that the United States Air Force maintained a small army and a rather small navy, the United States Army had some seaborne capability and a great deal of airborne attack capability, the United States Navy had some major aircraft carriers and battle fleets which had enormous numbers of strike aircraft as part of their military capability, and the United States Marines were always designed as a flexible force with flexible resources. Interesting questions arose as to which of the three major branches of the armed forces should have control of intercontinental ballistic missiles. In practice they each had their own systems. It was therefore felt that the growth of these four enterprises had led to a certain measure of redundancy. However, given the structure of the Joint Chiefs of Staff Committee, it was also observed that the Secretary of State for Defense would always be presented by the Joint Chiefs of Staff with their own solution to whatever problems emerged. Essentially the power of decision making rested not with the Secretary of State but with the Joint Chiefs of Staff. Readers may have entirely different views about what they regard as appropriate. However, Robert McNamara, as Secretary of State for Defense, it is reported, created civilian directors of theatre operations reporting directly to him. The Joint Chiefs of Staff were then told that if they wanted any military resource or any money to provide that resource they would have to negotiate with the directors of theatre operations, who were the budget holders.

departments may use the existence of such a policy to bid for extra funds but find it expedient to allocate some of them to equally worthy but competing activities. In short the very thrust for efficiency which functional specialism enables may render the policies less effective.

The idea of creating programme managers, across the functions and hence along the matrix, to co-ordinate such a policy initiative seems simple enough. However if the co-ordinators have less authority or micropolitical force than the functional managers then their co-ordination role will become one of messengers rather than mediators. A second-stage solution to this problem is to provide a programme or policy manager with the budgetary allocation and invite the functions or departments to bid for resources from the programme manager so that he or she can hold them to account and in turn be accountable for the policy initiative. Here the matrix managers have more resource power than the function heads. Hence it is clear that the idea of PPBS is the creation of a means of integration to ensure the adaptation to programme needs becomes crucial to the behaviour of departments. It is also clear that the idea of an internal market can be used here, for that is how functions obtain resources to do work.

Of course in any ongoing organisation as complex as a government it is unlikely that such internal market power will be the dominant mode of behaviour. Long-lasting organisations develop all manner of social structures, customs and histories which would mediate the crude application of these internal market arrangements. A slight insight into such social structures may be gained by noting the routes for promotion. For example, do the programme managers aspire to be departmental heads, or vice versa? Further consideration of the fact that government policy initiatives do not get created in a vacuum but are the outcome of considerable external and internal debate should give the sceptical good cause to doubt that simple structural changes would give rise to major changes. However PPBS stands as an interesting contribution to the pursuit of the rational in the allocation of resources in pursuit of organisational goals. Its very introduction might create some interesting political realignments.

A further technique used in pursuit of rational resource allocation in the achievement of goals is zero-based budgeting (ZBB). This requires all bidders for resources to assume no history or precedent and to justify from a zero base all resources sought in the budget. This somewhat unlikely approach, especially in organisations with ongoing commitments, might cause a deal of irritation and time wasting in order to satisfy the 'new manager' that previous behaviour was not perverse. It makes a good if dangerous weapon in the hands of a new manager, for in such an approach is an invitation to reassert authority and perhaps power. ZBB is susceptible to the same critiques as PPBS and all other prescriptions for the narrowly rational pursuit of resource control in the pursuit of goals. In simple terms, PPBS may be represented as in Figure 4.3. Note that in a PPBS system resources are allocated to functions by programme managers.

FIGURE 4.3   Resource Flows in PPBS

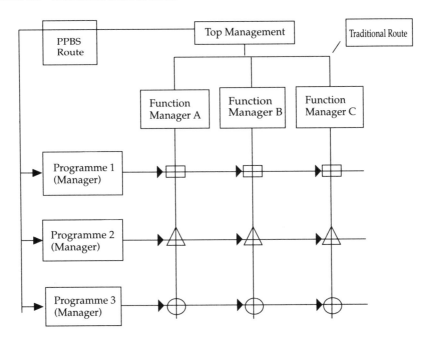

Note that in PPBS the programme managers are the primary conduct
of resources for their functions.

In functional goal disaggregated planning and budgeting, the function
managers bid for resources in the context of a prior plan. The programme
managers negotiate for resources from the function managers. In PPBS the
resources are given to the programme managers. The function managers have
to bid for resources from the programme managers. The programme managers could be held to have a more systemic view of the operations to product
outputs, and are likely to encourage further processes of adaptation. Clearly,
though, the pathways of differentiation and integration are significantly
different.

It is not at all clear that McNamara's attempt actually worked well, or that
the civilians ever did manage to get control of the military. Aaron
Wildavsky's (1975) study of the introduction of programme planning and
budgeting systems in the US Department of Agriculture suggested that its
impact as a means of changing resource allocation from that of the prior
bureaucracy was very modest indeed. The combination of traditional separation and major programmes seemed to create a life of their own, for, while
attempts might have been made to organise apparent management in a

different way by having programme managers, the substantive reality was not much affected. This could be seen as further support for the behavioural critique that social structures both endure and are of great significance. It is easier to change the symbolic representation of what is happening than it is to change the social structure and the grounded reality of the way people actually engage with their work and with each other. In any event, Wildavski's memorable conclusion to his study was that 'some butterflies were caught, but no elephants were stopped'. He found that the departments were the progenitors of programmes, they possessed the expertise to analyse and create; they were a major source of knowledge for the programme managers.

Of course, programme planning and budgeting systems seem to be the classic solution to the problem of matrix organisations. PPBS offers (see Figure 4.3) the product managers of matrix organisation the capacity to make the crucial decisions about the resource flows that create the goods and services for which they are responsible. If properly developed, PPBS gives them the data to enable them to manage the planning and control loops around their particular responsibility. We can see how internal markets can be developed (see Chapter 7).

The question arises as to the efficacy of these approaches. One of the more interesting studies of budgeting in the UK government observed that, in any given financial year, the most any government could affect the overall level of budgets was of the order of 1 per cent and the most they could affect the distribution or redistribution of resources amongst the programmes and ministries was probably not much more than that. This means that, as in any large organisation, the impetus of past commitments and the limited rationality, together with the political processes of bargaining and negotiation, suggest that incrementalism is not merely inevitable but also, according to Braybrooke and Lindblom (1963), a desirable process for managing major institutions. The arguments of the incrementalists contained in Braybrook and Lindblom essentially state that, because of plurality, the pluralism of values, limitation of knowledge, the weight of past decisions and the continuity of programmes, the ambiguity of goals, the shifting relationship of means to ends, the bargaining between one sector of activity and another and so on, the processes of mutual adjustment and incrementalism are inevitable if an organisation is not to fragment.

As noted earlier, the rationalist attack on incrementalism was to create the notion of zero-based budgeting; that is, managers were supposed to justify anew all resources to be required for the following planning period. The basic idea is clearly difficult in operation yet, as a kind of mental discipline, it offers some opportunities for reflective rigour. It suggests that it might be possible to look at an organisation in action and develop a critique from a zero base and then ask, firstly, how the particular current configuration of resources came to be and, secondly, whether that is the most effective configuration of resources that can be used to achieve what the organisation and differentiated units now wish to achieve. So ZBB has a helpful critical contribution to make, providing it is more than an analytical exercise and is connected to the operating, day-to-day reality of the managers concerned, where future activities are the result of past decisions.

The rediscovery of programme planning and budgeting systems

Johnson and Kaplan (1987), in their critique of management accounting and control, argued that the systematic structures of cost accounting did not make much of a connection with the systemic problems of managing an enterprise. To recapitulate a little, the structures of traditional cost accounting, especially such things as full absorption costing, fit beautifully with the notion of the functional bureaucracy, in that they are a classic case of decomposition and disaggregation of hierarchic elements to lower-order activities. If it is important that the bureaucratic functions work together, then this programme of systematic accounting, taking no cognisance of the need to manage interdependence, is likely to produce an accounting structure with limited usefulness.

The manager of the fish-finger factory (see Box 4.3) had, through the use of systematic accounting, become a rather poorly paid servant of a retail operation. Had the factory managers had a systemic notion of accounting they would never have got themselves into this predicament. They needed such an analysis to enable them to see the relationship between the way in which they were using resources and the way in which they were allocating cost, so as to adopt a different business behaviour. Even if we accept the economic marginal resource – marginal cost analysis, it will be noted that the use of full absorption costing to reflect opportunity cost was unhelpful and inadequate. Kaplan and Johnson's critique is pretty much that story told over and over again. What Kaplan argued was that it was important to break this systematic notion of full absorption costing, and to actually create the idea of activity pools to which overheads could be allocated. Then these activity pools would be rigorously criticised (in other words, there would be the emergence of the ideas of zero-based budgeting in a new form) to decide upon appropriate cost structures, then the costs in the activity pools would be allocated to products on some reasoned basis. Now, clearly, this model of activity-based costing has some useful advantages in that it does introduce a critical review. With cost in its application it is, however, an alternative model of systematic analysis and is not necessarily a matter of systemic analysis. The reason why this is so is that it is using fundamentally the observation model of accounting rather than an explanatory model which might lie in economic theory or organisation theory for the behaviour of the firm.

In the late 1980s and early 1990s activity-based costing has become relatively widespread. It is being followed, at the time this chapter is being written, by the rise of activity-based management (ABM). Of course activity-

---

Box 4.3   Competing with oneself

In a fish-finger factory in Europe the company discovered that they had some excess production capacity. Their current brands were selling well and the product was acceptable in many markets. The company was approached by a major retail operation asking them to manufacture, with their spare capacity, some fish-fingers which would be slightly different and wrapped in the retail company's packaging, as an own-label (as it is called) brand. The fish-finger company, believing, rightly at that time, that there was no problem with competition with their own market, readily agreed and through the negotiation of volume contracts offered a very competitive price to the retailer. In the ensuing five to ten years the structure of cost accounting and its full absorption model were pursued until the company accountant noticed that the own-label business was now more than half of the total output, and that the own-label business was costed with a lower level of cost absorption than their own brand business because of the systematic structure of the accounting. The company had moved itself into a rather unpleasant corner, for its brand prices were under pressure in the market-place. It was a problem for the management to understand how they got themselves into this predicament and how they could get themselves out of it.

---

based management is nothing other than programme planning and budgeting systems rediscovered in what is recognisably a more practical and more grounded way. Activity-based management is the horizontal integration process which addresses the systemic issues of any enterprise, and with the reconfiguring of accounting data flows in support of ABM we can begin to see an encouraging development of accounting to support a systemic mode of management control and decision making rather than supporting a systematic mode. It is important to note that the problems of differentiation of task and decision authority, the issue of autonomy and the management of interdependence, are not fully resolved; they are only reconfigured. Inevitably the recognition of an activity constitutes the recognition of an interdependence which is essentially task-based. There would also be powerful and helpful interdependencies between different activity systems and the same functional bureaucratic system. An illustration of this might be that the existence of one activity might well make it possible to have a related activity (such as a similar product or service) and have a cost for doing both of them in the same enterprise rather lower than doing them in two separate enterprises. Some authors regard this as strategic cost management – finding cost savings as a result of the available interdependencies within a very complex system.

In the 1950s and 1960s Boeing developed the family of Boeing 707, 727 and 737 civil jet airliners. The commonality of the technology, design of some parts, and of the operating characteristics of aircraft in airline use enabled very considerable cost savings to be made by having the family of aircraft products made within the same organisation. That is, given the development of the 707, it was cheaper for Boeing to build the 727 and 737 than it would have been for another manufacturer to build similar aircraft. Of course this is to replicate the familiar problems of economics of product range and market scope.

Managing with uncertainty

The previous discussions of procedures for dealing with complexity are themselves a matter of order and ordering. We hope that the reader is not too caught up with the approach of order and stability to forget that what one sees in a financial plan, especially one which is projected on a spreadsheet as single-point estimates over ten years, might be one where the problem of uncertainty has been set aside. For we live in a state of uncertainty about the future of the universe. We cannot predict anything accurately; the best we can do is to create some understanding of probability distributions of distant events. The fact that nearly all financial plans are couched in single-point estimates (presumably drawn from unknown probability distributions and therefore unknown likelihoods of being achieved) provides us with something of a puzzle, for why would that be so?

The behavioural critique of the economic theory of the firm from Cyert and March (1963) included the observation that managers set out to avoid uncertainty. We suspect that we all have a great deal more sympathy with avoiding uncertainty than engaging with it, to which task both Donald Michael (1973) and Donald Schon (1983) encourage us. Schon wrote that the denial of uncertainty merely leads one to live in a disconnected way and it was imperative to have thought structures and behaviours which did connect parts of our experience and understandings. Schon and Michael agreed, though, that managers must learn to live and work with uncertainty and might, in particular, explore the way in which the anxieties that seem to stem from uncertainty bump into the defences that managers and organisations mobilise within themselves. Michael argues that only if future responsive planning systems are created can organisations come to terms with uncertainty and create the essentially intelligent, goal-seeking, adaptive organisations which are necessary. So in terms of our functional quartet of goals, integration, adaptation and social structure, Michael is recognising clearly that the social structure has to bear the costs and difficulties of managing uncertainty through personal and organisational adaptation. He argues that this can only happen if individuals within the social structure learn to give each other support and, further, that in an uncertain world the only likely outcome of quasi-certain financial planning, indeed any other human activity, is that we will get it wrong. If we close down the notion of getting it wrong, either by punishing wrong-doers or by creating a climate within which getting it wrong is unacceptable, we will merely replicate conservative, limited, inward-looking and life-denying organisations (you may well work in one of those!). In order not to do that the social structures, that is the people and the way they work together, have to develop the competence and the capacity to learn. It is in this arena, this awareness of the self and behaviour and the awareness of organisational processes through which defence structures are mobilised against anxiety, that Michael makes his sharpest contribution. He argues that managers need considerably more knowledge of themselves, much greater interpersonal sensitivity and a much greater capacity for giving each other support if we are ever able to enter a future responsive learning organisation that can cope with the ambiguities and uncertainties which face it.

It might be thought that what is being argued for here is something that looks rather like what is believed to have been the management style of some Japanese corporations in the 1980s. In these organisations, goals and programmes were formulated after lengthy processes of discourse and dialogue, examining a wide range of possibilities and ensuring, as best they can, that they create understanding of the world they work in, how they work together in it, how to cope with surprises and opportunities, and how to reflect and then learn anew about the world as they encounter it. To some extent that may be a reasonable description. In cultures of high dependence, where people are not primarily anxious about whether they belong, these processes appear to be possible. In cultures of egocentric ambition, competition and fight, which characterise the Anglo-Saxon world, it would appear to be more difficult to do that. What seems to be needed in the Anglo-Saxon world is a process of social adaptation to enable the social structures to function effectively in handling the problems of high uncertainty of markets and technologies. It is important to note that the techno-structure is inanimate and the anxieties that are provoked by uncertainty are provoked inside people and do not float in some kind of institutional miasma where they can be located, packaged and locked in a spreadsheet.

The problem of uncertainty can lead organisations to create and mirror the varieties of chaos which they face. They do not deal with the uncertainty, rather they let it tumble in across their defences and randomly disturb what were believed to be orderly patterns. An example of this would be a financial plan subject to a multivariate sensitivity analysis with no exploration of managing consequences. Another would be the presentation of the future of the enterprise as a probability distribution of the net present value of future expected cash flows, with no understanding of the loss function of the decision makers. The problem of uncertainty disturbs the apparent stability of budgeting and the patterns of expectation. It certainly radically disturbs what one thinks one is doing when one measures events. Even more significantly, the accounting measurement is difficult, for the nature of observation of the past as a basis for future predictions in an uncertain world is highly problematic. What becomes clear here is that the nature of observation of the past to infer exact predictions in an uncertain world is a highly difficult business. Statisticians lead us to think about variability, measures of variability and issues of sampling. So if the problems of observation and measurement are difficult then the elicitation of meaning is even more difficult. What the problem of uncertainty does is focus the requirement for interpretative analysis as part of the control loop, rather than mere resort to observation and comparison of what is observed by what was expected. The issue of uncertainty leads us to have disturbed pictures of expectations and possibly inadequate measures of phenomena as they actually occur. Therefore some much richer frame of interpretative analysis is required to enable those in the position of controller to actually come to some judgement as to the antecedents of observed activity and what might be done to shape future activities.

This takes us back to the beginning of this chapter, where we touched upon the difference between decision making and control. What seems to emerge here is support for Geoffrey Vickers' (1965) general proposition that managers, in using procedures for control, do not, and perhaps should not, make decisions, and nor should they believe that they do. Rather, he argues, and we agree, that managers need to form appreciations of what they are setting out to manage. The appreciation is the multidimensioned, multitheoried understanding of the complexities and uncertainties of the domains in which they find themselves in relation to the environment. This notion of an appreciation then creates the context within which action might be considered and resource patterns shifted. It provides the basis for Jalland's notion of a planning compact. What this does, then, is relate the techno-structure of control to the social structure of organisations, recognising that the techno-structure can contain the complexity, while the social structure contains the uncertainty.

Conclusions

We are essentially arguing here that the techno-structure of planning and control procedures is necessary, valid and very important, because it is the only process that we actually have in an adequate variety-reduced form that enables us at least to relate analytically the factor markets, transformation process and product/service markets of any enterprise. The limitations of the techno-structure of such control procedures is that it provides a category of observations, largely without an explanatory theory; it cannot deal well with uncertainty and it cannot, apparently, survive unscathed either the behavioural critique, the complexity critique or the uncertainty critique which we have offered. We are arguing that the way out of this is a linked frame of thinking which would enable us to locate the control procedures to the social structure of the organisation.

Note also that, in our view, the plan as created (with its attention to complexity – variety – and to uncertainty) is a description of the outcome of the control procedure which creates it. Hence the control procedure of planning provides the activity within which explanatory and predictive models are brought into use to provide the substantive arguments for the plan as selected. Thus the variety model for control of the enterprise as system is that of the planning process, and not the plan, while the uncertainty is contained by the people in the social structures.

CHAPTER 5

The context of control

Anthony J. Berry, Jane Broadbent and David Otley

Introduction: some general issues

In order to consider the context of control this chapter will examine issues outside the organisation, that is to say, the environment in which the organisation exists. This endeavour should not be seen as unproblematically imposing a strict delineation of the organisation and its environment, nor as a one-way relationship between the two. Thus, in order to examine the *context* of control, two prior points about the nature of control itself need to be raised. The first of these relates to the extent to which the locus of control is within or outside organisations, the second relates to the extent to which it is possible to differentiate the organisation from its environment. These two issues will be examined in turn.

The locus of control

Controls are conceived and can operate at different levels: internal to the organisation, conceived and operated within them and relatively concrete, for example, the management accounting systems. Other control systems are conceived externally, on a societal level, sometimes by governments, but operated within an organisation. Again these systems are relatively concrete, for example systems to cope with issues such as health and safety, or the requirements of the companies acts. On a more abstract level are the values and ethics of a society which influence the laws and controls which are possible as well as separating deviant from acceptable behaviour. An extreme example is the use of the death sentence as a tool of control. The death sentence is used far more in some societies than in others, and this, it is argued, is related to the values of the different societies. So the context of control is argued to relate, not just to concrete external issues, but crucially to the values and the ethics of the society in question. As members of organisations are also citizens in their societies this context is not just 'something out there', but is also related to the abstract and embedded controls which spring from inner values gained from membership of that society. This will be a central issue in the current chapter. There are interactions between the values of a given society and the structures which are produced within it. It must be recognised that values affect the structures which are created, but also these structures, in turn, provide contexts which might be constraining in themselves and which may not easily be changed. These relationships between the structures of society and the value systems have been studied in different ways. Some of the ideas of Anthony Giddens and Jurgen Habermas will be explored later in the chapter.

The organisation and its environment

If we wish to study the context of control and are focusing upon an examination of control within organisations, then we need a means whereby we can separate the outside from the inside and hence define what is the organisation and what is its context. It has to be recognised that the relationship between the organisation and its environment is likely to be complex. Contingency and functional theorists argue that an organisation should adapt to the environment, applying what might be seen as akin to a Darwinian logic. However it is argued that this gives too little emphasis to the actors in the environment to have an impact upon and shape an organisation. The population ecology view (Hannan and Freeman, 1977) argues that there is a natural selection process in which the organisations which are fittest for their environment will survive, whilst others will fail. Organisational ecology theory (Trist, 1976), on the other hand, sees the environment and the many organisations within it operating as a complex ecosystem, evolving together. The environment of any one organisation therefore comprises many other organisations and each one, in this situation, is part of the environment to the others. Any organisation can, therefore, influence that environment, and the latter perhaps is a negotiated context and is not independently and externally imposed.

One way in which the boundary between the inside and the outside of the organisation is defined is by legislation. In this chapter, the organisation will be generally assumed to be that defined by legal governance and the analysis will look closely at controls which are imposed (or are attempted to be imposed) by external bodies of varying kinds. External regulation of the legally constituted body will, therefore, be the main focus of interest. However, in a final analysis, we will return to the problem of defining the organisation and its environment and their interrelationships through consideration of the extent to which external controls can be said to be effective.

External regulation and its impact

We can now turn to the controls themselves. One influential source of control is the machinery of the law, developed through the regulatory and enforcement powers of government. This is not the only source of control, for trade and professional groupings may also provide regulation and enforcement, although this is most commonly viewed as self-regulation. The extent to which the regulations which are developed by both government and other associations accord with the values of society in general will be discussed later. The next section of this chapter will be primarily concerned with providing a discussion of the controls which exist.

Governmental legislation

As has been argued above, government legislation provides an important element in the context of control of many organisations. It provides a direct control over the actions of organisations in many different ways. It can create and bound the organisation. The UK Companies Act 1985 provides the regulative framework for the creation of public and private limited companies. This Act allows for the creation of a limitation of the liability which can be borne by the owners and defines the difference between public and private limited companies. The latter, in contrast to the former, have shares which cannot be traded publicly. They provide a framework in which companies can, through their articles and memoranda, define their relationships with the outside world as well as internal rules of procedure for the relationships between the shareholders.

UK legislation allows for the existence of other organisational forms: the Partnership Act, 1890, governs the relationships between partners in a business situation, the Building Societies Act, 1986 regulates building societies, the Charity Commissioners regulate the operation of charities, local authorities operate within a legal framework, as do health authorities. Without the requisite legislation the organisations in question could not exist in the form they do. The legislation provides broad control over the governance of all the organisations as well as defining certain levels of public and private accountability which must be met. The provision of annual accounts to shareholders in a limited company is a good example of how one level of accountability is promoted between the managers and owners of a company. It is interesting to note how much of the accountability which is imposed on companies is expressed in financial terms and is directed to a selected audience (Laughlin and Gray, 1988, p. 296). Thus external accountability and control have a tendency to be identified with accounting-based information.

Not only does this type of legislation impose organisational boundaries and therefore control the existence of organisational types, it also creates opportunities and possibilities for the control of and within the organisations which are created. The markets and hierarchies framework has been used in earlier chapters as a way of focusing on the controls within organisations. It must be recognised that, to allow for different types of organisational control, the environment in which either markets or hierarchies can exist has to be created. This point can be illustrated by the example of the National Health Service in the UK. Until recently the NHS has been organised as a hierarchy in which administrators through resource provision and professionals through a system of shared values, a clan culture, have been enabled to control the organisation. The National Health and Community Care Act 1990 has legislated for change, which, by creating structures for provision and purchase of services, requires a more market-based approach to the interrelationships in the service. This structure was not adopted spontaneously; it required the provision of a legislative framework before its implementation. Here we see that the external regulation which is provided by government is essential to the enablement of the particular form of control which has been adopted.

The actual structure which the government legislates to impose can, by its very nature, have profound implications for the control structures which are possible. The difference between the privatisation of British Telecom as a whole unit and the separation of the different water authorities into competing units illustrates the variety of possible structures.

Lindblom (1977), in the context of a critique of the competence of markets, shows the extent to which government has provided privileges which enable business to function in a market environment. The provision of limited liability confers business with a crucial privilege; other examples include tax incentives, influence in policy-making circles and legislation to control the labour force. Without this support business would not be able to function as it does and this raises questions, which cannot be pursued here in any depth, as to the extent to which the market really functions as an invisible hand. Imai and Itami (1984) provide a discussion as to the interpenetration of organisation and market in different settings. They examine the US and Japanese economies, and show how market ideas and organisational forms of resource allocation impinge upon each other in different ways in the two situations. Their work emphasises that, while they are analytically separable, in a practical situation the distinction between the market and organisational forms of resource allocation is not a clear one.

Other regulations are related to the relationships between the organisation and both the general community and its workers. Health and safety regulations, employment regulations and pollution controls are examples of this type of control. These define the obligations of the organisation in very specific ways and through inspection and enforcement they control particular activities directly. These regulations are therefore much more direct than the former controls (which relate to boundary definitions and the creation of a supportive environment); this type of regulation provides a framework of specific actions and requirements.

Given British membership of the European Community (EC), regulation of organisations from external parties will increasingly have an international dimension. Regulation from the EC is concerned with many areas of organisation and may well impinge much more in the future as transnational activities expand and as new treaties are enacted. The influence of the EC will be felt both on the issue of boundary regulation and in terms of direct intervention to define the actions of organisations in particular circumstances. Harmonisation of practices in the European Community is the aim of this institution and this is desired in the name of maintaining conditions for a free market within the community. As well as the more obvious ventures in, for example, harmonising accounting practices, the EC also provides requirements in wider issues such as the environment. This emerging power of the EC is an example of the use of transnational regulation to provide the context in which organisations and markets can function.

It has to be recognised that the legislative framework provided by government (national and the EC) is just a framework. Any formal control system cannot be comprehensive unless the context in which it operates is known completely and is predictable; this is likely only to be possible in very simple situations and the context of the social world is not simple. Because of this the legislation needs fleshing out and this may be done in a number of ways, sometimes through the legal processes in which case law is developed. Case law is an important vehicle by which the law is clarified in relation to specific situations, which then can be applied to related areas. Sometimes this fleshing out is through processes of administration. The delegation of powers to make decisions to responsible officials is one way in which this is achieved. For example, in the UK, the Education Reform Act and the National Health and Community Care Act both provide for the respective Secretaries of State to be able to rule on particular issues. Within the health service there are well used channels in which the policies of government can be communicated to health authorities, the bureaucratic structure providing for lines of authority from the Secretary of State to the operating units. Direct instruction in the framework provided by the general legislation is therefore possible.

Other external regulation

Not all regulation flows from government; some regulations may even be seen as the means by which government regulation is avoided. This type of control is introduced by groups working together on a voluntary level; adherence to them might be seen as the price of joining a 'club' or exclusive group. For example, the UK stock market has regulations which are amongst the most comprehensive controls which are imposed upon companies and these are administered by the body itself and not through the companies acts. If a company wishes to have a quotation on the exchange then it must comply with the requirements. These regulations can also be used to define boundaries. An example is provided by the concept of the 'Chinese wall' in stockbroking firms, created on the inception of the 'Big Bang' in the stock exchange. Broking and dealing can now be undertaken by the same firm, but confidentiality between and separation of the two areas is demanded. There is a requirement in the Stock Exchange Regulations to provide and presumably maintain an internal boundary.

Not all associations are so visible. Cartels, the association of firms in the same market acting together to control the market, are illegal in the UK, but have existed in the past and operate elsewhere. OPEC is a well-known current example of a group of producers who work together to control both oil production and oil prices. There are arguments as to how long and how effectively any cartel can exercise control, but some seem to flourish as examples of predatory monopolies.

Professional associations are another source of control. These bodies act to control entry into professions through education and examination programmes and have procedures for expulsion upon proof of unacceptable behaviour. They control the rules of conduct for their members and act as a lobbying body on their behalf in many cases. The UK accounting professional bodies fulfil all these functions. They control the educational process by setting minimum standards for registration as students and they have their own examination systems. Membership of these bodies is usually the result of both passing examinations and demonstrating a minimum of practical experience. The professional accounting bodies also have a great input into the setting of standards for the practice of accounting. They are closely involved in the processes of generating Financial Reporting Standards (FRSs), which outline the way in which accountants should approach their compilation of financial data; again there is a sense of harmonisation of practice. This is a way of achieving data which will help the functioning of the capital markets and allow a fairer assessment of the results of companies by the general public. Again this regulation can be seen as a way of achieving the conditions in which a market can function.

On another level it could be that the professional associations exist to protect the values which are implicit in membership of those groups. The control of the profession by the profession is argued for in the context of the expertise of the particular group. Professional judgement and expertise are argued to be such that they cannot be legislated for; implicit in professional control is a concern for the protection of the 'culture' of the profession. The medical profession, with their central value of medical autonomy, and the academic community who value their academic freedom are both communities who work hard to maintain their professional autonomy and (as they see it) their integrity. The issue, as far as we are concerned in this chapter, is that the values of the professional grouping act as a strong control on the behaviour of its members. The regulations which are formally produced stem from those values and are produced in some cases as a means of maintaining the autonomy of the profession to regulate itself.

Trade associations might agree codes of practice on a voluntary basis as a way of protecting both their independence of behaviour and also the confidence of the general public. The scheme operated by the Association of British Travel Agents (ABTA) to protect holiday-makers when travel firms get into financial difficulties can be seen as controlling the trade and protecting public confidence. Trade unions, similarly, impose controls upon their members as well as trying to control, through national negotiations of wages and conditions, the employers of their members. They seek to control the employer–employee relationship for the benefit of their members. In so doing the trade unions become part of the environment of employing organisations as well as being organisations in their own right. This type of interrelationship is illustrative of those in the organisational ecology model of Trist (1976).

QUANGOS

Quasi-autonomous non-government organisations (QUANGOS) can also be used as a means of control. These are set up by government action but are argued to have autonomy from them, acting to control other organisations 'objectively' within a policy framework, rather than 'politically'. For example, regulatory boards have been set up to control the prices and profits of the utilities which have recently been transferred to private ownership and which, because of their near monopoly, could possibly exploit the general public through their pricing policies. The Office of Water Regulation (OFWAT), the Office for Electricity Regulation (OFER), OFGAS, concerned with the gas industry, and OFTEL, the regulator of the Telecommunications industry are examples of such organisations.

Overview

This overview of some sources of regulation is not exhaustive, but is illustrative. It does provide some indication of the nature of regulation and also the difference in scope. A regulation which provides a boundary for an organisation or one which provides an environment should be differentiated from a regulation which defines actions more closely. The different sources of external control are also worthy of note. It can be seen that there are multiple sources of regulation. The question which will be asked in the next section of this chapter is how this regulation actually works to achieve control. The existence of regulation does not mean that it necessarily achieves what it intends, neither does it explain why organisations take notice of regulation. The answers to these questions are crucial if we are to understand the context of control and it is to these we shall turn in the next section.

Regulation: how does it work, why does it work?

Legislation does not always 'work'. People do not always do as they are legally required. A drive along any of our roads will illustrate the extent to which speed limits, for example, are interpreted and indeed broken. Police officers have publicly admitted that they will not prosecute those exceeding the speed limit on UK motorways by 10 miles per hour or less. This effectively means that one can travel down a motorway at 80mph with little fear of prosecution for speeding. The short history of the Community Charge gives another example of the manner in which legislation can fail to control the behaviour of large numbers of the community; it also illustrates the danger to the legislators of implementing laws which are not acceptable to large numbers of the community. It could be argued that the fall of the UK prime minister, Margaret Thatcher, from power in 1991, was to some extent the result of the reception of the 'poll tax' and its lack of compatibility with the values of great numbers of the community. These examples provide a base from which to discuss the relationship between the regulations which exist as formal and concrete structures in society and the less tangible elements, the prevalent societal values or culture.

Many social theorists have given precedence to either the structures in society or the subjective role of the individual. The work of Marx, for example, stresses the importance of the structures of society, in particular the centrality of the capitalist mode of production. In contrast to this the work of Goffman is much more concerned with the way in which individuals shape their own social world, but does not concern itself with structural issues. Two theorists have attempted to link the two elements together to provide what they believe is a rather richer picture of society. We shall consider the work of these authors (although in a modest and limited fashion) because they provide some rationale for recognising the importance of both the tangible and non-tangible organisational elements in systems of control.

Anthony Giddens has developed a theory of structuration which aims to address the relationship between the structures of society and the systems made up by the interdependent actions of the individuals which make up that society. This approach highlights the relationship between very different elements; intangible elements such as meanings and values are linked to the more tangible structures. A brief introduction to the theory (and an application of it) is provided by Capps *et al.* (1989). Capps *et al.* use structuration theory as a way of exploring and understanding the role of culture in organisational control. The structures provide the rules and resources which people can use in social life and it is through their use that the structures are maintained and developed. This is what Giddens calls the duality of structure. Three forms of structure are suggested: meaning, morality and domination. Together these provide the rules which are linked to the communication of meaning, the norms which guide relationships and the power relationships between parties. Capps and her colleagues use this theory in the context of a case study in the NCB showing the set of practices which create and sustain the structures alongside the production of meaning. The study aims to show how interpretive studies of culture which look at meanings can be extended to include considerations of structure and power.

Jurgen Habermas also recognises the importance of intangible elements in the social world in which we exist, although he adopts a rather different approach. He differentiates the life world, the stock of taken-for-granted definitions and understanding we have of the world, from the systems of society. The systems of society are seen to be ones which are the product of the values and beliefs of the life world. There are mechanisms which intervene to 'steer' the systems in a way which is commensurate with the life world values. This is an abstract model of societal development which has been adapted for use on an organisational level by Laughlin, who argues that the organisation can be seen as a microcosm of society and has a life world, steering media and systems. Any process of change which is not led by evolution of the life world and which therefore is at odds with the values of the organisation is likely to be disruptive to the organisation and may not achieve what it set out to do. (Laughlin, 1987, 1991, provides a discussion of the issues which give much more detail for readers who would like to pursue the issues in more depth.) The value of referring to the work of Habermas is that it provides another articulation of the argument that the intangible aspects of organisational and social life are at least as important as the tangible ones.

Using ideas developed from the work of Habermas outlined above, along with those of some critical lawyers, Laughlin and Broadbent (1993) have examined the implications of legislation which is not in line with the life world of organisations or societies. In particular they have looked at the UK Education Reform Act of 1986 and the UK National Health and Community Care Act 1990. Their aim has been to see whether and to what extent these Acts are overreaching the life world demands and the self-reproductive processes of the organisations with which they are concerned. The implications of this are important in a consideration of the context of control, especially in the context of a discussion of the extent to which external legislation *can* control. This brings us back to the questions raised at the beginning of this section. Why do people obey laws and how is control achieved through external legislation? We argue that the law can only achieve control when it is in harmony with the life world of the context in which it is to be applied. If this is not the case, then, in the long term, either the law is ignored or the downfall of those who seek to impose the law or the down fall of the law itself are possibilities. Thus Sunday trading carries on in the UK and the prohibition of alcohol earlier this century in the USA was unsuccessful.

One set of answers to our original questions, how does regulation work and why does it work, can now be suggested. Regulation and control will succeed when there are in accordance with the values and beliefs which predominate in a society or an organisation. They 'work' because they are imposing controls which reflect the values and beliefs of most of society. This does not mean that all of society will conform – there will always be deviants and different shades of opinion in a society – we refer here to the acceptance and implicit acceptance by the majority.

It has to be recognized that the context of control is not simply the result of regulation. If values and beliefs are important components of control then they may be so deeply ingrained that they do not require formal regulation. This is apparent in the normative controls (Etzioni, 1961) and clan controls (Ouchi, 1980) mentioned in Chapter 2. Using a rather wider perspective, the question of why controls succeed can be related to the notion of their legitimacy (Weber, 1948). Authority is gained through the legitimacy which is accorded to those who seek to control and legitimacy is achieved in a number of ways. Modern society is seen as being oriented towards systems of control which achieve their legitimacy through democratic, legal, rational structures such as those we have discussed earlier. On the other hand, legitimacy might be achieved through tradition or charisma. These possibilities will be considered in turn.

Traditional authority lies with those who have traditionally been accorded that right. This is a situation in which the values of the society are such that particular relationships are the norm and to some extent this type of authority is similar to that encompassed in clan control or normative control. For example, in some societies age traditionally receives deference from youth and authority therefore relates to the role or position held by particular people. Weber uses patriarchy as an example of an important type of domination which rests on tradition. In this situation, control can be exercised by a person who holds a given role because he or she is the holder of that role and for no other reason.

Charismatic authority, on the other hand, is achieved by those with (or perceived to have) extraordinary qualities, and authority therefore lies with that particular person. Religious leaders or national leaders such as Mahatma Ghandi, Mother Theresa or Adolf Hitler might be seen as examples of this type of leader and control can be achieved by these people through the authority of their persona. This type of control is substantially different from that based upon either legal – rational or traditional authority as it is personality-led and may appear at random. For charismatic authority to be achieved the person in question must have the support of substantial numbers in an organisation or in a society. If this is achieved, the person in question will have a great capacity to control and this will indeed be an important element in the context of control.

The possibilities of achieving control through external regulation

This last section of the chapter will seek to reflect on what the context of control might be seen to be and the extent to which external regulation is an important component of that environment. The importance of various kinds of regulation in providing a context for the control of individual organisations cannot be denied. The extent to which market or bureaucratic control is enabled by the external regulatory framework in existence is clear, and actors in the environment can be powerful determinants of control. Legal and external regulation have also sought to try to define the boundaries of organisations, having been more successful in some cases than others. The intertwining of the affairs of the companies which were controlled by Robert Maxwell shows how the attempts to provide boundaries and maintain them can be breached by those who wish to do so.

The extent to which the external environment is constitutive of the organisation or is actually constituted by the organisation perhaps remains open. In some cases there is little doubt that the organisation is constrained by the environmental context in which it exists: on the whole people and organisations do not go out and break the law. Also people and organisations do react to cultural values; issues of social welfare are now common in Western societies. However it is equally possible for organisations to have a great influence on their own environment either directly or indirectly. The main employer in a small market town in the south of England was seen by local residents to exert an 'unfair' pressure on the local planners because of its threat to relocate if new offices did not receive planning permission. It seems likely that there is a two-way interchange and that there will be variability in the direction in which the power flows. For those who are designing controls an awareness of the possible environmental influences is essential; the judgement as to what that context is and what its effect may be cannot be specified away from the actual situation.

The other central issue for those who seek to develop controls systems is whether the systems they develop will produce the control required. External regulation is imposed with the expectation that desired effects can be achieved in this fashion. Members of parliament, for example, who promote legislation, do so on the premise that desired consequences will follow, that they can change things! The argument that has been presented in this chapter is that controls can only work when there is some alignment between the spirit of the control and the values of the organisation or the society in which the control is placed. One exception to this has been ignored and that is where there is the presence of direct coercion or physical restraint. Thus controls in a situation of slavery or in a prison may work in a rather different fashion (although even in situations like this conflict is possible).

If we restrict ourselves to a discussion of situations where direct or physical control is not the case, then the question has to be asked as to how we can develop external controls which are effective. In this case the argument for law which reflects the values of the organisation or society as a whole is essential. It is also perhaps sensible to use what has been called 'reflexive law' (Teubner, 1983) that is, law which deals with broad frameworks within which practical problems can be resolved. It is a law which defines processes within which answers are enabled. It does not seek to define answers directly. This type of law recognizes that controls which are developed with one particular situation may not transpose either spatially or temporally. This would seem to be a good model for developing systems of control on both a micro and a macro level. It allows for the possibility for controls to develop and mutate as need require. If this type of law was developed, regulation from external sources would not only have the chance of being accepted and therefore effective, but also it would have the potential for longevity.

There is also an ethical dimension to the existence of regulation. Regulation is needed in many cases not only to control, but also, to provide a framework of sanctions for those who contravene the law. These are essential because people are sometimes naughty! There are always people who will break the laws which we set. Thus there needs, morally, to be some way by which the bounds of acceptable behaviour are set and the penalties for breaking them defined. For this reason it is important that external regulation can work. However it is important to underline once again that the regulation will be stronger when it relates to a firm value foundation, held by the community which has imposed the control. One further question (which this chapter will not seek to answer) can be raised as a point for discussion. Is there any law or regulation which can be stated unequivocally? Is there a point about which, morally, there is no debate, and external regulation can and should be imposed unilaterally?

Summary

This chapter has been concerned with the context of control and has focused on the effect of external regulation in defining the context. We have examined the role that external regulation has in defining the boundaries of the organisations and the relationships between them. Regulation has been seen to come through the rule of law and through the voluntary association of groups of individuals and organisations. It has been argued that for regulation to be effective it must have a strong association with the values of those it seeks to regulate, or the law will either be ignored or will have the potential to undermine the law-makers. The use of reflexive law, a law which defines the processes by which agreement as to the nature of particular controls is achieved, is suggested as this law will have the mutability to deal with changing values and circumstances.

We cannot pretend that this is the whole story of the context of control; we have addressed areas which give rise to both passion and conflict and these issues can be illuminated by people from many other disciplines, for example, political scientists, sociologists or novelists. Deeper insights can be achieved by extending the boundary of our considerations and we encourage the interested reader to do this. On a practical level, it is clear it is essential to consider the context of control if any attempt to achieve control is to be made. The extent of the success of any attempt will relate to the interplay of the actions and their context.

PART II

Issues of Control

CHAPTER 6

Accounting systems and control

Anthony J. Berry, Jane Broadbent and David Otley

Introduction

The aim of this chapter is to consider the role of accounting systems in organisational control. Every organisation, be it small or large, business or family unit, has some type of accounting system. Accounting systems provide a fundamental way of handling high levels of complexity by the imposition of a set of standard operating procedures; this provides a major strength of accounting as a control system. However weaknesses also stem from the imposition of standard systems in complex situations because inventive human minds find ways of reporting desired results through the manipulation of the system rather than by behaving in expected ways.

Simon *et al.* (1957) suggested that accounting information serves three major functions: attention directing, problem solving and scorecard keeping. Control involves all of these functions. Attention must be directed to the process being controlled when results are not as expected. The idea of management by exception follows directly from this approach. Accounting provides data for problem solving which may be proactive or reactive, in this latter case dealing with issues highlighted by the attention-directing function. Accounts for scorecard keeping are the result of a process which examines the extent to which the organisation as a whole as well as the individuals within it meet the performance targets set. Performance evaluation of managers and the business units they direct is heavily dependent upon accounting-based measures, such as profit, return on investment, residual income or value added.

In this chapter we shall be concerned with the attention-directing and scorecard keeping functions of accounting-based control systems as they are central to the formal and routine control of the organisation. Problem solving, whilst a familiar feature of organisational life, tends to be ad hoc, reactive and rarely a simple routine. However routinely collected data are often the basis for problem recognition and are used extensively in finding solutions, so there are close linkages between attention-directing routines and decisions taken in respect of unique problems. Hence we will also consider the use of accounting data in problem solving. A final note of caution should be sounded before moving on to look at these areas in more detail; as the earlier part of this text has illustrated, control is related to many issues, other than accounting. Accounting is just one element used in systems of control, albeit the central concern of this chapter.

Problem solving: techniques for gathering and organising data for accounting-based control

The generation of data and information about the internal operations of a firm is the focus of management rather than financial accounting, the latter being geared to provide information for formal and external purposes and for legal controls. Management accounting is often defined as providing information for decision making or problem solving. These management accounting approaches will be outlined in this chapter. For a more detailed examination, the reader is referred to standard management accounting texts (for example, Emmanuel *et al.*, 1990, provide an overview of the area; detailed accounts can be found in Arnold and Hope, 1990; Drury, 1992; Wilson and Chua, 1992). The approaches which we shall outline are concerned with providing information for short-term and long-term decisions about activity and with the ascertainment of total product costs. However, before considering specific techniques, a more general point about the limited nature of the models which underlie management accounting should be noted.

Many management accounting techniques are based on a simple first order control loop. This model suggests that control requires the formation of objectives, the development of plans (using predictive models) to achieve these objectives, measurement of the extent of such achievement and, finally, the monitoring of variances from plan to see if any corrective action is required (Otley and Berry, 1980). Management accounting models tend not to give full consideration to all the stages of this process, mainly focusing on the implementation of plans and the monitoring of variances. The formation of objectives is often taken as unproblematic; the debate as to whether we can talk about the goals of the *organisation*, or whether we really should refer to the goals of *coalitions* or *individuals*, is often neglected; and the micropolitics of the organisation are thus ignored. The process of scanning of the environment for opportunities has also received scant attention (King, 1975). Much of the investment appraisal literature is based upon the assumption that suitable projects will present themselves without any effort on the part of managers.

Furthermore the development of predictive models has been glossed over, despite the fact that the use of appropriate predictive models enables pro-active, feedforward control to be used. Feedforward control may be less expensive than reactive feedback control, which can only rectify errors already made. By planning to avoid predicted consequences which are undesirable, considerable savings can be made. Most of the predictive models in management accounting are rooted in economic theories which see 'profit maximisation' as the main business objective. The maximisation of the present values of cash flows has been used as a surrogate for profit maximisation. However this is not always the reason for which people enter business, as Box 6.1 illustrates.

We now turn to a short overview of the main techniques of management accounting.

Short-term decisions

An important issue for managers is the effect of short term changes in activity on the financial results. Techniques have been developed to provide an analysis of the effect on costs of levels of activity in the short term. These techniques also enable the examination of the profitability of operating at different activity levels. The interested reader should examine chapters concerned with cost structure, marginal costing and cost–profit–volume analysis in management accounting texts. This approach is based on the fact that some costs can, in the short term, be seen to vary in proportion to volume of output (variable cost)

Box 6.1   Comparisons for performance?

A comparison scheme for hotel businesses sought to provide hoteliers with an analysis of their financial results. Comparison with the regional average, it was suggested, would enable them to identify areas where they were stronger or weaker than this average and so indicate areas where performance might improve. The scheme was not well supported. Many hoteliers argued that they operated in a pleasant south coast resort because they enjoyed the lifestyle. For them improving financial results was not a prime issue as long as a standard of living satisfactory to them was being achieved. This illustrates that to focus solely on objectives of profit maximisation can give an impoverished account of why people enter business and what they seek to achieve. We need to be sensitive to the variety of motivations managers may have when considering the use of techniques based on a narrow, economic perspective.

whilst other costs (fixed or period costs) do not change with variations in volume. However the categorisation of costs into fixed and variable components depends upon the time horizon of the decision being considered. In the very short term, most costs are fixed; in the long term, all costs become variable. It is therefore vital to consider the time span of the decision being taken before embarking upon a cost analysis of this nature.

Of key importance is the 'contribution' each unit of production makes. Contribution is defined as the difference between the variable cost of production and the selling price of each unit. Total contribution can therefore be found for any level of activity (within the relevant range) by multiplying the contribution per unit and the activity level. Contribution accumulates, first, to cover fixed costs, then to provide profits. Profits are not, therefore, earned incrementally with each unit of production sold. A given level of activity is required to reach 'break-even point', the point at which contribution is sufficient to cover fixed costs. This approach allows the calculation of costs and profits at different levels of production and can be used as a feedforward control device to aid decisions as to whether particular activities will be profitable. Where there are limiting resources or production bottlenecks, the idea of measuring the contribution per unit of limiting resource is a widely applicable heuristic, popularised in texts such as Eli Goldratt's *The Goal* (Goldratt, 1984).

The contribution approach can also be used as a basis for decisions about whether a firm should make components internally or buy them from outside suppliers. If spare capacity exists (and only then), the relevant comparison will be between the internal variable cost and the external purchase price . The fixed costs which will be incurred whether the new production goes ahead or not can be argued to be irrelevant in this situation. Thus the focus of interest is the marginal cost of the decision, which may be obscured by the widespread use of full-cost absorption accounting systems which allocate fixed costs to units of production.

The contribution technique can also be used to aid some pricing decisions, particularly in secondary pricing situations, where there is spare capacity. Here we may choose to adopt the principle that any contribution, however small, is better than no contribution. Thus a lower price may be accepted than that usually charged, provided that variable costs are covered. It must be remembered that short term decisions do, however, have long-term consequences. It is to these long term decisions we now turn.

Long-term decisions

In the long term all costs are variable and one of the costs which assumes significant importance in long-term decisions is the time value of money. We are generally concerned with a situation in which an initial investment is made now which will produce expected benefits over a number of future years. The estimation of the magnitude of these future benefits is a significant difficulty faced by all investment appraisal techniques, and most tend to assume the existence of good predictive models. In practice we usually have only rather poor models and are forced into performing sensitivity analyses to examine how our decision might be affected by variations in estimates.

There are several different approaches to the appraisal of long term investments. Three approaches will be examined in this section: net present value techniques, payback and accounting rate of return. The mainstream management accounting texts deal with these techniques under the heading of capital investment appraisal and provide detailed discussion of the benefits of the different approaches.

The theoretically favoured techniques to appraise long-term decisions focus on the incremental cash flows which are expected to be generated. The reason for this preference lies in the assumptions about the objectives of the firm which are linked to the maximisation of shareholder wealth. Evaluating new activities on the basis of maximising the net present value of the expected future cash flows provides a surrogate for the maximisation of shareholder wealth.

Net Present Value (NPV) methods take estimated incremental cash flows over the life of a project and discount them to their present value. Discounting is undertaken to account for the fact that cash received in the future has an opportunity cost when compared with cash received now. To be acceptable, an investment must have a positive net present value at an appropriate discount rate. Another derivative of this approach is the calculation of an internal rate of return (IRR). This rate is simply the discount rate at which the NPV of an investment becomes zero. Here the decision rule is that an acceptable project must have an IRR better than some predetermined hurdle rate. Whilst these approaches are not technically difficult to implement, there are problems in both deciding the discount rate to be applied and forecasting future cash flows.

The problem of estimating an appropriate discount rate to be used in NPV calculations has engaged academics for some time. The discount rate can be argued to depend on both the cost of capital to the firm and the specific risk associated with the project. In practice the weighted average cost of capital to the firm as a whole may be used to give a discount factor to be used in all capital appraisals. Another refinement is to attempt to relate the discount factor to the risk of the particular project, and its interrelationship with other investments. As the discount factor determines whether the NPV is positive or negative it is vital to ensure this is an appropriate estimate. It is also important to ensure that inflation is properly dealt with. If cash flows are estimated in real terms, then a real cost of capital must be used; if estimated in nominal terms, then a nominal rate is appropriate. Although this seems straightforward, all too often it is observed that the discount rate used is inappropriate to the basis of cash flow estimation used.

The forecasting of the project life and its associated future cash flows is also problematic, as the application of the most sophisticated techniques to wrong estimates will not give good results – Garbage In, Garbage Out! Predicting the future is always difficult and cash flow prediction is no different. Hertz (1964) offered one solution when he argued that the use of Monte Carlo simulation on probabilistic cash flows to produce a probability distribution of NPV estimates was the best we might achieve. In his favour it can be seen that this at least provides the decision maker with an assessment of the probabilities of loss and gain, should the project be undertaken.

It should be noted that surveys designed to detect whether the adoption of these 'sophisticated' techniques do provide 'better' results as measured by increased earnings per share have not been able to show significant relationships (Haka *et al.*, 1985). There are various reasons for this and these may have a relationship to the context of their use as well as practical difficulties in their application (for an overview, see Northcott, 1991, 1992). Indeed some studies have shown an inverse relationship between the use of sophisticated evaluation methods and subsequent performance. However this may well be an example of reverse causation: that is, poorly performing firms are more likely to use sophisticated appraisal methods in an attempt to improve their performance.

In the face of such problems of estimation of both cost of capital and cash flows, many firms adopt the less sophisticated technique of payback, which is the length of time the initial cash investment takes to be recuperated by the cash flows generated by the scheme. This is a much used and well understood technique, with the advantage of simplicity. If the cost of capital is about 20 per cent, then a three year payback rule will provide a fairly robust criterion for project acceptance. Some firms use it only for smaller schemes, some in conjunction with other approaches, but others use it in isolation. A more sophisticated variant is to calculate discounted payback period, which at least provides one estimate of the time period over which the firm is at risk from its investment.

Debates as to the strengths and weaknesses of the diverse techniques are recounted in the texts. Suffice it to say at this stage that the discounting techniques are theoretically superior, but are not always used. However their adoption is spreading (Pike, 1983, 1988), perhaps as the result of business education. There is a danger that the techniques may be used to justify decisions which have in effect already been made. If, for example, an NPV calculation does not achieve satisfactory results, then the cash flows or the discount rate might be changed to provide the result which is required. It seems unlikely that a manager would put forward any plan which does not appear to meet a firm's current criterion of positive NPV or required payback, as it would be rejected at first sight. However managers may well be influenced to adjust the estimates in order to promote projects which they believe to be desirable for their own purposes.

The choice of the appraisal technique is complicated by the existence of another approach, the accounting rate of return (that is the ratio of profit generated by the scheme to the initial – (or average) – investment). This provides another way of appraising investments and is important, because it is also often used to appraise managers' performance. It is seen as theoretically inferior to NPV because it deals with profit flows rather than cash flows, and these can be manipulated by the application of different accounting policies and techniques. NPV deals with cash flows, which are argued to be more objective and less subject to manipulation than profit flows, which are seen as more subjective. (Interestingly this argument ignores the manipulation which can also bias cash flow estimates!) Different accounting rates of return can be obtained from similar schemes which are accounted for using different accounting policies. In particular, ARR raises problems of asset valuation. Despite these problems it is used, probably because it produces results similar to the familiar measurement of return on capital employed (ROCE), used to appraise results post hoc.

A fundamental conflict can arise between capital investment appraisal methods, which are based on discounted cash flows, and subsequent managerial performance assessment, which is based on accounting profit and return on investment measures. A 'good' project (on NPV criteria) may have poor accounting returns in its early years; conversely, a 'poor' project can show good accounting returns initially. Thus a manager may be reluctant to propose a project which is clearly in the firm's best interest because it would adversely affect his or her performance reports in the short term. This conflict between future-oriented investment appraisal techniques and historically oriented accounting measurement techniques is difficult to resolve. The most straightforward suggestion is that the financial impact of a new capital investment should be incorporated into future budgets when it is accepted. The responsible manager's performance should then be monitored in terms of achieving the budgeted figures, rather than any preset ROCE target.

As the application of each of the techniques has different aims, and the prescription for action might be different under each, appropriate action cannot be easily decided. The forecasting of future cash flows always provides the opportunity for biasing and manipulation in the interests of individuals and against the interest of the organisation as a whole. If appraisal of managers' performance is linked to the results produced, manipulation will always be a problem and can only be minimised (for example, by the use of post-audit techniques) rather than eliminated.

Data for routine control

Information about the costs of existing products or parts of an organisation's operation is also needed for decision making and control. In particular, total costs for each product are needed for the valuation of inventories in the financial accounts. The technique of absorption costing traces to the cost object those costs which can be directly identified with that object. It then allocates the other indirect costs between the units produced. The total cost of each cost unit is thus the direct cost of each unit plus the share of indirect costs apportioned to it. Absorption costing is, therefore, a systematic approach to the construction of total cost information. As well as providing estimates of total cost for the financial accounts, this approach gives information which can form a basis for comparison between different operating units or provide information which might be useful in pricing cost objects. The basis of 'sharing out' the indirect costs can be problematic as it is an arbitrary act. This is not necessarily a problem in itself but, when the figures produced are not recognised as arbitrary and then become the basis of decisions, problems can arise. Johnson and Kaplan (1987) have offered a critique of the relevance of management accounting because of issues such as this. Full-cost information can give only a general indication of long-term viability of a product (if appropriately constructed), whereas variable cost information provides a sound basis for short-run decision making.

Activity-based costing (ABC), latterly developed into activity based management, has been devised as a more defensible approach to the problem of calculating the cost of a product, department or service. ABC is a systematic approach but, unlike absorption costing, it seeks to relate costs to the cost object in alignment with the actual processes of transformation it undergoes. This requires an analysis of the 'cost drivers' within a business. For example, the cost of filling an order for £100 of goods is likely to be similar to the cost of filling an order for £10 000. The cost driver in this case is therefore the number of invoices rather than the value of the invoice. Allocating costs by the use of cost drivers is argued to produce a more 'realistic' cost, although it must be recognised that it still involves arbitrary allocations. Identifying and examining the cost drivers can focus management attention on the activities which cause costs to be incurred.

The above techniques provide the foundation for many of management accounting's virtues as well as the problems which arise from inherent shortcomings. Some of these problems relate to the issue of observing and classifying costs in the ways required to use the techniques, but other problems relate to the difficulty of using the techniques in a context which requires prediction. However these basic techniques provide the elements of the 'tool-kit' which can be used to approach the main problems which management accounting is asked to answer.

Attention directing: budgetary control

The implementation of a system of accounting-based control needs more than just the techniques for calculating costs noted above. Systems for co-ordinating the information generated and integrating it with the other business information in functional areas such as production and marketing are also required. Thus, whilst accounting-based control of the business could not be enacted without the tools to calculate relevant costs, the process of control is carried out through a different set of activities, those of budgeting. Budgetary control forms the foundation for the other two functions of accounting information systems, attention directing and scorecard keeping. It involves the development of plans for action, expressed in financial terms, and the monitoring of subsequent activity to monitor the extent to which plans have been achieved.

Emmanuel *et al.* (1990) alert us to the fact that budgets fulfil many different purposes within an organisation. Beside being an important element in enabling the process of decision making, some possible roles that budgets may serve include:

1. authorisation of actions,
2. a means of forecasting and planning,
3. a channel of communication and co-ordination,
4. a means of motivating organisational members,
5. a vehicle for performance evaluation and control.

The first four roles are oriented more to attention directing; the fifth is more related to scorecard keeping. Different elements of control are to be found in the different roles. In different organisations, each of the above roles may be given a different emphasis; a budget which is designed to serve one purpose well will probably be less effective at serving other purposes. Thus the design of a budgetary control system is essentially a set of compromises and will result in each purpose being served to a greater or lesser degree.

Budgets as authorisation

Formal authorisation of spending limits is one way of controlling the actions of subordinates. Thus school governing bodies now have the responsibility, delegated from the Local Education Authority, to spend within a preset budget. They can spend that budget as they wish (within the requirement to provide education), but they cannot spend more than the set amount. In contrast to this idea of a global sum, a budget may be much more detailed and used as a means of authorising spending only on particular line items, such as salaries or building maintenance. The extent to which a budget is delegated as a total figure, rather than item by item, defines the extent of the control which is being attempted. A line-item budget is very much a behaviour (action) control.

The scope for controlling resourceful human beings by simple devices such as budgets is limited by creative attempts to modify the control which is being sought. For example, cash-limited Health Authorities, it is alleged, hold back invoices for payment at the year end in order to stay within their authorised cash budget. Thus activity exceeds that which is recorded and budgeted for, yet the cash budget is met. In other circumstances activities may be halted even though profitable production could be continued, because budgetary spending limits on direct materials have been reached. This latter situation may be the perverse achievement when a budget is given line by line to the manager of a cost centre. A less detailed situation where managers are given profit targets may produce better results, but inevitably the detailed controls are fewer. Indeed greater control may be achieved by the reduction of the number of individual controls (Drucker, 1964).

There is a tension between retaining centralised control and delegating decisions to an operational manager. A local manager should have greater knowledge of that environment and delegation to him or her will mean that better decisions can be taken more rapidly. However the local manager may make decisions which are good for that local operation but which do not accord with the overall needs of the organisation. This tension between knowledge of what is feasible (generally concentrated at lower levels) and knowledge of what is desirable (generally concentrated at higher levels) is a notable feature of all budgeting systems. Responsibility for either a cost centre (in which the decision of the extent of each budget item is centrally controlled) or a profit centre (where there is greater delegation of decisions as to the budgetary elements) is therefore qualitatively different, as is the control achieved. Decisions about the type of control to be exercised must recognise these tensions.

Forecasting, planning and communication

The second set of roles, forecasting and planning, come into play when developing a budget. Horngren (1981) defined a budget as 'A quantitative expression of a plan of action and an aid to co-ordination and implementation. In most cases the budget is the best practical approximation to a formal model of the whole organisation: its objective, its inputs and its outputs.' An alternative definition is 'a forecast of the financial implications of an operating plan', which also indicates the predictive role inherent in the budgeting process.

The third role of budgeting suggested, that of communicating and co-ordinating, is also suggested by this definition. The way in which these functions are served can best be illustrated by examining the stages of budget preparation. The nature of the control process can also be illustrated. The interested reader can find more detail of these issues in the mainstream accounting texts (Arnold and Hope, 1990; Drury, 1992; Wilson and Chua, 1992); here, yet again, there is only space for an outline to be presented.

Preparation of any budget first requires the forecasting of future activity from all parts of the organisation. Activity levels for the diverse areas must be decided upon and then expressed in monetary terms using the forecasts of economic activity price changes and so on. These individual plans are then amalgamated into an organisational budget (the master budget), which co-ordinates all the different functions, balancing, for example, production and selling plans.

This process of budget preparation will involve communication between different functional areas in the organisation. The type of communication engaged in is important in the formation of perceptions about the budgeting process by the different organisational members. A 'top-down' approach, in which plans are imposed from above, may well lead organisational members to consider the budget as a severe constraint. Suspicion and subversion of the budget and the budgeting process can result. The active participation of budget holders and the possibility of their negotiating the final budget outcome, that is, a 'bottom-up' approach make it less likely that the budget will be the focus of organisational conflict. But it should be recognised that all budgeting is both top-down and bottom-up. The budget circulates up and down the organisation in several iterations involving negotiation and bargaining. 'Top-down' and 'bottom-up' refer only to the starting-point, and there may often be little to choose between them as approaches. Much more important is the way in which changes are negotiated and communicated.

The accounting literature suggests that the generation of budgets should follow the organisational structure of responsibility and accountability. It should also be as detailed as is needed to ensure co-ordination. Organisational structure does not necessarily determine the type of control system to be operated, for it can be altered in order to achieve a configuration which allows the desired control, including budgetary control, to be applied. In particular, the alignment of cost centre or profit centre responsibilities may be changed in line with a desire to change the type of control desired.

A budget may be based upon standard costs. The forecasting, planning and co-ordination requirements are particularly stringent in this case. The standard costing approach defines standards for material and labour usage as well as standard costs for each of the quantified elements. Based on the philosophy of scientific management which sees 'one best way' to achieve a result, the 'best way' is decided upon and costed. The process therefore finds a predetermined standard cost for the production of a unit and results will be analysed to see if these standards have been achieved. The use of this technique allows a detailed analysis of results to find out exactly where standards are not being achieved, and represents strong behaviour control. Explanations for non-achievement can then be sought and remedies may be applied. Decisions may also have to be taken about the level of variation to be tolerated before investigations are instigated. It would be misguided to expect complete accuracy in developing, or adhering to, standards and judgements as to the action taken in response to variances which have to be made. Variances may not always be the result of poor performance; it may be that the standards set were inappropriate. The development of a standard costing system can be expensive and the use of a poor set of standards means that much time may be spent investigating deviation from standards which are the result of poor standard setting and not poor control. Because of the expense of generating good standards, standard costing is best applied in situations where there is a standard product that is produced in large numbers.

Because the system of standard costing provides such a tight system of control, products and services are now often deliberately 'standardised' in order to achieve such control. Although common in mass production, this idea is being carried across into service organisations. One example of this is the generation of Diagnosis Related Groups (DRGs) in the National Health Service. DRGs are groups of medical problems which have similar diagnoses and are seen to require similar treatment, generating similar costs. They were developed as the basis of reimbursing medical insurers in the USA, but are now being seen as a way of distributing resources and controlling expenditure.

Thus, in different ways, the process of budget preparation achieves the focus for forecasting and planning and provides the channel for communication and co-ordination. However budgetary control requires that a further stage of activity be followed.

Motivating and evaluating performance

After the budget is produced and the activity to which it relates is undertaken, then information on actual results must be collected. This is in line with the fifth role of budgeting, that of feedback control. Such control will be sought by action to both remedy the situation where budgets are not being achieved and to feed back to update the planning process. This information about the alignment of actual and budgeted performance can also be used as the basis for performance evaluation. Further the fact that performance is evaluated in this way means that achievement of budget targets should also provide a source of motivation for organisational members.

In the context of motivation we can investigate the effect of budgets when they are used to provide targets for individual performance. Tosi (1975) provided evidence that performance is better when clear, defined, quantitative targets are provided. While a difficult target tends to motivate higher performance, if a target is so high as to be perceived as unattainable (and is not accepted by the individual who is responsible for its achievement) results are likely to be worse than if a lower, but accepted, goal was set (Locke, 1968). This phenomenon was also demonstrated by Hofstede (1967). This book carried on the investigations started by Argyris (1952) into the effects of budgets and targets on human behaviour. The conclusions which Hofstede reached were as follows.

- Budgets only motivate if they are 'owned' by the manager concerned.
- Provided the budget does not exceed the most demanding target which an individual accepts, the results will increase in line with increasing difficulty.
- Participation in budget creation facilitates acceptance of budgets.
- Cultural and organisational norms as well as individual personality affect managers' reactions to particular budget targets.

The title of Hofstede's book is an apt one as there is much gamesmanship in the setting of budgets. Participation in budget setting, for example, can be helpful in ensuring the acceptance of budgets, lead to improved communication and can decrease the likelihood of distortion and manipulation of information. However it can also provide the opportunity to bias the budget. For example, slack may be built into targets (Lowe and Shaw, 1968) and managers may affect budgets (Schiff and Lewin, 1970) more than budgets affect managers (Argyris, 1952). This is particularly likely where the achievement of budget is linked to remuneration.

Cyert *et al.* (1961) showed that the forecast projections of the same set of figures differed according to the label attached to them. Thus a lower rate of increase was estimated when the figure was labelled 'sales' than when it was labelled 'costs'. It is likely that the forecast is made with regard to the consequences of error and a conservative estimate of sales or a generous estimate of costs provides less threat of non-achievement of the target. The work of both Lowe and Shaw (1968) and Otley (1978) showed that the biased estimates might not always be in the direction of setting easier targets. In a situation where current performance was poor, managers might feel obliged to promise better for the future and overestimate future performance. This could provide them with the time and opportunity to continue in their jobs in the hope of solving the problems.

The usefulness of participation is also contingent on the culture and the personality of different managers. Those who feel that they are in control of their own destiny react more positively to participation than those who feel they are the victims of destiny (Brownell, 1981). The latter group exhibited poorer performance when participating in budget formation, possibly as a result of increased stress from an environment they perceived as uncontrollable and uncertain. Bruns and Waterhouse (1975) suggested that participation was most useful in decentralised organisations which were engaged in tasks of a well-defined and structured nature.

The findings relating to the use of budgets as motivators suggest that there is likely to be some tension when budgets designed to motivate are used as vehicles for performance evaluation. This is because a good motivational budget will always be slightly more difficult to attain than the performance which can be achieved. Managers evaluating performance need to bear this in mind and not treat small adverse variance too harshly. Those using budgets as a basis for planning must also remember that the estimates may contain bias for reasons which are entirely rational from the point of view of the manager who has prepared the budget, but which may undermine some of the usefulness of the budget from the point of view of the organisation as a whole.

While there will be some intrinsic satisfaction in achieving a set target, a major source of motivation lies in the rewards which are often contingent on achieving target performance. In this sense the budget can be seen as an important tool of performance evaluation, and may be used as such by senior management. If achievement of targets is necessary for achieving reward, then an important catalyst for bias has been constructed. This bias will be quite difficult to detect in the processes of negotiation which precede the setting up and agreement of targets.

Thus budget-based incentive schemes should be designed in such a way as to try to ensure that the individual's behaviour in achieving rewards is in line with the company objectives (Hopwood, 1972). This may mean that good performance is not necessarily the same thing as successfully meeting budget targets. Indeed there are organisational structures where the control and reward of performance are not best achieved by such detailed control. Accounting measures may still be used in such circumstances, and it is to a consideration of these controls that we will now move.

Scorecard keeping: performance evaluation and accounting controls

The requirement to adhere to detailed budgets is perhaps most useful as a control in a situation where responsibility for costs alone is delegated to the manager. The reporting of line-by-line results against budget allows for problems to be pinpointed by the delegator. If the responsibility delegated is for the achievement of given levels of profit, the line-by-line detail of the budget is of central interest to the manager to whom responsibility is delegated, but not to the delegator. In this case, a profit target is often used as a means of control. Performance is evaluated by the achievement of these targets. The logic of this type of control is that those who have responsibility are closest to the conditions in which operations are carried out and know best how to achieve results.

This type of logic achieves its fullest expression in the context of the divisionalised company. Here the control of the company is delegated to those in operating divisions who are considered to be closest to the environment and who can therefore make the 'best' decisions because of this local knowledge. In these situations the use of return on investment (ROI) or residual income (RI) measurements can be used to measure the performance of managers. ROI looks at the profit which is generated in comparison with the asset base used to generate that profit, expressing it in percentage terms. RI adjusts the profit figure attained, introducing an imputed interest charge for the financing of the assets used. Managers will be given specific targets and, while detailed control of day-to-day operations is not required, the overall target result must be achieved. Bonus payments are often used to enhance the motivation of managers to achieve the required targets. The use and development of performance measures are not straightforward and problems can arise for many reasons, as suggested by Emmanuel *et al.* (1990, p. 176):

- Organisations have many objectives and purposes which cannot be measured easily or effectively by single measures of performance.
- Organisations often require that co-operative action be taken. Trying to measure individual performance will not necessarily reflect the co-operative aspects of tasks and may be dysfunctional in that individuals may pursue actions which enhance their individual ratings at the expense of the organisation's best interests.
- The specification of tasks and targets in advance may be a fruitless task because of the ambiguous nature of managerial responsibilities.
- Not all aspects of performance, especially such issues as quality or morale of staff, which are increasingly being stressed as important in the modern organisation can be measured in quantitative terms.
- The measurement of results may not be adequate to reward effort, especially when the environment has not been as was expected when targets were set.

The overall problem is that reward systems reward report results and not behaviour. This leads to the situation where managerial behaviour is geared towards the achievement of reported results. In a situation where the environment is rapidly changing the standards against which results are assessed may be inappropriate. The retention rather than renewal of fully depreciated assets may be the result of their beneficial effect on achieving ROI targets (Dearden, 1962). The purchase of a new asset will increase the capital base upon which the profits generated are to be assessed, as well as generating depreciation charges against profit. This may be dysfunctional where, for example, new investment which would improve the competitive advantage of the firms products by achieving better quality is being postponed.

The research findings on the issues of participation in budget setting must be borne in mind when performance is being assessed. One finding by Kenis (1979) is worthy of inclusion here as it extends the discussion beyond that of budget achievement. In his study, Kenis notes that, while budget achievement was improved by participation, there was no relation to other measures of overall job performance. Studies by Ivanevitch (1976), Milani (1975) and Steers (1975) show relatively insignificant connections between budgetary characteristics and job performance. This must alert us to the fact that quantitative evaluation might have little effect on overall job performance. This may be the result of the fact that managers may have no control over some important variables, no matter whether they are involved in the construction of the budget or not. Evaluation styles can vary however. Merchant (1981) found that large, decentralised firms with diversified activities tended to operate administrative rather than personnel controls. Greater stress was given to formal controls such as budgeting and lower levels of managers participated in developing budgets.

Hopwood (1972) studied cost centre managers in a sequentially independent situation and argued that three diverse orientations to evaluation could be identified. In each case there are different approaches to the linkage of performance and rewards.

1. A budget-constrained style: here a rigid insistence upon the short term achievement of the budget is the central feature.
2. A profit-conscious style: here the general effectiveness of the unit's operations is the central feature. The approach is more flexible than that in the budget-constrained style, and budgetary information is supplemented by other information. Thus a manager who has a good explanation for over-spending may still be evaluated favourably.
3. A non-accounting style: in which budgetary data are seen as relatively unimportant and other measures of managerial performance are used.

Managers who were evaluated in a non-accounting style were less cost-conscious than those evaluated using accounting-based styles. Those managers who were evaluated using the budget-constrained style reported higher levels of stress, poorer relationships with colleagues and a greater tendency to manipulate financial reports than managers evaluated under a profit-conscious style.

Otley (1978) repeated some of Hopwood's work in the setting of independent profit centres. He thought that, in the chosen setting, budgetary information would represent a more adequate measure of managerial performance than in Hopwood's study. He found style of evaluation had little impact on job-related tension or on manipulation of data. Performance evaluation based on budget achievement led to an emphasis on the short term, but, apart from this, provided an effective management style. Otley also found that performance affected the choice of management style, with better performing managers being more likely to be evaluated in the more flexible style. Thus the choice of the way to use budgetary information in performance evaluation is a complex matter, with the potential to generate unexpected side-effects.

Hirst (1981) studied the effect of different environmental conditions. Where there is a high level of uncertainty, accounting measures are seen as providing a less complete description of performance than in a more stable environment. Govindarajan (1984) supports this position, suggesting that in a highly uncertain environment more subjective evaluation procedures are likely to be adopted. These studies suggest there are two central issues that need to be resolved in each specific situation. First, the impact of the control system depends on the way in which accounting information is used by managers and the rewards that are contingent upon its achievement. Secondly, the effect of high reliance on budgetary measures of performance is contingent upon the extent to which we can be certain of the linkage between managerial behaviour and desired results. This is often quite low and is made more ambiguous in an uncertain environment. Reward systems must be designed with this in mind and must be tolerant of occasional failure, especially in situations where innovation may be needed.

Individual differences between managers must also be borne in mind, and there is some indication that the cognitive style of individuals will affect the structure of the information which will be of most use to them. Highly aggregated data, such as balance sheets and formal accounting reports, are of most use to high-analytic types (those who use conceptual models to understand situations). Low-analytic types (who see situations more holistically) are better served by disaggregated raw data (Benbassat and Dexter, 1979). Macintosh (1985) also suggested that information should be supplied in a manner which is consistent with a manager's cognitive style.

Another important individual difference relates to the extent to which individuals accept personal responsibility for what happens to them. Those with an external locus of control see events as being outside their control, those with an internal locus of control see events as the result of their own behaviour. The latter group performed best when involved in budget setting, the former group when targets were imposed.

This short overview of the literature relating to performance evaluation suggests that there are inherent difficulties in providing suitable measures of performance, that the style by which individuals are evaluated by their superiors will affect performance and that individual differences and the state of the external environment are all important factors for consideration in designing systems. All these complexities suggest that the design of performance evaluation systems, as part of a control system, is complex and difficult to determine away from the particular situation and the individuals within it. What works in one place for a certain set of people may not work in another situation or even in the same situation when different individuals are involved.

Closing comments

An overview of the uses of accounting-based controls shows how diverse the roles served by such controls are, as well as the various interlinkages and tensions which exist within and between the roles. Despite this complexity, accounting is clearly an important element of control and is generally perceived to be so. It is now being introduced into areas which have previously had little financial control at an operational level – schools, probation offices, the arts, hospitals, universities and voluntary organisations. Because of this level of influence the synergies and tensions associated with the use of accounting based controls need to be clearly understood if we are to exploit the virtues of accounting and not be prey to the weaknesses and dysfunctions which can be created by its misguided use.

If we return to the simple control model upon which management accounting is based (that is, where an objective exists for an activity in a quasi-stable environment which can be described by a predictive model, and where it is possible to measure what has been achieved and allow monitoring to take place) we can see the type of environment in which accounting based control is likely to work best. It is a situation in which certainty and well defined relationships exist. The irony is that it is in precisely these circumstances that any approach to control will be most easily applied. Where there is a more uncertain environment, where interdependencies are least easily defined and where the future is most difficult to predict we are most in need of some way to help us achieve control. Here any accounting-based approach to control is of least use because it relies on the ability to predict and translate predictions into financial values. Despite the variability of the circumstances in which accounting information is appropriate there is little variability in its application in Western societies. But accounting still provides the articulation of the one measure which can serve to aggregate or contrast information from all aspects of a diversified business, monetary value. However flawed it may be, it can be argued that it is still the best control we have available to us.

Nevertheless there is some disquiet about the central role of management accounting information in management control. Johnson and Kaplan (1987) have raised the issue of the relevance of the type of information which management accounting produces. While there is some contention as to the adequacy of the account these authors offer (Ezzamel *et al.*, 1990, Hopper and Armstrong, 1991) their book has provided the impetus for a debate on the direction which management accounting should take. Linked to this debate has been a closer inspection of the techniques adopted by Japanese companies, which are less financially oriented, and consideration has been given to the question of whether Western companies can learn from their Eastern counterparts. The outcome of these deliberations will be important for the development of accounting-based control and for management control in general. There are unlikely to be simple solutions, but the complexity of the task should not discourage us from undertaking an attempt to seek the resolution.

CHAPTER 7

Divisional control

M. Broadbent and J. Cullen

Introduction

Chapter 3 has already considered both how an increase in an organisation's size may lead to problems if a centralised and unitary control structure is maintained and how divisional structures were developed to balance the problems of allowing sufficient specialisation and yet providing an integration of the tasks carried out. That chapter further stated that divisional structures may lead to suboptimal decisions being taken by divisional management. The work of Williamson (1970, 1975) was used to support the notion of multidivisional (M-form organisations) as a medium for control to cope with the growing complexity of larger organisations and particularly those operating in 'diverse' product markets. M-form organisations are argued to integrate the concept of markets and hierarchies within one organisation, at divisional level through the market considering day-to-day activities, and at the group or head office level, through hierarchies setting strategies for the divisions. Put more distinctly, strategic decisions are vested in top management whereas operating decisions are the prerogative of divisional managers (Ezzamel, 1992, p. 5).

Contingency theory approaches to control, introduced in Chapter 2, argue there is no one 'optimal' way to structure an organisation, but that structure should reflect the environment in which it is found. The contingency literature suggests that environmental complexity is significantly correlated to the extent of decentralisation and that a strategy of product diversification has caused many organisations to divisionalise their structures (Chandler, 1962). Lorsch and Allen (1973) linked greater market differentiation and independence between products to divisionalisation along product lines, while organisations operating in integrated markets tend to remain non-divisionalised.

Chapter 4 introduced the notion of subsidiarity as a means of coping with complexity; in this case task and decision authority should be delegated as close to the point of enactment as possible. The principle of subsidiarity does not imply either a divisional or unitary form but leads to a consideration of the relevant and appropriate location of task and decision authority which, as argued above, leads to a separation of strategy and operational decision making and control for divisionalised companies.

Having linked back to the threads developed in the initial chapters of this text, we aim in this chapter to explore the issues raised in greater detail, initially returning to the arguments put forward by Chandler and others, before moving towards a control model for divisional companies and consideration of the ensuing problems that creates. The traditional approaches to control, through an accounting information system, will be explored, as will non-accounting controls (for example, Kaplan and Norton, 1992, 1993). The assertion of the separation of strategies and operational decision making will be questioned using, inter alia, the work of Goold and Campbell (1987a, 1987b).

The M-model arguments revised

Dermer (1977) emphasises that an understanding of the way an organisation structures itself through differentiation and the allocation of responsibilities through decentralisation is necessary in order to study control. Organisations differentiate their activities into subunits so each faces a more homogeneous and manageable environment. Differentiation can take many forms, the two major ones being differentiation by function and by product. Decentralisation determines the organisational structure, the scope of each unit and its potential range of activities. Differentiation determines what each unit is capable of doing, while it is decentralisation that determines what decisions it is responsible for and determines the range of discretion allowed to each subunit within the organisation.

Ezzamel and Hilton (1980a, 1980b) bring these two concepts together by classifying decentralised structures as 'functional' or 'federal'. Functional decentralisation is the delegation of decision-making power to lower levels of management on the basis of functional specification, for example production or marketing, while federal decentralisation involves the partitioning of the firm into two or more quasi-autonomous subunits, divisions or business units, whose activities are co-ordinated primarily through price mechanisms such as product lines, customers or geographical location.

Loft (1991), writing about the history of management accounting, suggests that at the turn of the nineteenth century the US economy had several huge vertically integrated firms, successfully adopting a centralised (or U-form) organisation structure by employing decentralised decision making through differentiation into highly specialist units. Hence top management could co-ordinate activities and direct strategy and policy. Johnson and Kaplan (1987), using the Williamson (1975) argument, maintained such large companies recognised the benefits of a well managed hierarchy over those of market exchange(s). The firms were not at this stage divisionalised: they were decentralised and it was not until after the First World War that divisionalised companies started to emerge, well known examples including Du Pont and General Motors.

The links between decentralisation and environmental uncertainty are well stated in the contingency theory literature. The work of Burns and Stalker (1961) who identified the categories mechanistic and organic organisational structure lead to research suggesting that environmental complexity is significantly linked to the extent of decentralisation within an organisation. The work by Chandler (1962) linked product diversification with decentralised structures and was supported by Lorsch and Allen (1973). This led to the conclusion that, as firms differentiate their products, divisionalisation will arise as a consequence of the resulting independence of different lines. This argument can be augmented by the analysis of technology as a contingent variable. This can be illustrated by the work of Woodward (1958a) and Perrow (1967, 1970) who maintain different organisational structures are a reflection of their technologies. This work suggests that, if a large company which operated in several diverse product markets and which used several different production technologies were to decentralise, divisionalisation would be the likely result.

Such a conclusion is supported by the general systems theory literature, which argues that organisations, like individuals, seek to cope with their environments. If the environment is uncertain and highly complex then the creation of subunits or divisions within an organisation as a 'coping' mechanism would seem appropriate. Thompson (1967) summarised this approach, stating that organisations cope with uncertainty by 'creating certain parts specifically to deal with it'.

The arguments put forward so far within this chapter follow those of Chandler (1962), supported by Johnson and Kaplan (1987), summarised by Loft (1991) as follows: 'that the environment caused large companies to follow certain strategies, which in turn 'caused' the multi divisional company'. This is not to suggest there is certainty about this. Loft questions this assertion, suggesting an opposite line of causation that may be equally as valid, 'that large companies' strategy of trying to dominate the market by driving competitors out, or swallowing them up, lead to monopoly and oligopoly and in turn to bureaucracy and wastefulness'.

Returning to the mainstream literature, Scott (1971) summarised the development of a firm into four stages, linking these with organisational structure and their respective attributes (see Figure 7.1] Scott (1971). The Scott matrix views the development of organisational structures through growth in size and complexity. Initial growth in size is seen as leading to the development of

FIGURE 7.1   The Scott Matrix

	Owner manager	Growth in size	Growth in complexity but central strategy	Highly diverse, no central strategy: set by business units
Stage	I	II	III	IV
Product line	Single	Single	Multiple	Multiple
Distribution	Single	Single	Multiple	Multiple
Organisational structure	Little or no formal structure	Functionally based and integrated	Product market based and quasi-autonomous	Product market based and largely autonomous

Source: Four strages of Organisational Development adapted from Scott (1971).

decentralised, functionally based organisations. With increased complexity the structure becomes product based and quasi-autonomous, with strategy held centrally – the classic multidivisional company. The final stage suggests that, as organisations become so diverse, the holding of a central strategy is replaced by the delegation of individual strategies to divisions or strategic business units. This matrix presents a logical progression of structure, but any large diversified company may be adopting different control mechanisms for different divisions at any one point of time – so control for a core business division will be different from that of a peripheral business unit. Such arguments will be developed later in this chapter using the work of Goold and Campbell (1987(a), 1987(b)) and Miles and Snow (1978).

Control with multidivisional organisations

The major advantage of decentralised and multidivisional organisation in particular is that it allows different layers of management to 'concentrate on those issues with which they are best placed to deal' (Emmanuel *et al.*, 1990a, b). The M-form organisation, if applied appropriately within organisations, should provide for effective performance and profit maximisation (Williamson, 1975) through the following three attributes. First is the efficient allocation of resources within the organisation. If the organisation is compared to a capital market, where lenders with surplus units are seeking out borrowers requiring those units for investment through a risk–return trade-off, then headquarters or central management is allocating resources between divisions on an equally competitive basis. Funds raised externally are obtained at a lower cost than any individual division could obtain, they are then allocated on a competitive basis between divisions and the efficiency of these funds is monitored through the use of performance indicators, so providing a control loop for the allocation of these resources.

Secondly, by the delegation of day-to-day and operational decision making to largely autonomous divisions, the communications channels to higher levels of management are not overburdened by the detailed information filtered out at lower levels. Such information channels can be used for summarised information flows and strategy dissemination. The concentration by divisions in particular areas of activity also reduces information flows, as interdivisional transactions are reduced.

Thirdly, the M-form minimises suboptimal behaviour. The vesting of strategic decisions with top management and the day-to-day operating decisions at divisional level reduces the risk and complexity of the decision making, as each is specialising at different levels. Because the organisation is a collection of interdependent units, transactions between these units will reduce the potential for opportunistic behaviour, which would be encouraged in transactions external to the organisation. The use of control systems and performance-monitoring devices, linked to a flexible reward system, may ensure optimal behaviour. Headquarters can, if required, mediate in disputes between divisions expediently without recourse to legal intermediaries.

According to this theory, hierarchies are only liable to replace markets if it is more economical to organise transactions through such hierarchies, so any managerial costs of divisionalisation must be less than those incurred by operating through the markets. The delegation of decision making to divisional managers will automatically increase the managerial costs through increased monitoring to ensure that delegated authority is not misused. Scapens and Roberts (1993) argue that decentralisation is often ambiguous because of a mismatch between the commercial unity of a division and the arbitrary divisions created by the system of profit centres. This ambiguity is supported by Otley (1990) in a case study of British Coal. As divisional level managers are given greater decision responsibility, they in turn expect greater rewards for that increased responsibility and a share in the success of the divisional activities.

It is possible for the performance of one division to be enhanced at the expense of the total organisation and the sheer competitive nature of divisionalisation may breed separatist attitudes and overcompetitive behaviour amongst divisions. Since the loss of central control through decentralisation and divisionalisation means a higher incidence of non-programmed decisions (Emmanuel *et al.*, 1990) for divisional managers, it is essential that these decisions are taken using judgement and intuition which is organisationally goal based, rather than solely divisionally based.

The use of divisionalised structures may be counterproductive where there are excessive interdependencies between divisions, for example where the organisation goal is indivisible amongst divisions, or where organisational resources are so complementary that separation between divisions reduces the scope for scale economics. The interdependencies of production functions may require high management costs to manage the relationships and may negate any benefits obtained from divisionalisation. Hopper (1988) argued that such costs arose from the requirement to have corporate controls over the managerial labour process, and the growth of management itself necessitated its management through monitoring processes.

Williamson (1970, 1975) argued that the divisionalised organisational structure possesses the requisite control apparatus required for profit maximisation:

1. an incentive machinery, including pecuniary and non pecuniary rewards, which can be adapted to monitor the behaviour of divisional managers towards the goals of central management;
2. an internal audit system which reviews and evaluates the performance of divisional managers;
3. an allocation system which assigns resources (cash flows) to the highest yielding projects after evaluation of divisional investment proposals.

He further puts forward the procedures for the implementation of divisional structure, as follows:

– identification of divisional boundaries;
– assignment of quasi-autonomous status for each division, so determining the extent of division autonomy;
– allocation of company resources to divisions;
– the use of performance measures and reward schemes to monitor divisional activities;
– the performance of strategic planning wherever possible.

Ezzamel and Hart (1987) suggest the management accounting literature has devoted little attention to the identification of divisional boundaries , the assignment of quasi autonomous status to divisions , and the performing of strategic planning. We hope to redress this balance by considering just these issues in the following section before considering the traditional accounting approaches to divisional control, to be followed by a broadening of the performance measures and the development of the strategic planning issues.

Controls in divisionalised organisations

This discussion will draw heavily on the work of Ezzamel and Hart (1987) who maintain that divisional control emphasises both financial and structural control devices, that these interact and, to some extent, constrain one another.

They state the overall control apparatus can encompass a variety of individual controls which may relate to:

- defining divisional environment,
- determining divisional size,
- defining and co-ordinating divisional interdependencies,
- determining the extent of divisional decision-making autonomy,
- characteristics of information and information flow,
- designing an internal audit system, and
- designing appropriate reward systems.

The above act as interacting decision variables which may constrain managerial action and which may be subject to other managers' manipulations. Each will be considered in turn.

The divisional environment will be a subset of the environment faced by the total organisation. The degree of differentiation required by each division to meet the demands of its environment will create internal diversity. The greater the differentiation the greater will be the problem of integration between different divisions. Divisions operating in relatively certain environments will rely on more formalised organisational practices, whilst those operating in environments reflecting greater complexity will have less formalised systems. The greater the environmental variety the greater the potential for disunity and dysfunctional behaviour amongst divisions, yet each division is unlikely to be fully independent of other divisions. The organisation needs to achieve integration between units to remain a whole. Lorsch and Allen (1973) maintained that the greater the differentiation between divisions the harder the task of integration, with a resulting complexity of integrative devices; task forces, committees, divisional specialists working at head office and so on. Within conglomerate companies, by definition highly diverse and operating in different product markets, Lorsch and Allen (1973) found performance evaluation systems that had direct linkages between performance in a financial sense and monetary rewards, while, in vertically integrated firms, having greater interdependencies and facing a similar environment, the performance evaluation systems were more formally administered with less emphasis on financial results and more on operating criteria.

Divisional size may reflect a compromise between economic efficiency and administrative efficiency. While classical economics would have us believe there are optimum sizes for particular units, divisional managers may have valid personal reasons to extend plant size beyond this norm for their own rewards. Similarly head office staff may limit plant size below this norm to ensure that the power base of individual divisional managers is not enhanced.

The issue of divisional interdependence includes the relationships between central management and divisional management, between divisional managers themselves, divisional managers and their operating units, and between operating units within any one division. The interdependencies (Ezzamel and Hart, 1987) could take several forms, and relate to demand and transfer pricing issues as well as issues of technological interdependency as well as behavioural effects. Each must be co-ordinated to avoid managers pursuing behaviour which is dysfunctional for the organisation as a whole but which may further their own interests. It is suggested that, in order to improve the effectiveness and usefulness of various accounting procedures, accountants have to team up with organisation designers and behavioural scientists.

The level of autonomy granted to a division manager is stated clearly in the work of Williamson (1970, 1975): central managers take strategic decisions, whilst operating decisions are vested with divisional managers. Williamson argues that the mixing of these decision levels may lead to suboptimal decision making and a reduction in organisational effectiveness. The evidence cited is a product of studies within traditional US divisionalised companies, yet more recent work by Goold and Campbell (1987a, 1987b) illustrates the sometimes clouded nature of the two levels of decision making, particularly for strategic business units (see Scott, 1971, Figure 7.1).

Even within the strategic business unit and the more traditional division it is essential that central management maintain the decision process which allocates resources amongst competing units. It is this process which can regulate the growth of any one division and its ultimate size and importance within the whole organisation. The rationing of resources to divisions that do not conform with central strategies may be a powerful incentive to conform.

Ezzamel and Hart (1987) maintain a commonsense view about the amount of decision discretion granted to divisional managers in that it would 'presumably imply that division discretion should be limited in decision areas characterised by excessive interdependencies, as well as in areas of critical importance to the organisation as a whole'. Lorsch and Allen (1973), in the study already quoted, found divisional managers within conglomerates had greater autonomy in their decision making than vertically integrated organisations. Other academic studies seem inconclusive and conflicting. The logical view would suggest that divisional managers facing environmental uncertainty which is different to that of the organisation as a whole, operating with few interdependencies, would have a greater range of decision responsibilities than the divisional manager working in contrary circumstances.

Information flows between levels of management reduce the level of uncertainty in which they operate. If decentralisation and divisionalisation is to work through the notion of subsidiarity, then ex ante information gathering for decision making should be done at the appropriate level; equally ex post information should be reliable for performance evaluation. Information characteristic and information flows will vary according to the reliability of the data. When output is difficult to observe and verify then the focus of information is likely to shift to 'softer' information flows. There has been much criticism of the use of 'hard' accounting information for the evaluation of divisional performance measures: see, for example, Ezzamel *et al.* (1990), who argue for the use of soft information for performance evaluation. Other proponents of this approach include Kaplan and Norton (1992, 1993) whose work will be discussed later.

Ezzamel and Hart (1987) considered that the internal audit of divisional organisations can operate at three different levels: advanced, contemporaneous and ex post. The advanced level involves reviewing a divisional proposed course of action; contemporaneous evaluation entails continuous monitoring of divisional performance; ex post evaluation involves end of period performance evaluation. Williamson (1970, 1975) views audit as a necessary cost of using a hierarchy as opposed to a market. The audit function, he argues, is necessary to attain the greater efficiencies generated by internal transactions.

'Traditional' accounting methods for the measurement of divisional performance

Next we provide an overview of the issues involved in providing accounting measures of divisional performance. The bulk of the literature is contained within management accounting texts, many of which assume that management accounting exists in splendid isolation rather than being a subset of management control!

Measures of divisional performance are usually financially based. There is substantial research evidence (Reece and Cool, 1978; Vancil, 1979; Tomkins, 1973) demonstrating the continued use of profit measures and return on investment ratios as the main measures of divisional performance. Solomons (1965) gave three reasons why some sort of index of divisional profitability would be useful.

1. as a guide to central management in assessing the efficiency of each division as an economic entity;
2. as aid to central managers in assessing the efficiency with which divisional managers discharge their duties;
3. to guide divisional managers in making decisions in respect of the daily activities of their own divisions.

While the three reasons provide a basic rationale for the use of divisional performance indexes within one organisation, Skinner (1990) maintains that a further economic justification for the use of performance indexes is inter-firm comparisons, where results of one division can be compared with those of the results of a whole company in a similar industry. Recent developments in company segmental reporting also highlight this external focus. Solomon concentrates on central managers and divisional managers to the exclusion of operating managers whose efficiency has a direct link to profitability. The three reasons stated by Solomon do agree with the Williamson (1970,1975) arguments that, through effective resource allocation and performance evaluation by central management, divisionalised organisations can pursue the notion of profit maximisation.

A major challenge facing this approach is to devise performance measures which do not encourage divisional managers to pursue policies that are beneficial to their own division but detrimental to the organisation as a whole. Shillinglaw (1982) suggests three rules with which divisional profit measures must comply before they can be regarded as acceptable; summarised by Drury (1985) they are:

1. divisional profit should not be increased by any action which reduces total organisational profit;
2. each division's profit should be as independent as possible of performance efficiency and managerial decisions elsewhere in the company;
3. each division's profit should reflect items which are subject to any substantial degree of control by the divisional management or his (or her) subordinates.

Traditional measures of divisional performance include profit, return on investment (ROI), residual income (RI) and discounted cash flow (DCF). Each will be considered in turn.

Profit

Profit is an appropriate measure of performance if the divisional manager has decision responsibility for all the variables within its calculation. There are, however, problems concerning profit measurement, profit definition and profit calculation, and the issue of common costs, common revenues and transfer prices. Absolute profit can be defined in many ways using different accounting bases. Which level of profit is applicable may also present problems – contribution margin, direct divisional profit, controllable divisional profit, income before taxation or net income.

Return on investment and residual income

Return on investment (ROI) or return on capital employed (ROCE) are very commonly used indexes of managerial and divisional performance levels. Skinner (1990) indicated that surveys from a variety of countries have shown that about 70 per cent of divisionalised companies use profit, most often in the form of return on investment ratios, as their main measure of divisional

Box 7.1   How to reject an acceptable investment

A division within a large conglomerate has achieved a fairly consistent ROI of about 20 per cent for the last five years. This is above the return for the company as a whole which has varied from 11 per cent to 15 per cent over the same period with a cost of capital estimated to be 10 per cent. The divisional management team are considering a new investment in advanced manufacturing technology. The new investment ROI is estimated at 18 per cent with a positive net present value of £68 500 and an internal rate of return of 14 per cent. The divisional management team have decided not to submit the new investment to headquarters for approval as it would reduce the ROI of the division in the short term.

financial performance. Return on investment has many advantages: it is a true efficiency ratio focusing attention on both assets and profits; it is a measure which is widely used (and abused) by managers; it provides a basis for comparison of performance between divisions, between divisions and outside companies and between divisions and alternative investment of funds. ROI is a ratio, which divisional managers will be required to maintain or improve over time. A divisional manager may be able to maintain the ratio by replacing assets as necessary and making progress improvements, but there is no strong encouragement to make the division grow in size, hence the use of absolute profit in parallel with ROI. Horngren (1962) has suggested that the change in ROI is often more significant than its absolute level, whilst Amey (1969) argues that profit maximisation must be the true objective.

The use of ROI can lead to the suboptimisation of resources. Divisional managers may reject new capital investment projects which are in the company's best long-term interests by having a positive net present value, because of the effect such a project would have on the short-term divisional return on investment. (See the example in Box 7.1 above.) Because new projects usually originate at operational levels within companies (King, 1975; Bower, 1986) it is possible for divisional management to filter out such projects before central management know of their existence. While the bulk of academic literature supports this view, Lillis (1992) repudiates this generalist conclusion in her work on three large divisionalised firms.

Solomons (1965) argued that the use of residual income overcomes these difficulties. Residual income imputes a cost of capital on the investment base which, when deducted from profits (or net earnings) gives an absolute figure rather than a percentage, like ROI. The charge for capital would be useful for evaluating performance and for guiding investment decisions. Divisional managers, he argues, would have an incentive to pursue all projects that have estimated internal rates of return greater than the cost of capital as this could increase absolute residual income. In the short run, Solomons also argued that residual income is the long run counterpart of discounted cash flow, so making it consistent with the wealth maximisation of model classical economics. This latter assertion has met with much criticism from Amey (1969) who argued, amongst other things, that the cost of capital may be inappropriate. ROI, regardless of the definitional problems of its two components; profit and investment, does provide a measure of efficiency. Such a measure, however, may encourage managers to pursue short-term goals and have a very narrow view of the organisation objectives. Swieringa and Weick (1987) maintain that a measure like ROI at least initiates action within the organisation, whilst Covaleski et al (1987) links this internal measure with the external pressures from the financial markets.

Financial measures of performance tend to concentrate on the short term, that is the effect of actions on the current financial year. In fact the time scale may be even less: Tomkins (1973) found that in British divisionalised companies a very large proportion (46 out of 53) appraised their divisions against detailed financial budgets on a time scale of one month or less. So projects which reduce short-term financial performance are likely to be held back by divisional managers unless specific provision is made for them in the capital budgeting process.

The use of financial performance targets results in divisional managers making decisions which are consistent with the achievement of a corporate finance objective, but this ignores the fact that organisations have multiple objectives, many of which cannot be easily measured. This narrowness of objectives will be considered in some detail after the next section on the use of discounted cash flow techniques and the issue of the divisional cost of capital.

Discounted cash flow

The discounted cash flow approach to divisional performance attempts to compare the expected net present value of the division at the beginning and at the end of a given period. It has clear links to the economic value concepts of financial accounting which have not been adopted for corporate financial reporting. While future cash flow may be difficult to estimate, the academic and practical problem is the establishment of a discount rate or cost of capital for application to the estimated cash flows.

The establishment of such a discount rate is highly problematic. Less formal approaches may include the use of past divisional returns, returns achieved by a company comparable to the division, budget returns of the division, the average return of industry in which the division operates or management judgement. More formal approaches may include the weighted average cost of capital adjusted for risk levels, or the use of the capital asset pricing model (CAPM) to derive covariances for divisional returns. The establishment of a weighted average cost of capital for a division may be computationally difficult – there are problems with gearing levels for divisions, the issue of the holding company not holding securities issued by divisions and traded in capital markets, although Williamson (1970, 1975) likens the relationship to a capital market.

The use of a CAPM approach has several computation problems, including the following.

1. Thode (1986) argued that four conditions need to exist before the CAPM could be adopted: the selection of a company of equal business risk to the division, the proxy company's business risk can be quantified; no scale economies or other synergies exist; and the growth opportunities of the division exactly match those of the proxy companies. Thode further argued that it is highly unlikely that such conditions will exist jointly.
2. There is a potential problem which may arise because of the changing expectations of managers having applied a single corporate rate in the past to using different rates for each division (Welch and Kainen, 1983). Some divisions may have projects rejected which otherwise might have been accepted, so having implications for divisional growth, profitability and management rewards. The change may be culturally unacceptable to divisional managers.
3. The use of divisional costs of capital to evaluate all projects in a division is likely to bias divisional managers in favour of riskier projects. A portfolio of projects of high, medium and low returns is normally present. Adherence to one cost of capital to evaluate all projects in a division may mean rejection of low-return but low-risk projects.

Grinyer (1986) has argued that the CAPM approach which emphasises systematic risk will not be adopted by managers who are subject to total risk.

The discounted cash flow model needs careful consideration but currently a profitability index like ROI is the dominant divisional measure of performance. This emphasis on accounting measurement and asset valuation has resulted in broad-based criticism of performance appraisal techniques which will be reviewed within the next section, which considers recent developments in divisional performance measurement.

Developments in divisional performance measures

Traditionally there has been a tendency for management accounting control systems to concentrate solely on internal issues. As indicated earlier in the chapter, there has also been a tendency for these control systems to focus solely on financial measures of performance. It has been well documented that financial measures of performance tend to concentrate on the short term (that is, the effect of actions on one year's profits, return on investment or residual income). Projects which harm short-term financial performance are likely to be held back by a divisional management team unless specific provision is made for them in the capital budgeting process. We have argued earlier that, if too much stress is placed on the corporate financial objectives, this may mean ignoring the fact that organisations have multiple objectives, many of which are not easily measured in financial terms. To use one key measure of financial performance is almost sure to produce dysfunctional behaviour as regards one or more other objectives. Other objectives may relate to sales growth, market share, employee relations, quality or social responsibility. It is to the need to link financial measures of performance to non-financial measures of performance that we now turn.

Many readers will be familiar with the work of Bromwich and Bhimani (1989), who pointed out that there was mounting empirical evidence supporting the need for management accounting to become more externally focused to enable the organisation to look outwards to the final goods market. This followed a call for strategic management accounting by Simmonds (1981), to be further developed by Bromwich (1990). While discussing the joint use of financial and non-financial measures of performance, we must simultaneously discuss the link between performance measures and the strategy being followed by the organisation.

As early as 1979, Parker produced a paper which put forward an argument for a balanced assessment of divisional performance to be measured by a composite mix of quantitative and qualitative indices. Parker (1979) argues that much of the traditional divisional performance literature appears to be based upon a simplistic and unrealistic view of corporate and divisional goals: 'Given the existing range of changing corporate and divisional goals, the divisional profit test taken by itself is inadequate as a measure of any division's progress towards the attainment of the corporate goal set' (p. 316). He went on to suggest an alternative approach to divisional performance measurement which accountants could adopt for the benefit of the decentralised company as a whole. The suggestion (p. 317) was that accountants should:

- discard the belief that accounting measures should be used to promote goal congruence among divisional managers;
- recognise the need to preserve some degree of autonomy in divisional operations;
- review the possible methods of assessing divisional performance with a view to accounting for the needs and objectives of all levels of management above and within each division;
- move beyond the single divisional profit-based index to provide an expanded number of measures of divisional performance which account for a broader range of success criteria.

Parker suggested the following as possible additions to the traditional profit/ROI measure:

- financial management ability – stock and asset turnover, gearing ratio, sources and application of funds, fixed asset statistics such as age, maintenance expenditures, depreciation policies;
- productivity – profit before interest and tax.
- marketing – sales volume, market share, sales effort indicators (for example, visits per customer);
- research and development – research and development costs to sales, research and development cost per employee, project performance indicators;
- social responsibility – social budget, narrative report;
- employee relations – lost time accidents, hours lost as a percentage of hours worked.

Other writers (Dearden, 1968; Kaplan, 1984; Johnson and Kaplan, 1987) have suggested before and since that profit/ROI is too narrow a view. However Parker's main argument is that there is a plurality of objectives for a company and its divisions and that there must therefore be a more balanced view of performance and the indicators used to appraise it.

This idea of a balanced view has been further developed by Kaplan and Norton (1992, 1993). They introduced the idea of a balanced scorecard (see Figure 7.2) which represents a set of measures aimed at giving managers a fast but comprehensive view of the business.

> The balanced scorecard includes financial measures that tell the results of actions already taken. And it complements the financial measures with operational measures on customer satisfaction, internal processes, and the organisation's innovation and improvement activities – operational measures that are the drivers of future financial performance. (Kaplan and Norton, 1992, p. 71)

An important feature of this approach is that it is looking at both internal and external matters concerning the organisation. The balanced scorecard introduces the idea of competitor benchmarking in relation to new product introductions and technology capability. Another important feature is that it is related to the key elements of a company's strategy. Different divisions may be following different strategies and the items in the balanced scorecard would therefore need to reflect these differences. A final important feature is the fact that financial and non-financial measures are linked together. There is no suggestion that financial performance measures should be discarded altogether. Periodic financial statements remind managers that improved quality, response time, productivity or new products only benefit the company when they are translated into improved sales and market share, reduced expenses or higher asset turnover. An illustration of the way the balanced scorecard could

FIGURE 7.2   The Balanced Scorecard

Financial perspective		Customer perspective	
GOALS	MEASURES	GOALS	MEASURES
Survive	Cash flow	New products	Percent of sales from new products
Succeed	Quarterly sales growth and operating income by division		Percent of sales from proprietary products
Prosper	Increased market share and ROI	Responsive supply	On-time delivery (defined by customer)
		Preferred supplier	Share of key accounts' purchases
			Ranking by key accounts
		Customer partnership	Number of cooperative engineering efforts

Internal business perspective		Innovation and learning perspective	
GOALS	MEASURES	GOALS	MEASURES
Technology capability	Manufacturing geometry vs competition	Technology leadership	Time to develop next generation
Manufacturing excellence	Cycle time Unit cost Yield	Manufacturing learning	Process time to maturity
Design productivity	Silicon efficiency Engineering efficiency	Product focus	Percent of products that equal 80% sales
New product introduction	Actual introduction schedule vs plan	Time to market	New product introduction vs competition

Source: Kaplan and Norton (1992), p. 76.

be developed within a divisionalised organisation is given below in Box 7.2 taken from Kaplan and Norton (1993) (see also Figure 7.2).

Box 7.2

FMC Corporation is one of the most diversified companies in the United States, producing more than 300 product lines in 21 divisions organised into five business segments: industrial chemicals, performance chemicals, precious metals, defence systems, and machinery and equipment. Based in Chicago, FMC has worldwide revenues in excess of $4 billion.

If we were going to create value by managing a group of diversified companies, we had to understand and provide strategic focus to their operations. We had to be sure that each division had a strategy that would give it sustainable competitive advantage. In addition, through measurement of their operations, whether or not the divisions were meeting their strategic objectives.

If you are going to ask a division or the corporation to change its strategy, you had better change the system of measurement to be consistent with the new strategy. We acknowledged that the company may have become too short-term and too internally focused in its business measures. Defining what should replace the financial focus was more difficult. We wanted managers to sustain their search for continuous improvement, but we also wanted them to identify the opportunities for breakthrough performance.

A new measurement system was needed to lead operating managers beyond achieving internal goals to searching for competitive breakthroughs in the global market-place. The system would have to focus on measures of customer service, market position and new products that could generate long-term value for the business. We used the scorecard as the focal point for the discussion. It forced division managers to answer these questions: How do we become our customers' most valued supplier? How do we become more externally focused? What is my division's competitive advantage? What is my competitive vulnerability?

We decided to try a pilot programme. We selected six division managers to develop prototype scorecards for their operations. Each division had to perform a strategic analysis to identify its sources of competitive advantage. The 15 to 20 measures in the balanced scorecard had to be organisation-specific and had to communicate clearly what short-term measures of operating performance were consistent with a long term trajectory of strategic success.

We definitely wanted the division managers to perform their own strategic analysis and to develop their own measures. That was an essential part of creating a consensus between senior and divisional management on operating objectives. Senior management did, however, place some conditions on the output.

The extract describes an organisation where the divisional managers were involved in the process of strategic analysis and it is to this area that we now turn our attention. As mentioned earlier in the chapter, the work of Williamson (1970, 1975) is based on the premise that central managers take strategic decisions, whilst divisional managers are vested with operational decisions. We will now look at a range of literature which challenges this particular assumption. The main thrust of this literature is the need to accommodate, within the divisional performance measurement system, the fact that many divisional managers are responsible for the development of their own business strategy. Simons (1990) explains that business strategy refers to the way a company competes in a given business and positions itself among its competitors. This contrasts with corporate strategy which Simons (1990) explains as being concerned with the determination of which business(es) the organisation chooses to compete in and the most effective way of allocating scarce resources among business units.

As part of the discussion on the work of Kaplan and Norton (1992, 1993), the need to link the performance measurement system to the key elements of a company's strategy was highlighted. The point was also made that different divisions within the organisation may be following different strategies and consequently the items in the balanced scorecard would need to reflect these differences. Hall (1978) described how General Electric, recognising the need to differentiate between divisions, introduced the concept of Strategic Business Units (SBUs). Hall outlined (p. 394) that the SBU concept of planning is based on the following principles:

– the diversified firm should be managed as a 'portfolio' of businesses, with each business unit serving a clearly defined product-market segment with a clearly defined strategy;
– each business unit in the portfolio should develop a strategy tailored to its capabilities and competitive needs, but consistent with the overall capabilities and needs.

Hall (p. 396) identified four steps which are required to operationalise the concept of SBUs:

1. identification of strategic business elements, or units;
2. strategic analysis of these units to ascertain their competitive position and long-term product market attractiveness;
3. strategic management of these units, given their overall positioning;
4. strategic follow-up and reappraisal of SBU and corporate performance.

Using the concept of strategy as a position, Hall emphasised the need for different performance measurement and appraisal systems for business units holding positions in the different strategic classifications of dogs, question marks, stars and cash cows. However, as part of a critical evaluation of the SBU process, he suggested that organisations had generally failed to develop the managerial control aspects of the process. He found it illogical to go through the process of SBU analysis and then to continue to measure and reward SBU management on annual performance against a profit target.

> Most firms have gone only half way with the SBU concept – they position the product market segments and then go right on rewarding and promoting managers on traditional criteria. In the end the companies which make the SBU concept work will be those which change all management systems; developing and rewarding SBU managers differentially depending on their SBU position and the strategic handling which is appropriate for their element of the portfolio. (Hall, 1978, p. 402)

This link between strategy and control systems formed the basis of further work by Govindarajan and Gupta (1985) and Simons (1987a). Govindarajan and Gupta (1985) examined the linkage between strategy, incentive bonus systems and effectiveness at the SBU level within diversified firms. The results of the study can be summarised as follows: (a) greater reliance on long-run criteria (for example, product development, market development, personnel development, political/public affairs) as well as greater reliance on subjective (non-formula) approaches for determining the SBU general manager's bonus contributions to effectiveness and (b) the relationships between the extent of the bonus system's reliance on short-run criteria and SBU effectiveness is effectively independent of SBU strategy.

The study by Govindarajan and Gupta therefore provides empirical support for the idea that, in terms of SBU effectiveness, the utility of any particular incentive bonus scheme employed in an attempt to influence the SBU general manager's behaviour is contingent upon the strategy of the focal SBU. Simons (1987), again using the concept of strategy as a position, carried out an empirical study which investigated the relationship between business strategy and accounting-based control systems. Building on the Miles and Snow (1978) typology for identifying generic strategies (prospector, defender, analyser), Simons (1987a) studied firms classified as either prospectors or defenders to determine whether management control systems differ between the two groups. He found that successful prospector firms seem to attach a great deal of importance to the use of forecast data in control reports, set tight budget goals and monitor outputs carefully. For prospectors cost control is reduced. In addition, large prospector firms appear to emphasise frequent reporting and the use of uniform control systems which are modified when necessary. Defenders, particularly large firms, appear to use their management control systems less intensively. In fact negative correlations were noted between profit performance and attributes such as tight budget goals and performance monitoring. Defenders emphasised bonus remuneration based on achievement of budget targets and tended to have little change in their control systems.

Goold and Campbell (1987a, 1987b) took this debate a stage further by carrying out a major piece of empirical work looking at the management of diversification in 16 large UK companies (1987a, b):

> For senior managers at the corporate headquarters of most large companies, diversity is a fact of life. The portfolio of these companies frequently includes businesses from several industries, at different stages of maturity, with different growth option and different financial performance. Understanding and controlling each of the businesses in a portfolio of this sort is a severe test of corporate management. (Goold and Campbell, 1987, p. 42)

Goold and Campbell identified three main different central management styles (strategic planning, strategic control and financial control) and three main philosophies for building and managing a diverse portfolio (core business, diverse business and manageable business). A brief description of the different philosophies and management styles is shown in Figure 7.3.

An important finding from the Goold and Campbell work is that companies tend to employ a uniform style across most of their businesses, and that changes in style rarely occur. Companies with a core business philosophy tend to adopt a strategic planning style. Those with a manageable business philosophy adopt a financial control style. Companies operating a diverse business philosophy use a strategic control style. This relationship is highlighted in Figure 7.4. Comparing Figure 7.4 with the Scott (1971) matrix (see Figure 7.1) the Goold and Campbell analysis discusses specific control issues within stages III and IV in more depth by considering different management philosophies and styles associated with these different stages.

The idea of strategic control is of particular interest to us in terms of the degree of decentralisation given to business unit managers. This links into the concept of Strategic Business Units, discussed earlier in the chapter, introduced by Hall (1978). The essence of this decentralisation is the location of the primary responsibility for proposing strategy and achieving results with the business unit manager and not with central management. Companies, in this situation, decentralise strategic responsibility in order to ensure that strategies are based on a detailed knowledge of specific products markets, to increase business level 'ownership' of strategy, and to reduce the overload on the chief executive and senior management. Goold (1991) agrees with these objectives but emphasises that such decentralisation can only work well if two basic conditions are fulfilled:

- The centre must be able to determine whether the business is on track with its own strategy. Unless the centre knows when to intervene, decentralisation becomes abdication of responsibility.

FIGURE 7.3   Different Philosophies and Management Styles

PHILOSOPHIES

Core Business

Company commits itself to a few industries and sets out to win big in those industries.

Manageable Business

The emphasis is on selecting businesses for the portfolio which can be effectively managed using short-term financial controls. There may be extensive diversity in terms of industries, but there is homogeneity in the nature of the businesses.

Diverse Business

The emphasis is on diversity rather than focus. The centre seeks to build a portfolio that spreads risk across industries and geographic areas, as well as ensuring that the portfolio is balanced in terms of growth, profitability and cash flow.

CENTRAL MANAGEMENT STYLE

Strategic Planning

Corporate management in Strategic Planning companies believe that the centre should participate in and influence the development of business unit strategies. Their influence takes two forms: establishing a planning process and contributing to strategic thinking. In general they place less emphasis on financial controls.

Financial Control

Financial Control companies focus on annual profit targets. There are no long-term planning systems and no strategy documents. The centre limits its role to approving investments and budgets, and monitoring performance. Targets are expected to be stretching and once they are agreed they become part of a contract between the business unit and the centre. Failure to deliver the promised figures can lead to management changes.

Strategic Control

The centre of Strategic Control companies is concerned with the plans of its business units. But it believes in autonomy for business unit managers. Plans are reviewed in a formal planning process with the objective being to upgrade the quality of the thinking. However the centre does not want to avocate strategies or interfere with the major decisions. Control is maintained by the use of financial targets and strategic objectives.

Source: Goold and Campbell (1987b), p. 27.

FIGURE 7.4   Management of a diverse portfolio

	Philosophies		
	Core business	Manageable businesses	Diverse Businesses
Diversity across industries	Low	Very high	High
Diversity across types of businesses	Fairly low	Low	High
Style at centre	Strategic Planning	Financial Control	Strategic control
How mismatches avoided	Core business mainly responsive to Strategic Planning	Portfolio selection and retention of 'manageable' businesses	Structure into homogeneous groups
Growth	Mainly organic	Mainly acquisition	Organic and acquisition
Drawbacks	– Limited industry diversity – Maturation of core businesses – Non core businesses	– Limits to acquisition-based growth – Vulnerable to aggressive competition – Does not build	– Low key centre – Limited central added value – Cultural complexity

Source: (Goold and Campbell (1987), p. 50)

– The business heads must know what will be counted as good performance by the centre. Without clear goals, the whole concept of decentralised responsibility suffers, since the conditions under which a business head can expect to operate free from central intervention are ill-defined (p. 69).

In the companies using a strategic control style, formal strategic control processes typically had the following key stages (Goold, 1991):

– Periodic strategy reviews for each business – the business proposes a number of specific strategic objectives or milestones and negotiates with the centre until they reach agreement. These objectives are non-financial indicators of underlying competitive position, and provide a longer-term, more strategic balance to financial objectives.
– Annual operating plans – explicit non-financial objectives derived from the strategic plan are often included alongside financial budget objectives in annual operating plans.
– Formal monitoring of strategic results – some companies combine this with budget or operating plan monitoring. In others it is a separate process.
– Personal rewards and central intervention – explicit strategic objectives are built into personal reward schemes and complement financial performance in guiding central intervention. Most companies avoid a formula-based link between achievement of strategic objectives and personal rewards, and prefer a more direct and flexible link.

The last two points in this strategic control process can be related to the work of Simons (1990), who introduces the idea of interactive management control as opposed to programmed control:

> Management controls become interactive when business managers use planning and control procedures to actively monitor and intervene in on-going decision activities of subordinates. Since this intervention provides an opportunity for top management to debate and challenge underlying data, assumptions and action plans, interactive management controls demand regular attention from operating subordinates at all levels of the company. Programmed controls, by contrast, rely heavily on staff specialists in preparing and interpreting information. Data are transmitted through formal reporting procedures and operating managers are involved infrequently and on an exception basis. (Simons, 1990, p. 136)

The focus of attention in Simons' work is business strategy and the way in which top managers use interactive control systems to monitor the progress of a business unit towards its business goals. Simons argues that the top managers make selected control systems interactive to monitor personally the strategic uncertainties that they believe are critical to achieving the organisational goals. It is also suggested, in a similar way to Goold (1991), that the use of interactive control systems can be linked to the use of subjective reward systems which are not formula based. Company B, for instance, in Simons (1990) has a reward system based on effort. As a result of the debate and dialogue that surrounds the interactive management control process, new strategies and tactics emerge over time. Simons (1990) therefore illustrates how management control systems are important not only for strategy implementation but also for strategy formulation. The work illustrates how interactive control systems can be used to manage emergent strategy (Mintzberg, 1978). Similar points are made by Dent (1990) who illustrates how embryonic management notions can become manifest through new systems of planning, accountability and performance measurement. These in turn can provide conditions of possibility for organisational reform and the emergence of new strategies.

Conclusion

The later parts of the chapter have discussed the way in which management control systems, particularly the use of a combination of financial and non-financial measures as part of a strategic control process, need to be understood in their organisational context. The overall issues of control within divisionalised companies is a highly complex mechanism, the linkages between strategy, structure and organisational content provide an opaque picture of control, which is not reflected in the clarity of the Williamson (1970, 1975) model. Hopwood (1987, 1990) and Dermer (1990) provide both theoretical and empirical debate about the way in which accounting needs to be seen in terms of shaping, rather than just enabling, organisational affairs. The approach taken in the development of strategic control in this chapter has been uncritical. A critique of strategic control is included within the next chapter.

CHAPTER 8

Strategic control

Alan Coad

Introduction

The study of management during the last three decades has been dominated by two concepts: strategy and cybernetics (Dermer, 1988). The resulting conventional wisdom has tended to be teleological. Strategy is usually described as management's definition of what the organisation should be doing. Control is then effected cybernetically, through goal-related feedback and adjustment. However there is another body of literature, more recent and rooted in a more empirical research tradition, which regards strategy and control as something other than the creation of top management. According to this perspective, organisations are made up of a variety of stakeholders attempting to satisfy their wants amidst a host of conflicts and constraints. Strategy in this light is not the prerogative of top management, but rather the outcome of organisational struggles. It is what the organisation actually does rather than what top management intends it to do. The resulting order is not the creation of an overall designer; rather it emerges from the collectivity of interactions of organisational actors (Mintzberg and Waters, 1985; Johnson, 1987; Dermer, 1988, 1990).

Research has indicated that strategic change is shaped by such things as administrative planning and control systems (Ansoff, 1979; Anthony, 1965; Goold and Quinn, 1990a); the perceptions and biases of key decision makers (Anderson and Paine, 1975; Schwenk, 1984) and political factors (Mintzberg, 1983; Pettigrew, 1985). Much of the conventional wisdom regarding the relationship of strategy and control has focused on the first of these, thereby, perhaps inadvertently, denying important aspects of organisational reality.

This chapter attempts to redress the balance somewhat. Initially it examines the concept of strategy and the conventional wisdom of the relationship of strategy and control. It then explores issues such as cognition, learning, ideology and politics to gain some understanding of the way they affect this relationship. Finally it attempts a synthesis of the ideas and considers the implications for strategic management.

Strategy

The term 'strategy' is probably one of the most ill-defined in the business vocabulary, having a wide range of connotations. Published definitions vary, with each writer adding his or her own ideas and emphasis. To some, strategy refers to a plan, the end product of strategy formulation (Newman and Logan, 1971). Some include objectives as part of the strategy (Andrews, 1971; Quinn, 1980) whilst others see objectives as what the strategy is to achieve (Ackoff, 1974). Many mention the allocation of resources as a critical aspect of strategy (Hofer and Schendel, 1978). Some prescribe a review of the market and specifically mention competitive position (Porter, 1985). To further complicate matters, some writers suggest that strategy is reserved for a formal logic, explicitly stated, that links together the activities of business (Ansoff, 1979), while others indicate that a strategy can emerge from a set of decisions and need not be explicitly stated (Mintzberg and Waters, 1985).

Clearly the word 'strategy' is used in different ways. However within this variety two major themes are evident. Firstly, there is the idea of strategy as a position. This concept involves identifying where an organisation locates itself in its environment. By this definition, strategy becomes the mediating force, or 'match' (Hofer and Schendel, 1978), between the internal and external context. In ecological terms, strategy in this sense is an environmental 'niche'; in economic terms, a place that generates 'rent'; in management terms, a product-market 'domain', the place in the environment where resources are concentrated. Strategy, by this definition, is a version of positional analysis, concerned with the status of an organisation relative to competition and other aspects of its environment. A feature of this concept of strategy is that all organisations can be said to have a strategy. Thus, while the match between an organisation's resources and its environment may or may not be explicitly developed and while it may or may not be a good match, the characteristics of this match can be described for all organisations (Hofer and Schendel, 1978).

The second major theme is the idea of strategy as a process. Landmark works by Chandler (1962), Ansoff (1965) and Andrews (1971) were among the first to propose the distinction between the process of strategy and its content. The distinction has tended to divide research ever since. Strategy process research has been concerned with the way strategy is formed and implemented, whereas 'what is being decided' has been claimed as the province of position-oriented research. Questions of 'who is involved in strategy' and 'why strategy arises' have been addressed by both groups, but in different ways. The business unit, the company and populations of organisations have been the focus of position research, whereas process research is largely preoccupied with the individual and the group. The question 'why' has been seen primarily as one of economic performance by position researchers, whereas process researchers have looked either to logical or behavioural rationales.

However this distinction between process and position research leaves both streams weakened, theoretically. Most scholars would agree that the content of a strategy is likely to be affected by the processes whereby the strategy is developed and implemented. Also it is possible that the processes are affected by the content and outcomes of previous strategic decisions. Close examination of positioning strategies (for example, Miles and Snow's prospectors, analysers, defenders and reactors) infers a variety of organisational processes. Moreover many of the prescriptions for the processes of strategy (such as Andrew's search of the environment to identify opportunities which may be exploited by company strengths) imply a search for environmental niches, that is positions.

This overlap of two key themes in the strategy literature is accommodated by Stacey's (1993) model of the strategy concept. He emphasises the importance of thinking of strategy as a game people play. This overcomes a tendency to depersonalise strategy. Much of the strategy literature infers an objective reality in which 'the organisation' moves in response to changes in 'the environment' (Glaister and Thwaites, 1993). Unconsciously we begin to see strategy in mechanical terms where one 'thing' moves in predetermined ways in relation to another 'thing'. This oversimplifies strategic management because organisations and their environments are not things, but rather groupings of people interacting with one another. By focusing on strategy as a game, we remind ourselves to examine the moves, countermoves and further responses by inter- and intra-organisational players which are the dynamics governing success or failure.

Stacey's model of this gaming process is shown in Figure 8.1. Starting at the left-hand side, we see that people in the environment of organisation A do something that people in that organisation discover. People in organisation A choose how to respond and then act upon that choice. These actions then have consequences for people in the environment, for example competitors, customers, suppliers, distributors and legislators. These then choose how to respond to their perceptions of the actions of people in organisation A. And so the game goes on. People both within and outside an organisation interact through a series of feedback loops resulting in discovery, decisions and action that control and develop their organisations.

Figure 8.1 illustrates that we can look back in time from the present to, and if we are able to perceive a pattern in past actions, we call this pattern the past strategy of the organisation. Similarly, if we are able to look forward to *tf*, we may discern a pattern, or strategy, in future actions. For Stacey, then, strategy

122

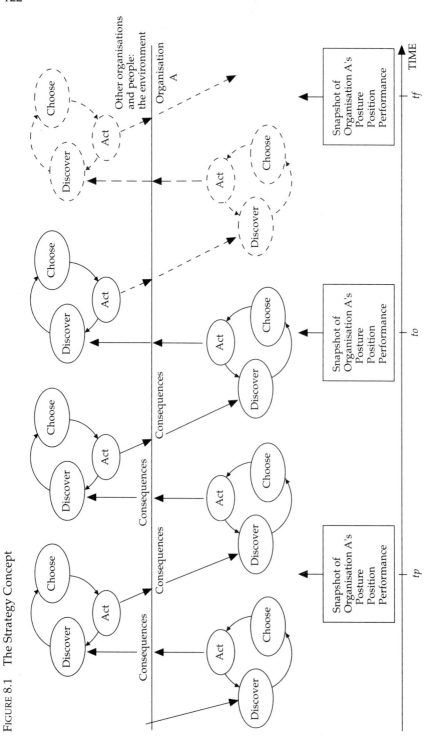

FIGURE 8.1   The Strategy Concept

Source: Stacey (1993).

is a perceived pattern in actions past or yet to come. The emphasis on perceptions in this definition is important because strategy does not have an objective reality independent of the observer: we cannot touch or feel a strategy. Strategy is a label that people apply to patterns in action. Moreover different people might apply different labels, focusing on different attributes of the unfolding action. This leads us to the concept of multiple realities, whereby different organisational actors perceive the patterns of the strategy game in different ways, which may lead to different prescriptions regarding how to act in the future. This concept of multiple realities and the attendant multiple rationalities will be examined further in the section on political factors, below.

Having explored the concept of strategy, it is possible to offer a working definition of what the present author understands by the term 'strategic control':

> Strategic control is concerned with the decisions and actions undertaken by organisational actors in response to perceived environmental patterns in organisational action, past or yet to come.

In particular, this chapter focuses on the way in which organisational actors make sense of their environment and how this, in turn, contributes to the development of strategies in the cultural, political and social milieux of organisations.

It is acknowledged that the definition above is much broader than that which is normally found in the literature of strategic management and management control. The conventional wisdom of strategic control tends to place emphasis on formal planning and monitoring systems. This conventional wisdom will be described in the next section of this chapter, and subsequent sections will examine some of the theories of organisational dynamics which imply a need for an expanded concept of strategic control.

The conventional wisdom

The term 'conventional wisdom' refers to those general prescriptions for success that command most attention in best-selling management textbooks and among practising managers. In respect of Stacey's three elements of the strategy process – discovery, choice and action – the conventional wisdom prescribes that the discovery phase should comprise some systematic appraisal of an organisation's strengths and weaknesses, its environmental threats and opportunities, together with a recognition of the values and expectations of influential stakeholders (usually assumed to be top management). This knowledge is then summarised in a form of position statement (such as a SWOT analysis) which gives an indication of where current strategies are likely to lead the organisation into the predicted future. If a gap exists between predicted performance and managerial expectations then the gap should be closed by selecting appropriate strategies. The 'choice' phase of the conventional wisdom, then, comprises the identification of possible strategies and their evaluation according to a favoured set of criteria. The criteria prescribed for assessing strategies are often summarised under classifications such as tests of 'fit' with environmental opportunities and threats, 'feasibility' in terms of the resource capability of the focal organisation, and 'acceptability' to the influential stakeholders. Together, these stages of discovery and choice are referred to as strategy formulation. In the conventional wisdom, the action phase involves a formal implementation of chosen strategies by designing an appropriate organisation structure, adopting a management style that will influence organisation culture in a way regarded as instrumental by top management, and establishing the appropriate control systems to check that actions align with managerial expectations.

It is acknowledged that this description is a simplification of the conventional wisdom of strategic management. However it presents a picture that will be familiar to readers of popular textbooks on the subject (see Dess and Miller, 1993; Johnson and Scholes, 1993; Morden, 1993). Moreover it should be emphasised that the conventional wisdom is not some monolithic, uniform body of explanation and prescription. On the contrary, it consists of a number of approaches that appear to be very different. For example, some writers (such as Andrews, 1971) regard strategy formation as a creative, conscious intellectual process of organisational design, whereas others (such as Ansoff, 1979) regard strategy as the outcome of systematic, formal planning and control. Nevertheless the coventional wisdom tends to adopt a teleological perspective in that perceived organisational order is assumed to have been put in place by a designer. It is assumed that organisations follow particular strategies because that is what their senior management have decided. Consistent with this belief in the designing influence of top management is the belief that the circular process of discovery, choice and action that is strategic management is a deliberate and intentional one (Stacey, 1993). The question of the validity of these beliefs will be dealt with later in this chapter. For now it is time to concentrate on what has conventionally been understood to be the relationship between strategy and control.

From the mid-1960s to the mid-1980s the dominant view of the connection of strategy to management control was based on the work of R.N. Anthony, who defined management control as 'the process by which managers assure that resources are obtained and used effectively in the accomplishment of the organisation's objectives' (Anthony, 1965). This definition distinguished management control from both strategic planning and operational control and led to the development of formal, systematic, organisation-wide, data-handling systems which are designed to facilitate management control (Machin, 1983). It is a perspective that has been reinforced by a tendency in the strategy literature conceptually to separate strategy formulation from strategy implementation. Hence strategic planning sets the strategies, management control checks they are being pursued appropriately. Control is effected through negative feedback. The management control system measures the performance of a process and compares it with a standard. If the performance fails to meet the standard, subsequent performance is adjusted to ensure compliance. The model is, therefore, essentially cybernetic, although a very simple kind of cybernetics is involved (Lowe and Puxty, 1989).

It was noted in Chapter 2 that Anthony's perspective brings into close alignment the concepts of management control systems and management accounting systems. For him, management control is built around financial information about revenues, costs and resources. The information covers both planned and actual levels, such as are found in a budget. In addition to financial information, the system may include data about volume of resources and number of personnel, as well as the quantity and quality of output. Plans are presented and approved at certain dates each year. Reports on actual outcomes are submitted, reviewed and evaluated in a prearranged sequence. Overall the management control process is depicted as an integrated one, encompassing programming, budgeting, accounting, reporting, analysis and corrective action.

Despite its plausibility and widespread acceptance, Anthony's model of management control has a number of serious limitations. Some of these have been referred to in Chapter 2. What we seek to emphasise here is the fact that a number of limitations came to be acknowledged in the strategy literature during the 1980s and led to a variety of prescriptions for systems of strategic control (see Hurst, 1982; Lorange *et al.*, 1986). In particular it was noted that Anthony's model stresses financial objectives and, via the medium of the budgetary control system, usually concentrates only on the coming 12 months. It pays little explicit attention to longer-term goals and objectives. Moreover, by virtually ignoring issues such as organisations' environments and their positioning relative to other entities, it fails to accommodate constructs that are fundamental to the concepts of strategy and control. Furthermore it plays down the potential of management control systems to influence strategy formation and draws unnecessarily restrictive boundaries around concepts such as management control and strategic planning.

The prescriptions for strategic control systems that emerged in the strategy literature during the 1980s broadly fall into two categories. Firstly, there are those elements of the system which are concerned with ensuring that the firm's strategy is on track. These may be referred to as implementation controls. Secondly, there are recommendations for systematic approaches to check that the present strategy remains relevant in changing circumstances. This is the role of strategic control systems which enable top management to respond to unforeseen external and internal developments with changes in strategy. These may be referred to as relevance controls.

Strategy implementation control is concerned with whether or not a firm's strategy is being implemented as planned. By analogy with budgetary control systems, this requires that objectives be established and performance measured against the objectives to assess whether strategy is going according to plan. However there is a fundamental problem here, in that strategic objectives tend to be relatively long-term. Hrebiniak and Joyce (1986) point to a tendency for managers to focus more on short-term than on long-term objectives. Controls set against objectives that are several years ahead will not be as influential as controls set against this year's targets. Therefore they suggest that strategic control systems should specify short-term goals (milestones) which need to be achieved in order that the strategy is implemented in the long term. The strategic milestones are not targets in themselves, but rather things which are realised on the way (for example, completion of a new factory). To strike a proper balance between long-term and short-term objectives, Lorange (1988) argues in favour of developing separate strategic and operational budgets which should be controlled against independently. His strategic budget is based on two elements. Firstly, it includes an allocation of resources necessary to change the direction of a particular business, that is, those resources necessary to implement a major change in business strategy. Secondly, the resources should be identified with specific strategic projects or programmes. Lorange suggests that the primary justification for a particular allocation of strategic resources is that it should enhance the firm or business unit's long-term competitive position. The operational budget, on the other hand, should include those resources necessary to maintain current operations at a successful level. For each organisational unit, Lorange suggests establishing strategic objectives (the eventual position competitively); strategic programmes and milestones (specific tasks en route to the strategic objectives); strategic budgets (the resources to be spent on strategic programmes); and operating budgets. Performance should be monitored against each heading and the reward system should, at least in part, be geared to the implementation of strategy.

Recommendations in the literature regarding the use of relevance controls are concerned with a much broader question: should the firm's overall strategy be changed in the light of unfolding events and trends? Hurst (1982) reasons that there are differences between strategic control systems and budgetary control. Strategic control requires more data from more sources, particularly external sources, and may be concerned with competitive benchmarks and with non-financial measures, as well as with long-term outcomes. Strategic control may therefore be less precise and less formal than budgetary control and is concerned more with the accuracy of the premises on which a managerial strategy has been based and much less with quantitative deviations from a standard. Premise control requires systematic and continuous strategic survelliance of internal and environmental factors to determine if the assumptions on which a managerial strategy has been based remain valid. It is argued that control processes such as these provide top management with the information they need to decide when to intervene to adjust strategy (Schreyogg and Steinmann, 1987).

We see from the above sections that there is no shortage of literature recommending the establishment of strategic controls. However, paradoxically, very few companies identify formal and explicit strategic control measures and build them into their control systems (Horovitz, 1979; Goold and Campbell, 1987a, 1987b). A recent survey (Goold and Quinn, 1990a) shows that only 15 per cent of those large companies in the UK which have formal planning systems use them as a standard against which to monitor actions. Goold and Quinn (1990b) question why this apparent paradox should exist. Is it because there is a significant lag between theory and practice? Or is it that the benefits of strategic control systems have been greatly overstated in the literature of the 1980s?

We may go some way towards answering these questions by returning to the idea that the conventional wisdom is teleological in nature. It pictures the firm as being guided by a comprehensive and explicit strategy which is systematically planned and co-operatively executed. It considers strategic decisions to be the domain of senior management. As management's definition of what the organisation is and what it should be doing, strategy articulates, shapes and justifies the context of organisational activity for all concerned (Dermer, 1988). The conventional wisdom admits that there are barriers to strategic control arising from systems complexity and behavioural and political factors (Lorange and Murphy, 1984). However these are mere stumbling-blocks; they do not negate the definition of success which is still measured in terms of managements' ability to deal with the issues it faces (Dermer, 1990). The conventional wisdom defines issues as events in the organisation's environment to which management must respond. Accordingly prescriptions are made to sharpen management's response by developing systematic approaches to environmental scanning.

However, as we have seen, there is a theory/practice gap regarding strategic control. The position taken here is that the teleological model of strategic management, whilst of value as a logical model in structuring debate and informing learning, does not describe strategic management in practice. Specifically it attaches too much importance to the role of top management in strategy formation. It is too optimistic about the possibility of synoptic, rational analysis by top management and co-operative execution of strategies. It fails to address such issues as the cognitive limitations on analytical and rational behaviour, the interaction of a variety of stakeholders in the location and definition of strategic issues or the exercise of choice at the interpersonal level. In short, it is a depersonalised model of management which fails to recognise the emergent nature of strategy. It is to these issues that we turn in the next two sections.

Cognition and shared mental models

The material in this section deals with organisational members' cognitive models of strategic problems and the factors which affect the ways they develop these models. This, in turn, affects strategic issue diagnosis, problem formulation and choice of action. Much of this perspective derives from work in the 1940s and 1950s by Nobel prizewinner H.A Simon, who laid the groundwork for the treatment of cognitive simplification in his discussion of 'bounded rationality' by suggesting that choice of action in the real world departs from the requirements of objective rationality because of human cognitive limitations.

Within the field of cognitive psychology, the construct theory of Kelly (1955) and the 'field expectations' of Tolman (1949) are both models of cognition which suggest that individuals have a coded perception of their world to which they relate new experiences. Their models indicate that managers will process environmental and organisational events through pre-existing knowledge systems known as schemata. Schemata are mental models which represent beliefs, theories and propositions that have developed over time, based on individuals' personal experiences and which allow them to categorise events, assess consequences and consider appropriate actions (Fiske and Taylor, 1991).

A number of researchers have argued that the brain's capacity to store information vastly exceeds its capacity to process that information (for example, Hyman and Anderson, 1982). As a result, there is a need for some sort of patterning of the information into larger units so that it can be managed. Furthermore, when faced with new situations, individuals seek to allocate the experience to an existing pattern. Schemata thereby provide frames for problems which make it unnecessary for organisational decision makers to expend the mental effort necessary to diagnose completely each element of a new strategic problem (Taylor and Crocker, 1983). Schon (1983) reasons that schemata provide managers with a repertoire of images, examples and actions such that when a new situation arises it is perceived as something already present in the repertoire. There is a tendency then to filter new information so as to focus only on those data which fit in with established mental models.

In a similar vein, Weick (1979) argues that schemata – he refers to them as 'perceptual sets' – are ready-made explanations that the actor carries from situation to situation. Futhermore he suggests that human actors do not react to an environment, rather they enact it; that is, they create meaning from environmental stimuli on the basis of attention to what has already occurred. Moreover what they understand to be occurring currently affects their perception of past occurrences. They thereby continually amend their mental models through their ongoing experiences or enactments. In this sense they invent their own environment. For Weick, environments are enactments by managers of the world in which they live; their 'reality' in terms of perceptions about the interactions of people inside and outside an organisation is not to be understood as an empirical reality but rather as a function of management cognition. Indeed it may be a mistake to think of managerial thought and managerial action as separable. When managers act, their thinking occurs concurrently; there is a presumption of logic in meeting a situation, so action is natural and thinking (in action) in turn endows the action itself with greater meaning (Weick, 1983). It may, then, only be possible for managers to make sense of what they are doing after they have done it. This reasoning has implications for our understanding of strategic control. In highly complex and turbulent situations, explanations of strategic change need to take account of the view that environments are invented or created in managers' minds and that they can often only make sense of what they are doing with hindsight.

One further consequence of using schemata to process information deserves to be highlighted. Their use allows individuals to reason by means of analogy. This enables people to speed up the process of recall and application to a new situation. We use analogies to make the novel seem familiar by relating it to prior experience. A basic form of learning uses some form of repetition to push schemata into the subconscious where they can be recalled and used very rapidly. The richer the stock of schemata, the more expert the person. This form of learning is referred to as 'single-loop learning'. A stimulus results in a reaction based on our previous experience. No attempt is made to retrieve and examine the subconsious schemata to test it for continuing validity. This carries with it a number of dangers in the strategic setting. The fact that the schemata being used to design actions are subconscious means that we are not questioning them. The more expert people are, the quicker they use subconsious models, and therefore the more readily they take for granted the simplifications and assumptions on which the models have been based. This is highly efficient in stable conditions, but in changing conditions it may lead to skilled incompetence (Argyris, 1990). This gives rise to the need for double loop learning (Argyris and Schon, 1978) where we learn by questioning and adjusting subconscious schemata.

However, so far the discussion has been at an individual level. Strategies are rarely formed by individuals alone. More usually they are the product of people choosing and acting in groups. It is worth considering whether the lessons from cognitive psychology have relevance at the group level. Sims and Gioia (1986) suggest that the schemata concept can be applied to management groups and used to describe similarities in assumptions and ways of processing information within the group. According to the authors, common types of schemata include implicit theories about relationships among variables within a company and its environment, and scripts, which provide directions for behaviour.

Beyer (1981) argues that there exist organisational ideologies that can be defined as a relatively coherent set of beliefs that bind some people together and that explain their worlds in terms of cause and effect relations. Other writers refer to similar sets of beliefs as 'paradigms' (Sheldon, 1980; Pfeffer, 1981). A paradigm is a set of beliefs and assumptions people have about the world. It is usually subconscious and therefore rarely questioned. As people live and work in a group they come to share ways of looking at the world. The paradigm flows from shared past experience and reduces the communication and information flows necessary to secure cohesive group action. This sharing of implicit models is often referred to as the culture of the group or organisation.

Of importance to our discussion about strategic change are the insights from researchers who have observed the tendency of paradigms to dominate organisations in a relatively conservative way. Sheldon (1980) argues that organisations may enter a 'paradigmatic state' in which they cease to adapt to their environment, or may simply adjust marginally within their paradigm. The paradigm tends to be quite robust, even in the face of potentially disconfirming evidence. Grinyer and Spender (1974) describe how managers will defend their paradigm by cycling problems through routines of adjustment and interpretation (single loop learning). Confronted by a challenge, for example declining performance, management are first likely to seek means of improving the implementation of existing strategy, perhaps by tightening controls. If this is ineffective, they may seek to change strategy incrementally, but still in a manner in line with the existing paradigm. Only if there is persistent disconfirming evidence will management consider abandoning the old recipe and shifting to a new paradigm. Similar observations are made by Argyris and Schon (1978) who provide illustrations of the difficulty managers have in moving from single loop learning, where they are making responses within established cognitive frameworks, to double loop learning, where they internalise divergent views which do not correspond to these frameworks.

These observations suggest that paradigms and their attendant strategies may not change readily in response to environmental change. This provides the phenomenon of strategic momentum (Miller and Friesen, 1980) where managers resist changes that conflict with their way of understanding their organisation and its environment until some crisis makes such resistance unsustainable. Johnson (1987) describes a typical pattern of strategic change in which the organisation is driven down a particular path by its own momentum, becoming more and more out of line with the requirements of its environment. When the resulting strategic drift has taken the organisation too far from these requirements, a revolutionary adjustment is necessary which involves breaking the old paradigm and establishing a new one.

In this section it has been suggested that central to the process of forming strategy are the cognitive systems of the people involved. In the previous section we examined the conventional wisdom of strategic management. This represents a particular paradigm, the assumptions of which suggest that strategy making is the domain of top management who through a systematic assessment of an organisation and its environment can identify and implement strategies that maintain an organisation in a state of dynamic equilibrium in which it is adapted to its environment. The implementation and control of strategies is assumed to be effected by an appropriate organisation structure, sophisticated control systems to sense environmental and organisational change, and the establishment of a strong organisational culture. It follows that the behaviour patterns of successful organisations are assumed to be ones of order, regularity and consensus around a stable belief system. However the empirical research of Miller (1990) and Pascale (1990) suggests that such harmony, consistency and fit achieved by organisations may be at one and the same time their strength and their downfall. Reinforcing their paradigm, the tendency is for companies in this position to concentrate on doing better what they already do well. This results in what Miller refers to as the Icarus paradox. As organisations keep modifying and building upon what initially made them successful, a momentum results which leads to disaster. Pascale emphasises the need to change today's dominant paradigm. The conventional wisdom which focuses on order, objectives, planning and control systems tends to emphasise doing the same things better. Consequently the existing paradigm blocks alternatives. Pascale argues for a new paradigm that recognises the non-equilibrium nature of innovative organisations and the connection between tension and creativity. For him, successful organisations demonstrate a paradox. On the one hand, they must achieve 'fit', that is coherence among units, central control and synergies; on the other hand, they also require 'split', that is decentralisation, differentiation, variety and rivalry. Split is required in order to develop new perspectives and innovative actions. This leads to the destruction of old paradigms. This need for fit and split inevitably causes tension, but Pascale regards this as creative tension that provokes inquiry and questioning and leads to a learning organisation which supports a continual dialogue between contradicting points of view.

Overall, then, a picture begins to emerge that innovative strategies will rarely flow from centralised systematic strategic planning. Instead most innovative strategies emerge from a complex organisational learning process. We will return to this theme in a later section. First it is necessary to consider another important facet of group dynamics: political factors.

Political factors

Underlying the conventional wisdom is what is referred to as a unitary view of organisations. This pictures organisations as being integrated wholes where the interests of the individual and the organisation are synonymous. It emphasises the importance of individuals subordinating themselves in the service of an organisation as a means of realising their interests and the common good (Morgan, 1986). The unitary perspective reifies organisations by regarding participants in organisational life as being united under the umbrella of 'organisational goals' which 'it' attempts to achieve in a team-like manner (Fox, 1974). Consequently organisations are pictured as harmonious, consensual phenomena existing for the pursuit of common ends. Conflict tends to be explained in terms of pathological causes (such as ignorance or antisocial behaviour), and it is seen as an unwanted intrusion. It is the role of the team leaders (top management) to eliminate or suppress conflict wherever possible so as to reinforce the team spirit. Power is regarded in such a way that it is limited to management; formal authority is the only legitimate source of power, and the rights and abilities of others to influence organisational processes are rarely acknowledged (Morgan, 1986).

It will be argued here that the unitary perspective not only inaccurately describes organisational life but also may lead to a suppression of dissenting views which are necessary for organisations to achieve creatively and innovatively a strategic advantage. An alternative to the unitary perspective is the pluralist view. This sees organisations as comprising diverse socioeconomic groups whose pursuit of sectional interests inevitably creates some conflict (Fox, 1974). Hence conflict between organisational stakeholders (management, workers and so on) is not abnormal: it should be expected. Morgan (1986) argues that conflict can serve both positive and negative functions. On the positive side, conflict can energise an organisation. It may counter tendencies towards lethargy, staleness and apathetic compliance. It may encourage forms of self-evaluation that challenge the conventional wisdom and established organisational paradigms. Consequently, it may help stimulate learning by keeping the organisation in touch with what is happening in the environment and by being an important source of innovation. In particular, a healthy attitude towards conflict may overcome pathological conformity arising from 'groupthink' and 'organisational defensive routines'.

Groupthink (Janis, 1972) refers to a tendency of some groups who work together over a period of time to produce poorly reasoned decisions. Group cohesiveness and a desire for consensus lead to a number of symptoms which include self-censorship by members who avoid speaking up against the majority opinion; a shared illusion of invulnerability; and erroneous stereotyping of people outside the group. These phenomena can then lead to serious deficiencies in the decision-making process. These include incomplete survey of alternatives, failure to examine the risks of the preferred choice; failure to reappraise initially rejected alternatives; and selective bias in processing information (Janis and Mann, 1977). Overall too few alternatives are examined, with the policy alternative first tabled often being the one adopted, whether it was sound or not.

Organisational defensive routines (Argyris, 1985, 1990) are patterns of behaviour deployed by people in an organisation to protect themselves from embarrassment and anxiety. A key defensive routine is to make matters undiscussable and to make the undiscussability itself undiscussable. So, for example, subordinates may refrain from telling their superiors the truth if it is likely that the truth may be something they will dislike. Of course the subordinates do not publicly admit they are doing this. Nevertheless their superiors know it is going on, because they do it themselves. The result is an undiscussed game of pretence in which all indulge and all know it is going on. The pay-off from the game is that it avoids confronting potentially embarrassing or dissonant situations. Argyris describes such defensive routines as barriers to organisational learning. They may become so entrenched that managers actually avoid discussing contentious open-ended issues altogether. This is particularly dangerous in circumstances requiring strategic control. Organisational participants may become desensitised to gradually accumulating changes in the environment and the prevailing paradigm will become reinforced by default.

The existence of rival points of view, recognised by a pluralist perspective, can do much to overcome such pathologies and improve the quality of strategic decision making. There are of course negative aspects of conflict. Too much of it can immobilise an organisation by channelling the efforts of its members into unproductive activities. Nevertheless it is a matter of balance because, as we have seen, too little conflict may result in complacency and lethargy.

The basic unit of analysis in the pluralist perspective is the interest group. Each unit is presumed to have its own perspective, its own rationality, and to operate consistently within the rationality (Cooper, 1983; Dermer and Lucas, 1986). The multirational nature of organisations generates conflict wherein stakeholders contend for the control of strategy. There is no presumption of managerial prerogative. Managerial plans do not necessarily determine the contents of the strategic agenda (Dermer, 1990). Strategic concerns may originate anywhere in the organisation and the role of 'change entrepreneur' can be assumed by anyone with the necessary motivation and ability: 'the strategic agenda emerges from the reconciliation of conflicting rationalities, not from the imposition of management's global scheme. Because no grand design is assumed to exist, organisational strategy does not necessarily need to make sense from any single perspective' (Dermer, 1990).

March and Simon (1958) suggest that each interest group recognises, defines and attempts to resolve into limited and manageable problems the uncertainty it faces. It then seeks to articulate and legitimise those problems for which it feels it has implementable solutions. Dermer and Lucas (1986) reason that it is probable that there is more than one model of controllable reality operating at any one time. Moreover multiple models imply the necessity for multiple control systems (even though only one system, that of top management, is acknowledged as legitimate).

For pluralists, sources of power are the media through which conflicts of interest are resolved. If we accept the assumptions of shared power, multiple realities and multirationality, it is likely that the formal, authoritative control systems cannot fully prescribe or predetermine behaviour. Because of mutual dependency and the need for mutual survival, differences between organisational units must be harmonised through processes such as negotiation and compromise. The role of each organisational unit is regulated, not only by a system of (strategic) control imposed by top management, but also as a result of negotiation with other stakeholder units. Thus Dermer and Lucas (1986) contend that actual control systems are, in fact, the emergent results of prior political negotiations between organisational units. An implication of this reasoning is that the conventional wisdom of strategy and control as it is taught (and practised?) does not reflect the whole of organisational reality.

Towards a broader concept of strategic control

In recent years, the strategy literature has begun to reflect a perspective that coalesces in the notion of emergent strategy (Mintzberg and Waters, 1985). Strategy in this light is not the prerogative of top management, but rather the outcome of organisational struggles. It is what the organisation actually does rather than what top management intends it to do.

By considering the ways in which cognitive factors interact with political factors, we may develop a clearer understanding of the ways in which strategic change occurs. This will have implications for what we understand by the term 'strategic control'. Below we present a simplified model of the strategic change process, which adopts a pluralist perspective. In this model, the process of strategic change begins with an event in the internal or external environment of an organisation. The event becomes known to individuals within the organisation either because they have direct contact with it or because it is communicated to them through the formal and informal systems of the company. Research suggests that the awareness of strategically significant events often exists in the organisation long before any action is taken to deal with them (Pettigrew, 1985; Schwenk, 1988). Indeed the event may be dealt with by local subsystem adaptation, rather than precipitating an organisation-wide response (Quinn, 1980).

According to the pluralist view, the organisation will comprise interest groups, each of which has a paradigm which will be used to interpret the event and define its significance. The paradigm will also suggest a possible response to the event on the part of the organisation. This response will tend to be consistent with the political interests of the group proposing it. Given sufficient motivation, the interest group will push for organisational attention to be paid to their issue and proposed solution. A complex process of advocacy and coalition building is required before the issue can be said to have gained organisational attention. Once an issue has gained sufficient support, in the sense that it is being discussed by people with sufficient power to do something about it, then the issue becomes part of the strategic agenda (Dermer, 1990). This process is often characterised by the interaction of multiple participants advocating alternative solutions to multiple problems that are being dealt with simultaneously (Cohen *et al.*, 1972; Pettigrew, 1985). Through this interaction, new understandings of strategic issues emerge (March and Olsen, 1976; Quinn, 1980). There is no overall framework to which organisational participants may refer when tackling issues on the strategic agenda because each issue is unique. Potential solutions become apparent through discussion with other members of the organisation, with customers, suppliers and even competitors. This progress of the issue is likely to have implications for participants' paradigms. They are in effect modifying old mental models and existing company recipes to come up with new ways of doing things. Thus the people involved with issues on the strategic agenda experience a real-time learning activity which results in new paradigms. These then form the basis for a new strategic orientation. This, in turn, may necessitate changes in organisational structure and information processing, which will, of course, take time. The new paradigm and its associated organisational implications inevitably create conditions for changes in political alliances and the relative power of interest groups. This may create a resistance to change which reinforces the notions of strategic momentum and strategic drift described earlier.

This simplification of the political and cognitive factors involved in strategic change is sometimes referred to as self-organisation. This is because no one centrally organises event recognition, issue framing, support building and choice of action. Self-organisation is a process of political interaction and group learning from which innovations and new strategic directions may emerge. It occurs when people form a group that produces patterns of behaviour, despite the absence of formal hierarchy within the group or authority imposed from outside it.

Concepts of emergent strategies and self organisation lead us to reconsider what is meant by strategic control. It is most usually portrayed as something to do with ensuring conformity with the central organisation-wide intent of top management. However Dermer (1988) argues that cognitive and political models view organisations as non-goal-oriented, non-instrumental social systems which are susceptible to change in infinite ways because their strategies can be affected to some extent by any stakeholder. For Dermer, control must therefore be redefined as that which causes activities and outcomes to happen. In this chapter, we have attempted to follow his advice, and hope that this is reflected in the definition of strategic control proposed on page 123. In this way, we broaden the concept so as to explicitly recognise that forces other than senior management can and do shape strategic evolution. Organisational effectiveness is no longer goal-related but can be evaluated only in terms of adaptability and, ultimately, survival.

Implications for management

We appear to have painted a pessimistic picture regarding mangements' abilities to effect strategic control. This is unintentional. What we have attempted is of a more realistic portrayal of the context in which strategic mangement takes place. It is a complex context in which simultaneously organisations require both stability to effectively implement current strategies via approximations to planning/monitoring forms of control; and instability to encourage innovation via political and group learning modes of decision making and self-organising forms of control. In this context, an important role for strategic management is one of effectively using their positions of power to influence the structural arrangements and dynamics of organisations so as to provide an appropriate balance between the stability of planning and monitoring systems and the discontinuities of learning and political behaviour.

Assuredly scholars are a long way from becoming prescriptive regarding the management of the inevitable tensions. The legacy of Burns and Stalker (1961) was an 'either/or' way of thinking about the design of organisations. There became a widely held belief that formal bureaucratic controls are inappropriate for organisations facing high levels of uncertainty. Changing contexts apparently require more organic practices: co-ordination is achieved through the use of informal, personal communications, rather than by rules and standard operating procedures. The implication is that organisations face choices between designs for order or for disorder, for consistency or for disturbance, and for continuity or for change.

We would argue that this dichotomy has been overstated. Katz and Kahn (1978) observe that organisations possess both 'maintaining systems', which insulate them from change and uncertainty and perpetuate the status quo, and 'adaptive systems', which stimulate innovation and experimentation. An issue which remains largely unaddressed in the literature is the extent to which the balance between these types of system may be designed through the conscious intervention of senior management, or left to spontaneous self-organisation.

Some indirect evidence is provided by comparing and contrasting the approaches to control taken by two large successful organisations described in case studies in the same text (Bruns and Kaplan, 1987). Dent (1987) describes the structure and processes of control systems at Eurocorp, a company which develops, manufactures and distributes a wide range of computing products. Simons (1987a, 1987b) describes the control processes at Johnson & Johnson, a company with business interests in pharmaceutical, cosmetic and health care products. Both companies are large organisations. Contingency studies suggest that increased size leads to task specialisation, especially where scale economies may be obtained. This in turn creates task interdependence and pressures for the development of bureaucratic planning and control procedures (Mintzberg, 1979). In addition, both companies face high levels of environmental uncertainty. Such uncertainty tends to produce pressures for decentralised decision making, giving discretion to those with specialised market knowledge, and may be best managed through organic arrangements (Mintzberg, 1979). What is especially striking is a comparison of the different ways in which the two companies cope with their challenging circumstances.

At a superficial level, Eurocorp's control systems appear to be designed according to traditional principles. Formal planning procedures exist. However they are not continuous activities. In the rapid rate of change in the company's product-markets, planning details quickly become obsolete. Planning creates corporate direction but, in practice, operational co-ordination is achieved through a complex pattern of spontaneous interaction. Dent argues that the structure of the control system is significant in supporting this interaction. Responsibility exceeds authority; managers depend on others to achieve their own unit's performance targets. This creates tensions in the organisation, encouraging unit managers to think beyond their functional tasks and to negotiate with managers of other units to act on their behalf.

In contrast, Johnson & Johnson cope with the learning requirements of an uncertain environment by formalising frequent superior/subordinate interaction. Simons distinguishes two types of control process. The first he terms 'interactive control' to describe situations in which business managers actively use planning and control procedures to monitor and intervene in ongoing decision activities. At this company, long-range and financial planning systems are used interactively: superiors are highly involved in negotiations with subordinates regarding revisions to plans and actual outcomes. The involvement is formally programmed and is an ongoing activity. However this interaction is set against a background of a second type of control process, which Simons refers to as 'programmed control'. This is used in areas of the business which are less exposed to uncertainty. Here managers direct their attention primarily to ensuring that predetermined control procedures are established and maintained by designated subordinates. For programmed control, managers intervene only if outcomes are not in accordance with predetermined standards.

Obviously, the richness of the case studies by Dent and Simons cannot be conveyed in two short paragraphs. The reader is encouraged to refer to the source material. Nevertheless we observe here two significantly different ways of coming to terms with some of the issues explored in this chapter. Both cases demonstrate the paradox of 'fit' and 'split' (Pascale, 1990). At Eurocorp, stability, central control and synergies (fit), are encouraged through the annual planning cycle, which examines broad competitive issues, allocates resources and establishes an attitude of profit consciousness through the specification of unit financial objectives. However new perspectives and innovative actions (split) are encouraged through decentralised decision making and overlapping responsibilities, which results in informal negotiations between managers of different units. Hence needs for double loop learning are primarily accommodated by horizontal interaction and self-organisation. In contrast, at Johnson & Johnson, stable activities are subject to programmed controls. The need continually to re-examine organisational paradigms is formally designed into the routine and frequent interaction between superior and subordinates.

Both approaches encourage organisational learning and the identification of strategic issues by people at lower levels of the organisational hierarchy. It may be that, to some extent, the approaches are substitutable, and involve certain trade-offs. Dent observes that the processes at Eurocorp are inefficient. They consume a lot of management time and energy. Without formal authority over other units, managers expend a lot of effort in persuasion of others. Sometimes there are suspicions that agreements may not be implemented. Levels of stress are high, and frictions emerge. Nevertheless it is far from clear that alternative approaches would be less costly. At Johnson & Johnson, interactive controls necessitate continual replanning and frequent communication between superiors and subordinates. These procedures are costly to operate.

If the approaches are substitutable, they call into question simple contingency frameworks which tend to infer that mutually exclusive modes of strategic control may be appropriate in different circumstances. We really need far more detailed case studies of the nature of those provided by Dent and Simons before we are in a position to describe more accurately strategic control in practice. The provision of these descriptions, together with consideration of the generalisability of findings, and the extent to which strategic control processes may be intentionally designed by top management, are some of the more important challenges facing researchers and practitioners in the years to come.

CHAPTER 9

Control of embedded operations spanning traditional boundaries

Anthony J. Berry

As so often in discussions of management control, we return to the seminal idea of Robert Anthony's three levels of control: strategic, managerial and operational. Earlier chapters of this book have been critical of this taxonomy, but it very serviceable as an ideal type from which we may extend our analysis. In this chapter we leave aside the issues of strategic and managerial aspects and turn to the consideration of operational control.

Typically, in management accounting and control texts, control of operations is handled through the establishment of budgets of various kinds (see Chapter 6). In this chapter we wish to take a broader view of operations, followed firstly by consideration of modes of control for networks, and secondly by consideration of financial control and clan control issues in what we shall term 'embedded networks' or chains of operations (Grabner, 1993). Embeddedness means that such a firm is linked by medium-and longer-term contracts to both suppliers and to purchasers in a complex chain of organisations, which themselves are similarly connected. In the first section of this chapter some of the characteristics of the embedded firm are developed. This is followed by a discussion of the problems of control in and of such chains. The issues for financial control are examined prior to an exploration of the social and organisational processes within and between partners in such chains.

Operations and organisations

We will consider operations from two standpoints: firstly, those which are wholly within a given organisation, and secondly, those that lie within and outside the boundaries of a number of participating organisations. In the first case we will be considering operations which are wholly under the control of the owners or managers of an enterprise. Such an operation might be simple and only inside one part of a complex organisation but it might also be an operation which requires the co-operation of many different organisation sub units. In Figure 9.1(a) we give a simplified example of an operation to produce products or services which require a series of steps from inputs to outputs through a convergent procedure. In the figure the transfers into and out of the organisation involve transactions at the boundary of the organisation.

The idea of boundary to organisation is used in two different ways: firstly, there is the legal and institutional boundary of the organisation, which is clearly marked by the usual transactions of purchase and sale of goods and services; secondly, there are the social and cultural boundaries of the organisation, which may be considerably fuzzier than the legal or transactional ones. These social and cultural boundaries are marked by individuals and sub-groups in an organisation.

In this first example the operating system is located wholly within the legal boundary of the organisation and the legal boundary is itself wholly within a country boundary. What is presented in this example is a firm operating in markets and acting as an independent trader. In Figure 9.1(b). the

FIGURE 9.1(a)   A Firm and its Boundaries within a Country

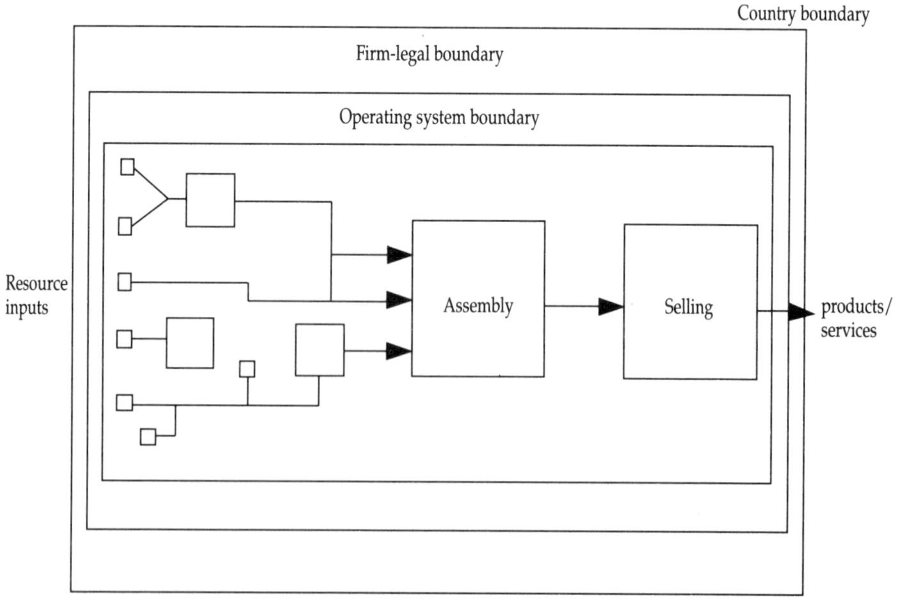

In this example, the operating system is within the firm and the firm is within a country.

FIGURE 9.1(b)   A Firm and its Boundaries across Countries

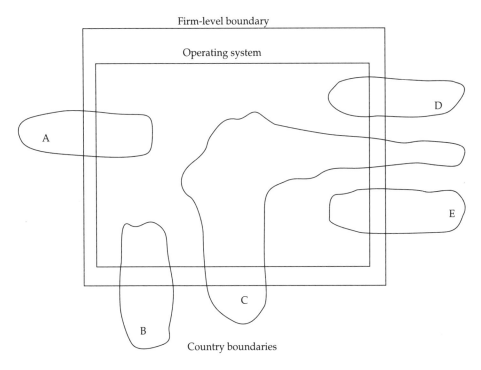

In this example, the firm operates in five countries, takes in resources from three countries and sells in three countries. The firm is essentially independent.

example is complicated by relaxing the country constraint and we can see that the steps of the operation still lie within the legal boundary but now take place in a number of different countries. Here a third idea of boundary is introduced, that of the country. An example of this is the Ford Motor Company in Europe, which operates on an integrated strategy, marketing and manufacturing process, so that engines might be made in Germany, Spain or England; the assembly plants might be in Belgium, England or Spain, or other countries; parts suppliers could be located in any Western European country or other part of the world, and the product marketed in all Western European countries and outside it. Indeed it is said that the automotive industry is one of the first truly global networks of provisioning and selling. Here there are complex issues in the legal control of Ford that cross the social, cultural, national boundaries , but the system that they are managing , as the final suppliers of vehicles to consumers,includes controlling the system which produces all of the parts for the assembly lines that they have established.

In Figure 9.2 the situation is made more complex by showing how the operating system to produce products and services has been modified by having the steps in the operation take part in legally separate organisations. In this latter case the firms or organisations are, to a greater or lesser extent, dependent upon one another for the functioning of the operating system. In this case, following the terminology of Grabner (1993), we refer to these organisations or firms as being 'embedded'. So we can see that this simplified example leads us to consider the problems of the control of operations within independent firms and within firms embedded in an operating system which includes other embedded firms. Some writers refer to these kinds of systems as networks, others as chains. Note that the boundaries which are applied to denote what is inside the system, network or chain are an arbitrary choice, perhaps based upon considerations of the relative significance of the contributions of the actors to the operation in question.

In the case of the embedded firms the operations of focus are inside and outside the ownership of the boundaries of the specific enterprises. An example here would be an operation to supply clothes at a retail shop which involves textile technology firms, dye makers, fashion designers, textile manufacturers, makers of trims, suppliers of computer-controlled production machinery, garment makers and assemblers, merchants, retail houses and so on working together to design, manufacture, merchandise, market and sell the

FIGURE 9.2   The Embedded Firms

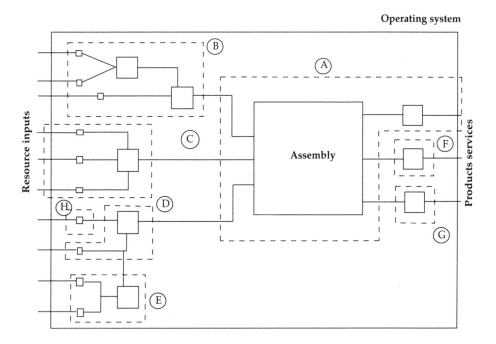

garments. So, in addition to the legal, cultural and national boundaries, we note that a fourth idea of boundary arises, that of technology. The relationship of different technological approaches in organisations would create considerable problems for the establishment of embedded chains. To overcome such difficulties would imply that the organisation was not technologically separate from other enterprises in the network or chain: for example, the imperatives of technological integration of production equipment and procedures and, of great interest for control, electronic data interchange will enter the operations of any one enterprise. Clearly, then, in any complex operational chain to produce goods and services which is typical of most advanced manufacturing countries, most of the operating systems that are established and managed involve transactions across all of these four boundaries.

Control in embedded networks

Two primary modes of control, direct control, that is direct personal supervision of those doing the work, and indirect control, that is supervision of work through mediating layers of organisation, are familiar. However in both, quite simple, organisations (see Box 9.1) direct control is difficult and, in complex organisations, direct supervision and oversight is hardly possible. Furthermore, rule-based control is difficult to establish and sustain in organisations which have high degrees of variety, both in terms of required skills and knowledge, geographical locations and technologies, and hence is clearly problematic in a firm in an embedded chain. Thus the control of the embedded networks of complex organisations becomes of interest.

Box 9.1   The African bus driver

An African bus driver in what is now Zambia had a bus route that meant his driving a bus away from his depot one day, and driving it back the following day. Sometimes a problem arose in collecting the ticket money. On a particular day, the inspector who had been given by the driver the proceeds of one of these two-day trips was rather suspicious of the small amount of money that had been handed in. He asked the driver, 'Is that all?' and the driver said, 'Yes'. The very large inspector then picked the driver up, turned him upside down and shook him, and a great deal more money rattled out of the driver's pockets, clothes and so on, over the floor. When all this was scooped up they came to an equable agreement about how much of this belonged to the bus company and how much belonged to the driver.

It appears that three different problems arise, both in the case of the operating systems in the independent firms and within the chain of embedded firms. Firstly, there is the problem of deciding which organisations will enter the chain. Secondly, there is the problem of establishing the operating system from which role, work demands, the nature of work and work organisation are derived (and which in turn serve as an experience from which changes might be managed). A common approach to managing this process can be found in the literature of project management, where the actors negotiate and agree to a programme for establishing the new system. Thirdly, there is the ongoing management of the now established operating system.

In order to begin exploring these problems we first consider a process of evolution from a 'firm' operation through a procedure of decentralisation (alternative hierarchic control) to one which is part of an embedded chain either through contracting out or through franchising. Operational control of complex and wide-ranging activities engender difficulties in reporting action and implementing decisions both because of the time lags and because of the degree of unexpected variety which local managers must handle. This latter point is often used as an argument for decentralisation, in order to make a contract for responsibility and accountability within the organisation, a form of control through hierarchies and rules, in order to minimise the variety that senior managers need to handle. Of course decentralisation as a form of differentiation designed to cope with external complexity and uncertainty leads to a need for new modes of integration between the decentralised units; for example, new rules emerge for transfer of products and services. When this becomes too difficult to manage (because of significance, the nature of interdependence and of complexity and uncertainty) then quasi-market related controls are allowed, in various forms, to enter the internal world of the organisation. Should these still leave control problems, the troublesome activities can be exported from the organisation in two primary ways: subcontracting for products or services instead of providing them internally, (and perhaps permitting a management buy-out to create the subcontractor) and franchising (for example, retail outlets) or selling off parts of operations instead of owning them.

Here we note that complexity and uncertainty of operations within the independent firm are seen to lead to variations of the control structures and procedures through changes in hierarchy and rules and forms of markets. These are not only matters from the technical system, for the issues and problems associated with motivation, identity, belonging and loyalty are used as arguments for franchising, where there is a procedure to regain control at the boundary by placing the ex-employee, now franchisee, firmly outside the organisational boundary. Here the problems of motivation are apparently solved by ensuring that the franchisee's self-interest is now aligned with the economic goals of the franchiser. Such a practice has occurred within the domestic bread and milk delivery business in the UK. In general we can see that organisational and environmental complexity and uncertainty can lead independent firms to develop approaches to control which can create our second case of the embedded firms in a 'chain' operating system. Of course these two examples – that of the independent firm and that of the embedded firm – are two ideal types which mark a continuum. It is probable that firms will operate in a close approximation to these. It is likely however that some firms will operate in a more hybrid mode, with some operations largely within their control and some embedded in networks or chains.

The imperatives which create such very complex chains of systems making up an operating system include the need to cope with behaviour of competitive actors in product markets. The need to cope with market uncertainty and volatility requires the establishment of operating systems which can be flexible in response to external environmental changes (particularly product market changes). However it is important that this whole operating system exhibits some characteristics of stability and predictability; that is, that the manner in which the linked organisations can work to actually produce goods and services for the market-place has a reasonable degree of likelihood of operating within the parameters that managers and actors in the system have established. Here we rediscover one of the eternal tensions in the design of control procedures, that which lies between the wish for stability and the wish to cope with change.

In the literature we notice the prevalence of this theme. For example, the system dynamics work of Forester (1961) demonstrated that if systems in a chain operate independently then dynamic instabilities may arise. This point is nicely illustrated by the brewery example in Senge (1993) where the interplay of retailers, responding on their own time scales to perceived growth in demand and perceived supply shortages by overordering in the expectation of rationing, led to huge overproduction. One solution to this kind of predicament when operating systems are open to discrete decisions is to include significant amounts of redundancy to prevent instabilities. This solution, which is to have excess operating capacity and to hold stocks of goods and services at intermediate stages in the chain, may be of lower cost than that delivered by large instabilities but is more expensive than the embedded firms operating the whole system or network in concert to minimise capacity throughout the whole system and stockholding at all stages, or perhaps persuading the consumers to hold stocks instead.

The broad question arises as to what modes of control might be applied to the three stages identified earlier, that is the membership, establishment and operation of these networks or chains. Here we suggest three 'ideal' types as a basis for discussion. These are control through (a) dominance, (b) collaboration and (c) competition.

By dominance we mean that the most powerful player in some part of the operating system is enabled to ensure compliance to his or her requirements by the relative weakness of the others. It is characteristic of many advanced manufacturing systems with many embedded firms that such complex operations are dominated by one of the actors. This domination exists in different forms, depending upon what power may be exercised by the various actors. For example, the 1980s saw system domination being exercised by retailers, as in the case of much clothing and foodstuffs in the UK. The domination was created by capture of retail channels through the creation of supermarkets, with lower costs of operation (reducing employment in retailing), provision of a wide range of goods in one place (customer convenience) and cost efficiency in purchasing and distribution. But domination elsewhere is in the hands of manufacturers, as in the case of motor cars, where manufacturers have considerable control over the retail operations through direct ownership but more commonly through tight franchising arrangements. In this industry such dominance has led to embedded suppliers being required to 'open' their internal accounts to the dominant actor. Further power may be the property of components suppliers, as perhaps in the case of certain computers where microchip technology and supply constrain downstream activities.

By collaboration we mean the joint control of transorganisational networks. An example here would be the development of aircraft, flight systems and engine technologies, where close collaboration between aircraft, component, engine manufacturers and air forces and airline companies is essential in order not only to design but also to operate embedded systems.

By competition, we mean that, by the day-to-day, week-to-week interplay of markets and competition, suppliers are able to supply and buyers to buy. In order to explore these types we need to consider the nature of the interdependence between the firms in the embedded chain. Before taking up that point it is necessary to consider the fact of differing time scales. It seems reasonable to argue that the time scales for the operation of an embedded system would depend upon the critical path of the system and would also be relatively short, of the order of months. In contrast it is argued that the time scales for negotiation of membership and establishment of such systems are relatively long and of the order of years, because of issues of materials, design and production technologies. By extension it is argued that the time scales for modification of such systems would be of intermediate duration. Following Miller (1976) we adopt a taxonomy of interdependence as follows: serial, that is activity A precedes activity B and so on; mutual, where activities A and B take place jointly and perhaps lead to activity C; reciprocal, where activity A and B are interactively related. In relation to an established embedded operating system we expect to find the interdependence of the embedded firms to be serial or mutual while, in relation to the process of negotiating and establishing such an operation, we expect the interdependence to be mutual or reciprocal.

Therefore, applying these ideas to an established embedded operating system, we expect the time scales to be short and the dependence to be serial or mutual and the form of control to lie in either dominance or collaboration. The competition mode of control is the least likely, for it supposes not only that the rationale for setting up the embedded chain was incorrect but that short-term switching of suppliers in such complex systems is feasible. Indeed it is possible to claim that for such a competitive mode to exist the operating systems must be simple and made up of available parts from alternative suppliers.

Extending these considerations to the processes of negotiating membership of complex chains we expect the time scales to be long and the interdependence mutual, and hence we expect the first mode of control to be competition; that is, organisations would bid and negotiate to take a role in a systemic chain. Then, after the partners have come together, the likely mode of control in the process of establishing such chains would shift to collaboration. Even so the most powerful actor in the chain could exercise a decisive influence in managing the market competition, perhaps by setting the criteria (such as quality or resources) by which others might be permitted to enter the competition. Where the time scales are long and interdependence in the design or creation of the chain is reciprocal, we would expect to find a collaborative mode of control. Here we expect to see joint working groups to ensure that the best compromises are reached. It is unlikely that such joint groups of embedded firms would then set up a competitive mode of control for part of this work. Of course in this argument we posit tendencies of control modes following a certain type. It is possible that, in any such chain of systems, all three modes of control will actually be observed to a greater or lesser extent in both the establishment and operation of the chains. The argument so far is to try to understand how the logic of the tasks of the embedded systems leads to mode of control. We need to also ask how the social and cultural processes in these embedded systems affect the control procedures, a question which will be taken up in the fourth section of this chapter.

A counterpoint to what some might see as the despotism of the powerful actor in the chain, effectively using power to gain the compliant behaviour of other embedded firms by essentially tying them in to a specified plan for the operation, is to work from the idea that three operations may be being managed at the same time. These of course are those referred to earlier in this chapter: negotiating a role, establishing an operating system and running it. The logic of the needs of the 'establishing' system are for cooperation and exchange such that the system established is the best overall compromise; the 'partners' in the chain need each other's energy and creativity and a willingness to understand the consequences of their actions for each other. In contrast the running of the operating system requires the embedded firms to stay with the plan. The paradox here of partnership in one mode and power in another leads to the idea of loosely coupled systems, which enables alternative logics to work in the network while the overall system has the requisite degree of stability and potential flexibility and renewal. Much writing on manufacturing operations is based on such a systemic logic; that is, the procedures for materials requirement programming and 'just-in-time' delivery arrangements have been established as modes of ensuring the operating integrity and efficiency of the system chains created. It is now clear that as several modes of control can be observed in any one embedded network. This explains why some authors write about control as being 'tight–loose', as they note the paradox of apparently conflicting control modes used around an operating system.

Financial control

Normally financial control is fitted into this world as a way of constructing statements of the resource inputs and tracing the way in which those resource inputs are transformed into outputs; much of the earlier discussion in Chapter 6 has addressed these questions. Within the system as established, the cost management models of either full-absorption costing or activity-based costing might be used. However it is clear that the idea of activity-based accounting aims to achieve a closer approximation (because they are descriptive models) to modelling the operations themselves. One might note the similarity of the idea of activity-based accounting to the ideas of programming, planning and budgeting, popular in accounting and management literature of the early 1970s.

The financial management and control of such embedded chains replicate the problems found in divisionalised organisations which have adopted investment centre control and varieties of transfer pricing policies for aiding the management of the interdependent operations across the divisions. All of the familiar problems of optimisation and suboptimisation reappear, with the added complexity of legal independence and perhaps a struggle to ensure that the economic returns to the participating firms are appropriate, however that may be determined. In the nature of collaboration of embedded firms one would expect to find specificity of assets for particular purpose, product or service specificity and probably knowledge and skill specificity in relation to the particular operating system. (This is not to argue that each firm is only involved in one such operating system, though such multiplicity does add complexity.)

If the appropriate control mode is that of dominance we expect the dominant actor to require openness of costing and the adoption of costing systems that ensure that the dominant actor can assess the cost structure, through relevant future time periods, of the whole operating system. To manage such a system the dominant actor must have some knowledge of the relationship of fixed and marginal costs as a function of time and activity volume of the whole system as well as an estimate of the way cost reduction programmes (all other matters being equal) can be designed and implemented by all of the partners. In this way strategic direction can be given, provided there is adequate understanding of market conditions over the requisite time scales. Of course the detailed arrangements would need to reflect the likely volatility in markets, so one would expect, as indeed there exists in the automotive supply system, a series of contract arrangements which permit variations in call off of volume and category of elements over appropriate time scales. In short it is possible to have flexible arrangements in the embedded chain even though these are established through asymmetric power relations.

Even if the appropriate control mode is collaboration we expect to find exactly the same management problems and the same need for cost data to be shared among the partners (which could include parallel providers of similar elements, that is multiple sourcing) to enable them to manage the operating system in the light of expected market conditions. Of course the likelihood of stable symmetric power relations is low, but there is no particular reason to doubt that a shared process can be applied, though skill in negotiation may create ripples.

The particular accounting arrangements for an embedded network are a matter of great concern. There is evidence from recent research that the accounting arrangements in large divisionalised organisations are designed to support financial reporting rather than management accounting and control. While matrix organisation structures have been developed within organisation, Jones and his colleagues (1993) reported:

> information overload, domination by the need for consolidation, the irrelevance of group information for operating subsidiaries, e.g. needs of financial accounts dominate the managerial accounting needs and control information dominates decision and action information.

Such research suggests that, if the problems of intra organisational networks are not readily addressed, those of interorganisational networks would be even more difficult. This point leads to the suggestion that a derivative of activity-based costing could be the basis for establishing the financial control structure for an embedded operating system, for it would follow clearly the character of the system itself. Whether the partners would be able to reconcile ABC for the system with their other accounting procedures would raise difficult technical questions. Note, however, that ABC is suitable for planning and reporting, but less appropriate for the decision issues, noted earlier, in the management of the system.

From this brief discussion of cost management we note that there are many other issues in the provision of elements of such operating systems. These would include quality, delivery agreements and compliance. Equally it is clear enough that the 'operation' to establish an operating system would need a different cost management procedure (more like a project management process focusing on effectiveness) from that of the operating system itself (more of a focus upon efficiency).

Embedded operations and clan control

The control modes of dominance, collaboration and competition can be related to Ouchi's constructs of hierarchies and rules and market-based control, which have been used in other chapters of this book as an heuristic framework. So far in this chapter collaboration has been addressed in a technical manner. Little has been said about the issue of clan based control. To illustrate the significance of these factors we consider the findings of a research project in the American automotive component supply industry, where alliances were made between US and Japanese companies. The researchers reported that the Americans concluded that they had learned nothing from the collaboration, while the Japanese had different views. However the Japanese were puzzled at the attitudes and behaviour of the US participants. It seems that the clan-based control with which the Japanese were familiar, based upon open discussion and sharing of problems, knowledge and data, was simply unavailable to the US participants, who expected a rules- or market-based (competition) control. Hence we observe the significance of the dynamics of competition and collaboration, for it would appear that the embedded firms of the Anglo-Saxon world expect power and dominance , rules and markets while the Asian organisations naturally seek to create a significant degree of clan based control where collaboration would exist both in the tasks and in the social and cultural systems.

Before jumping to familiar conclusions about differences in cultures, we may note that potential actors in the embedded firms must have the ability to contribute to the required reciprocal or mutual dependence. If potential firms cannot do so, then they are treated as accidental contractors and subject to market-based control. This idea explains why observers of Japanese manufacturing systems find complex embedded chains existing with some sweat shop contractors on their edges.

In these complex manufacturing chains, for example aircraft, cat food and cars, it may be necessary to create transorganisational workgroups so that the effective modes of collaboration can take place. So the paradox of the complex capitalist system manufacturing chains emerges. Capitalism is supposed to be about competition and we have shown how competition enters into the processes of negotiating for membership of embedded chains. However the establishment and operation of the embedded chains requires high degrees of collaboration through the working together of people to create the context for other participants in the organisations. This implies that there is an imperative to work at issues of mutualities and interdependencies both through contracts and through the notion of trust.

What comes into focus then is the need for apparently independent firms to work together in the operating system, or what some have called the 'virtual organisation' or, less helpfully, the 'boundaryless organisation'. Particular problems arise when we consider the issue of control across boundaries, whether they are internal or external to an organisation. We can begin to examine some of the difficulties with the example of a travelling salesman employed in an independent firm. The salesman spends most of his time at the physical and geographic boundaries of the operating systems of the enterprise. Such a person is in effect continually negotiating organisational boundaries.

The problem that arises is that the task boundaries of the operating systems may become changed by the salesman's negotiation of special terms and delivery schedules disturbing the previous programmes and requiring consequent ad hoc adjustments through the personal networks of the organisation.

Perhaps more importantly this simple example cause us to acknowledge the significance of the social and cultural boundaries of the operating systems. Note how these are modified or even blurred by the fact that such salespersons often find a greater sense of identity with the clients than they do with major parts of their employing organisation. As a consequence organisations have to introduce procedures to ensure that the salesperson's identity as an employee of the firm is continually reinforced. This problem is also encountered in governmental services, especially in the foreign services, where ambassadors might come to be more sympathetic to their accredited governments than to their own state. These problems arise with equal sharpness for the people who work in such embedded firms, for they now have to handle the conflicts arising from alternative modes, collaboration and competition, at the boundary of their firms. Of course this problem is as old as human experience but that marks it as difficult rather than trivial. A full discussion of the manner in which we might understand how to handle these issues is to be found in the extensive literature on boundary spanning roles.

In addition to the personal issues of boundary spanning it is important to note that the culture of partners in the chains may clash in subtle as well as more blatant ways. To assume that, because the technical characteristics of operating systems can be created and run satisfactorily, such systems will deliver expected benefits is to ignore the clan-based problems. Note how matrix forms of organisation were invented for divisionalised independent organisations as a means of creating coherence in the operating systems and dampening conflict among the divisions, yet it is clear that multinational firms still find that cultural issues pose major problems of organisational functioning, as the extensive literature on international management demonstrates. The cultural problems found in the example of the Japanese–American alliances reported earlier have been repeated many times as is shown by the extensive literature on joint ventures and strategic alliances. Indeed it is arguable that the Anglo-Saxons and the Asians are equally able, from an assumption of long-term self-interests, to see that an embedded system is appropriate, but it is more likely that the Asians, with their greater disposition to co-operation, will actually work the micro adjustment processes to realise the long-term benefits.

Systems do not always work

We have examined the control problems that arise in what we have called an embedded operating system. We have shown how the nature of the interdependence, together with consideration of time spans, affects the choice of control mode. For operations which are dedicated to the negotiation and establishing of embedded operating systems we suggest that the control modes would be competition and collaboration. For the operation so created we suggest that the likely control modes are collaboration and dominance.

In the case of the embedded operating system it appears that the control of the system must lie within it, for, although there may be asymmetric power relations or a dominant partner, there is no superordinate authority. This interesting and difficult state leads to a number of questions. Firstly, how do we create a control system that actually has the capacity to serve the partner's needs to learn about the inside of the system in relation to the outside? Neither the traditional ideas of financial control nor activity-based costing approaches can solve this problem. Neither have we done more than show how the broader approach to control in this chapter and in this book may provide a means of thinking about the parameters of the issues of control of embedded networks. A second question arises as to how control procedures can be designed to prevent the embedded operating systems becoming sclerotic when the actors cannot find the energy to recreate such complexity. Can the partners find ways of working away from the defensive routines that exist within organisations (for example, secretiveness, personal fiefdoms, the lust for power, conflict of ambitions or narcissistic leadership) and across organisations (fear and anxieties, failure of generosity, blaming the partner, using one system operation as a bargaining counter for another, failure in understanding the otherness of the partners, and so on)? The significance of the unaddressed and unmodified defensive routines is that they lead to an immobilisation of needed change and then to an inevitable shattering of trust, which in turn will shatter the embedded system operations.

Summary

In this chapter we have shown how the control problems of complex embedded systems follow from the tasks interdependence and time frames involved. We have shown that different control modes come into play at different stages in the negotiation, establishment and operation of such embedded chains. In drawing attention to the implications for the financial control of such chains we noted that we had recognised the limitations of current practice and suggested a broader framework for taking matters further. Finally, having developed the discussion from a technical standpoint, we argued that the major control problems for embedded chains would lie in what Ouchi termed 'clan control', that is in the social and cultural processes within and between the partners in such chains.

CHAPTER 10

Economics and control

Willie Seal

Introduction

In Chapter 3, the 'market' approach to organisation was discussed in the context of its pervasive influence on policy making in areas which were hitherto regarded as sancrosanct parts of the 'public sector' and thus organised via a combination of political, bureaucratic and professional controls. Indeed the policy influence of the 'subcontracting model' has become so dominant that it is sometimes hard to see how the drive towards marketisation and contracting out can be resisted! The aim of this chapter is to set out the economics approach to control from a critical perspective. It is suggested that the superiority of the market over hierarchy as the mode of allocation is not as clear-cut as some policy makers seem to think. Furthermore it is quite possible that forms of internal organisation with subtle forms of control are being replaced by transactionally inferior governance structures.

Control in economics

'Control' in mainstream economics is most usually seen as something which is exercised from 'outside' the economic system, generally by the government. Thus there are discussions on the impact of, for example, price and wage controls on inflation and unemployment, and on the effect of attempts to control public expenditure. Significantly 'control' is rarely seen as being an endogenous feature of economic systems. There are a number of plausible explanations for this neglect. From a technical point of view, mainstream analysis has focused on exchanges between individuals acting through equilibriating markets. Thus, under strict assumptions, general equilibrium theory has shown that this can lead to an optimal allocation of resources (Bator, 1957) with the consequence that other controls are unnecessary.

Other explanations of this neglect of control recognise historical and ideological factors. Historically, the beginnings of the subject (at least in the English-speaking world) are associated with Adam Smith's famous doctrine of the 'invisible hand'. Thus the problematic of classical through to neoclassical economics was the analysis of the way goods and factors of production which were allocated through markets were guided by the 'invisible hand' of the price system. The 'visible hand' which allocated resources within organisations such as firms was largely ignored. In as much as there was an 'economics of the firm', it focused on the way the profit-maximising firm's price and output were affected by the interplay between external market factors (such as the competitive structure of the industry) and a technologically derived production function (which determined costs).

The internal allocation of the firm's resources (the main focus of the management control and accounting literatures) was reduced to a number of simple decision rules such as equating marginal revenue and marginal cost or choosing projects with a positive net present value. Somewhat paradoxically these optimising rules have greatly influenced both management accounting and, as was argued in Chapter 2, management control literatures. This paradox of neglect and influence can be resolved by drawing on the distinction made in Chapter 1 between *systematic* and *systemic* approaches. Economics offers through its normative, microeconomic paradigm, a number of enticing decision rules which aid the development of *systematic* control. However, in its *systemic* version, it emphasises the superiority of decentralisation allocation via markets rather than internal organisation. Thus (with the obvious exception of the markets and hierarchies paradigm) the word 'control' is bracketed with other essentially 'non-economic' words such as 'organisation', 'hierarchy', 'authority' and 'process' dealt with by other disciplines.

The preoccupation with atomistic, self-equilibriating systems has been criticised at both macro and micro levels. At the macro level, the basis of Keynes's critique of the 'classical model' was that long-term disequilibrium could lead to 'involuntary unemployment'. Interestingly, in view of the earlier discussion of systems and cybernetics in the control literature, more modern reinterpretations emphasise 'disequilibrium' – the breakdown of a price system when decisions are based on non-equilibrium prices – in other words, the essence of the Keynesian critique was not that unemployment could exist in equilibrium but rather that the price system could send the wrong signals (Leijonhufvud, 1968). Even this somewhat limited perspective on control has been on the retreat at both theoretical and policy-making levels. The theoretical riposte to Keynes from economists has rested on 'rational expectations' and the 'new classical' model. At the policy level, these ideas have spawned various forms of monetarism.

Many modern Keynesians would have little difficulty in perceiving the economy as a 'cybernetic system' with all the associated feedback processes. However, as we shall see below, this perception of 'economics as a process' has fewer adherents at the micro level. Perhaps surprising in the light of their laissez-faire predilections, much of the recent criticism of the orthodox microeconomics, especially the so-called 'theory of the firm,' has come from the so-called 'new institutionalist' or 'contractual' economists. Contractualists reject what they would term the 'engineering' model of the firm which seems to emerge from the industrial economics literature. In their view, the production function is not technologically determined. Indeed contractual perspectives see it as being imperfectly specified as the result of informational asymmetries, bounded rationality, opportunism and other lacunae of the contractual world introduced in Chapter 3.

There are two main versions of contractual theory – agency theory and transaction cost economics.[1] From a systemic perspective, the agency vision is of an economy as a network of interlocking contracts (Jensen and Meckling, 1976). As we have seen in Chapter 3, the transaction cost paradigm sees the economy as a mixture of 'markets and hierarchies'. We may compare the two approaches with simple examples. To illustrate the markets and hierarchies (or transaction cost economics) approach consider a common managerial problem, the 'make-or-buy' decision on a component. In management accounting terms, the choice may be based on a simple comparison between the unit cost of manufacturing the component 'in-house' compared with the unit cost of buying the component from a subcontractor. The transaction cost economics (TCE) approach would put this decision in a wider and more comprehensive framework. For example, does the production of the component require investment in specialised machinery or specialised training for workers? If it does, then we have a situation of *asset specificity*. This raises the possibility that an external contract may be difficult to draw up and enforce because small numbers bargaining may be hindered by opportunistic behaviour by one or both parties. For this reason, it may be 'cheaper' to produce the component 'in-house' because of *contractual* rather than *engineering* problems. In other words, it is less costly to use a *hierarchy* than a market.

The agency problem can be illustrated by the situation facing the owner of a holiday bungalow who lives a long way away. The owner only uses the bungalow herself for a few weeks a year. For the rest of the time she rents it out to other tenants or holiday makers. The obvious solution is for her (the *principal*) to appoint a local *agent* to handle these sublets. The question is now, how can the agent be motivated and monitored? Probably the owner will decide to allow the agent a percentage of the rents. She will also expect the agent to send her regular accounts recording income and expenditure. She is unlikely to request that these accounts be independently audited but it is easy to see how agency theorists have used this line of reasoning to explain the spontaneous development of financial accounting and auditing in more complex agency relationships![2]

These two examples are admittedly in the 'Robinson Crusoe' tradition of economic reasoning. What they do not capture are some of the underlying behavioural assumptions and the sometimes contentious policy implications which have been drawn from these two approaches. We therefore need to take a more detailed and critical look at these issues.

Some problems with the 'economics' approach to control

One theoretical interpretation of the push for marketisation is that the agency, rather than the transactions cost, approach has triumphed! To agency theorists, the aim is to find the 'best' contractual arrangement – internal organisation is not an option because, in theory, it does not exist. The firm is a 'nexus of contracts' and 'a legal myth' (Jensen and Meckling, 1976). In the context of the issues discussed in Chapter 3, a control structure designed by an agency theory-influenced consultant would be different from a system designed by a transaction cost economics-influenced consultant, particularly one familiar with the works of Ouchi and others.

The equivalent issue in the private sector is the long running debate begun by Coase (1937) on the reason for the existence and boundary of the firm. Once again, as the discussion in Chapter 3 illustrates, this debate has influenced much of the recent management literature, whether it is 'sticking to the knitting' (Peters and Waterman, 1982) or divestment and management buyouts (Thompson and Wright, 1988). Indeed, rather than putting the policy issue in terms of 'private sector versus public sector' – the common currency of the popular debate – the question may be couched in the more general one of 'market versus non- market forms' of organisation. This problem has to be answered in the private sector as well as the public sector but, as we shall see below, the forces influencing the 'choice' of contractual arrangements are quite different from those operating in the political sphere.

The limits to contracting

Williamson has always argued that a prescriptive application of transaction cost economics involves a *comparative institutional* methodology (see, for example, Williamson, 1985). Secondly, in their explanatory version of institutional change and development, both the transactions cost and agency paradigms draw on versions of *natural selection* theory. Thirdly, in contrast to agency theorists, Williamson has acknowledged and defended the role of the *authority relationship* in effecting transactional efficiency. We now turn to a critical examination of each of these issues, after which we will see how contractual theory may be applied to organisational choice problems.

Alternative types of organisation with different transaction cost characteristics

Transaction cost economics suggest a number of alternative governance structures, with spot market exchange at one end of the spectrum and hierarchy at the other. Between these extremes lie other forms such as franchising, long-term contracts, 'inside contracting' and quasi-vertical integration. We have already seen that there are other organisational forms such as the 'clan'. We may add various forms of participatory models. These may range from the pure labour-managed firm to the informal forms of participation associated with the Japanese firm (the J-firm – see especially Aoki, 1984, 1986, 1990a, 1990b).

Labour-managed firms are usually dismissed by both transaction cost and agency theorists on theoretical and empirical grounds (Jensen and Meckling, 1979). In view of the immense success of Japanese industry and the numerous attempts to copy features of Japanese organisation, the J-firm cannot be so easily ignored. A variety of governance structures is also characteristic of most 'public sector' institutions. If we consider the forms of organisation in the public sector, it would be a gross error to characterise them as being simple hierarchies. Indeed the danger of contracting out is that the subtle forms of social and professional control are replaced by contractors who actually *do* use primitive hierarchical forms of organisation.

The comparative advantage of different forms of non-market governance structures depends on contingency factors such as the task or the level of uncertainty in the environment. For example, in terms of technological development, the clan plays a crucial role since it is in activities such as research and development that performance ambiguity is likely to be high and formal output controls are not only ineffective but actually dysfunctional. Furthermore if, as is often argued, technological progress is as much reliant on the ideas of ordinary workers as it is the responsibility of the designated researcher then the innovatory advantages of social arrangements are further augmented.

Other models of the firm offer a superior adaptive response to environmental uncertainty compared with the simple hierarchy. For example, Aoki's models of the firm emphasise that good *horizontal* communication between functional areas is more important than the vertical communication up and down the conventional hierarchy in dealing with *emergent* problems (Aoki, 1986). His approach emphasises *participatory* or *bargaining* models of the firm which seem to make fewer normative demands than the clan. This organisational form is more explicable in terms of the self-interest rather than self-abnegation of the worker (Aoki, 1984, 1990a, 1990b). Indeed, in contrast with the classical capitalist firm, co-operation is based on a more equal constitutional footing between shareholders and employees, with the management acting as a sort of mediator. The firm is seen as a 'nexus of treaties' rather than a 'nexus of contracts' (Aoki, 1990a).

Non-economists often criticise economists for basing all their theories on a narrow version of self-interest. A less common criticism is that they tend to argue that people are the same, whatever the organisational environment. Thus, if behaviour does vary between different institutional settings (such as between the public and private sectors), it is because the *cost and reward structure* differs, not because people are 'different' and/or 'better or worse'. Although there are good methodological reasons for this assumption (without it, any behaviour could be explained by the 'people are different' argument), it ignores the potential benefits generated by governance structures because they actually seek to 'make people different/better'. For example, a 'clan' would be relatively uninteresting if it was simply a by-product of a specifically Japanese culture and not, as Ouchi argues, a type of firm or organisation that can be created through socialisation (Ouchi, 1980, 1981).

Can we be sure that the best contractual modes are selected?

A second criticism of the new 'institutionalist economics', although it is generally more applicable to agency that to transaction cost theory (Putterman, 1986) is the assumption that 'efficient' organisational forms will be selected through a form of natural selection. The use of biological analogies in social science has attracted a number of general and specific criticisms.

Methodologically there is a danger that survival becomes its own justification – that the 'survival of the fittest' is a tautology (see Langlois, 1986). In response to this criticism, Jensen (1983) argues tautologies may be useful heuristic devices in the development of refutable theories. A second charge against natural selection theories is that they are 'Panglossian' in that they tend to support the status quo as the 'best of all possible worlds' (Tinker, 1988). This charge may be rebutted on both theoretical and empirical grounds. In the specific context of management control, a firm may face an environment where conflicting pressures induce contradictory practices (Seal, 1993). For example, firms such as Hanson or GEC that have been successful predators in the market for control do not develop management styles which enhance success in the product market (Goold and Campbell, 1987a, b). Organisational, as with biological, adaptation is a compromise meaning that survival traits in one part of the environment may weaken the firm's ability to compete in another area. Thus survival does *not* imply optimal design. As well as conflicting pressures, institutional development is a product of *path dependencies*. Thus organisational forms which might be optimal in one historical period may have been wiped out in a previous period when conditions were different (Nelson and Winter, 1982).

In his critique of competitive selection, Dow (1987) raises the issues of power and appropriability. We will be looking at power in the next section. The issue of appropriability is that 'selection can ... be expected to operate on firms as a function of their profitability in a given market environment' (Dow, 1987, pp. 31–2). Dow makes the point that the survival of a firm in a capitalist economy depends upon the ability of the entrepreneur to capture the benefits of a particular governance structure in the form of profits. Thus, while a non-capitalist governance structure such as a labour-managed firm *may* generate larger transaction cost savings than the classical capitalist firm, these benefits will be diffused throughout the workforce. The advantage (from a survival point of view) of the capitalist firm is that the '[smaller] benefits of control by capital can be concentrated quite easily in the hands of a single agent, by bringing all physical capital under the umbrella of common ownership' (Dow, 1987, p. 32).

Although it is possible to rebut general criticisms of selection theory, it is easy to understand why it has such a tainted reputation in the social sciences. Indeed the problem with so much of the 'new institutionalist' literature is that, although writers such as Williamson, Jensen, Meckling and Fama may be able to defend their use of selection theory against *general* criticisms, it is relatively easy to find *specific* examples of tautological and Panglossian reasoning in their work. More damagingly at the policy level, crass invocation of selection theory by politicians and consultants may be used to provide support for the fashion for the application of 'business methods' in the public sector, arguing that, if they have withstood competitive pressures in the private sector, they must possess some universally optimal properties.

Authority, power and efficiency: the labour process debate

The transaction cost paradigm unambiguously espouses the efficiency-enhancing properties of the authority relationship and is quite prepared to engage in debate with the labour process school. It recognises that the need for management control is a direct consequence of the assumptions of costly information and bounded rationality. In contrast the neoclassical tradition is coy about the role of authority and power. For example, Alchian and Demsetz (1972) even suggest in a renowned passage that the employer has no more power over the employee than the grocer has over a customer. Perhaps more surprisingly, neoclassical theory also lacks an explicit theory of ownership. Ownership, at least in popular interpretations of capitalism, is usually in-extricably linked to both power and authority.

Putterman (1988) argues that a theory of ownership emerges once the sim-plicities of the neoclassical world are left behind. The neoclassical firm is a 'production function to which a maximand profit has been assigned' and argues that the 'owner' of such a firm possesses the right to select the production programme and appropriate the residual (p. 247). There is no need for this person to actually own a resource such as capital. In the new institutional economics, the owner of the firm 'must do more than simply determine a production programme and collect the profits; he must also *manage*'. Putterman criticises much of the economics literture because it tends to 'obscure a central aspect of the nature of production organisation in the capitalist economy; precisely, the ownability of the entity that undertakes the task of organisation, and the exclusion of factors hired by that entity from control and residual rights' (Putterman, 1988, p. 256).

The role of authority is an area of transaction cost economics that has attracted much critical attention from radical economists. Some have argued that hierarchies are more to do with power than with economic efficiency (Marglin, 1974). The well-known 'putting-out' debate revolves around whether factory production replaced cottage industry for efficiency or power reasons. Rather than being a transaction cost solution to problems of cheating, embezzlement and high stocks, Marglin argues that 'the success of the factory, as well as its inspiration, was the substitution of capitalists' for workers' control of the production process' (1974, p. 46).

Dow, another critic of the transaction cost paradigm, focuses on the function of authority in transaction cost economics, although its function is supposedly to 'restrain the opportunism which would otherwise infect market exchange' (Dow, 1987, p. 19). What is there to control the opportunism of the higher levels of authority? Rather than restricting themselves to controlling opportunism among subordinates, Dow observes that 'agents holding positions of authority might use data obtained through internal audits to gain strategic advantages over lower level parties, use fiat to settle disputes in ways to suit themselves, or impose self-serving incentive systems' (1987, p. 20).

Some policy implications

In the light of recent megafrauds in the UK and the increasing divergence between corporate performance and director remuneration, Dow's observations on managerial opportunism seem particularly pertinent. In other areas, the bias of the transaction cost paradigm is less clear-cut. In view of the reputation that transaction cost economics has in the minds of radicals, it is somewhat ironic that it may actually be used to defend hierarchies against the contracting out model. The contemporary relevance of this debate is that, paradoxically, most of the modern debate about the boundary of the firm (or the scope of the 'public sector') is concerned with institutional changes in the opposite direction – away from hierarchy towards 'contracting out'!

There are differences, of course. The contracts are not generally going to independent artisans, as in the pre-industrial era, but to firms with their own characteristics of internal organisation. Thus the relevant comparison is not simply between market and hierarchy but between different types of internal organisation which are now linked by market rather than hierarchical links. Whilst transaction cost economics may not actually support hierarchical governance structures, the ambiguity of its prescriptions may actually produce more caution in policy makers' minds. Dow suggests two major difficulties. Firstly, we cannot always separate the transaction from the existing governance structure; secondly, bounded rationality and opportunism means we cannot identify an efficient governance structure *ex ante*.

The first problem is a serious obstacle to making transaction cost logic fully operational. In order to choose an appropriate governance structure, we need to be able to identify independently a transaction. This might be relatively easy in the production of widgets but it is far more difficult in the service tasks which are typical of the public sector. For example, if one of the dimensions for identifying a transaction is asset specificity, then the level of human asset specificity seems to be an endogenous function of the governance structure rather than an exogenous factor helping to determine it. For example, the UK prison service has developed high levels of human asset specificity based upon a 'relational team', yet recent decisions to contract out many of its activities suggest a different judgement about the nature of 'transactions' in the prison service!

This example is also relevant to illustrate the second of Dow's criticisms. Much subcontracting of former public sector services is based on a sort of franchise process. This requires forecasts about *ex post* behaviour and contractual safeguards against problems such as 'opportunistic quality degradation'. However 'perfect' contractual design itself conflicts with the transaction cost assumption of bounded rationality. As Dow (1987) puts it, 'the mere existence of positive transactions costs may suffice to prevent transaction cost minimisation' (p. 28).

Contractual safeguards rely on accurate measurement of both quantities and quality of output, yet one of the difficulties in managing so much of the public sector is the lack of agreed output indicators.As was discussed in Chapter 3, if output cannot be satisfactorily monitored then control must be based on 'behaviour control' rather than 'output controls' à la Ouchi (1977).

In conclusion, contrary to the suspicions of many non-economists, transaction cost economics is either extremely difficult to operationalise or biased towards internal organisation rather than market organisation. Thus, if governments *are* choosing to subcontract to the private sector (ignoring, for the sake of argument, any venal or corrupt motives), it is because they feel that the nature of transactions will not be changed by changes in contractual arrangements. Secondly, they are confident that there will be sufficient *ex ante* competition between contractors. Thirdly, they can design contracts which monitor and punish any *ex post* contract opportunism by the franchisees. In short, they are operating in a world of unbounded rationality and zero transaction costs – a world familiar to the more formal versions of agency theory but alien by assumption to the world of the transaction cost and incomplete contracting paradigms.

Notes

1. See Seal (1993) for an extended critical comparison of the various forms of agency theory and transaction cost economics, with specific reference to issues of accounting and management control.
2. For example, a more complex agency relationship exists between the managers and shareholders of a mature corporation where typically there has been a separation of ownership and control. Jensen and Meckling (1976) and Watts and Zimmerman (1979) have used the potential conflict of interest between shareholders and managers (as well as other parties such as debtholders) to produce a voluntaristic theory of accounting and auditing. For criticisms of this 'Positive Accounting' school, see Christenson (1983) and Lowe *et al.* (1983).

CHAPTER 11

Performance indicators and control in the public sector

Peter Smith

The public sector poses particularly challenging problems of control. Almost by definition, there are no competitive markets for its products, and it is not subjected to the traditional discipline of financial markets. Instead strategic control must be secured through political processes, which can take many forms. With the rapid reduction in the cost of data collection, governments are increasingly relying on various types of performance indicator to inform the political process, and thereby secure control of public sector management. The purpose of this chapter is to examine the implications of the use of performance indicators (PIs) for managerial control of public sector resources.

The first section sets the scene by tracing the recent history of performance indicators in the UK. PIs are expected to fulfil many roles in securing control of public sector organisations, and these are examined next. It is argued that the principal criterion for introducing a PI system is that its benefits should outweigh its costs. The third sections therefore investigates the principal benefits that PI schemes can be expected to generate, while the forth examines their associated costs. Next issues relating to the implementation of PI schemes are discussed and the chapter ends with an appraisal of the strengths and weaknesses of PIs in securing control of the public sector.

Introduction

During the 1980s, fuelled by the ready availability of cheap information technology, the practice of publishing information about the performance of the public sector became widespread. The principal purpose of these developments was to enable various interested parties to secure control of public sector resources. In the UK, no part of the public sector escaped the scrutiny of the performance auditor. This section describes some of the more important developments.

The first scheme receiving high-profile promotion by the UK government was the 'Local Government Comparative Statistics' initiative (Department of the Environment, 1981). This formed part of a code of practice that local governments were urged to follow when publishing their annual reports. Every report was to include the authority's performance on a range of about 50 indicators, set beside data from other 'similar' authorities. The indicators were principally related to costs and manpower. The similar authorities were selected by the local government itself, and a wide variety of practices was adopted (Ashley Smith and Smith, 1987). The Chartered Institute of Public Finance and Accountancy published an annual volume listing the indicators for every authority (CIPFA, 1982). However the initiative appeared to have very little tangible effect on public, elected representatives or local government (Chandler and Cook, 1986).

The National Health Service (NHS) in the UK is a central government programme, but is administered by local health authorities. The central government uses PIs as a central part of its mechanism for controlling the activities of these local administrations. In 1983 a series of reports was published documenting for each Local Health Authority 123 performance indicators relating mainly to costs (Department of Health and Social Security, 1983). These thick volumes had little immediate impact. However they were soon replaced by an enhanced package of over 400 indicators, made available in machine-readable form (Department of Health and Social Security, 1985). The government rapidly developed computer software to give rudimentary analysis of the data. In 1987 it published an expert system to help the performance auditor make sense of the vast volume of data (Department of Heath and Social Security, 1987), and commissioned an introductory guide to the PI system (Department of Health and Social Security, 1988). The performance indicators now form a central part of the system of performance review in the NHS, whereby District Health Authorities are held to account by Regional Health Authorities, which are in turn accountable to the central government. Thus this set of PIs is central to securing control of the NHS.

Many other PI schemes have been put in place. For example, the Committee of Vice Chancellors and Principals (1987) initiated a series of performance indicators for UK universities. The process of public sector performance measurement then reached its apotheosis with the publication in 1991 of the 'Citizen's Charter' (UK Government, 1991). Intrinsic to this initiative was the notion that only by making available information about the activities and achievements of public services could those services be held properly to account. Accordingly a series of charters for individual services was produced, amongst the first being a 'Parent's Charter' for schools (Department of Education and Science, 1991) and a 'Patient's Charter' in the NHS (Department of Health, 1991).

The Parent's Charter contains a number of measures intended to make schools more sensitive to the demands of parents. Amongst them is the intention to publish 'league tables' of public examination results, truancy rates and destinations of pupils leaving school. Coupled with this reporting initiative was the establishment of a right of parents to express a preference for the school their child should attend, offering parents some sanction against poor performance.

The Patient's Charter also includes provisions for the publication of performance data, including waiting times for outpatient appointments, waiting times for inpatient treatment, and waiting times for ambulance services. Associated with these data are a series of patient rights, including guaranteed admission for inpatient treatment within two years of being placed on a waiting list.

Perhaps the most ambitious PI initiative associated with the Citizen's Charter has been the set of performance indicators developed for local government by the Audit Commission (1992). Development of this package was complicated by the fact that UK local government still enjoys some autonomy from central government, and so can within limits specify its own priorities and targets. As a result, a national unified system of performance reporting may be inappropriate. Nevertheless the Audit Commission has devised a system of over 200 PIs which seeks to allow some local autonomy, yet forces local authorities to present comparative performance data.

Thus the performance indicator philosophy has permeated most of the UK public sector. The first developments had little impact, principally because there were few sanctions attached to continued poor reported performance. However, especially since the introduction of the Citizen's Charter, real sanctions, for example in the form of client choice, have forced public sector organisations to pay increased attention to their activities as reported in PIs.

Roles of performance indicators

The publication of performance indicators is intended to serve a number of objectives. Most fundamental is the desire to secure *accountability* of the public sector organisation (the agent) to its principals. Stewart (1984) suggests that accountability can be secured only if two conditions obtain: first, the agent must have to give an account of performance to the principal; and second, the principal must be able to hold the agent to account. The title of this chapter reflects the need both for a report of performance and for the associated ability to act on the report, and thereby to control the public sector organisation.

Agency theory has been developed principally in the context of the corporate sector (Baiman, 1990) in which the identification of principal (owner) and agent (manager) is relatively straightforward. The pattern of accountability in the public sector is far more complex. Consider, for example, the case of a local government housing department. There are various 'stakeholders' in such a department, each of which might consider itself a principal. Examples include the chief executive of the local government; the local elected representatives; the central government; the local taxpayers; the housing department tenants; the broader public, including potential future tenants; and auditors acting on behalf of one or more of these parties. To a greater or lesser extent, each of these parties has a legitimate interest in the performance of the department, and might seek to exercise some control over its operations. Thus the simple model of a single principal is hopelessly inadequate as a reflection of the rich pattern of accountability that obtains in the public sector.

Notice in particular that the users – or *potential* users – of public sector services should be able to hold those services to account. In the corporate sector, when product markets are competitive, customers do not expect to exercise direct control over management because they have the strong sanction of taking their custom elsewhere. In contrast, most public services are local monopolies, and there are few real sanctions available to users. In addition, many potential users of services or other interested parties do not have direct experience of the quality of service delivered. For example, many citizens have legitimate interests in the performance of police or personal social services, even though they cannot be explicitly identified as clients of those services. To secure accountability it therefore becomes desirable to furnish such parties with some mechanism for controlling the performance of the services.

A strong framework of accountability is thought to be necessary for the pursuit of the accountant's notions of efficiency and effectiveness. If the pattern of accountability is faulty, it can be argued, managers may have no incentive to use their resources efficiently. Such considerations are likely to be the principal concern of the funders of the organisation, such as taxpayers and the central government. Similarly, without accountability, there may be no incentive for a public sector organisation to pursue the objectives of its principals, and so effectiveness might suffer. While most stakeholders will have an interest in effectiveness, it is perhaps service users who have the most immediate interest in it.

However, once PI schemes have become operational, it soon becomes clear that they are addressing issues broader than efficiency and effectiveness. For example, in assessing the NHS scheme after it had been in place for a number of years, Baroness Trumpington (1987) suggested that its main role was the promotion of *equity* between individuals and between geographical areas. The extension to equity considerations emphasises why it is important to consider the broader concept of *control* as the principal purpose of PI schemes. In the corporate sector, control might be considered synonymous with the promotion of efficiency and effectiveness. The interest of owners and customers is in persuading the company to produce goods required by product markets and securing rates of return that satisfy financial markets. Any company failing to do so runs the risk of bankruptcy. However in the public sector control might have wider connotations, first because the principals are more diverse, and second because there is much less consensus about what the public sector should be doing.

The emphasis on control raises the issue of who is exercising the control on behalf of whom. The mechanism for securing control is the prevailing pattern of accountability. In practice most accountability structures have developed in an arbitrary manner, and are the outcome of the vagaries of historical accident. There is no ineluctable model of accountability. As a result it is difficult to generalise about how control over a public sector organization is exercised. Thus, for example, UK local government is controlled in part by local electors, who are periodically able to pass judgement on their elected representatives in local elections. In addition, the central government feels it too has a legitimate interest in local government, and has adopted the right to control expenditure and implement a wide range of more detailed controls. On the other hand, the NHS is directly run by the central government, albeit on an agency model, with local Health Authorities having no elected members, and very weak local patient representation, in the form of Community Health Councils. The citizen wishing to effect a change may therefore have to seek influence via a very circuitous route, perhaps needing to put pressure on the secretary of state by lobbying a local member of parliament.

Thus the citizen with a legitimate interest in public services often has very imperfect sanctions with which to affect the management of local services. The principal mechanisms are various forms of political pressure, including voting, and migration to areas with a preferred pattern of public services. These alternatives may be either ineffectual (as in the case of voting) or very costly to the individual. There is therefore a difficulty in persuading the citizen to take an interest in the performance of public sector organisations. This insight has informed many of the recent PI developments in the UK. For example, the Citizen's Charter is intended to make it easier for ordinary people to assess the performance of the public sector, and to give them an incentive to do so.

A parallel, alternative strategy to overcome the problem of lack of public interest is the creation of expert audit offices, which are intended to act on behalf of citizens in scrutinising public sector performance. In England and Wales, this role is undertaken by the National Audit Office (for central government) and the Audit Commission (for local government and the NHS).

As the above examples have shown, PI schemes have traditionally been considered under two headings: those that are designed for external stakeholders and those that serve internal management control purposes. These external and internal purposes can be considered analogous to the external and internal accounting functions in the corporate sector. The two types of PI scheme can be thought of as serving respectively the *political* and *managerial* control of the organisation. An example of the former is the set of PIs which English local governments are advised to publish in their annual reports. The explicit objectives were 'to give [local taxpayers] clear information about local government's activities; to make it easier for electors, [taxpayers] and other interested parties to make comparisons of performance of their authorities; and to help [elected representatives] form judgements about the performance of their own authority' (Department of the Environment, 1981). On the other hand, the set of PIs developed for the NHS address managerial control, were intended 'to help [managers] assess the efficiency of the services for which they are responsible' (Department of Health and Social Security, 1983).

Increasingly, however, there is emerging a third type of control, in which the principal is a purchasing organisation, disbursing public funds, and the agent a quasi-autonomous provider in receipt of those funds (Carter and Greer, 1993). The relationship between purchaser and provider is guided by a formal contract, through the terms of which the principal seeks to control the agent. PIs might form an intrinsic part of the contractual arrangement. This third type of control might be called *agency* control. Here an example from the UK is the Benefits Agency, the organisation which is responsible for assessing and paying social security benefits claims. This is held to account by the central government through the medium of a range of performance indicators and associated targets, such as 'to pay the correct amount [of income support] in 92% of cases' (Benefits Agency, 1993).

At the interface between the external world and the public sector organisation is the board of governors. Anthony and Young (1984, p. 649) consider the most important stimulus to improved management control in non-profit organisations to be 'more active interest in the effective and efficient functioning of the organization by its governing board'. In general, governing boards are held accountable to external stakeholders by various mechanisms, such as elections or patronage. Thus, when PI schemes are aimed at external stakeholders, if they are at all effective, they are likely to influence the decisions of the governing board. And so, in turn, they will influence the *internal* management of the organisation. The external PI scheme will thereby be internalized. Consequently this chapter makes no distinction between the various forms of scheme described above, and seeks instead to examine the influence of all types of PI on the internal control of the public sector organisation.

Two models of management implicitly underlie the traditional public sector PI scheme: a model of production, and a model of control. These two models indicate respectively what the PIs are seeking to represent, and how they are subsequently to be used to effect change. Architects of PI schemes usually appear to have in mind a standard neoclassical production model, in which inputs are consumed by an organisation. Some production process takes place and a set of valued outputs emerge. The outputs eventually have an outcome in terms of their impact on society. Within this framework there are usually four types of PI, seeking to measure different aspects of activities: environment, inputs, processes and outputs. Some authors distinguish between intermediate measures of output and eventual outcome (Jackson and Palmer, 1989). However it is very rare for any PI scheme to be able to address outcome issues, so for practical purposes it is reasonable to ignore the outcome aspect of performance.

The model of control is based on the notion of managerial cybernetics discussed in Chapter 1. PIs serve the various stages of the cybernetic model by enabling principals to set quantitative targets for management. Performance can then be assessed in relation to these targets. Any deviation can be examined, remedial action proposed and revised targets set. Thus the principal objective of the PI scheme is to facilitate estimation of the production function confronting the organisation, so that best practice can be identified and *achievable* targets set. The criterion for judging the PI scheme should therefore be the extent to which its benefits – in terms of more sensitive control – exceed its costs. The following sections set out the principal benefits and costs associated with a PI scheme.

Benefits of performance indicators

The relevant benefits and costs arising from PI initiatives are those impinging on the external stakeholders. As discussed above, the putative benefits might arise in the form of the greater efficiency, effectiveness, equity and probity of the public sector. Costs include the direct costs of collecting and disseminating data, and might also emerge in the shape of unintended dysfunctional consequences of PI schemes. This section seeks to categorize the various benefits. Costs are treated in the next section.

The principal benefits claimed for PI schemes can be considered under six headings:

1. clarifying the objectives of the organisation;
2. developing agreed measures of activity;
3. gaining a greater understanding of the production process;
4. facilitating comparison of performance in different organizations;
5. facilitating the setting of targets for organisations and managers;
6. promoting the accountability of the organisation to its stakeholders.

Although forming an important component of most PI schemes, the measurement of inputs – as expressed in costs – is usually relatively straightforward. Indeed, many early schemes, such as the Local Government Comparative Statistics initiative, concentrated almost exclusively on inputs, in the form of personnel and costs. Increasingly, however, schemes are seeking to address much more interesting questions, namely: what is going on inside the black box known as the production process; how are the valued outputs (not to mention eventual outcomes) to be measured; and what light do the PIs cast on the performance of the organization? The first step in devising a PI scheme is therefore to identify the processes and objectives of the organisation. In itself, this procedure might prove valuable. It requires explicit statements of methods and goals which hitherto may have been muddled and ambiguous. If it proves possible to make such statements, the organisation may be given a clearer sense of purpose, and the efforts of staff at all levels can be focused to common objectives.

However one of the aspects of public sector management which distinguishes it very clearly from management in the corporate sector is that identification of objectives may be difficult or even futile. Different stakeholders often hold different expectations with regard to a public sector organisation. For example, parents, employers, the community at large and the central government might wish to emphasise very different outputs of the secondary education sector. Even within a group of stakeholders (say parents), there might be a great mix of requirements. And the priorities of all groups might change over time. In the end, of course, schools must reconcile the possibly conflicting demands made on them. But to make explicit statements of objectives might show that they are favouring one group of stakeholders at the expense of another, and preclude the flexibility needed to adapt to changing demands. It is therefore important to emphasise that identifying objectives is not a trivial process, and may in some circumstances even be dysfunctional.

Having identified processes and objectives, the next requirement is to devise measures of the phenomena of interest. Only by identifying unambiguous and consistent measures is it possible to compare the activities and achievements of the organisation, either with its own performance in previous periods or with that of other organisations in the same period. These two types of comparison – dynamic and cross-sectional – are the only realistic methods of gaining some idea of the production possibilities of the organisation, as there rarely exist ideal, engineering benchmarks of performance. It is therefore imperative that the definitions of any measures used are clear and not open to 'creative' misinterpretation by different management teams. They should therefore be readily audited, to minimise misinterpretation or even fraud.

In practice, many aspects of public sector performance are very difficult to measure, and the measurement process is often dependent on data provided directly by 'front line' workers, the very people whose performance is to be assessed. For example, the measurement of medical caseload requires information on the diagnosis of patients, which is provided by doctors. If such data are to be used in judging the efficiency of those same doctors, then they have a very strong incentive to maximize their apparent workload by assigning their patients to diagnosis groups with a high workload 'tariff'. It is almost impossible to control such activity by external audit, as there is considerable scope for discretion in matters of clinical judgement. In any case, any large-scale audit would be infeasible. As a result, much of the public sector relies on the good-will of staff to extract useful performance data, and so obtaining their support in implementing any PI scheme is imperative.

Measurement is only the beginning of the comparison process. The phenomena measured must be incorporated into a model of the production process before any useful comparisons can be made. The modelling stage is often particularly difficult because our understanding of the means whereby public sector inputs are converted into outputs is very imperfect, particularly when environmental circumstances have a significant influence on outcome. Smith (1990) gives five reasons why variations in PIs might be observed between organisations: they might be pursuing different objectives; they might have different environments; they might face different resource costs; they might report their performance differently; and they might have different levels of efficiency. The purpose of modelling is to disentangle these causes of variability.

Modelling is therefore an essential aspect of almost all comparison. In the corporate sector, businesses have the option of closing down operations if the environment is adverse – for example if local pay rates are very high, or local transport infrastructure is poor. Indeed, if the business is operating in a competitive market, such closure may be essential if the business is to remain competitive. The need for modelling the production process sensitively is therefore relatively modest in most competitive product markets.

In contrast, most public sector organisations have to continue operating regardless of how adverse the external environment might be. There is what one might call a 'geographical imperative' regarding the location of services such as schools, hospitals and refuse collection. As a result, the modelling stage is crucial, and the performance analyst must seek to take full account of the external environment when coming to judgements on public sector performance. In the schools sector, for example, there has emerged the notion of the 'value added' by schools when judging their examination results (Gray *et al.*, 1990). That is, performance is judged, not on crude examination results, but on the results secured in relation to the capabilities of the children as measured when they entered the school. The intricacy of the statistical models developed in the education sector is evidence of the complex process involved in coming to informed judgements about performance once it becomes necessary to take account of environment. It is often best to think of uncontrollable environmental determinants of performance as additional inputs into the production process, augmenting the set of more conventional physical inputs.

The next stage in analysis of performance is to come to a judgement on the performance of the organisation of interest. Dynamic or cross-sectional comparison yields benchmarks against which its achievements can be measured. From this analysis, some statement can be made about the *desired* level of performance, and so targets can be set in terms of the dimensions of performance encompassed by the PI scheme. In itself, the publication of comparative data might introduce pseudo-competition between public sector organisations. Implicit in the comparison process there might be rewards and punishments for management boards and their staff which lead the organisations under scrutiny to pursue measures which improve their performance, as reflected in the PIs. However it may be that publication alone is not enough, and that targets must be associated with an explicit incentive scheme for organisations or the managers within them. Thus, as well as facilitating retrospective appraisal of past performance, the PIs can play a central prospective role in servicing the system of targets and rewards – whether implicit or explicit – adopted by the external controllers of the organisation.

For example, in the UK Benefits Agency, a key organisational objective is to clear 67 per cent of child benefit claims within 10 days (Benefits Agency, 1993). The senior management of the organisation can therefore be held to account on clearance rates such as these, and they in turn can hold to account the management of individual offices using the same PIs. However, as noted above, in doing so they may need to take into account the different environments (reflected in the complexity of claims) in which different offices must operate.

In summary, therefore, the PI philosophy entails identifying objectives, measuring progress towards those objectives, assessing performance, setting targets and ensuring that incentives are compatible with progress towards targets. The cybernetic model of management control underlying the PI philosophy is intended to bring numerous benefits relating to management control. The identification of objectives might clarify the organisation's mission, and enable it to nurture a shared sense of purpose amongst staff. Quantifying objectives enables targets to be set at all levels in the organisation, to which incentives can be attached, and forces managers to address trade-offs between conflicting objectives. The performance assessment process can generate an enhanced understanding of the production process underlying the organisation's activities. And it is possible that the entire PI culture might enhance the organisation's accountability to outside stakeholders, enabling them to secure better control.

Costs of performance indicators

Although many of the potential benefits listed above are palpable, and can be observed in many public sector organisations adopting the PI philosophy, no PI scheme is without associated costs. As the Audit Commission noted when developing its PI scheme for UK local government, the direct costs of collecting, analysing, auditing and disseminating data can be considerable (Audit Commission, 1992). And there are a large number of less obvious but possibly more pernicious potential costs, in the form of unexpected behavioural conse-quences of publishing performance data. These are examined in this section.

The possibly dysfunctional consequences arise for two fundamental reasons. First, it is very difficult to implement the principles set out in the pre-vious section. To a greater or lesser extent, most PI schemes fail to reflect all the nuances of organisations' purposes and activities. This might be because some of the processes and outputs are elusive and difficult to identify or because – although identifiable – they are difficult to capture in simple PIs. And second, controllers have only a limited ability to process the data emerg-ing from a PI scheme, and so may be misled into making faulty inferences about performance. These two limitations can be thought of as respectively malfunctions of the PI *sensing* mechanism and malfunctions of the *response* mechanism.

Following Smith (1993), it is possible to examine the unintended conse-quences of PI schemes under eight headings: (1) tunnel vision, (2) sub-optimisation, (3) myopia, (4) measure fixation, (5) misrepresentation, (6) misinterpretation, (7) gaming, (8) ossification. Tunnel vision, suboptimisation and myopia reflect different aspects of incompleteness in the PI scheme. If managers are given incentives to pursue targets reflected in PIs, then they are implicitly being given incentives to ignore aspects of performance not encom-passed by the scheme. Thus if, as is usually the case, some valued aspects of performance are not captured by PIs, there is a risk that they will be ignored by management. The scheme induces tunnel vision.

Suboptimisation is the pursuit by managers of narrow local objectives at the expense of the objectives of the organization as a whole. It is a very real danger in the public sector, in which many of the outputs are the result of co-operation between a number of agencies. Such co-operation is endangered if each of the agencies is asked to pursue its own agenda. The enhancement of joint outputs is in general not attractive to a manager given explicit perform-ance incentives, because it entails the co-operation of individuals beyond his or her direct control. Thus, even if joint objectives can be incorporated into a PI scheme, it is likely that managers will give them less priority than objectives more within their direct control.

Myopia is the neglect of long-term objectives. This phenomenon is endemic to any PI scheme. Either the controller waits for all the long-term conse-quences of activity to unfold before coming to a judgement on performance – in which case the judgement may be too late to be useful – or a judgement is made before the long-term consequences have become evident – in which case the evaluation is incomplete. Long-term issues are very important in many public sector programmes, particularly health and education.

Most *measures* of performance are only imperfect reflections of activity or progress towards an objective. Therefore, if managers are held to account with such imperfect measures, dysfunctional consequences may result because it is in their interest to enhance performance as measured, and not necessarily to maximise valued outputs related to the underlying objective (Kerr,1975). This phenomenon – measure fixation – was endemic to the Soviet Union (Kornai, 1992) and results from the impossibility of capturing all the subtleties of performance in a limited number of indices. For example, in the UK National Health Service, managers have been set the target of ensuring that no patient waits more than two years for an operation (Department of Health, 1991). Managers have pursued this target with zeal, yet the outcome may have been longer waiting times for patients awaiting serious surgery, as hospitals have concentrated on reducing the *longer* waiting times of those in need of relatively minor surgery. This outcome may not have been intended by the controller (the UK government).

We have already noted the danger of excessive reliance on PI schemes leading to misrepresentation, which can take the form of 'creative' reporting or fraud. Creative reporting is legitimate, but entails the deliberate use of judgement to show the organisation in the best possible light, and may lead to biased perceptions of activity. Examples include smoothing – the deliberate choice of the time period to which to assign an event (Ronen and Sadan, 1981). Fraud is illegitimate manipulation of data, and is an ever-present danger when auditing is costly and complex, as in the public sector. Misrepresentation of any type is likely to be dysfunctional because it leads to the controller receiving misleading messages about processes and outputs.

The problem of misinterpretation is brought about principally by the need to take account of environment, and the intrinsically complex transformation processes inherent in much of the public sector. In addition, notwithstanding the efforts of bodies such as the UK Audit Commission, there is a great shortage of expert intermediaries able to cast dispassionate light on performance data. Often the only experts available to interpret such data are employees of the very organisation the performance of which is under scrutiny. Such observers clearly have an incentive to put their own efforts in the best possible light, and so their interpretation may lead to biased perceptions about the organisation's performance.

Gaming is the deliberate distortion of behaviour by management to secure strategic advantage (Jaworski and Young, 1992). For example, managers might deliberately underperform year after year to avoid being set more demanding targets. They can blame such underperformance on external factors and the controller is often in no position to gainsay such judgement. The incentive for gaming arises because, although managers might be given a reward for outperforming their targets, the subsequent penalty is that all future targets will be 'ratcheted' up by the controller in the knowledge that enhanced performance is possible. As a result, unless they are given an incentive to *improve* targets as well as simply achieve them, managers may opt to achieve chronically mediocre performance (Weitzman, 1976). The scope for gaming therefore arises because of shortcomings in the incentive scheme and long time horizons amongst managers.

Setting up any PI scheme is a costly and complex process. It is tempting for controllers to assume that, once designed and implemented, the scheme can be left unaltered. However, if it is not to ossify, it must be kept under constant review. New challenges and opportunities constantly arise, and should be incorporated into the PI scheme when relevant. In addition, one of the means of insuring against gaming behaviour is to lead managers to expect that the criteria of success will be periodically changed.

Thus there exists a wide range of potentially serious adverse consequences arising from the implementation of PI schemes. The next section considers ways in which these might be mitigated.

Mitigating dysfunctional consequences

Numerous strategies exist to counter the unintended and possibly dysfunctional consequences of PI schemes. Amongst the most important are the following:

1. involving staff at all levels in the development and implementation of PI schemes;
2. retaining flexibility in the use of PIs, and not relying on them exclusively for control purposes;
3. keeping the PI system under constant review;
4. seeking to quantify every objective, however elusive;
5. measuring client satisfaction;
6. seeking expert interpretation of the PI scheme;
7. maintaining careful audit of the data;
8. nurturing long term career perspectives amongst staff;
9. keeping the number of indicators small;
10. developing performance benchmarks independent of past activity.

Involving staff at all levels (1), retaining flexibility (2) and keeping the PI scheme under constant review (3) are strategies which acknowledge that no PI scheme can offer a perfect representation of the production process, and that control mechanisms are inevitably imprecise. The controller must recognize that, unless applied with some sensitivity, PI schemes are doomed to fail in all but the simplest circumstances. And it is important to recognize that many aspects of performance in the public sector are resistant to quantification. Rather than try to force the organisation into a rigid straitjacket of PI control, it may be more appropriate to adopt a mixed strategy, in which other modes of control are also adopted. For example, as discussed in Chapter 3, Ouchi (1979) notes that production processes in which outcomes are difficult to measure and the transformation process imperfectly understood – characteristics of much of the public sector – may be better suited to the 'clan' control of peer pressure and shared objectives amongst staff. It is noteworthy that the culture of the UK National Health Service has changed dramatically on the introduction of an internal market for health care in 1990, from that of clan control to that of agency control, in which performance data play a much more important role than hitherto. Attention to (1), (2) and (3) might alleviate many of the unintended consequences of PI schemes.

Measuring progress towards every objective (4) and measuring client satisfaction (5) are different strategies for seeking to encompass all salient dimensions of performance into the PI scheme. The measurement of every objective, however roughly done, is increasingly being recognized as a key component in non-financial performance measurement in the corporate sector (Kaplan and Norton, 1992) and is essential if important dimensions of performance are not to be neglected by managers. Yet the prospect of capturing all aspects of public sector performance in a manageable number of measures is daunting. The strategy of seeking measures of client satisfaction is one way of sidestepping this massive measurement problem. Measures of outputs are after all only proxies for their impact on clients. The problems involved in measuring satisfaction are, however, very considerable. More fundamentally, the identification of 'clients' is very difficult, perhaps including taxpayers, non-users, future generations and governments, as well as the more obvious class of clients – service users.

Expert interpretation of data (6) is needed because of the complexity of assessing performance, and the lack of incentive for individual citizens to undertake such analysis. Clearly public audit offices fulfil this role, and are also able to undertake audit of data (7). There remains the problem, of course, of who audits the auditors, and how their effectiveness is judged.

Strategies (1) to (7) are likely to be applicable to most PI schemes. The remaining strategies are designed to address specific dysfunctional phenomena which may arise in particular circumstances. Nurturing long-term career perspectives (8) is designed to encourage staff to address long-term objectives. The difficulty of capturing long-term issues in PI schemes is reduced if staff expect to be in post to experience the consequences of their attention to long-term issues. It should be noted, however, that long-term career perspectives may encourage gaming amongst staff, as they seek to maintain modest performance targets into the future.

Keeping the number of indicators small (9) reduces the scope for misinterpretation and increases the ability of the principal to exercise meaningful control. However it may compromise the objective of developing a comprehensive PI scheme, and may encourage gaming. It is noteworthy that, in seeking to develop a PI scheme for English local government, the Audit Commission (1992) came up with a package which did not 'cover every service' and did not deal with 'individual services in excessive detail'. They recognized that the limitations of the scheme would leave 'some commentators dissatisfied'. Yet the package includes over 200 indicators.

The need to develop independent benchmarks (10) is brought about by the ability of individual managers or organisations to appeal to uncontrollable external circumstances as the reason for their apparently poor performance. There will always be organisations for which no comparator is available – for example, schools operating in uniquely disadvantaged areas. And some public services are natural monopolies with which few comparisons are possible. It is possible that, with careful use of modelling techniques such as data envelopment analysis (Ganley and Cubbin, 1992), benchmarking might be possible in public sector services with simple production processes where a number of comparable organisations exist. However such circumstances are relatively rare, so the scope for benchmarking is limited.

Not all of these strategies for averting dysfunctional consequences are relevant in every situation and some, such as nurturing long-term career perspectives, may be helpful in minimising some adverse consequences but aggravate others. Nevertheless the list indicates that there do exist means of addressing many of the unintended costs of performance measurement. The wise controller must seek to balance the costs of implementing these strategies against the benefits they might bring in terms of control.

Conclusions

Performance indicators are assuming increased importance in most public sectors for a number of reasons. One is simply that over a short period the costs of collecting and disseminating data have reduced dramatically. Another is that public sectors are increasingly being reorganised away from monolithic structures towards agency arrangements in which small policy units purchase public sector services from quasi-autonomous agencies. The resulting arms' length relationship between purchasers and providers must be serviced by performance data, where before internal control could be by more informal means. It is noteworthy, therefore, that no discussion of PIs can be made in isolation from the organisational structure they are intended to service.

This chapter has viewed the use of PIs within a cost–benefit framework and asserted that the acid test for a PI scheme should be that its benefits should exceed its costs. A number of benefits claimed for PI schemes have been identified, and it has also been noted that a number of unexpected costs might arise when implementing PI schemes. Strategies exist to mitigate some of the adverse consequences associated with PIs, and again the benefits of implementing these strategies must be weighed against their costs.

The discussion suggests that, if handled carefully, the provision of more performance data may be beneficial to the performance and accountability of the public sector. However one cannot ignore the manifest dysfunctional consequences that arose in the former Soviet Union when an attempt was made to run an entire economy through the medium of such data. Only by careful attention to the considerations set out here, and by keeping a sense of proportion about the limitations of PIs in securing control, can the worst consequences of excessive reliance on performance indicators be avoided.

CHAPTER 12

Organisational culture and control

Kim Langfield-Smith

The term 'culture' has been used to describe many forms of human collectives – nations, ethnic or regional groups, organisations, professions or occupations and families. In this chapter the focus will be on cultures that characterise an organisation. The study of human groups as cultures owes its origins to the early writing in anthropology of Margaret Mead (1928), Malinowski (1922), Radcliffe-Brown (1952) and, more recently, to Lévi-Strauss (1967) and Geertz (1973). Aspects that are now associated with organisational culture have been studied in the organisational behaviour literature by writers such as Whyte (1948), Dalton (1959), Blau (1955) and Roy (1960). However it was not until the 1970s that cultural perspectives began to emerge in organisational research and the terms 'organisational culture' or 'corporate culture' came into popular and academic use. For academic researchers, culture became a framework for understanding and attributing meaning to the structures, systems, events, interactions and other phenomena that take place in organisations. In the popular press, the interest in culture has focused on managing (or changing) culture, or creating an awareness of the influence of an organisation's culture on organisational success. Several popular management writers have suggested that an effective culture can be planned and implemented rationally. It is only very recently that academic researchers have begun to investigate the significance of culture for control systems.

In this chapter we will discuss the concept of organisational culture as used within organisational research, and its relevance to the design and operation of control systems. This area of research is complex and fraught with competing definitions and viewpoints about the nature of organisational culture and of control. When organisational culture is viewed as embedded in the wider sociocultural system, it becomes a metaphor for understanding the organisation (and its control systems). Alternatively organisational culture can be viewed as an organisational variable, in the same way that we consider organisational structure or technology. Thus culture can be viewed as part of the organisational context to be considered in the design of control systems, or as a tool to be managed to achieve better control and organisational effectiveness.

Clans and clan control

We can begin our discussion of organisational culture by considering the closely related idea of clans. Within a transactions cost framework, Ouchi (1979) described three different organisational control mechanisms: markets, bureaucracies and clans. Each of these mechanisms needs certain minimum social and information requirements to operate. These are shown in Table 12.1. Market mechanisms require there to be a shared norm of reciprocity, and control is achieved through price mechanisms. Reciprocity refers to the notion of trust. It is necessary for each party to a transaction to be assured that the other is acting honestly, and this reduces transaction costs. All information relevant to the transaction is captured in the price. In a bureaucracy there is the additional social requirement of agreement on the legitimate source of authority. The norm of reciprocity takes the form of 'an honest day's work for an honest day's pay'. Control is achieved through formal rules. The most demanding mechanisms are clan controls which require that the members of an organisation share a range of values and beliefs on the forms of proper behaviours, and have a high level of commitment to those behaviours. Thus, within a clan, control is achieved implicitly. It will be noted that Ouchi's description of the clan bears some similarity to Etzioni's normative organisations.

Clan controls are most effective in certain types, or parts, of organisations where the outputs are ambiguous and difficult to measure, and where behaviour controls are inappropriate because the transformation process is unknown (Ouchi, 1980). The imposition of output or behaviour controls, which might be used within a bureaucracy, can actually impede effective control within a clan by encouraging behaviour that is not consistent with

TABLE 12.1   Social and informational requirements for
organisational control mechanisms

Type of control	*Social requirements*	*Informational requirements*
Market	Norm of reciprocity	Prices
Bureaucracy	Norm of reciprocity	Rules
	Legitimate authority	
Clan	Norm of reciprocity	Traditions
	Legitimate authority	
	Shared values, beliefs	

organisational goals and objectives, or by directly intruding on the day-to-day smooth functioning of the organisation. A research laboratory in a pharmaceutical company, or a medical centre, might place reliance on clan controls. In both situations formal and inflexible accounting controls may impede workflow and redirect attention to aspects that do not lead to desired outputs. Clan controls are subtle and not visible, particularly to the casual outside observer. Key aspects of the control system are rewards that attach to displaying the correct attitudes and values. These may take the form of some ritual or ceremony that serves to reinforce those same attitudes and values. For example, in a university the awarding of degrees is signified by the ritual of graduation, which emphasises the rewards obtained through scholarship.

Ouchi's (1980) model of markets, bureaucracies and clans is dominated by the nature of the economic relationships between parties within an organisation. In particular, the condition of trust, or reciprocity, in a clan is based on members' beliefs that co-operative behaviour is a good way to achieve higher output, which can ultimately result in long-term financial equity. However Alvesson and Lindkvist (1993) suggested that there are clans where there are other bases of trust. They distinguished between the *economic clan* of Ouchi, and the *social clan* and *blood relationship clan*. In a social clan, commitment and reciprocity are based on the individuals' needs to belong and communicate with other members as part of an organisation. Thus these organisations satisfy the emotional and social needs of its members. A blood relationship clan is connected to a 'biological imperative'. That is, clan relationships and trust are based on family relationships that dominate that organisation.

While organisations that can be described as pure clans are rarely found, many organisations rely to some extent on clan control. Examples include hospitals, schools, research groups, legal firms and public accounting firms. A characteristic of these types of organisations is the high level of commitment that can be found among employees, the careful selection of individuals by the organisation, stability of employment and extensive socialisation processes (often through formal qualifications and schooling) during which people come to internalise certain values.

The social requirements of a clan rely largely on the existence of shared values and beliefs, and organisational commitment, which are also characteristics of *organisational cultures*. The idea of organisational culture has increased in popularity over the past decade. However, it is complex and problematic, because of different understandings about the nature of the construct.

What is organisational culture?

Organisation culture has been addressed by many researchers (Pettigrew, 1979, 1985; Schein, 1984; Gagliardi, 1986; Meek, 1988) and it has been given a range of definitions. Meek (1988), in a critique of organisational culture research, described culture as encompassing multiple aspects: symbols (including language, architecture and artefacts), myths, ideational systems (including cognitive systems and ideology) and rituals. Morgan (1986) regarded 'shared meanings, shared understandings, and shared sense making' as different ways of describing organisational culture. Organisational culture was regarded as the 'process of reality construction that allows people to see and understand particular events, actions, objects, utterances, or situations in distinctive ways' (Morgan, 1986, 1.28).

Cultures have a stock of knowledge, including recipe knowledge and social typifications (Sproull, 1981). Recipe knowledge includes the routine performance programmes and standard operating procedures that guide actions in particular situations. Social typifications are the shared understandings which are acquired through socialisation and interaction of the people within a group and are influenced by its distinct language, environment and history. Culture is conveyed to organisational members through sentiment, beliefs and attitudes and thus appeals to the emotional elements of individuals (Pfeffer, 1981). It is an elusive concept because of its intangible and amorphous nature. While culture is manifested through behaviour, it should not be confused with overt behaviour patterns.

Organisational cultures are perpetuated by myths or stories which act to reinforce cultural values. These stories may be a series of memorable events in the company's history that become part of the 'organisational folklore'. For example, they may be concerned with the way the leader started the organisation – his drive, his vision and the band of pioneers that surrounded him (Clark, 1972). There is the element of myth surrounding some of these organisational stories. In some situations organisational stories may be consciously (or strategically) developed, but often emerge 'naturally' over time. These stories may take on the character of myths and the content may subtly change over time, especially when first-hand witnesses to the event become fewer. Stories, or more specifically myths, may be used to present cultural values to newcomers. These stories may present the social prescription of 'how things are done around here', the consequences of compliance or deviance, and the social categories and statuses that are legitimate within that organisation.

At Hewlett Packard, the stories surrounding Bill and Dave were stories that emphasised and legitimated the management philosophy of the company (Box 12.1). The symbolic nature of stories and myths makes it difficult to interpret the underlying message or meaning, especially for people external to the culture. However, these types of stories perform an important control function as they transmit and reinforce the cultural values and shared perspectives of organisational members. They provide a more effective method for co-ordinating work and operations than formal bureaucratic control, as they can be persuasive in their message and are easily remembered.

Box 12.1   Hewlett-Packard

Hewlett-Packard was founded in the 1940s in the USA by Bill Hewlett and Dave Packard and together they created a strong culture charac- terised by innovation and strong team commitment. These founders practised a hand-son management style that emphasised an enthusiasm for work, and encouraged an atmosphere of problem sharing and open exchange of information and ideas. These values were reinforced by frequent meetings which provided opportunities for interactions and sharing, and social interactions such as the ritual 'beer busts' and 'koffee klatches'. Over time myths and stories were passed on to new members which helped to sustain the cultural values created by the founders. These include stories of the early days when Bill and Dave started the company in Bill's garage and the family oven was used to make some of the first products.

The overall message that was transmitted by the culture was that of trusting and valuing employees. In the difficult times of the 1970s, the strength of the culture and the commitment of the management and staff was tested when instead of retrenching [sic] employees, staff took a 10 per cent decline in pay and worked a nine-day fortnight. Again the emphasis on team spirit and sharing was possible, even in difficult times.

Source: Morgan (1986), p. 124, adapted.

Accounting and control systems can be an important component of the organisational culture in that they can demonstrate the way that an organisa- tion views the world, and help to reinforce a particular view of reality. An example of the role of these systems in the changing culture of a railway company is described in Box 12.2.

Organisational subcultures

The popular management literature (for example, Peters and Waterman's *In Search of Excellence*) has encouraged the idea of strong unitary organisational cultures. However it is more likely that organisations contain subcultures. A variety of factors may contribute to the emergence of these subcultures within an organisation: the introduction of new people from outside the organisation, unique work roles and departmental perspectives, dense boundaries or loose couplings of various organisational groups, the introduction of new

---

Box 12.2   The symbolic role of accounting systems in a railway company

In some organisations accounting and control systems have an important symbolic role, but in others they may have no particular significance. Dent (1991) provided an interesting study where he illustrated the significance of these systems in effecting a cultural change.

In a large European railway company the accounting activities and financial reporting systems were incidental to the running of the business, as the dominant culture of the company was focused on the railway. For over a century the railway was viewed as a public service and the purpose was to run trains. Profitability was secondary to railway engineering and the logistics of running trains. The cultural knowledge was that if the organisation provided the nation with a transport infrastructure then they would be financially supported by the government.

However, in an increasingly resource-constrained environment, business managers were appointed and we were assigned responsibility for developing strategies that would improve financial performance. The pressure to adopt a business culture saw 'the train' as decreasing in its symbolic significance and with the help of accounting activities there was a shift of importance from the train to the customer. Rail transport came to be regarded as a product or service and the railway was viewed as a profit-seeking enterprise. Systems of accountability and organisational structures centring upon the business managers were created. The assumptions underlying those systems – rationality, authority, organisation and the time – gradually permeated the knowledge and the values and beliefs of the organisation and became the dominant culture.

---

technologies, social and ethnic groupings, and professional affiliations. Some of these subcultures (for example, those based on nationality or professional affiliation) may have their sources outside the organisation's boundaries.

Subcultures within the one organisation may have some similarities, but there may also exist disparate subcultures that actively compete for dominance or persist in an uneasy symbiosis (Martin and Siehl, 1983). The dominant culture is often associated with the senior management perspective, which through access to power and resources is actively reinforced by managerial decisions and actions. Some organisations successfully function with discordant subcultures. These subcultures can maintain their distinct identities by being 'loosely coupled' to other subcultures or subsystems. This can be achieved by physical or geographical isolation of a department or, for example, by releasing a section of the organisation from the demands of the budgeting and formal management control systems. For example, to foster creativity the research and development division of a corporation may be allowed to manage itself, free from the control systems imposed on the other sections of the organisation.

National cultures and organisational culture

The impact of national cultures on organisational culture is a complex area for research, but has implications for the design of control systems in multinational companies. Can the same structures, reporting systems and formal controls that are used in the head office of a company be used effectively in overseas branches?

It is tempting to associate Japanese cultures with Japanese companies, or German cultures with German companies. However there may be distinct differences in culture within the one nation. In these times of increasing globalisation, and with the growth of transnational corporations, the isolation of particular characteristics of national cultures becomes even more problematic. It may be more useful to consider the influence of 'societal' cultures on organisational culture. Societal cultures focus more on subcultures of a nation, which may be based on ethnicity, region, class or profession. For example, Birnberg and Snodgrass (1988) considered that in many Japanese-style societies managers come to an organisation having already learned the need for group consensus, the role of subset of actions and activities and the nuances of language in conveying meaning. These societal values lead to a control system that places less emphasis on bureaucratic rules and incentive systems.

While national cultures may influence the style of organisational culture, there are many examples of multinational companies that have more in common with the dominant organisational culture of the parent company than with their national culture. IBM has commonly been presented as a company that has a strong global organisational culture that emphasises respect for the individual, service orientation and the pursuit of excellence (Hofstede, 1985). Internalisation of the dominant shared values in international companies is often achieved by transferring staff between overseas posts, conducting centralised training and conferences and imposing standardised management and control systems. Foreign subsidiaries may also develop cultures that contain aspects of both their national and parent company cultures. It is only recently that the differing national cultures within multinational companies and their effect on control systems design have been researched (see, for example, Chow *et al.*, 1991).

What is the relevance of culture for control systems?

To understand the relationship between organisational culture and control, we need first to consider different assumptions that can be held about the nature of organisational culture (Smircich, 1983; Allaire and Firsirotu, 1984). First, we can view an organisation as a *sociocultural system*. Under this approach culture becomes a metaphor for the organisation. Culture is portrayed in terms of systems of cognition and beliefs, patterns of symbolic discourse or manifestations of unconscious processes (Smircich, 1983). Control systems can be viewed as part of the sociocultural system, and will both reflect and be a part of the organisational culture. To study organisational culture we would consider organisational structures, functioning and evolutionary processes, as organisational culture is assumed to be enmeshed within the social structures of the organisation. Issues of dissonance and incongruity between the culture and the other components of the organisation have no relevance, as these are assumed to be part of an attuned whole.

The second approach is to regard organisational culture as a separate *organisational variable*. That is, culture is a conceptually separate component of the organisation, either being located in the minds of the members of the culture or arising from shared meanings and symbols. The organisational culture is revealed by the patterns of the attitudes and actions of the organisational members. It is within this view that we can advance the idea that an organisational culture can adapt, and may be intentionally changed or designed. For example, many popular management writers (Peters and Waterman, 1982; Deal and Kennedy, 1982) view culture as a management control tool, which can be changed to enhance organisational performance. Also, under this approach, control systems can be viewed as an outcome of, as well as a precondition to, organisational culture (Jelinek *et al.*, 1983). Culture can be viewed as providing a context for the design of control systems and may itself be a source of control.

Culture as the context for control

Flamholtz *et al.* (1985) view organisational culture as an independent variable. They present a model of organisational control that explicitly considers organisational culture as a component of the control context (Figure 12.1). Culture was described as facilitating control when the control system is consistent with the social norms of the organisation – or as inhibiting control when it is at variance with the shared norms, values, management philosophy and practices. Culture itself was recognised as a control mechanism in organisations where knowledge of the transformation process is imperfect and where the ability to measure output is low. This is consistent with Ouchi's (1980) preconditions for clan controls. Culture becomes the source of control through messages contained in rituals, stories and ceremonies which relay to organisational members desirable behaviours. Thus culture is not only a context for the design of control systems but, in certain organisations, may itself be a mechanism of control.

Culture has also been described as a filter for perceiving the environment that sets the action and decision premises of individuals within an organisation (Birnberg and Snodgrass, 1988). Culture influences the effectiveness of a control system in two ways. First, culture can affect which aspects of a control system are perceived by an individual, so that certain stimuli are sought and others are ignored. Secondly, the culture can affect any value judgements made about those perceived stimuli. Birnberg and Snodgrass focused on the

FIGURE 12.1 Framework for Organisational Control

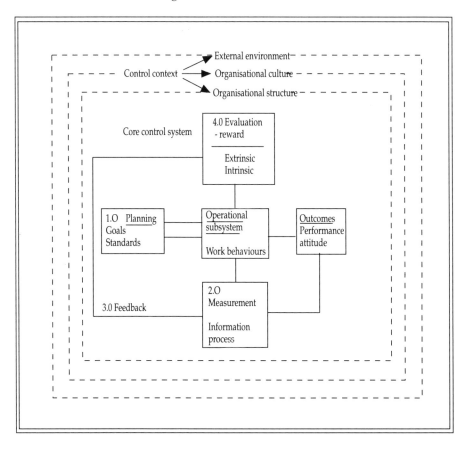

Source: Flamholt, Das and Tsui (1985), p. 38

degree of homogeneity of a culture and the differing values placed on co-
operation to explain the different types of control systems that may suit particular culture – co-operation mixes. A group is considered to have a
homogeneous culture when there are few differences between the values,
beliefs and behaviour of its members, and heterogeneous where differences
exist. Where there are heterogeneous cultures in the one organisation, those
groups will react differently to the same control processes – they will perceive
and interpret control mechanisms in different ways.

A model is presented in Figure 12.2 that explains the degree of formality of
the control system under four possible states. In cell 1 we have a homogeneous culture and high value is placed on co-operation by its members. In this
situation the members of the culture possess a common set of values, and
where these are consistent with the organisation's goals there is less need for
an implicit (formal) control system. One objective of formal controls is to communicate and reward certain behaviour; however this is not required in the

FIGURE 12.2   The Role of the Control System under Differing Culture–
Co-operation Mixes

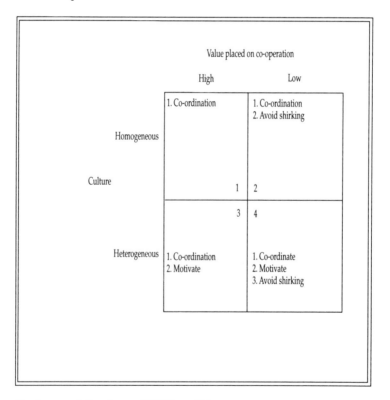

Source: Birnberg and Snodgrass (1988), p. 451

situation in cell 1 because of the sharing of values. Therefore the role of the control system becomes one of co-ordination, achieved by communicating information for informed decision making. The cell 1 situation describes *the clan* (Ouchi, 1979) and clan control. In cell 3 there is a high value placed on co-operation; however, because of the heterogeneity of the culture, controls are needed to both co-ordinate and motivate workers to achieve organisational goals. In cells 2 and 4 the value placed on co-operation is low, so control systems would include mechanisms such as participation, bureaucratic rules and firm-wide incentive systems to facilitate goal congruence. According to Birnberg and Snodgrass, the Japanese culture is an example of a cell 1 situation and US organisations are cell 4 (or perhaps cell 3). Compared to Japanese companies, in many US organisations there are disparate values and individuals are more concerned with the way their actions affect themselves, in preference to the group. Of course, these generalisations about the cohesiveness of Japanese companies and the nature of the group ethos in both Japanese and US companies have been questioned in recent years (see, for example, Hammond and Preston, 1992).

Inferring the nature of the organisational culture

If we accept that the nature and homogeneity of an organisational culture must be considered in the design of control systems, then we are assuming that a culture can be separately identified and studied. However, if culture is such a nebulous concept and if much of the culture resides in the unconscious shared assumptions and values of its members, how can the nature of the organisational culture be determined?

Schein (1985) suggests that an organisation's culture can be inferred and understood by considering its visible artefacts which also act to reinforce the culture. These include the organisational structure, the information and control systems, formal goals and mission statements and myths, legends and stories. However the inferences that we can make from observing formal structures and responsibility systems are limited and their significance should be interpreted with care. For example, a formal structure that is apparently highly centralised with very little delegation of decision-making responsibility could suggest that the senior management has low regard for and trust in the abilities of the more junior managers, and believes that they cannot be trusted. Alternatively this structure could be chosen because senior management enjoys the day-to-day involvement in operational decisions. Another possibility is that the structure was imposed by the parent company or was an historical choice, and the formal structure may bear little resemblance to the informal arrangements under which decisions are actually made. Management may not bother changing the irrelevant formal structure, as it is not considered to be an important issue. So, while the nature of formal structures might be important in understanding a culture, there are many competing interpretations that can be made.

An organisation's formal control system may reflect aspects of the organisation's culture – but only if the controls are actually attended to by managers. Once again there may be little correspondence between the informal (actual) control processes and the formal aspects. However even apparently unused control processes may be regarded as rituals, and can perform a useful function within the organisation. Apparent contradictions between formal and informal control systems may suggest conflict to an observer, but to insiders may be important features of the culture. For example, in a company which is dominated by engineering or marketing concerns, accounting controls may form a ritualistic function. The accountants may be content to prepare cost-based performance reports and all managers may take part in budgeting meetings. However everybody may know that effective control and performance is related to new product design and successful product launches. Alternatively such apparent conflicts could be a cause of stress and disruption, creating an even wider rift between functional cultures and engendering frustration among accountants regarding their 'rightful place' in the organisation. An example of the role of the finance function in the production culture of the National Coal Board is discussed in Box 12.3. In this situation the finance function was allowed to exist although it conflicted with the dominant culture.

Box 12.3   Achieving control in the National Coal Board

In a study of management control in an area (region) of the National Coal Board, Berry *et al.* (1985) provide an excellent account of the interaction of control and organisational culture. Budgets and financial reports were prepared for each colliery in the area and managers were held formally accountable for results; however financial planning and control systems were not the dominant mode of organisational control. The area was dominated by a culture which emphasised production and technology. This was heavily reinforced through socialisation processes which, even for colliery or area managers, was reinforced by underground mine work early in their careers, limited technical education and living in the coal mining communities. A high value was attached to loyalty, local knowledge, experience and skills which were reinforced through the stories and myths of the coal mining industry. These myths were built around the role of the battling miner who performed a dangerous and difficult job in a hostile environment, but always with the support of his colliery manager. Mine workers and area managers shared common loyalties to 'our pit' and there was a strong belief in the protection of the miners' fair share of output targets and earnings. The maintenance of the myth of the colliery as a 'self-contained, technical entity' also became an effective way of controlling non-miners and non-engineers, who had not experienced the same socialisation. Beside this strong culture, financial considerations were marginal and tended to be the concern of head office managers, or those few senior managers who were placed into the area from the head office. Accounting reports and budgeting systems were largely ignored by area managers and were not allowed to intrude on the real production-related issues. The researchers found the content and form of these accounting reports curious, but suggested that the creation of more accurate economic statements might not be welcomed as it could lead to a shift in power, and thus affect the maintenance of the dominant culture.

The NCB was managing through vertical and horizontal decoupling which allowed each part of the organisation to maintain its own distinct identity and concerns. Strategic and planning issues and models, and capital expenditure analyses were the domain of the head office and this knowledge was generally not conveyed to areas. Any long-term planning at the area level was confined to geographical feasible capacities. This lack of communication helped to maintain morale and stability in the areas, in the face of a declining coal market and limited finance. Horizontal decoupling occurred in the separation of finance and operations and while this partially reflected the differences in occupational cultures it also satisfied the role of managing the inherent ambiguity and uncertainty of the industry by again protecting the production core. However the role of finance became one of legitimisation and ritual: accounting reports satisfied external requirements and gave the appearance that the area followed conventional accountability and efficiency practices. The specific characteristics of the area, which depended on and was reinforced by the maintenance of the strong mining culture, provided a means for control in the face of change and uncertainty so that any attempt to integrate systems and move towards a more financially-oriented business culture might be counterproductive.

The formal mission statement, or even the goals of an organisation, may not derive from the shared beliefs and assumptions of the organisational members but may reflect the senior management culture, or may indicate the new future cultural direction for the company. However in designing control systems we need to be aware of the way in which the values communicated in the mission or goals differ from those of the dominant culture of the organisation. Organisational myths, legends and stories abound in any organisation where there is a strong culture. Often these are used by senior management to reinforce the new values of a culture. Sometimes they develop from lower levels of the organisation. They may reflect the dominant culture or a subculture, and may even carry a subversive meaning. They are often some of the earliest messages conveyed to new members of an organisation. In the earlier example of Hewlett-Packard, stories and myths were very important in sustaining the strong culture.

Organisational culture as a management control tool

It is clear from the above discussions that there is a view that many aspects of organisational culture provide control, and in some situations more effective control than that based on explicit rules. Many popular management books operate on the premise that culture is an important variable that can be managed and manipulated in organisations, to achieve greater control and effectiveness.

Creating a *strong* organisational culture

Organisational cultures have been described as 'weak' or 'strong'. Strong cultures are those to which members are strongly committed, which is said to provide control advantages. Strong and enduring organisational cultures are often said to be initiated by a strong leader, for example the group's founder, or an influential reformer (Clark, 1972; Pettigrew, 1979; Schein, 1985). There are many theories about the way in which founders, or new managers, can create a strong organisational culture. Gagliardi (1986) described the process of 'idealisation' where beliefs are transformed into organisational core values and assumptions. When organisations are created, leaders will have a vision for that organisation and will direct operations using their specific sets of beliefs and values. If the leader guides the organisation to success and the members recognise this, over time this *way of doing things* will become accepted by subordinates. This reduces the need for the leader to directly control the members' activities. It is the shared experiences of success that help to develop and strengthen organisational beliefs and values. The causes of the successes become ideals or values that, over time, become important in their own right. With successive generations of organisational members these values are increasingly taken for granted, and they become the assumptions that underlie the organisational culture. They influence the more tangible aspects of the organisational culture – the work practices, the rituals and symbols – and will protect and sustain the culture. The culture is perpetuated and may grow in intensity as shared experiences increase and as the memories of success are enshrined as organisational sagas or myths. The Hewlett Packard example, presented earlier in this chapter supports this theory, involving a successful company with a strong culture led by strong founders.

It can be argued that the mere sharing of core values and assumptions provides a powerful source of control through the internalisation of corporate objectives and goals, and reducing the problems of goal incongruence. However Kotter and Heskett (1992) found that organisations with weak organisational culture were likely to be just as successful as those with strong organisational culture. One reason for this is that a strong culture may become an obstacle to change and a strong but misdirected culture may 'lead intelligent people to walk, in concert, off a cliff'. Also, strong cultures, or subcultures, within organisations may be at variance with the senior management culture and conflict with the organisational goals.

A less harmonious view of cultural development is presented by Schein (1985, p. 222) who describes the situation of a new organisation where the leader is surrounded by strong individuals who are unwilling to accept the leader's vision, assumptions and beliefs. This may result in conflict, negotiation, compromise, resignations and either good or bad outcomes for the organisation. Similarly, in an established organisation, the entry of a new leader may be conflict-free – the process of embedding new assumptions and values occurs through Gagliardi's processes of idealisation – or may be fraught with resistance and conflict.

Strong organisational cultures have been held up as keys to success in many newly industrialised nations, especially in Japanese companies. The example of the Matsushita company is described in the Box 12.4. Many advanced manufacturing philosophies based on Japanese models have been distilled and promoted in Western companies. The success of these programmes in non-Japanese companies depends on an ability to change the underlying management philosophies and cultures of the workplace. However the historical influences that contribute to Japanese culture are very different to the US or UK experiences, and may cause Japanese practices to be less successful when introduced into non-Japanese companies. For example, one theory is that Japanese organisations combine the traditional cultural values of the rice field with those of the samurai. This creates organisations that have an elitist managerial hierarchy and feudal worker/master relationships. To Western observers, this gives the appearance of a submissive and deferential workforce. However, unlike the situation in many Western countries, where people gain their self-respect through competing against a system to emphasise their individuality, Japanese workers may achieve self-respect through service within an organisation (Morgan, 1986, p. 116). This is not to imply that Japanese practices cannot be successfully introduced in non-Japanese countries, or that practices from other countries than Japan cannot be adopted in other countries. It merely highlights the influence that national cultures may have on organisational cultures and the difficulties of implementing practices within a different national context.

Box 12.4   The culture at Matsushita

In the early 1980s the Matsushita Electric Company was ranked as one of the 50 largest corporations in the world. Its products were sold under the brand names of National, Panasonic, Quasar and Technics. The founder, Konosuke Matsushita, was very influential in shaping the future of his company. He believed that the firm had an inescapable responsibility to help employees' inner selves, which could best be realised by managers being trainers and developers of character, not exploiters of human resources. A technique of 'self-indoctrination' was used where every employee was asked at least each second month to give a ten-minute talk to his work group on the company's values and its relationship to society. Matsushita was the first company in Japan to have a song and a code of values. One executive said, 'It seems silly to Westerners, but every morning at 8.00 a.m., all across Japan, there are 87,000 people reciting the code of values and singing together. It's like we are all a community.' The basic principles, beliefs and values of the company were as follows:

Basic business principles
To recognise our responsibilities as industrialists, to foster progress, to promote the general welfare of society, and to devote ourselves to the further development of world culture.

Employees' creed
Progress and development can be realised only through the combined efforts and co-operation of each member of our Company. Each of us, therefore, shall keep this idea constantly in mind as we devote ourselves to the continous improvement of our Company.

The seven spiritual values
1.   National service through industry
2.   Fairness
3.   Harmony and co-operation
4.   Struggle for betterment
5.   Courtesy and humility
6.   Adjustment and assimilation
7.   Gratitude

Source: Pascale and Athos (1981) pp. 50–1.

Cultural change

The term cultural change is used to describe the natural evolution of a culture, or more commonly it is used to describe the process of introduced cultural change. In the organisational theory literature, change is often described as either *first order* or *second order* change. During first order change, the organisation searches for a solution to problems but is constrained by the limits of the shared belief systems. Different behaviours from a range of possible behaviours are combined into different sequences, but these all lead to solutions that lie within the boundaries of the existing cultural paradigm. A system, or an organisation, 'cannot generate from within itself the conditions for its own change; it cannot produce the rules for changing its own rules' (Watzlawick *et al.*, 1974, p.22). Thus, it is extremely difficult to break out of this self-directing search, or even to conceive of alternatives that lie outside the existing cultural assumptions. Janis (1972) described the concept of *groupthink*: when individuals in a group are dominated by collective belief structures, they will sample the environment in an increasingly narrow manner, so that those beliefs become reinforced. The inability to solve the organisation's problems may result in confusion and in the culture losing its cohesion as the experiences of failure intensify.

Second order change is said to take place when an organisation finds that it is no longer effective in managing the problems within its environment. This may involve a complete change of culture, a discontinuity or transformation of the cultural paradigm, or incremental change where the organisation goes through periods of transition. The new manager who might initiate a new culture is not constrained by the existing cultural assumptions, so may be able to question the current beliefs and values.

The success of any change will depend on a variety of factors, including the extent to which new behaviours, and the new beliefs and values on which they are based, conflict with the old cultural values and assumptions. The degree to which the organisational members can collectively experience the success of the new behaviour patterns is also an important factor. It must also be remembered that, while there may be a change in the dominant culture of the organisation, subcultures may remain unaffected. There is the view that not all parts of an organisation need to change, and that a degree of cultural fragmentation may even be desirable (Weick, 1976).

Advanced manufacturing philosophies such as total quality management (TQM) and 'just-in-time' systems (JIT) rely heavily on employee involvement and empowerment. In particular, TQM practices require not only changes in work practices, but changes in attitudes and values of all employees, which for many companies implies a cultural change. Formal bureaucratic controls are often regarded as inconsistent with these approaches, especially those that concentrate on controlling the individual, rather than the group. The types of controls that are cultivated in these systems are clan controls. Individuals are encouraged to work in groups, to support their fellow workers in that group and to be self-motivated though accepting responsibility and commitment to a high-quality product or service.

Embedding and transmitting culture

Schein (1985, p. 224) described five mechanisms used by senior managers to embed and transmit culture:

1. what leaders pay attention to, measure and control;
2. leader reactions to critical incidents and organisational crises;
3. deliberate role modelling, teaching and coaching by leaders;
4. criteria for allocation of rewards and status;
5. criteria for recruitment, selection, promotion, retirement and excommunication.

These mechanisms may be used deliberately or may operate unintended. It is interesting to note that, apart from the second item, all these mechanisms are elements of the formal or informal management control processes. Thus the processes of reinforcing or embedding a culture may act to create control.

The first mechanism is described by Schein as one of the best methods for managers to communicate their orientation and the aspects that they believe are important. This is achieved through designing formal control systems, or simply by managers' remarks and questions that are consistently geared to certain themes. Formal controls will include performance evaluation and reward systems and routine reporting systems. An example of the informal processes would be if the company's new orientation is to emphasise customer service rather than market share, when the senior manager may give important signals during a planning meeting by asking how certain product changes or other activities will affect the level of customer service. Emotional outbursts and other reactions may also be used by managers when they feel that an important assumption is being violated. This will further reinforce the priorities and values that they wish to transmit. Signals are also created by what is *not* reacted to. However such messages will lose their effect if they are not consistent with the managers' behaviour. The example of the quality drive in a university department (Box 12.5) demonstrates the importance of providing a consistent message.

Simons (1990) explained the role of management control systems in influencing the strategy formulation process and effecting change (Figure 12.3, p. 198). He argued that senior managers choose to make certain control systems interactive and to programme others. Programmed controls are delegated to staff specialists, and senior managers are only involved when there

---

Box 12.5   Promotional criteria in a university department

Traditionally universities have placed far greater emphasis on research quality than on the quality of teaching when evaluating its academic staff. However, with the increased pressures on universities for increased *accountability* of funds, many institutions are placing greater emphasis on evaluating the quality of teaching and explicitly considering teaching skills as an important promotional criterion. However many senior academics who owe their high position to research expertise, and not necessarily teaching skills, find it difficult to change their priorities, especially when it comes to considering applications for promotion of more junior staff. So, while research and teaching may be given comparable status in formal documents of criteria for staff promotion, in many cases these 'new values' are not carried through. For many the shifting of priorities amounts to a change in values, and perhaps even a cultural change.

Thus, while the new cultural message may be that quality research and quality teaching are necessary for 'good academics', any inconsistencies over what is considered important by some senior university staff when considering applications for staff promotions may weaken the new initiatives.

Any control aspects that could be achieved through performance evaluation and reward systems are also jeopardised by inconsistencies between the espoused values and the enacted values.

---

are problems. When controls are used interactively, managers actively monitor those controls and intervene in day-to-day decisions of subordinates. This provides an active forum where important issues can be debated and challenged, and managerial values and preferences are clearly signalled. Interactive controls are those that focus on the strategic uncertainties in the environment. Organisational learning takes place as managers become more aware and respond to the opportunities and threats that the strategic uncertainties present.

The way that an organisation, and a senior manager, deal with a crisis may reveal important assumptions and closely held values. The leader's reactions can provide a rapid learning experience for other managers and employees. When the SPC fruit canning company faced a crisis, the managers explained the difficult situation to the shop-floor workers. The managers themselves showed their commitment to the company by taking a decrease in pay and, such was the level of trust between managers and workers, the workers also agreed to accept lower pay levels. This is described in Box 12.6.

FIGURE 12.3   Process Model of the Relationship between Control Systems, Business Strategy and Organisational Learning

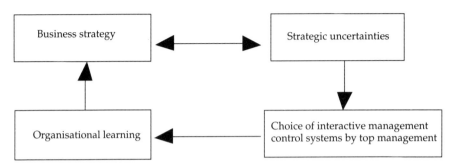

Source: Simons (1990), p. 138.

Box 12.6   The SPC Fruit Canning Company

SPC Limited was established in 1917 in a fruit-growing valley of Australia and by 1990 was the largest Australian canner and exporter of deciduous fruit. However a series of expensive and poor decisions left the company heavily in debt and the dissatisfaction with management led to a board room coup. The shareholders, mainly local growers and employees of SPC, sacked most of the directors and elected a new Chairman, who was himself a grower. A local store owner, Jeff Tracy, was employed as the General Manager and he admitted: 'I don't know anything about fruit and I didn't know anything about production, but I do know about people'.

The previous culture was that of blaming the workers when things went wrong, and there was resentment by workers. Tracy created a climate for change. There was a flow of information to keep employees informed of the companies activities and problems in an attempt to improve the poor employee relations. An advisory committee of workers met weekly with Board members and the employees were always welcome to talk to Tracy in his office. However, the company was close to bankruptcy and redundancies of 25% took place. The survival of the town was dependent on the survival of SPC and the employees worked with management to help solve the company's problems. In a secret ballot 93% of employees voted to accept a lower wages package.

The new management demonstrated that they were serious about cost cutting at all levels, and they were there on the job at all hours working with employees. Reserved car parks were abolished, after-drinks sessions were held with Tracy and the managers to get to know staff. Board members were working on weekends on the hot and messy production lines. New ideas from employees were listened to and acted upon and the Board and CEO were 'Jeff' and 'John'. The communications newsletter became very important and contained messages of unity and commitment for all staff.

Profitability returned in 1991 and wages were restored, with the promise to reimburse much of the wages lost, and a profit-sharing scheme was negotiated. The Chairman stated that the new unity between employees and management was a major contribution to the turnaround.

The SPC is an example of a successful cultural change that took place in a very short time. The survival of the local town and community was heavily dependent on the survival of SPC. This factor, and the close personal identification of the employees, management and shareholders with the company and their history of shared experiences were major contributors to the success of the change.

Source: A. Sinclair and J. Baird, *SPC: New Deal*, by Melbourne Case Study Services, University of Melbourne

---

Explicit role modelling, teaching and coaching are a part of training employees and communicating assumptions and values of the new culture. This is where senior managers, by virtue of their access to resources and systems, have distinct advantages over other competing cultures within the organisation. Strategic planning weekends, or retreats, are often used to present new ways of thinking and to foster joint experiences in a setting removed from the day-to-day company situation.

The criteria used for awarding rewards and granting status create a learning experience for staff, especially if accompanied by formal appraisal sessions. However the espoused rewards may differ from the actual reward system. The formal rewards that accompany good performance may be emphasised in performance appraisal sessions, but individuals may know that it is other aspects that are actually rewarded. These types of inconsistencies may create perceptions of inequity. This may cloud any 'cultural message' that management is trying to reinforce. The example given of conflict in espoused values and enacted values in a university illustrates this.

When people are assimilated into a culture, changes may need to be made to their existing assumptions, values and beliefs before the values and beliefs of the new culture can be accepted. By hiring people who already share some of the cultural assumptions and values, a culture can be self-perpetuating and the need for formal bureaucratic controls can be reduced. This is helped by people self-selecting: choosing to work for organisations where they see the company's values and vision as consistent with their own self-image.

Conclusion

In this chapter the notion of organisational culture has been considered and various theories about the interaction of organisational culture and control have been discussed. However, because of the intangible and ambiguous nature of organisational culture, it is important when examining theories and research findings about organisational culture and control that we consider the assumptions made about the nature of organisational culture.

If organisational culture *is* the organisation, merely an idea that characterises one organisation from another, then to talk about changing the culture or control systems implies changing the very nature of the organisation. By understanding the culture of an organisation, or the subcultures, we can gain insight into the way control is achieved in an organisation; control is embedded within the culture, within the organisation.

The control advantages that arise from a strong organisational culture are an area that has not been addressed in conventional control systems theory. However can it be assumed that strong cultures are convenient resources or components of the organisation that can be managed to provide effective control? From a managerial viewpoint, culture can be looked on as a tool of control only if those shared values and beliefs are consistent with the dominant management culture and the organisational goals. Whether organisational culture can be used or manipulated as a management tool is debatable, and any notion of designing an effective culture rests on the idea that culture is an identifiable artefact of an organisation. Theories of cultural change highlight the importance of a leader with a strong vision being able to create a new culture or change an existing *ineffective* culture. However empirical evidence of the success of such ventures is sparse. If organisational culture is a metaphor for the organisation, rather than a distinct organisational artefact, then theories about effective or ineffective cultures, and prescriptions for changing the culture, have little relevance!

PART III

Practices of Control

Management control systems of Japanese companies operating in the United Kingdom

Istemi S. Demirag

Introduction

This chapter reports the results of a recently completed research project on Japanese companies' operations in the UK. The project focuses on Japanese companies' management control systems, corporate strategies and performance measures for their operations in the United Kingdom. The extent to which these differ from those adopted by companies based wholly in the UK is an issue to explore, given the current interest in Japanese approaches to management.

The literature on management control systems of multinational companies and their strategy indicated that the link between the two were not clearly spelt out. This was mainly because the strategy literature used various typologies and definitions (Hambrick, 1984; Langfield-Smith, 1993). This resulted in fragmented research findings, with often conflicting results. Similarly, different definitions are given to management control systems. Moreover organisational effectiveness or performance are measured using different standards. It is therefore hoped that the results of this study will help to fill this gap and show how management accounting, when used as a control or performance evaluation tool, can help to achieve strategic objectives (Dent, 1990a, 1990b; Simons, 1987, 1990; Govindarajan, 1988). The overall intention of the project was therefore to describe Japanese companies' strategy and their management style and control systems for their UK operations (Daniel and Reitsperger, 1991; Demirag and Tylecote, 1992a, 1992b). Rather than impose a particular strategy typology on companies, we have attempted to describe Japanese companies' strategies both at business and at operational level in Europe. The study also highlights some of the problems these companies are experiencing in the European markets and how they are dealing with these problems. Where appropriate, significant differences found between this study and UK company practice, as reported elsewhere, are highlighted in the chapter.

The first section provides an overall description of the research methods used for the study. The second section describes the results of the study. It highlights management control styles of Japanese companies' UK operations and it describes how Japanese companies are using management control systems to achieve continuous cost reductions and other strategic objectives (see, for example, Goold and Campbell, 1987a). It also points out some of the management control problems the companies are experiencing in the UK. For the purpose of this study, organisational forms and responsibilities, corporate strategies, capital investment techniques, and types of performance evaluation and remuneration systems are used to describe management control styles of Japanese companies. The last section provides an overall summary of the results.

An overall description of the study

Case study approach

Given the complexity of the subject the research used a multilayered case study approach with three Japanese multinational groups (companies) with manufacturing subsidiaries located in the UK: Group A, Group B and Group C. 'Face-to-Face' interviews with senior management located in the UK at the regional and divisional subsidiary management levels were conducted for each participating group. Participation in the study was obtained from the Japanese parent company management by a research team based in Japan. All interviews, which lasted on average four to five hours, were tape recorded. I spent two years interviewing 31 managers, and participated in several meetings. I also had access to some confidential management reports and other documents. From the interviews, I developed and administered a questionnaire among the senior managers in each of the companies in order to cross- check my perceptions and interview notes. The study sought explanation of the empirical situation. Throughout the study, for each management level, I assured the confidentiality of the information, so that honest opinions and perceptions were captured in the study. It is for this reason that the results of the study are analysed in aggregate form only and there is also no mention of the individual companies or persons who participated in the study.

The companies

Two of the case study groups, Groups A and B, were in consumer electronics and the third, Group C, was operating in the motor car industry. The companies were chosen on the basis of their willingness to participate in the interviews. For each of the selected three case study groups interviews were carried out with the Japanese regional company management teams, cascading down to the lower level of management, within the same company. The lower level management included both the UK divisional and business unit management.

The results of the study

Organisation forms and management responsibilities

The study found that the Japanese companies at the parent company level had strongly decentralised divisional profit responsibilities with highly autonomous and powerful manufacturing plants (referred to as 'works') focused on target results. This was supported by strong central management committee functions and mobility of personnel throughout the organisation within the units or between them. Regular monthly and quarterly financial reviews were carried out, but these were not central to the planning process. The UK operations can best be described as functional management. Each functional management reported to general management in the UK and functional and product management in Japan. In this complex matrix organisational structure, several levels of interaction in the decision-making process were visible. This was particularly clear to us in the area of the design function. In general the companies' basic philosophy was that a design team was responsible for profit. However, because the design function in the UK was relatively new, that type of design department with profit responsibility was not completely achieved in the UK. Instead the finance department supported the design department and the other departments in producing profitable products. This involved preparing profit forecasts for each product and then discussing these forecasts with the design and other, related departments. The finance department also assisted in the continuous costing of the models produced. In addition, in this matrix type of structure, purchasing departments had the prime responsibility for materials used in the products. The companies also had, within their design function, a section known as 'Value Engineering for the Customer' (VEC) responsible for reducing the cost of products. Design teams were also knowledgeable about the alternative materials which could be introduced into current or future models.

The Japanese companies were found to be rather single-minded, perhaps rather bureaucratic, in many of the things they did. All the business units fed the top management with information necessary for formulating and implementing strategic plans. This single-minded commitment was a difference that could be identified as being a Japanese strength relative to the Europeans. There was much less flexibility in the strategic planning sense in the Japanese companies. Once plans were established they were vigorously followed and implemented. It is worth noting that the bureaucratic approach to business plans is still maintained despite the growing internationalisation of Japanese business. Underlying cultural attitudes in Japan still induce a conservative approach to business overseas. The influence of parent company practices is also apparent in terms of the power structure of the overseas divisions within the organisation. Traditionally manufacturing and engineering functions have higher status in Japan and this point is reinforced by one of the managers interviewed:

> Well, you are starting to touch on things like the work ethic. The Japanese system, as you well know, is not one that encourages entrepreneurial flair. It comes up, it doesn't come down in terms of the style of the management of an operation or a company. Although in its environment the company was creating ideas, it was not allowing the market momentum to filter upwards, which is what the Japanese have done, I guess, in most segments they have approached. But remember that much that we do here in the UK is a reflection of what is driven from the Tokyo side. I do not think our company is a good example of a consumer-led company. I think that it is more industrial manufacturing in its attitude. It may well be one of the Japanese companies that will, during the course of the next 5 or 10 years, not be in consumer products and who will find that its investment return is better suited in other industries.

The difficulty of co-ordinating products against the wishes of the powerful manufacturing 'works' is to some extent alleviated by the way managers are trained in Japanese companies. As managers often move from one manufacturing plant to another, from one division to another and, more recently, from Japanese operations to overseas plants, the Japanese managers are expected to understand the problems of communication and be able to co-ordinate products across divisions, manufacturing plants and overseas operations.

This type of management training contrasts very sharply with the training of British managers, as is explained by one of the managers:

> I know that many of the very high level people in our company, directors and others, have an engineering background or technical background. A very important factor is that people have worked in factories in manufacturing and have experience of factory situations and how to create profit and run factories efficiently. Many of the senior people are not based at Head Office, they are based at factories. To be General Manager of a factory is a very high position, very high. It is very common within our company, and I think in many Japanese companies too, to move from headquarters

or from central office area to a factory and then to return to headquarters function. There is no similarity to the Western style where people sometimes become Directors having never worked in a manufacturing outlet, but have some academic or technical background of another type.

In addition to the unique Japanese style of management with bureaucratic command structure and good bottom-up communication channels, actual organisation structures of the companies also ensured that decisions made at headquarters level were sensitive to all parts of the company and reflected the interests of the organisation (see Figure 13.1). Even though most of the businesses were divisionalised with profit responsibilities, in co-operating and planning their activities managers at each level of the organisation put the interest of the organisation first in the decisions they made. The fact that each manager at one stage of his or her career may have worked in other divisions seem to have influenced this strategic type of planning. Yet, in one of the companies, I also came across problems relating to the co-ordination of product policies within the European markets; as one of the sales managers explained:

> In our head office in Japan there is a division for consumer products which is responsible for all consumer products. They should, of course, balance the interests of the various product groups. The works, traditionally, in our company have had the power and possibility to decide which product to develop, to manufacture, which product to sell at which price. There was hardly any overall co-ordination and any possibility to develop an overall strategy. The difficulty this division has on the production side, I also have it in the Sales Company here in Europe. I should be able to say, 'Well, Germany perhaps is suffering a little bit, but Italy is making a profit and overall in Europe we are still happy because we are still making a profit', but that is not the case. When Germany is making a loss no-one cares about what we are doing in Italy or Spain or other countries.

When I discussed this point further with managers, I found that the recently set up European co-ordination centres were specifically designed to solve this type of product co-ordination problem within Europe. In the next section, we discuss these problems as part of the companies European strategies.

Corporate strategies and management control styles

All three of the companies had a mission statement which tended to be expressed in terms of philosophy and ethics. However this was combined with more specific strategy statements, pointing out the importance of, first, market share and then profitability, at the local subsidiary levels. As one manager commented:

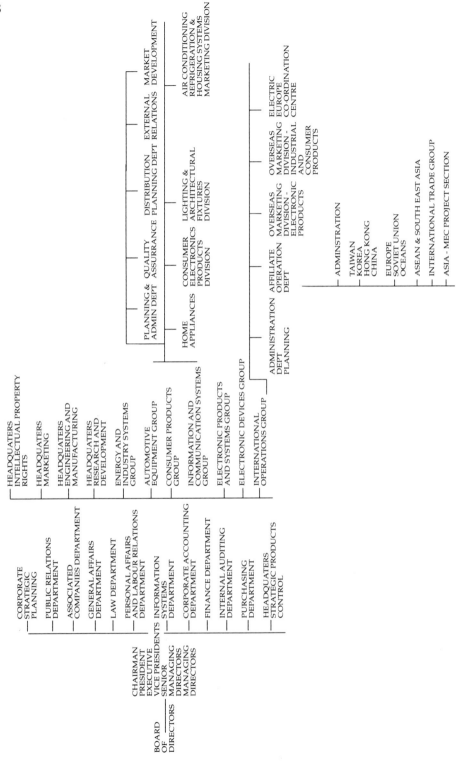

FIGURE 13.1

By my understanding the corporate mission of our company is to contribute to society. That is our final target. To human beings, not only in Japan, all over the world. But we need a profit to contribute to local society in Europe, the States or in Japan. So profit is a means of achieving the final target. Of course, to increase the profit, to some extent we need the market share or some position in the market, especially for the mass production. We need some sort of penetration in the market. The most excellent companies in the world, not only Japanese companies, but European companies, need market share in order to have profit and to contribute to their societies. So I think the market share is a factor.

Japanese companies involved in consumer products in the project are now posing the question, 'Should we stay in consumer goods?' In order to answer the question, they are evaluating the return and the loss in terms of exposure that the brand would enjoy, world wide and within the markets in which they operate. The most valuable thing the companies appear to have is their brand name. As one marketing manager explains:

> Largely our company is not a marketing company, it is an engineering company. It does not find the involvement in consumer products as interesting as its industrial involvement or its chemical involvement or its nuclear involvement. It is not the thrust of the business. But of course within Sony it is; Morita is driving a consumer company and he is very unusual for a Japanese. He is perhaps the only entrepreneur that I have ever met, he does drive the business, and the question will be of course what happens when that entrepreneur eventually dies, or retires or moves on. Because he is creating this momentum, there is a great difference between him and the Japanese style. But he, Morita, is dependent on consumer products, we're not. Sony is in consumer business; I don't know what the figures are, about 90% and the other 10% is professional studio equipment; that might not represent 10% but that is assuming that sort of ratio, 90% of their business is consumer products. Last year 13% of our business was in consumer products.

An understanding of the perception of UK subsidiary managers as to how management control systems (particularly performance evaluation measures) of their groups related to the overall corporate strategy was an important step in this research. It was found that the Japanese companies in the study had adopted a strategic planning type of management control style. Parent companies used divisionalisation but they did not fail to participate in and influence the development of divisional strategies by establishing demanding planning processes and making contributions of substance to strategic thinking. In general companies placed less emphasis on accounting and management control systems than on achieving smooth production or good quality products. Performance targets were set flexibly, and were reviewed within the context of long-term strategic progress. The pay-off to strategic decisions was sought in the long term, and it was accepted that there might be problems along the route to building up the core businesses.

The companies appeared to have been organised by functional departments supporting strong product groups in order to devolve strategic decision making. This matrix type of organisation required reviews at several levels: functional, product group and, more recently, geographic levels with a variety of inputs for the decision-making process. In these complex matrix organisations, strategic planning appeared to have sacrificed some clarity regarding responsibilities, initiative and interaction in and among business units. This was evident in the case of consumer electronic divisions and in particular in Group A. However this approach proved useful and appropriate where the existing portfolio of businesses had little overlap.

Relevant literature on UK companies indicated that many British companies are using a combination of management control styles, but I feel it might be difficult to find a 'correct formula' for success. This is because all styles must cope with basic conflicts or tensions that exist in the role of central management. Clear responsibilities are highly desirable as they enable tight control on a business unit, which in turn leads to more motivation to perform. Broad responsibility and autonomy at the business unit level leads to a greater sense of responsibility and support efforts to meet long-term objectives, but at the same time strong leadership produces purpose and direction.

Both strategic control and planning may be consistent with divisionalisation in organisations. However, if a profit centre is adopted with clear responsibilities, as in many UK companies with the financial control style, then it is difficult to have a matrix form of organisational structure designed to bring people together over major decisions. In these organisations, development of an organisational strategy might be carried out by managers closest to the business, but at the same time imposing strong leadership from the centre would not be consistent with the profit centre approach. Similarly tight controls cannot be combined with softer response to performance evaluations. A strict financial control regime might therefore be inappropriate with strategic planning. This is probably why some UK companies strike a balance between the extreme profit centre approach and strategic control which contrasts sharply with the Japanese companies' strategic planning style.

There appeared to be a strong willingness among the Japanese parent company managers to propose ideas for business units. Companies were generally concerned with market share, improved efficiency and cost reductions.

While all the companies were still largely dependent on parent company functions and manufacturing, there appeared to be clear moves in all the companies to have independent geographic centres set up. Although the basic design in all the companies was carried out in Japan, companies were increasing their design capabilities locally. All the companies had set up their European co-ordination centres with the intention that these would become independent units in the future.

European co-ordination centre: a means of compromise?

All the three companies have recently set up European co-ordination centres in order to co-ordinate the sales and manufacturing efforts of their companies.

They all operated on the basis that the factory was a profit centre. One of the roles of the European co-ordination centre was to redress the balance of power between the powerful works based in Japan and individual manufacturing and sales units scattered around Europe. Many Japanese companies started production in the UK only after 1985 and have not yet been able to incorporate British production into their previous sales network adequately. The setting up of the European centres was also designed to improve the distribution of the British production into other European sales companies. This reorganisation of the European control and distribution systems has been one of the crucial and urgent problems for the Japanese companies.

The reasons behind setting up the European co-ordination centre have been put by one of the managers in that new division as follows:

> What we are trying to do is to set up an office in London with product specialists for the European market. I would like to have two product specialists for each product area, one Japanese product planner and one European product marketing manager. The two, as a team, should understand the various European markets, Italy as well as Scandinavia, Holland as well as Spain and be able to define on a European level what product is necessary, a little bit more long term.

One of the managers indicated that the most important question in the last ten months had been how to set up the European co-ordination centre:

> In order to continue, to expand our business here in Europe we have to know in which direction Europe is going, to a single market perhaps. That is not so easy to explain in a short time. The United States of America is also a very big market but they are a single unit. In Europe, there are twelve different countries. They are going to a single market with a lot of directives from the EC government, so conditions are quite turbulent or changeable. In America when we proceed to business it is far easier than in Europe. For example, now we are going to have digital TV. European countries are going to have different systems, compared to the Japanese NHK systems or the American systems. With such a trend we have to get information, otherwise we cannot continue in the future.

One of the roles of the European co-ordination centre was to redress the balance of power between the powerful works based in Japan and individual manufacturing and sales units scattered around Europe. As one senior manager from the European co-ordination centre explained:

> The first step was to gather information on a European base. The second step was to have a strong power base here to propose the requirements in Europe to Japan. That's a very important role. So you see Europe as one market and you can speak with one voice, rather than different people going to Spain and then Japan and saying, we need this and that. The third step is to make decisions in Europe so that we can conclude most of the management decisions here; how much or how to invest the capital. Now this European Co-ordination Centre is the liaison office of our head office. We have not got the authority to make decisions here yet. When we

move into the third stage, we will have to re-organise for that part. This should be a holding company or an independent organisation.

In order to accomplish the objectives of the European centre, one of the companies established 'task forces' based at the European centre. This involved establishing 18 different task forces; nine product divisions/business units and a further nine functional teams. The functional task forces included, for example, distribution, tax or finance. Each task force had ten members. In all, 180 people were involved, but the same people could be in more than one task force. The task force teams often met the consumer products task force team from the parent factory, or the headquarters people. The objective was to get a consensus or an understanding at the same level and to speed up communication. Each task force team had a leader. The leaders were Japanese people working in the manufacturing side, and sometimes they came from the sales companies in Europe.

Manufacturing versus sales corporation

It was a surprise to find that the Japanese companies separated their manufacturing and sales elements and allowed them to operate quite independently of each other. Each had its own profit responsibility. The Japanese ethos seemed to be that, when you keep the sales separate from the manufacturing, the company as a whole is likely to benefit from the ensuing negotiations between these units. Each side will drive the other to be more effective and efficient. However I found that when there were small margins to be made it became difficult to conclude a satisfactory negotiation. It was often the stronger side which came out as the winner and traditionally it was the manufacturing works which had the greatest power in these negotiations. The sales companies in the UK were responsible for the UK sales, but sales to other overseas countries were handled from the manufacturing units. There were also links with the consumer product group and group sales headquarters in Japan. The problems of co-ordinating the activities of sales companies with manufacturing plants were expressed by a senior UK sales manager:

Each factory, or each sales company, is trying to optimise its own result, of course not looking at the total picture and the consequences that a certain decision may have on other products. To give an example, we have a leading position in the market for full-size camcorders. It is a relatively small segment, it is maybe 6 to 7 % of the market in Europe, but it is a profitable segment and it is a very stable segment. Now the factory has decided to drop one full-size camcorder, the top segment. This influences sales and profitability of other products. We are most likely to lose our market leader position in that small segment and thereby we become less interesting for dealers. It is becoming much more difficult in some areas of Europe to try and increase our television sales, because one factory decided that one product was not profitable enough and forgot completely about the impact that decision would have on other products. Although the sales companies were unhappy about it the factory decided to stop it. Instances like this are constantly occurring.

The problems created by the separation of sales companies from the manufacturing plants also contributed to the failure of market information being fed into the decision-making process of Japanese parent company managers from relevant works. As one marketing manager commented:

> People from the works and the factory, as from all Japanese companies, I think, have always been very active in visiting countries and sales companies. One of the problems, I think, is that they are Japanese people, they generally don't speak too much English and certainly they don't speak Italian and Spanish and French or German even. So when they come into the country, they first of all visit our sales company – most of the time they just spend in the office of the Japanese who is representing the company in that country. When they go out they go out with the Japanese – they visit a few stores, but they don't really talk to the salespeople, they certainly won't talk to consumers and I think it is impossible for them to really get a good feeling and understanding of the market.

Managers pointed out the problems of co-ordinating plans with the manufacturing plants in Japan. According to some managers interviewed, the negotiations between the Japanese and the local manufacturing plants did not appear to be independent. Furthermore certain preconditions such as providing a profitable budget and meeting medium term plans had to be satisfied.

Capital investment decisions

In my discussions with the senior British subsidiary managers I found that the senior parent company managers required long and complex formal procedures for major investment decisions. They were also often involved in detailed reviews aimed at key businesses. The centre appeared to be closely involved in most areas and there was a definite 'top-down' approach. A strong commitment to the corporate review of business strategies and plans was apparent in all the companies. All the parent companies retained the right to review and sanction capital investments but in most cases these were initiated by the business units. This was normally a part of the strategy review process. It was rather rare for the centre to reject proposals, and the process was more like a check on 'homework'. Major new initiatives were funded and managed centrally, with increasing willingness to invest massively behind a new strategic direction. Managers appeared to have taken a company-wide perspective which reduced the importance of the financial implications of a particular project. Projects seemed to be evaluated in terms of their contributions to the whole company and the significance of the financial decisions on a particular project was of secondary importance.

Overall there appeared to be less emphasis put on financial control than planning. As one manager indicated:

> I think in our company we are very concerned with profit. Also we are concerned with being seen to be a good employer and producing products and items which are required for people to enjoy or to improve their lives. I think what we want is to establish an operation which will exist comfortably in its environment; it will not be subject to peaks and troughs of the employment cycle or severe growth/depression periods. A company that will be able to operate over a long time and therefore will give some security of employment to those people either directly employed or involved through business relationships. To do that it has to be a company which is growing in sales value or through profitability or both.

The companies appeared to have developed structures and processes which allowed them to combine short-term financial focus with long-term strategic vision and planning. While companies stated that they used discounted cash flow and payback for the appraisal of new major projects, they did not seem to provide the essential decision criteria. The pressures to meet short-term financial targets were not allowed to detract from long-term progress. This approach did not permit short-termism such as was found in some of the UK companies studied by Demirag and Tylecote (1992a).

A senior manager in Group B also pointed out how strongly decentralised divisional profit responsibilities focused on short-term results were balanced by strategic vision and planning in his organisation.

> Clearly you are not going to make a profit out of consumer products in terms of just the hardware during the course of, say, the next 5 years. So it is very difficult for a management board to actually make a decision to invest in something that they know in the short term is not going to show them adequate returns. Because there is too much capacity in the consumer electronics business. What you are potentially doing is squeezing margins and some of the bigger ones will just drop off and say they don't want to play this game. They can only keep pumping money in for so long and then say, 'I give up, I don't want this any more.' Clearly the industry is going through that dip in terms of new development. We are now waiting for High Definition Television (HDTV), being the longer-term goal for the consumer electronics industry, being a profitable opportunity. Whether you get this depends on how much money you wish to invest to get there, not just in the product but also in the brand. You can't just put it on hold for four or five years and come back, by which time the brand will have been desecrated. I think the fundamental question is: does a Japanese corporation believe the consumer exposure is important to the rest of their business?

Performance measures

The findings showed that there was a considerable similarity in performance measures used in all the three groups studied. Companies placed significant emphasis on the overall corporate performance. Financial calculations appeared to have been integrated into productive and market assessments. Definition of performance was wider than that used in many British companies; I found that the companies studied placed much more emphasis on design, production and marketing than on financial control measures. At the same time I was told that increasingly profitability measures were becoming important in performance evaluations. Given the recent emphasis on decentralised operating policies for the foreign subsidiaries, this was not too surprising. Profit budgets, sales budgets and cash flow potential from the company to Japanese operations were also found to be important measures used by the companies. However it is worth mentioning that return on investment (ROI) was not ranked as a useful financial measure by any of the companies. I also found that companies often used several performance measures relating to product costs; these included break-even point, fixed and variable cost, personnel cost, sales per head, and profit and loss per head. Among the comparative measures, comparisons with other similar manufacturing units of the firm in different countries and earlier period balance sheet and income statements were ranked as the most useful comparative measures.

Japanese companies are very conscious of the fact that, if it is not possible to reduce costs or keep market share and prices high enough to earn a reasonable margin, it may not be possible to stay in a particular business line. They use market-driven product costing where prices are established on market conditions. They appear to be more concerned with market position than short-term profitability, as one manager argued:

> In consumer products especially, you can only get more profitable, I think, through increasing the volume of activity up to that level whereby you can be strong and secure. What that level is in Europe, of course I can't tell you yet. The only way you can make profit is through growth and cost reduction. As I said before, the level of profitability in consumer products is not significantly high – we are not talking 10% returns, we are talking about 3%.

This view is based on the principle that, if you can maintain or increase your market share, you can reduce cost per unit produced. This in turn will enable you to cut market prices and keep competitors out of business. In the longer term this will lead to more profitable businesses. After establishing the market price, companies determined a profit margin which was consistent with the firms' long-term strategy. The difference between the market price and the profit margin determined the cost of the products. Once the cost is determined, standard costs are established by the departments which contribute to the production of the product, assuming no innovation. Between these two estimates the organisation selects a target cost. When production starts, each department tries to cut its cost down so that the target costs become closer to the ideal. This is very different from the standard costing systems employed in many UK companies, as the target costing employed by the Japanese companies is more a function of prices than of ideal standards, but the target cost established for production managers is very close to an ideal standard.

The companies did not appear to be much concerned with the way overhead allocation techniques measure costs. However much concern was expressed as to how the allocation techniques encourage employees to reduce costs. In one of the companies studied I found that overhead was allocated according to the number of parts, and an overhead surcharge was applied against the non-standard parts. This was a good example of a company which was trying to cut the number of parts needed, especially the non-standard parts, for producing a product.

There was some scepticism over the use of financial measures among the senior management, who were more concerned with longer-term performance indicators such as R&D activity and percentage of new products introduced. While there was concern for profit-related financial measures, emphasis appeared to be placed on market share growth and maintaining it, thus indicating a longer-term perspective. It became apparent to me that companies were paying more attention to their informal measures of performance than formal ones. Companies indicated that their management viewed financial measures only as an aid to decision making. As the companies did not care much about financial performance I was not surprised to find that none of the companies appeared to make the distinction between the performance of the operating units and the managers' own performance.

Profit budgeting

A formal system of annual profit budgeting was common to all the case study companies. UK management was held responsible by the parent company management for meeting these budgets but in subsequent discussions with the senior managers I found that parent company managers were understanding and sympathetic towards the variances from the budgets.

The yearly budgets for the whole organisation were prepared in Japan after each country independently reported their figures in local currencies. The process of establishing budgets involved discussions and negotiations with the parent company management after each manufacturing plant submitted a proposal for its production plans to Japan, having consulted the European co-ordination centre on market conditions in Europe. Once the production plans were agreed, manufacturing units prepared their budgets for the following year. In preparing the budgets, sales companies guaranteed purchase of the next six months' projected sales. The Japanese manufacturing plants 'works' were also involved in these production plans because approximately 30–40 per cent of materials and components were imported from Japanese plants.

It was interesting to discover that Japanese parent company management generally set financial targets. These were initially developed by the local managers and they included profit, return on investment and return on assets. The annual profit budgets were then prepared by the UK management after consulting either the parent company management or, where applicable, the European headquarters. In all cases these budgets were formally reviewed by the Japanese parent company management who rarely changed the proposed budgets. The overall philosophy appeared to aim at a consensus position, through constructive dialogue and negotiations in which both top and lower levels of management reached agreement on realistic levels of achievement.

The detail of the profit budgets depended on the situation but generally they included income statement and balance sheet with appropriate supporting schedules which included cash flow and capital expenditure statements. Profit objectives in budgets were determined mainly by improvements from previous time periods and forecasts of economic conditions, and on the basis of the company's global objectives. All the companies reported actual performance of profits against monthly budgets and profit budgets were revised every six months, if necessary. I found that companies measured variances against original and revised budgets. A detailed analysis of variance by causal factors was carried out but the analysis of variance caused by exchange rate changes was always ignored.

Currency choice of performance measures

All the three companies indicated that financial statements presented in terms of sterling (local currency) provided them with better understanding of the performance of their companies' operations and their management (see Demirag, 1986, 1988). Statements prepared in local currency reflected the local environmental conditions and were more useful in planning and control than statements expressed in parent currencies after foreign currency translations. From in-depth discussions with the senior managers it was found that companies generally preferred local currency statements for convenience reasons, as sterling statements were more familiar to UK operation staff. However it was surprising to find that their policy to evaluate foreign subsidiary performance in yen or in local currency did not vary between subsidiaries. This might be because foreign management control systems used by Japanese foreign manufacturing companies were not tailor-made for the requirements of each foreign location and instead they were exported from their Japanese parent companies. None of the companies translated their profit budgets into yen for performance evaluation purposes. Similarly companies did not adjust their profit and loss account or balance sheet statements for price-level changes. I noticed that none of the parent companies sent a copy of the translated yen statements. This situation left foreign subsidiary managers unaware of their performance in parent company currency terms. This may not matter much as British managers are evaluated in local currencies. It is perhaps for this reason that the budgets were sent to Japan in local currency and then they were translated into yen by using some company fixed standard rate. When they evaluated the actual performance relative to the budget they used the same corporate fixed rate used in setting the budgets. They also used the actual rate at the end of the budget period to translate the actual results. This was generally for financial reporting rather than internal evaluation reasons.

It would appear that the companies were trying to do two things: first, by using the same budgeted fixed rate at the end of the budget period, they were finding out the deviations in profit as a result of changes in local operating environment; secondly, by using the actual exchange rate at the end of the period, they were determining total deviations from the budgets, including the full impact of exchange rate changes on managers' operating performance. Companies in the survey rarely used hedging for foreign currency movements and when they did this was not co-ordinated on a company basis.

Responsibilities for currency risk management

Foreign exchange risk management programme was either relatively decentralised or completely decentralised. All the companies had a manager or managers acting independently or as a group who were formally charged with the task of managing the exchange risk for their companies.

The companies did not seem to be concerned with the policy impact of accounting standards and were more interested in the underlying economic activities. This is different from the findings of studies on UK and US companies where accounting policies and standards influenced companies' actual operating decisions. The Japanese companies in this study and also in a recent study by Bromwich and Inoue (1992) indicated their interest in areas like target costing, achieving the desired 'yield ratio', reducing costs, and improving quality and distribution systems, rather than in financial controls. It is perhaps for this reason that the Japanese companies in the study ignored foreign currency translation gains and losses for the purpose of evaluating managers' own performance in the UK. Similarly foreign currency transaction gains and losses seemed to be managed according to the budgeted rates provided by the parent company management. While the gains and losses were separately reported, they did not seem to be directly related to any particular manager's performance.

It was interesting to notice that most of the manufacturing units in the UK sold their products in local currency so they did not have any adverse affects of exchange rate movements on their operating profits. This was probably because all their output was sold to their sales companies in different countries and the individual sales companies abroad had the responsibility to manage their own currency exposure. The companies' basic philosophy on exchange rate was that there was no incentive to be in a gain or loss situation: the objective was to be neutral, so you covered everything you could according to the budget rate. The decision whether to cover the current situation or not was determined by the subsidiary managers' own forecast of exchange rates. If their forecast rate was more favourable than the budgeted rate then they would have the incentive to take cover.

Performance rewards

All company members who were below the grade of middle manager had an annual salary review by a 'company members' board' which included representatives of a union, middle management, senior managers and an executive manager. I saw their role as to try and come up with a consensus recommendation on wage review. When they failed to reach an agreement, a negotiation between the company and unions took place. Arbitration was used as the final step if there was no agreement. It was also found that in addition to this annual review there was an assessment procedure for every company member twice a year. This was based on either nine or ten factors which had been established for several years and which were subject to a review by a joint working party under the auspices of ACAS, who came up with some amendments to it, such as time keeping, absence and overtime working, and others such as responsibility, creativity and reliability. Some other smaller schemes to encourage participation and reward accordingly were also found . These included methods of improving quality, stock control, efficiency and reducing costs. Performance of senior and executive managers was generally rewarded on informal evaluations, taking into account financial and non-financial performance criteria as previously discussed under performance measures.

Conclusions

The strategic objectives of the Japanese companies operating in the UK were on the whole directed towards sales and market share growth within the European Community countries. In one of the companies separation of sales companies from manufacturing seemed to have caused some problems in relation to product planning and design which were found to be generally reserved for Japanese parent companies. All the companies have recently set up their European headquarters partly to deal with these problems of centralisation in these areas. Although investment decisions involved bureaucratic procedures, strategic considerations dominated the decision process. In contrast to some of the divisionalised UK companies, Japanese companies operating in Britain were not yet subjected to short-term pressures. However it is difficult to speculate as to what things will look like in a few years' time when the vastly increased pressures for profits arising from the recent revaluation of the yen and recession have worked through the system. It was found that in general companies paid less attention to financial control systems than to achieving smooth production or good quality products. The Japanese companies in the study accorded market share the highest importance among the performance measures used for internal evaluations. While profitability measures were given increasingly high importance, they were used with great care so as to obtain consensus position through constructive dialogue and negotiations in which realistic levels of objectives were attained. This approach to performance evaluations was very different from those found in many of the UK companies, where financial controls were strictly used in order to increase short-term profits at the expense of longer-term benefits in areas such as research and development and management training. Financial rewards were awarded for reducing product costs and improving working environment, but job security, opportunities for promotion and workers' welfare were also used as other benefits available to the employees. Foreign currency risk management focused on only large transactions as most sales were made in local currencies. The use of a company forward rate for operating budgets protected local managers from any adverse impact of currency changes on their operating performance.

Notes

The author wishes to thank the research boards of the Chartered Institute of Management Accountants, Matsushita Research Foundation and Sheffield University Research Funds for providing financial support for the project.

The author is also indebted to many individuals for their encouragement, help and advice, in particular to Kiyoshi Ogawa, Tomoaki Sakano and Yoshihide Iwabuchi, who have also helped to set up interviews with senior Japanese managers in Britain; to Peter Armstrong, Andrew Tylecote, Jane Broadbent, Olav Jull Sorensen, Richard Laughlin, Tony Berry, and to Keith Harrison and others who commented on an earlier version of the paper presented at the British Accounting Association Northern Accounting Group in September 1993; and to the managers who co-operated and gave so much of their precious time whose names will remain anonymous for confidentiality reasons.

A copy of the questionnaire is available from the author on request.

CHAPTER 14

Management accounting: the Western problematic against the Japanese application

Karel Williams, Colin Haslam, John Williams, Makoto Abe, Toshio Aida, Itsutomo Mitsui

Management accounting (MA) in Japan as practised by a group of leading companies is often described and compared to the principles of MA in the Anglo-American tradition as exemplified in leading texts. Western textbook MA is shown to be a poor basis for productive intervention because it rests on a defective implicit model of manufacturing production which takes a single-product, single-process view of production and neglects the gains in labour and capital efficiency which can be realised by low stocks, small batches, faster set-up and improved layout. Little attention is paid to new product planning and development, whereas leading Japanese firms give these aspects of practice a privileged place corresponding to investment project appraisal in Western theory. The Japanese application of MA is shown to be of both intellectual interest and practical importance: it enables the exploitation of points of intervention which have been invisible (mostly) in the West, allowing Japanese companies to generate continuous cost reduction.

The object of analysis in this chapter is the difference between Anglo-American and Japanese management accounting (MA). We started to answer this question by acquiring information on the Japanese application of MA in manufacturing firms through an investigation of practices in some Japanese car and electronics companies. During the spring of 1990, in Japan, we interviewed senior management accountants in two large car companies (Toyota and Nissan) and three electronics companies of varying size (NEC, Sony TV division and Kenwood). These sources did not provide a straightforward answer: instead they revealed to us a methodological problem about how to analyse similarity and difference.

Many of the elements of Western MA can be found in Japanese firms which use calculative formulae like standard costing, budgeting or discounted cash flow (DCF). But the frequency of the elements is different when, for example, DCF is not universally used in investment appraisal. Furthermore the relation between the elements is different: as Monden (1990, p. 30) observes, standard costing is mainly used for financial reporting, not for MA. Increasingly it was realised that these differences of relation amounted to much more than just shifts in the nuances with which accounting formulae were interpreted and used. When we reviewed our interview material, we were impressed by quite radical differences in the articulation of accounting with (non-financial) market and productive calculation, as well as with forms of intervention in manufacturing practice.

What our research does show is that there is a substantial disjuncture between the Anglo-American theory of MA and the Japanese application. We argue that this disjuncture centres on a difference of representational presuppositions where the practice of Japanese firms rejects the assumptions of Western theory. This difference is of considerable importance to any Western firm whose practice is consonant with Western theory and it may also have significance for the way MA is generally taught in the West.

This said, it is necessary to enter a few cautionary comments and disclaimers. This chapter concentrates attention on one particular aspect of manufacturing activity, the part played by management accounting. We argue that the use made of MA in Japan, together with the considerable constraints on its use, is more beneficial and effective than the techniques highlighted in the leading Western MA texts. From this perspective the Japanese companies are rightly credited with intellectual foresight and productive virtue. If Japanese manufacturing was being viewed more broadly then other, rather darker, aspects of Japanese practice would demand more attention, as well as a more critical approach to the exaggerated claims often made by Western writers about the extent of Japanese productive superiority. We have attempted to confront each of these broader issues elsewhere, in work which questions the exaggerated and uncritical Japanolatry of much Western social science (Williams *et al.*, 1991, 1992).

The problematic of Western MA

Our account of this problematic is based on a reading of a number of American and British MA textbooks. In them it is clear that the standard techniques not only limit the field of the visible but also promote an implicit model of production which is largely contradicted by the current engineering knowledge of manufacturing production (see, for example, Schonberger, 1986). This engineering knowledge discloses many distinctive features of manufacturing activity which are mostly invisible in the MA textbooks. Point by point, the assumptions and assertions made in the textbook exposition of calculative formulae can be contrasted with the knowledge of production in mainstream production texts such as Hayes *et al.* (1988) and in articles such as our own on specific aspects of manufacturing (Williams, 1989a, 1986, 1991). In the six points below, the theses of production engineering are set against the antithesis of MA.

Thesis 1: modern manufacturing is a complex multi-process activity where many of the problems and opportunities arise from the reduction of waiting time and queues between process points.

Against this, in conceptualising production, Anglo-American MA focuses on the brief moments when value is added through conversion rather than the long intervals of waiting when costs are incurred. The standard techniques promote an analytic perspective focusing on the single product, process department or investment project. Synthesis through documents like the master budget is profoundly unilluminating because estimates of sales and production have to be broken down so that they connect with the analytic techniques and categories used in lower-level responsibility centres.

Thesis 2: stock reduction is an imperative which realises large benefits because 'stocks hide problems' like line imbalance and machine unreliability. The cost of stocks is high mainly because stock movement requires (unnecessary) indirects.

Against this stocks are virtually invisible in MA texts which still sometimes treat inventory turnover only as a liquidity ratio which measures debt-paying ability (for example, Ricketts and Gray, 1988, pp. 601, 607–8). MA texts never realistically compute the cost of stocks: the general assumption is that inventory costs equal the opportunity cost of the money tied up in stocks (Horngren, 1981, pp. 494–7). This is true even in texts which seem to cover other possibilities. One such recent text gives a list of costs of holding stocks: it is headed by the opportunity cost of the capital which is then followed by 'Insurance and Property taxes'. Not only is 'handling' low on the list, it is unexplained and appear not at all in ensuing discussions which feature only the capital and ordering costs (Wolk *et al.*, 1988, pp. 307–11).

The point about high stocks and more indirects is never taken on board because overhead is a vague residual category which includes everything except materials and direct labour. Overhead is allocated (rather than decomposed), so overhead items can be listed without examining their relative importance (Ricketts and Gray, 1988, pp. 28, 559; Wolk *et al.*, 1988, pp. 165, 173, 181; Horngren and Sundem, 1991, chs 10 and 16; Horngren and Foster, 1991, pp. 35–7, 40–1). The presentation of overhead as 'joint costs which benefit several products' (for example, Ricketts and Gray, 1988, p. 94) encourages the notion that all overhead is necessary. Discussion does not focus on how overhead can be reduced because 'the most important thing to note about manufacturing overhead is the fact that ... it is not easily traceable to specific units of output' (Wolk, *et al.*, 1988, p. 19).

Thesis 3: with fixed capital equipment in manufacturing, the most important issue is 'not what you have but how you use it'. Capital and labour productivity can usually be steadily raised by modifying machines for specific tasks and designing short-travel shop layouts.

Against this, MA texts assume that capacity and efficiency are fixed at the level set by 'currently available standards based on efficient operating conditions' (Ricketts and Gray, 1988, pp. 341–2, 357). Machine modification and better layout are ignored presumably because low-cost improvement is too paradoxical for the discourse (Horngren and Sundem, 1991; Allen and Myddleton, 1987; Anthony, *et al.*, 1984; Horngren and Foster, 1991). And the implicit technical determinism of the upper limit is reflected as language slips towards a narrow concept of control as policing the negative variances (Ricketts and Gray, 1988, pp. 321, 350, 354, 356) or implying that, if there are no exceptions or deviations from planned performance, management need not spend precious time where it is not needed (Wolk *et al.*, 1988, p. 302).

Thesis 4: faster set-up and changeover is essential if high rates of machine utilisation are to be maintained as batch size is reduced. Small batches are essential in a low-stocks, mixed-model factory.

Against this, set-up and changeover do not figure at all in Ricketts and Gray's main text where factories run without incurring these costs (Ricketts and Gray, 1988, chas 2–5). In other MA texts, set-up is discussed in the sections on EOQ which treat set-up as a fixed parameter in relation to which batch size should be adjusted as a dependent variable (Drury, 1988; Horngren 1981) or, having said set-up time can be substituted in Economic Order Quality (EOQ) formulae for order costs if management is interested in optimum batch size, evade any need to evaluate this alternative by asserting that 'the switch in application is straightforward' (Wolk *et al.*, 1988, p. 311).

Thesis 5: modern manufacturing remains a remarkably labour-intensive activity where internally controlled labour typically accounts for 30 per cent of costs and 70 per cent of value added.

Against this, the Anglo-American MA texts rarely have anything sensible to say about labour's share in costs or value added because labour, apart from direct labour, is bundled into such general categories as overheads as part of the process of allocating costs. Standard costing focuses attention on direct labour which is generally supposed to account for less than 10 per cent of manufacturing costs. This diverts attention from the more important issues about indirect labour and the embodied labour in materials.

Thesis 6: materials and components usually account for 50 per cent or more of costs and these items can be controlled through design to cost in the development stage and through constructive relations with suppliers.

Against this, MA texts are nearly 100 per cent preoccupied with production. They say little about the design and development phase and nothing about the scope for cost reduction in that phase, while the standard category of 'research and development' either does not appear (Wolk *et al.*, 1988) or hardly appears (Horngren and Foster, 1991, p. 411) or suggests that development is a necessary expense (Ricketts and Gray, 1988, pp. 180, 495). In discussions of make or buy and other issues (Wolk *et al.*, 1988, pp. 416–19; Ricketts and Gray, 1988, p. 270) it is throughout assumed that assembler-manufacturers have an arms'-length financial relation with suppliers.

The problem is not simply that MA restricts the field of the visible; it also comprehensively misspecifies the points of intervention and causal relations in the activity of manufacturing. For these reasons we cannot accept MA's own assurance that it delivers neutral relevant information for decision making. In manufacturing, this claim is an unsustainable pretension which covers up a tendentious account of the interests of the firm and a completely inadequate guide to the problems and possibilities of manufacturing activity. Any subject (academic or manager) who attempted to use the discourse to define the field of the visible would literally not know what to do in a manufacturing firm. When Ricketts and Gray (1988, pp. 179–80), for example, discuss how managers might reduce costs they immediately focus on materials and direct labour; the two options presented are to use less expensive materials or buy capital equipment to take out (direct) labour. Their field of the visible does not include the two more interesting and effective options of improving process efficiency through layout and set-up improvements or reducing overhead through stock reduction which saves indirect workers.

The broad characterisation of Anglo-American MA which has been presented is substantially confirmed in the findings of a recent study based on a large-scale examination of the textbooks (Scapens, 1991). The 'core material has not changed substantially during recent decades' (ibid., p. 12); 'the terms cost accounting and management accounting now tend to be used synonymously in textbook titles' (p. 10); 'current management accounting textbooks give particular attention to the classification of costs as fixed or variable' (p. 15); 'the measurement of performance in terms of variance ... is the primary method of managerial control' (p. 17); economics was the dominating influence and profit maximisation 'accruing to the owners of the business' the basic motivation (p. 23); whilst practitioners found it difficult to implement the techniques being taught (p. 33).

'Textbooks, in particular, and the accounting education process, more generally, are still firmly grounded in the traditions of the past' (Hopwood, in Clark *et al.*, 1985, p. 230) and the major changes in 'manufacturing operations are hardly anywhere reflected in contemporary cost accounting courses and materials' largely because it was exceptional 'for an accounting major to take a course in production, manufacturing processes or technology (Kaplan, 1985, pp. 223–4). The new directions which were flagged related to accounting's involvement in 'organizational power structures' and especially the 'rise to power of the corporate accountant and financial manager' as a 'phenomenon of the Atlantic fringe countries' (Hopwood, 1985, pp. 232–3). If these issues were important in themselves, they only related obliquely to our concern with

MA's relevance to the productive aspects of manufacturing; though it is fair to acknowledge Mackey's (1991) chapter in Ashton *et al.* (1991) which directly addresses production.

Much the same message is conveyed by recent books bringing together essays from a number of academic researchers in America and Britain (Bruns and Kaplan, 1987; Ashton *et al.*, 1991). These register the dissatisfaction felt by 'leading edge' scholars at the gap between accounting research and practice. It is also recognised (Ashton *et al.*, 1991, p. 4) that what has been embodied in the textbooks 'entailed the application of neo-classical economic theory to the problems of decision-making and control'. The models and techniques were attempts to programme the decision-making and control processes. It was assumed that the objective of management decision making is to maximise the wealth of shareholders. Such professional self-criticism is to be welcomed but it does not make redundant our own strictures because the 'issues in management accounting' are mostly concerned with the techniques of, and technical developments in, Western MA. In this sense the approach (Anglo-American) is insular. The key issue is to demote purely economics-based techniques from their overriding dominance and to make more room for social, legal and behavioural considerations. The allocation of costs (Ahmed and Scapens, 1991) and transfer pricing (Ezzamel, 1992) are reworked on this basis.

Such concern might appear to be more directly confronted in other examples of the 'worrying about MA' literature, exemplified by Johnson and Kaplan's (1987) recent well-received text. It is part of our contention that this literature proposes what might indelicately be termed 'largely irrelevant' reforms of MA because it remains within the original problematic which defines largely imaginary problems. To illustrate this point we will take a brief closer look at the text of *Relevance Lost*.

Johnson and Kaplan's title embodies their conservative problem definition. These authors do not query the object of profit; indeed they insist quite explicitly that the role of MA inside hierarchies is to generate substitutes for the price signals which the market would otherwise provide. Johnson and Kaplan's problem is simply that twentieth-century American management accounting has used relatively crude techniques which generate incorrect and irrelevant signals for internal use. They particularly criticise the general adoption, after 1918, of simple systems which absorb overhead by applying a multiplicand to the direct labour used in products and processes. In their view this simplifying procedure reflects the malign influence of external financial reporting requirements and the high costs of pre-electronic, manual data processing. The multiplication exercise is adequate for financial reporting purposes as long as all the overhead is absorbed, but the exercise allocates overhead to individual products on an arbitrary basis and thus does not generate adequate and accurate MA information on the cost of individual product lines. Procedures such as standard costing may have adequately represented manufacturing in an earlier era, but various developments, such as the growth of overhead and the substitution of capital for labour, have rendered the old formulae obsolete.

Johnson and Kaplan's solution is unitary with their problem definition. After accepting the validity of the neo-Kantian correspondence in an earlier historical era, their reform proposal must take the form of a neo-Kantian project. Their solution is to refine the techniques of MA and attach costs more precisely to products and processes so as to restore the lost correspondence between accounting reason and productive being. In product costing, the aim should be to determine long-run costs of production by subdividing overhead costs and attaching them to individual products. In process control the aim should be to understand short-run variation in costs by identifying the heterogeneous cost drivers specific to the activity. This second project is pressed by the current advocates of activity-based costing who take up the internal reform project of restoring a lost correspondence. Through its insistence on identifying relevant cost drivers, activity-based costing (ABC) does make new concessions to the diversity of different businesses, but that still allows the old technical objective of attaching costs to products to be secured and the privilege of the technique to be reasserted.

Critical MA does not succeed as a defensive move within the problematic. Many of the technical problems of cost accounting are practically insoluble when for example, it is not always possible to allocate selling expenses accurately to individual products. The general MA concern with predicting the future creates further problems. In DCF, for example, the financial values depend on productive and market estimates of operating efficiency and market share. More fundamentally, even if all the technical estimation problems could be solved, the reform proposals do not confront the problem that having better financial numbers within the MA problematic does not mean knowing what to do.

This issue is nicely brought into focus by one of Johnson and Kaplan's examples where they discuss the case of a manufacturing firm which, after MA reform, discovers that 23 per cent of a plant's products account for 85 per cent of total dollar sales and 400 per cent of the plant's profits (Johnson and Kaplan, 1987, pp. 240–41). The activity of throwing light on dark corners tends to be treated as an end in itself in critical MA. But, of course, the practical question is, what should the firm do next? The costing information provides no basis for deciding whether the company should accept low profits or losses on some of its lines, whether the unprofitable lines should be deleted, or whether prices should be raised. There can hardly be a simple financial answer to the question of whether the firm should carry on as a full(er) line producer. Furthermore the costing information provides no guidance as to whether and how margins on the unprofitable lines might be increased by expedients such as shorter, cheaper set up which would improve margins on short-run, low-volume products.

In response to such criticisms, the classic Anglo-American MA defence is that it is 'better to know the financial numbers'. As Johnson and Kaplan (1987, p. 241) observe in their discussion of the example we have cited, 'there are many actions we can contemplate or take once we understand the problem'. That defence may have common sense on its side, but it is hardly convincing after the inadequacies of the MA problematic have been exposed. A manufacturing firm which knew the numbers in a MA problematic would be disabled rather than empowered by that knowledge. It would be altogether more sensible to reject the problematic of MA and, in our view, this is what Japanese manufacturers have done to their considerable advantage.

The Japanese application of MA in a production and marketing-centred system

In practice it is seldom possible to make a complete break. Thus the Japanese do not eschew or proscribe all MA techniques, but they apply these techniques in a different way in a production and marketing-centred manufacturing system where the techniques are used by firms that break with the problematic of MA. In Japanese firms financial calculations are integrated into productive and market calculations; the result is a three-dimensional view which denies the universal representational privilege of financial numbers. Furthermore the integration of different kinds of calculation broadens out the definition of performance and identifies new points of intervention in a way which undermines the privilege of financial guidance techniques; in Japanese firms the main practical emphasis is on productive and market intervention rather than orthodox financial control. The absence of financial control can partly be explained by the economic context: the interviews were conducted in the spring of 1990 before the onset of the recession. But this particular chronological context does not explain the preoccupation with productive and market interventions. These points can be illustrated and exemplified if we begin by considering the difference of Japanese practice in the appraisal of divisional or affiliate performance and in the appraisal of investment projects.

There is less emphasis on the appraisal of divisional or affiliate performance in Japan because of institutional differences; Japanese manufacturing favours a loose affiliate structure rather than tight divisional organisation and, at every level, there is less stockholder pressure for the distribution of dividends. In appraising affiliates, Japanese companies do not use ROI and RI measures exclusively, as in the theory of MA or much current American practice. As Monden emphasises, Japanese companies use a variety of heterogeneous measures; these include productivity, sales growth and market share as well as ROI and RI. This is a significant difference because the Japanese measures incorporate a broader multidimensional view of market and productive as well as financial success.

Investment project analysis is again much less important in Japan for institutional and practical reasons. Most large Japanese manufacturing companies have been cash-rich and rationing funds between competing investment projects has not been a real problem; for much of the 1980s, firms like Toyota diverted funds into various kinds of financial activity because their manufacturing businesses could not absorb the operating surplus which they generated. When interviewed in 1990, senior Japanese management accountants who had operated in this context had difficulty in answering questions about the appraisal of abstracted, individual projects. They insisted that it was necessary to take a company-wide perspective which made the financial numbers on the particular project a secondary consideration; at Toyota we were told:

> if the figures do not appear to be favourable, we try to understand the merit from the point of all Toyota. And if we judge it worthwhile, we do it ... Because the project is evaluated in [terms of its contribution to] the whole company, the importance is calculated not only in figures.

Again, this is a significant difference because the company's interest is not defined as the sum of an iterative series of financial decisions on individual projects.

The DCF calculations which feature so prominently in Western textbooks and in American practice have had a relatively minor place in Japanese companies. It is possible to find large, well-run companies like NEC which never make DCF calculations, and other companies like Toyota which make DCF calculations, but quite explicitly do not use them as a decision principle. The Japanese approach to investment is to think in terms of cash flow and payback: in all three electronics companies, the simple rule of thumb was payback 'within three years' or 'in two to three years'. For Westerners, it seems paradoxical that firms which take a relaxed whole company view of investment should at the same time insist that they expect, and generally achieve, a short-term payback. For Japanese managers, the two positions are not paradoxical or incompatible. Rapid payback is regarded as unproblematic because they put great emphasis on practical intervention for cost reduction, which is very different from the Western textbook stereotype of financial calculation for cost maintenance. Cost reduction is achieved in two phases: first, in the product planning and development phase and, second, through managing operations.

The Japanese break with the Western problematic of MA because they attach great importance to the phase of development before production begins, which is almost completely ignored in the Western MA textbooks. The irrefutable argument for this is that most of a product's cost is determined in the design stage before it goes into production. Japanese management accountants also insist that model changeover and the introduction of new models is the point at which the firm naturally makes its major investment choices. Generally, in Japanese practice, product planning and development occupies the place corresponding to investment project appraisal in the Western problematic of MA. In that problematic it is assumed that firms can be guided to financial success by the allocation of capital to more profitable projects. In Japanese practice, the emphasis is on the attainment of target levels of cost which will not only safeguard profit but also maintain or increase market share and sales revenue. As we will argue later, capital expenditure is controlled indirectly through the procedures which limit and reduce costs in model development.

The general Japanese approach to new product development could be described as design for cost reduction and the role of financial calculation in this process is to serve as the relay between productive and market calculation. Design for cost reduction is implemented in different ways because the problems and opportunities vary according to the nature of the product. Cost reduction is relatively straightfoward in quasi-commodity product lines. In television, for example, Sony told us that the main consideration was simply to reduce the number of components in the new chassis which are introduced at three-yearly intervals. Kenwood's approach was similar, but rather more abstract and financial, because the aim here was to reduce the ratio of material costs to sales or cost of sales. But in the development of complex mechanical engineering products, like motor cars, Japanese firms use elaborate systems of cost planning on spreadsheets which are designed to dramatise the internal trade-offs at the same time as they illustrate the connection to the market.

In Nissan, the 'product manager', who is responsible for the development of one new model, is given a 'contribution target' for profit by top management. The unorthodox definition of contribution (as revenue – materials + direct labour + depreciation + R & D) had been introduced because it suited the task of new model cost reduction in this particular business; the manager who had designed the spreadsheet knew, and did not care, that it did not define contribution in the correct Western way. At Nissan, the basic rule is that the product manager has to make the contribution which is set so that overall costs have to be reduced. But the product manager is free to spend more on one item such as capital equipment if he can make savings elsewhere, for example in direct labour. The connection to the market is established by the provision for detailed projections of units sold and prices realised on cars produced and sold at home and overseas; this allows the product manager to consider the consequences of different kinds of pricing strategy in various markets. The spreadsheet also allows the product manager to consider feedback linkages; for example, more expenditure on development may generate product features which increase sales revenue.

Some Japanese companies put most of their effort into cost reduction in the product planning and development phase. Nissan, whose factories have never operated at anything like the Toyota level of integration, claimed: 'We changed our approach from the old approach of minimising cost in the production phase to the new approach of taking account of cost reduction in the planning phase.' However the other four companies we interviewed saw cost reduction in the production phase as a necessary follow-up to cost reduction in planning. A firm like Toyota maintains its traditional obsession with increasing operational efficiency and continuously improving labour utilisation.

Generally Japanese management accountants (like the line managers we interviewed in an earlier research trip) are convinced that the aim of production management should be cost reduction through 'Kaizen' steps to improvement, rather than cost maintenance through the normalisation of negative variance. As Toyota's senior management accountant observed: 'We always seek Kaizen, not only maintenance of present cost.' And there can be no doubt that reductions in production cost are regularly achieved in firms which privilege this objective. Indeed in some firms a Kaizen assumption is built into the firm's internal operating procedures; at Sony TV, for example, the division sells its products to the parent organisation at a transfer price which is reduced by 10 per cent each year.

Japanese practice demotes and marginalises cost accounting to show which product is more profitable: Nissan told us cheerfully 'we threw it away' and some companies like Toyota appear never to have used cost accounting for internal MA purposes. In the Japanese system profitability should be guaranteed by design intervention before the product goes into production. And, once the product is in production, product line or batch costing is of little interest to volume manufacturing companies whose factories operate mixed model lines and feature rapid low-cost changeover. The more relevant consideration is costs incurred or resources consumed at the factory and shop level where companies track and enforce progress through budget and target systems. If budgeting is used extensively in Japanese manufacturing firms, its articulation to production is quite different. In the Western problematic of MA (negative) financial variance against a (constant) standard is used as an indicator of the need for intervention. In the Japanese practice of factory and shop Kaizen (tightening), financial standards are used to enforce constant productive improvement which is indicated by physical measures.

The philosophy of Japanese manufacturing companies in MA, as in organisational design, is to strip out unnecessary intermediate layers. In the production phase, the aim is to move directly from financial targets, which are set by top management for each factory, to direct physical measures of process efficiency at plant or shop level. The overall picture in our five companies corresponds to what we sketched in an earlier article on car press shops (Williams, 1991). As a result, in Japanese practice, the balance between financial and physical calculation is tilted very strongly towards the physical. The incorporation of the physical breaks the universalism which is such a characteristic feature of the Western MA problematic because the physical measures vary according to the nature of the plant and process. In a NEC semiconductor plant the measures are yield and machine utilisation, whereas in a car company press shop they would typically be power-strokes per man-hour and die changes per month.

As far as one can judge, there is no general retreat from labour-centred measures. Many Japanese firms remain preoccupied with the reduction of (direct and indirect) labour hours. Toyota told us that labour supplied 50 per cent of the Kaizen cost reduction inside the company, although labour only accounted for 30 per cent of total costs. And, although each TV set now contains only one and a half hours of labour, Sony claimed the reduction of labour hours was still a priority because all the company's competitors were capable of redesigning chassis to incorporate fewer components. The focus on labour in production arises partly because materials and component savings are usually obtained in the design and pre-production phase when investment is also fixed; thus the responsibility of the factory managers in companies like Toyota and Sony is simply to ensure 'labour and machine utilisation'. Whatever the operational targets, the factory level imperative is the same: production managers must intervene continuously and positively to improve the physical indicator so that the budget target becomes attainable.

If we sum up the argument so far about Japanese practice, our account of enterprise calculation shows how MA is broken into pieces and used instrumentally in Japan. The recombination of elements realises productive and market objectives which have the same status as financial results; it also finds new points of intervention and new outcomes such as continuous improvement. These valuable results, which arise from the integration of productive, market and financial calculation are safeguarded by a number of heuristic principles which are respected in most Japanese manufacturing firms. Four of these principles are briefly described below.

Organisational integration of the MA function as a staff contribution to a team effort

It is well known that the Japanese economy operates with a tiny number of externally qualified accounting specialists; in 1986 the total number of professionally qualified accountants in Japan was 7837 (Choi and Hiramatsu, 1987, p. 186). From our point of view, we would argue that an external pedagogy of accounting and the mass production of certificated accounting specialists is unnecessary in a national manufacturing sector which depends on company-specific articulations of financial, productive and market calculation; the companies we researched met their own needs for MA specialists who could apply MA in their individual house style and would thus know what to do.

The detail of departmental organisation varies. In some firms one head office department is responsible for both management accounting and financial accounting; in other firms the two functions are carried out by separate departments. Whatever the organisational form, the number of head office specialists engaged in MA is very small. The larger of our two car companies, Toyota, employed more than 90 000 worldwide; its central accounting department employed just 80 executives in management accounting (excluding female clerical workers). The largest of our electronic companies, NEC, employed 40 000 worldwide; its central accounting department employed 180 executives in management accounting (excluding female clerical workers).

The number of executives employed in staff management accounting posts at the plant level is not very much larger in companies such as Toyota or NEC. Accountants are often to be found on detachment in product or project-centred teams. Much of the important work on new product development is carried out in teams which include an accountant. Nissan and NEC both operate a system of product managers who run mixed function teams; while Toyota explained, 'We make a team consisting of product planner, marketing, manufacturing and accounting.' Intractable problems of shop floor Kaizen are attacked in the same spirit by a project team.

The dissolution of accounting knowledge into other forms of knowledge and practices of intervention

This is the discursive principle which is the corollary of organisational integration. The dominance of this principle is given away by a variety of indicators, most important of which is the attention which Japanese companies give to non-accounting problems and priorities. A good example of this order of priorities is the attention to low stocks and small batch production which is such a striking feature of Japanese manufacturing practice. The issue of low stocks is not problematised because Japanese management accountants have an altogether more sophisticated accounting knowledge of the cost of stocks than Western MA. The priority arises because Japanese management accountants are part of a team which is prepared to accept production engineering arguments to the effect that 'stock hides problems' because the team gives production engineering knowledge an equal or higher status than accounting knowledge. Thus, at Toyota, the senior management accountant argued that the 'visible benefits' of stock reduction in Profit and Loss terms from reduced inventory investment were outweighed by the 'more important ... invisible benefits' of production benefits, especially the ability to run mixed model lines in a small batch factory.

When the invisible benefits are accepted as real, our conclusion is that Toyota and other Japanese firms are operating outside the problematic of Western MA because accounting knowledge does not delimit the field of the visible or define the priorities of the firm. The practical assertion of different priorities then depends on the integration of different forms of calculation plus the support of appropriate practices of intervention. For example, cost reduction targets in development are only achieved because they are supported by the techniques of value analysis and value engineering which are generally used to take out materials and component cost in the design stage. The ruthless financial short-termism of Japanese manufacturing does not lead to productive retreat (as in so many Western companies) because it is tied to constructive productive intervention.

Intelligibility of accounting information so that (cost reduction) tasks, which are inherently difficult, do not appear unnecessarily complicated

The emphasis on intelligibility is clearest at the plant and shop level where the preference for simple physical measures is always justified on the grounds that such measures are intelligible at the shop-floor level. And in the Japanese scheme of things every worker must be his own accountant, just as he is his own engineer. Thus, in Sony TV, the view was that even labour productivity measures were too complicated, abstract and indirect for shop-floor use; the division's factory managers were expected to translate a request for 10 per cent labour productivity improvement into 'remove one worker in ten within so many months'. From this point of view product costing was disparaged because it was always unintelligible to the uninitiated. Nissan claimed to have abandoned standard costing partly because 'the workforce didn't ... understand it' and costing failed to provide 'incentives or motivation'.

The principle of intelligibility is not confined to the shop-floor; it is honoured at all levels of the companies studied, even in their top echelons where capacity for abstract, conceptual thought is not a problem. Considerable effort is put into the development of company-specific analytic spreadsheets which list pertinent variables (rather than standard accounting categories) and thus show at a glance what has gone right or wrong. Table 14.1 shows the spreadsheet summary of divisional performance which is used at main board level in Nissan. In this income statement, used for both marketing and manufacturing divisions, the director can at a glance take in the trend of production and sales, the importance of exchange rate fluctuation, the progress of in-house Kaizen and cost reductions on newly developed models as well as the prices of bought-in components.

Adjustment of accounting practice to productive and market circumstances

We have already described the adjustment of accounting categories to variable productive circumstances, so it may be worthwhile to add something here about the incorporation of the market into enterprise calculation. A pattern of differences and similarities emerged from our interviews with the

TABLE 14.1 Divisional income statement

No. units sold

Total revenue

Net sales

Marketing costs

Operating profit (A)

Expected no. of units

Expected profit (B)
Difference
(A) – (B)
Sales increase/decrease
Production change
Sales rate changes
Fluctuation in exchange rate
Shipping costs
Total
Changes in invoice price
Discounts
Change in marketing costs

Profit/loss a/c of fixed costs

Cost reduction of in-house manufacturing

Fluctuations in purchasing prices

Cost reduction of newly developed models

R & D

three electronic companies. Only large, successful Japanese companies have the internal financial resources to make long-term market calculations. But all three of our companies make the same short-term payback calculation which is determined by an external variable, the speed at which the product market moves.

Companies like NEC and Sony can afford to carry unprofitable product lines on national markets if they believe that presence in these areas is important for their productive capability or global marketing plans. NEC is the world's largest producer of semiconductors but its managers admitted that investment in semiconductors, as in computers, did not meet their payback criterion. Sony admitted much the same about its presence in the American TV market, which others had abandoned, but then argued: 'it is very important for us, the US market is so huge and only a company looking for long-term business and the company which has enough money to invest and survive, can buy the market.' The small Kenwood electronics company was not in this category of being able to 'buy the market'. Although Kenwood was using its established hi-fi business as a cash cow, the company was so short of funds that it could only afford research into the next generation of production.

Despite the difference in financial resources, the same basic 'within three years' payback rule was adopted in all the companies because they faced the same market and product-life time horizons. Two to three years (with cosmetic facelifts) is the typical chassis life of consumer electronics products and all companies aim to recover their investment (including model-specific R & D) in the production run so that investment can be rolled over into the next generation of product. The companies also believe that it is impossible to forecast market volumes and prices for specific products over a period longer than three years. Thus a Kenwood manager argued that all the consumer electronics firms made the same payback calculations because 'even in bigger companies, the market situation is the same ... [and Japanese] companies do not chase dreams'. Significantly he then added the point that a five-year payback would be financially acceptable to his company but that was irrelevant because his company could not forecast the market that far ahead.

If our view of heuristic principles and forms of calculation has any novelty, it is because Japanese accounting practice is so often discussed as though it represented an incremental development of Western MA or can at least be added to Western MA as a supplement. Thus Bromwich and Bhimani comfortably conclude that what the West needs is evolutionary not revolutionary change in Western MA:

> If firms in the West place greater emphasis on meeting cost objectives from the Japanese, this should not be taken to mean that Western firms are at fault and ought to adopt the Japanese view automatically. A combination of the best of the two approaches seems a sensible aim. (Bromwich and Bhimani, 1989, p. 43)

But that conclusion can only be justified by an analytic reading which breaks down Japanese practice into a series of disconnected elements which can be added to any other kind of MA practice. We would dispute the conclusion and deny the premise. As we have argued, the reading of Japanese practice should be focused instead on the relation between the accounting elements, their relation to non-financial calculation and forms of intervention as well as the supporting heuristic principles. It is the combination of internal system and external connection which generates the possibility of continuous cost reduction for a manufacturing sector which is not operating in the textbook problematic of Western MA. Against this background, the project of borrowing and adding discursive elements to Western MA would be intellectually incoherent and practically ineffective.

Conclusion

As we explained in the introductory section, our aim was to contrast the Western (Anglo-American) theory of MA and the Japanese application. We have not yet investigated the application of management accounting in American or British firms, where the range of variation in practice is probably larger than in Japan. The large company British spreadsheets which we have seen are within the textbook problematic and take no account of Japanese practice. But it is not possible to come to any conclusion on American or British practice without much more knowledge. It is only very recently and slowly that 'management accounting research is starting to confront management accounting practice' (Hopwood, 1985, p. 227).

The verdict on the Western theory of MA, as represented in the common texts, is however clear enough and depressingly unfavourable. Any student who had acquired the principles of management accounting from a Western textbook would need re-education before he or she could work usefully in an accounting role inside a Japanese manufacturing company. If the aim is to encourage Western manufacturing companies which wish to close the performance gap with Japan, as we have argued elsewhere, then that is a difficult task. But Britain and America might usefully begin by discouraging the professionalisation of management accounting through external certification and redirecting the university departments and schools which do little except teach orthodox accounting techniques.

Note

The British authors have worked together as a team for the past ten years. Team publications include many articles and books such as *Why are the British bad at Manufacturing?* (1983) to 1992: *The Struggle for Europe* (1989). Their first article with I. Mitsui was published in *Critical Perspectives* (1991).

CHAPTER 15

Management control in an airline

C. Wilkinson

Introduction

This chapter describes and critically evaluates some of the management control processes in a large international airline, specifically those controls which concern the production and usage of management accounting information. The major activities to be examined include those of planning and budgeting, cost management and the evaluation of performance of the airline as a whole, its operations and the managers who are responsible for them.

The airline industry is highly cyclical in nature as demand for its product is heavily influenced by world economic trends, and as a result the profitability of airlines is extremely volatile by most standards. The industry is undergoing considerable structural change through a process of deregulation which is intended to remove many practices which have been perceived as anti-competitive by governments and international agencies such as the European Community. The combination of these factors has resulted in an unprecedented increase in competition between airlines on a global scale as markets which were traditionally protected become subject to 'open-skies' policies in the 1990s. Thus the need for efficiency in operation and effectiveness in resource allocation decisions have become major concerns for airline managers in recent years. Management accounting practices which are intended to serve these ends by providing useful and relevant financial information and performance measures clearly have a vital role to play in the overall management control process of any airline.

However it can be argued that many of the standard techniques of management accounting are not well suited to an airline environment. An airline can be seen as a network of interdependent operations in which many costs are common to the whole network rather than directly attributable to any specific product or service. Responsibility for operations follows functional roles rather than products because of the highly specialised nature of those functions, so costs are accumulated and controlled within functional areas, such as engineering or catering. Revenues, on the other hand, arise and can only be meaningfully accumulated by specific route products, so any attempt at matching costs to revenues for the purpose of evaluating operational efficiency must be heavily dependent upon arbitrary processes of allocation covering almost all significant cost items except fuel.

Airlines are a service industry in which product is consumed as it is produced. The product cannot be stored, so ideally production and consumption should match. In practice production levels and their associated costs are determined well in advance of consumption, when the flying schedule is planned and published. Most operational costs then become fixed, so in the short term it is demand management rather than output decisions which determine the financial efficiency and profitability of the airline. The management accounting system must address the needs of managers who are responsible for short-term demand management and longer-term capacity planning as well as the needs of those primarily concerned with operational efficiency, cost management and adherence to financial plans or budgets. This chapter attempts to assess how effectively the management accounting and related control systems in one large airline help managers to deal with these issues.

The airline industry and its environment

Fuelled by an ever-increasing demand for business, personal and leisure transport, the world airline industry has grown steadily throughout the latter half of the twentieth century. In some periods the rate of growth has been spectacular and at other times more modest, broadly in step with changing world macro-economic trends, but industry pundits confidently expect demand to continue to grow until well into the twenty-first century. Against this background of expected long-term rising demand, airline managers have from time to time to cope with significant year-to-year fluctuations in passenger numbers.

Another key characteristic of the industry is the trend towards deregulation in what has traditionally been a highly regulated environment. The structure of the industry is such that most nations have one national airline, often state-owned, which dominates its domestic market for internal and international flights. The dominance of the national carriers in their respective markets is no accident, since market entry has been rigidly regulated by governments since the early days of the industry. International routes in particular have traditionally been subject to a high degree of regulation, not only in safety and security matters, but also in terms of which airlines can operate between countries, at what capacity and the level of fares which can be charged for a standard class journey. Capacity constraints are usually the result of inter-government agreements, where governments are keen to protect the market share of their own airline, and standard fares are regulated by the International Air Transport Association (IATA). In effect no airline is allowed to fly just wherever it wishes, or to determine unilaterally the prices charged to its customers on many of its routes. Some routes are subject to revenue-sharing agreements, under which total route revenue is shared between carriers in some predetermined ratio, irrespective of the share of route passengers actually achieved by each carrier.

By such forms of regulation and collaborative actions, many airlines have been shielded from the normal competitive pressures of commercial life. Once an international route licence had been granted, the airlines involved (typically two, one from each country concerned) enjoyed a duopoly within which price competition was forbidden. This situation still continues today in many cases, but now an increasing number of routes are being 'deregulated', that is, opened to new airlines and freed of restrictive price controls.

Deregulation has already happened within the USA on internal routes, though these routes are still closed to foreign airlines by international agreement. The other major route network which is in the process of deregulation is the international network between member countries of the European Community. Some routes within the EC, such as London–Amsterdam, are now officially open to any EC-based carrier, without price control. The inevitable consequence of such changes is that increasing competition will threaten the traditional market dominance of established carriers on routes, at the same time providing opportunities for airlines to compete in new markets from which they have previously been excluded. Although the process of deregulation is still just beginning, it is clear that its effects upon the world's major airlines will be profound, as they evolve to meet the new threats and opportunities presented to them.

For the large national airlines such as Lufthansa, Air France and British Airways it is unlikely that their dominance of their respective domestic markets will be seriously challenged in the short term. However the threat of increasing competition is of considerable concern to their managers. Profitability levels can vary quite widely between routes, depending upon levels of demand, price and cost structures. It is the more profitable parts of an airline's route network which will attract the attentions of competitors and which therefore need to be strenuously defended.

Given free market access by competitors and the possibility of real price competition, the defence of market share on a profitable route is both vital and problematic. Established carriers would prefer to avoid price competition, with its immediate effects on profit margins, and so attempt to shift the focus of competition to quality of service factors such as punctuality and comfort. New entrants tend to focus on price in order to gain a foothold in the market, but then also shift to service quality to improve their margins, as evidenced by Virgin Airlines on the North Atlantic routes. Competition can also be expected to lead to increased costs in marketing and advertising. Before deregulation, passengers had less choice of carrier and so, in times of healthy demand, marketing expenses could be relatively light. All of these factors indicate increasing pressures on costs as well as price levels across the industry. The overall effects of deregulation have thus been to increase consumer choice while placing many airlines under severe financial pressure. The fates of Pan Am and TWA are testimony to the size of the challenge faced by airline managers as they adapt to the new order with limited degrees of freedom to act.

Cost structures are largely fixed in the short to medium term, the major cost items being those associated with owning, maintaining and flying a fleet of aircraft and the cost of employing staff at the home base and at many locations around the world. In the short term, those costs which vary in relation to passengers flown are little more than a small proportion of fuel and catering costs, so total costs are fairly insensitive to fluctuations in output and revenues. In times of declining demand or market share, airlines are generally reluctant to reduce capacity, and in any case their ability to do so is constrained by practical considerations. For example, in the short term, there would be little point in using a smaller aircraft on a particular route unless another route could benefit from using a larger one, given a stable aircraft fleet. An alternative tactic would be to reduce the frequency of flights on a particular route, but this has its own drawbacks. Quite apart from the difficulties of coping with a rearranged schedule in mid-season, failure to utilise previously allocated landing and take-off slots could jeopardise an airline's right to those slots in the future. If a slot is not used, it can be reallocated to another airline which then takes over the right to continue using it. Therefore any decision to cut capacity by withdrawing a flight at a busy airport could have long-term implications for competitiveness on the route concerned. For these reasons, airlines have little scope to change their total costs in response to short-term variations in demand. They must therefore ensure that they run their operations as efficiently as possible at all times and maintain capacity utilisation rates in order to minimise unit cost per passenger.

The following sections describe the management control systems in 'Inter Continental Airlines' (ICA), a major international airline, to illustrate and comment upon the way these control objectives are pursued in practice. The controls which are discussed are those of a financial or management accounting nature. This focus is not intended to imply that other types of controls are not important, but merely reflects the particular concerns which are uppermost in senior managers' minds at the time of writing.

Management structure and responsibility accounting

ICA is a large and complex organisation, and as such any attempt to describe it in detail would be both lengthy and quickly outdated because of the frequency of change in the organisation structure. However there are certain characteristics of the organisation which seem to endure, and which are described below.

The board of directors of ICA consists of the chairman, the chief executive, the finance director and several non-executive directors. Although the board fulfils the statutory responsibilities of a board of directors, day-to-day management responsibility lies with the executive board, consisting of the senior managers who are responsible for the various functional areas of the company, including sales and marketing, flight crew, cabin crew, engineering, legal, logistics, human resources management, information management and so on. The size of each functional area in terms of costs or people employed varies from the relatively small, such as legal, to the very large, such as engineering. Within each functional area there are a number of smaller units and subunits, each headed by a senior manager.

In responsibility accounting terms, the functional areas can be regarded as being either revenue centres or cost centres. Where profit centres exist, these tend to be in peripheral areas of activity, such as running a travel agency chain, or selling various services to other airlines. Within the major business area the marketing function, which includes all sales activity, is the aggregate revenue centre. All other functions, either operational or support areas, are cost centres. Within the marketing function, there are product managers who have responsibility for the major products or brands, which are the various classes of cabin accommodation – first class, business class, and economy. In this context, a product is a brand, not a route. These managers are responsible for decisions concerning the advertising and promotion of the products, pricing and levels of service provided, but are not directly accountable for all of the cost implications of their decisions which make demands upon the operations area. For example, if a product manager decided that the maximum acceptable length of a check-in queue for business class is three people, this would have staffing and hence cost implications for ground operations. Though such a decision may be justified in terms of maintaining a quality of service differential over executive class services offered by competitor airlines, the cost of its implementation would not be borne by the product manager's main budget, which is concerned with revenue items only.

The major responsibility for revenue generation lies with the sales function, which is divided into geographical regions and then into individual countries or groups of countries. Thus the initial aggregation of revenues is on the basis of where the sale of tickets occurs, rather than by individual route. In many cases the apportionment of the value of a ticket to particular routes is inevitably arbitrary. For example, if a customer in Mexico buys a ticket for a journey from Mexico to London, on to Cairo then back to Mexico direct, the last leg of the journey would have to be travelled with another carrier, as ICA does not fly Cairo to Mexico. There are inter-airline rules in operation which apportion revenue between ICA and the second carrier, but for the ICA legs of the journey there is no objective, non-arbitrary method of allocating the remaining revenue between Mexico–London and London–Cairo. (The fare would be different to the sum of three single tickets, purchased separately, for the separate legs of the journey.)

Within the operational areas cost responsibility follows functions, not routes. The majority of costs are incurred by activities which are common to many or all routes, rather than by routes directly. For example, the cost of baggage handling is a common cost of all routes which start or finish at a particular airport. The cost of maintaining an aircraft is a cost common to all routes on which that aircraft flies, of which there may be several.

The purpose of including the above examples at this stage is twofold. Firstly, in relation to the issue of organisation structure and responsibility accounting, they illustrate the difficulty of assigning profit responsibility for individual routes, as only a small proportion of costs can be influenced or managed at the individual route level. Secondly, they illustrate that the assessment of route profitability which is done (see later) has an inevitable degree of arbitrary cost and revenue apportionment contained within it, and therefore its results need to be interpreted with considerable care.

Given the degree of separation between responsibility for costs and revenues described above, the question arises of who is ultimately responsible for the profitability of the airline as a whole. The answer to this can only be that it is the chief executive, to whom the various cost and revenue centre managers report. Below this level, the managers are not in positions from which they can make well-informed trade-offs between cost decisions and their likely revenue implications for individual products, be they brands or routes. This is a rather unusual state of affairs. In typical manufacturing organisations it is a fairly simple task to analyse revenue by product line and the majority of costs will be either direct or apportionable on some reasonable basis between a limited number of products. In many service organisations profitability can be computed at subunit level as both costs and revenues are generally attributable to the same organisational subunit at least, if not specific products. However the problem is not unique to airlines. Any organisation which operates a large network-based service, be it a railway company, a telephone company or a mail delivery service, faces a similar situation in which costs are incurred by the activity of maintaining the network as a whole, and are therefore largely fixed, whereas revenues are earned from customers who, individually, use only a small part of the total network operation.

The budgeting process

Budgets and the operating plans upon which they are based are prepared for the two seasons which make up the ICA year, summer (April to October) and winter (November to March). The seasons are budgeted for separately because the scheduled flying plan and the scale of operations differ significantly between them. The budgeting process is the same in each case.

The first stage in the process is the specification of broad targets for revenue, expenses and manpower levels by the chief executive, based upon the desired level of improvement over the previous corresponding period. This sets expectations lower down the organisation as to what levels of performance will be acceptable. Then follows the issue of assumptions concerning macroeconomic trends and market forecasts, which are used by marketing to determine the flying plan for the season. The plan concerns routes to be flown, their frequency and capacity. The plan is then developed into a detailed schedule of operations by the logistics department, a process which, though technically complex, is handled smoothly by a team of specialists who are experts in the area.

In practice, changes to the schedule are relatively few from year to year, partly because of IATA's system of allocating landing rights at airports. Any airport has a maximum capacity in terms of the numbers of aircraft movements and passengers which can be handled in a given period of time. All major airports already operate at or near their capacity, so landing rights are a scarce resource. From season to season, landing rights are allocated on the basis of previous use of a specific landing 'slot'. For example, if ICA had a landing slot at 4.00 p.m. on Tuesdays at New York JFK last year, they have first claim on the same slot this year. Given the scarcity of slots at major airports, airlines are reluctant to give them up because of the difficulty of getting them back later, and because keeping slots is a very effective way of preventing competitors from establishing new routes.

Once finalised, the operating schedule provides the basis upon which many operating costs can be forecast, just as a production plan precedes a production budget in a manufacturing organisation. It is also the basis from which the revenue budget can be estimated, given the assumption of price levels and load factors for passengers and cargo. The revenue budget is submitted to the chief executive for approval at this stage, and is either accepted or returned for revision, which may involve subsequent changes to the schedule.

The next stage in the budgeting process is the issue of business plan packs to cost centre budget holders, which contain pro formas showing the cost information to be provided. The pro formas contain details of actual expenditures for the corresponding season in the previous year. Each budget holder is required to compile the budget for the coming period and to provide commentaries on significant variance from the previous the year's plan. Individual cost centre budgets are consolidated into departmental budgets by the finance function for review by department heads. The budgets are then submitted to the chief executive and finance director for review, and any amendments required by them will be communicated back down the chain.

The following quotation from a budget holder provides a view of this process from a line manager's perspective.

In practice, what tends to happen is that the budgets are constructed in some detail by line managers and reviewed upwards through the hierarchical chain with adjustments at most stages, usually reducing the costs. It seems that these cost budgets are always reduced even further by the chief executive – the cuts were particularly severe in the Summer 1989 plan – on a top-down basis. The line manager is then faced with an arbitrary cut to the plan despite having formulated it in significant detail. This then creates demotivation and low morale amongst the management team.

This quotation illustrates the difficulty faced by functional managers who do not have a global view of cost and revenue trends across the airline. Whilst they may strive to be more efficient than before, and may have a good understanding of what is feasible in terms of local performance, they cannot, by the nature of their work, have as clear an understanding of necessary performance levels across the whole organisation as the chief executive who has to balance the forecast revenue, cost and required profit equation.

The reality of the budgeting process is that, once the schedule has been fixed, the level of activity in many parts of the airline is also fixed. For example, the flying schedule effectively determines the engineering maintenance workload. Therefore most cost savings have to be the result either of efficiency gains or of cuts in discretionary activities such as staff training, refurbishment of ground facilities or purchasing new equipment. Whilst senior management would generally prefer saving to result from efficiency gains, which generally means reductions in staff numbers, cuts in discretionary activities are generally less painful to implement and are likely to be preferred by many cost centre managers.

Cost reporting systems and cost management practice

At the level of the operating unit or departments within the main functional areas, there is no single company-wide cost reporting system. Each functional area has its own cost-reporting system which draws data from the common general ledger system.

Responsibility for the provision of cost data lies with the accountants within each function. Although there is a central management accounting department, its role is concerned with overall company performance and route performance monitoring, not with cost monitoring in functional areas. Each function has its own team of accountants, whose role is to provide a service to that area. This seems to be sensible in principle, as there is little commonality between the accounting information needs of, say, engineering, catering and marketing. According to the accountants who provide the service, managers are able to receive cost reports to their own specification. The general ledger system is capable of producing reports with a high level of detail, with comparisons between actual spending and budget the previous year, or whatever is required by local management.

So, in principle, each functional area and every individual cost centre manager within it have the means of receiving cost reports to their own specification of content, layout and frequency. However in practice the system does have its critics amongst the managers who receive the reports. To work effectively, the system depends upon managers being able to specify their requirements to their accountants, and to ensure that the data from which reports are compiled are accurate. Some managers appear to lack sufficient technical understanding of accounting and or motivation to review and improve the cost information they receive. Some report that entries frequently appear under incorrect cost codes, causing managers to regard the system as unreliable and contributing to some degree of ambivalence about the budgetary control process.

Both of the above points reveal that in some cases cost control is not always regarded as a high priority, even amongst managers who, nominally at least, hold budget responsibility. This tendency is not evenly spread across the whole airline, however. Those functional areas which are essentially production-oriented, such as engineering and catering, appear to be more budget-conscious than others. These are areas in which cost standards can be most easily set using industrial engineering principles, as opposed to areas in which the 'right' cost level is largely a matter of judgement based upon changing notions of appropriate levels of customer service.

ICA has undergone a marked shift in senior management priorities during the past decade, from a preoccupation with increasing customer perceptions of quality throughout the mid-1980s, which was achieved with great success, to a focus on cost control as the recession of the early 1990s began to take effect in the form of a decline in demand across the whole industry. It does appear that, in those parts of the organisation where the drive to improve quality of service levels was most apparent, little attention was paid to cost management during the period of rising passenger numbers and high profit levels. Lack of attention to budgetary control in these areas allowed cost reporting systems to deteriorate through lack of necessary updating as business needs and operating practices continued to change. When the market downturn came and management needed to focus on cost control to achieve profit targets, some parts of the organisation found that they no longer had the reporting systems necessary to manage costs effectively.

This problem was recognised by ICA's senior management, who in 1990 instigated a wide-ranging review of overhead spending. This activity value analysis exercise was akin to a form of zero-based budgeting, in which all activities were evaluated and questioned, with a view to cutting out those activities which were not considered essential, and thus saving their associated costs. The first phase of the exercise considered 11 'overhead' departments, which employed approximately 4000 (that is, about 40 per cent of the non-operational staff). The analysis and evaluation took about four months, using a team of 30 managers who were seconded to the project from their usual jobs. The exercise identified £40 million of potential cost saving, or 16 per cent of the cost of all activities evaluated in this phase, which could be achieved within a two-year period. The majority of these savings were payroll costs.

A common concern amongst managers involved in the project was that, even where savings were achieved as a result of this exercise, there were insufficient ongoing budgetary or cost control measures to ensure that overhead costs did not steadily creep back up to their former levels. The majority of managers recognised that better cost control was essential for the airline to remain profitable, since costs had been rising faster than revenues for some time. On the other hand, many doubted that they had the control systems required to manage costs on an ongoing basis and thought that they would take some time to develop. Ad hoc attempts to reduce the fixed cost base such as that described above may be necessary from time to time when costs are perceived to be 'out of control', but in themselves are not substitutes for adequate controls in the hands of those who bear responsibility for cost management.

Monthly management accounts

Management accounts are prepared each month by the central accounting function for the executive board. These accounts consist of a series of reports which cover several aspects of the financial performance of the company and its operations. They include monthly financial accounts (income statement and balance sheet), cash flow analysis, detailed cost and revenue centre reports, schedules of capital expenditure and an analysis of route performance. As is usual in most companies the purpose of these accounts is to enable senior management to monitor performance and progress towards the anticipated year end outturn and to identify functions (or routes) which are underperforming in some respect. Heads of functions are expected to account for significant operating variances by providing explanations as to the causes and what actions they propose or are taking to remedy the problems.

The production and purposes of these accounts is fairly unremarkable in that those activities would be regarded as standard practice in almost any organisation. They provide a mans of 'keeping the score', a comforting ritual which confirms that all is well or, if not, at least the impression that things are being controlled, that attention is being directed at problems which need to be addressed. The one slightly unusual aspect of this management accounts system is the lack of integration between these company-wide summary accounts and the cost-reporting systems specified by and tailored to the needs of lower-level managers. In most organisations the management accounts would serve as the major cost-reporting vehicle. This is not the case in ICA.

Whether or not this hinders control to any significant extent is difficult to assess, but it does have the potential to create translation difficulties as the level of analysis moves from the company to function to department.

The evaluation of route profitability

ICA evaluates the financial performance of each of its routes by allocating operating costs to them and comparing these costs with route revenues. The costs allocated in this process are all costs which are directly attributable to the activity of flying aeroplanes, such as aircraft depreciation and maintenance, fuel, cabin crew and flight crew costs, catering, insurance, landing fees and so on. All non-flight related costs such as marketing, selling and the costs of service departments are excluded. By means of a rather complicated process of allocation, all operational costs are assigned to routes using a variety of allocation bases. For example, crew costs are allocated on the basis of duty time, fuel costs on the basis of distance flown and according to type of aircraft, catering costs on the basis of passenger numbers and so on. The extent of cost allocation means that route costs cannot be precise, but the system seems to be a reasonable compromise between accuracy and expediency.

Within these limits route costing serves a number of useful purposes in addition to allowing the airline to meet certain obligations to provide data to industry authorities. It provides a basis for evaluating fare levels, and it serves as a cost model which is complementary to that which is based on functional costs. Most importantly, it provides an indication of the relative profitability of different routes when the cost data are combined with route revenue. Like route cost data, route revenue data can in some cases be difficult to assess with precision, for reasons already explained, but, within the limitations of the exercise, the degree of accuracy is considered to be acceptable. The difference between revenues and costs is normally referred to as route profitability, but because marketing and other central costs are not allocated to routes, the 'route profit' is actually a measure of route contribution to central overheads and profit. Nevertheless as such it still provides a reasonable guide to the relative profitability of routes and an indication of the economically strong and weak parts of the network. Route performance is evaluated regularly, using three key measures which affect profitability:

1. yield – the average revenue earned per passenger carried on the route;
2. unit cost – the average cost of providing each seat on the route;
3. load factor – the proportion of route capacity sold.

Relative route profitability is expressed in the form of a 'profit index', which is defined as the ratio of total route revenue to total route costs. Thus a break-even route will have an index value of one. Using the three measures defined above, the profit index can be computed using the formula:

profit index = yield × load factor/unit cost

Analysing route results in this way facilitates understanding of route economics and can provide pointers to ways in which the performance of a route may be improved. For example, improvement on a route which already has a high load factor must come from either increased yield or reduced unit costs, whereas a route which has a low load factor may be improved by increasing the seat occupancy rate, perhaps at the expense of reducing yield.

The relationship between yield, unit cost and load factor is critically important in airlines and in many other service industries whose costs are largely determined by their planned level of operations which, once decided, cannot be changed easily in the short term. If a route's load factor falls, it is unlikely that a smaller, cheaper aeroplane could be substituted unless another route required a larger plane at the same time. Therefore the capacity and costs associated with any route are effectively fixed for the season at least, and typically a year in advance owing to planning constraints. This means that, in the short term, route performance can only be improved by increasing capacity utilisation, or yield, or both together. Achieving both may be difficult, since this would mean selling more seats while raising the average fare paid.

In the longer term, the relationship between a route's load factor and profitability provides a useful analytical device for aiding decision making about future resource allocation. For example, a route with a high load factor but low profitability may indicate that capacity should be reduced, whereas high profits associated with a low load factor would suggest the need for further marketing expenditure to stimulate demand. So long as the limitations of the cost allocation and route profitability computations are recognised and taken account of in the decision-making process, this type of analysis appears to serve a useful role in the long-term planning of the route network.

Managerial performance evaluation and reward system

Throughout ICA every manager's performance is formally assessed each year by reference to a set of criteria known as 'key result areas' (KRAs) which are individually agreed between managers and their direct superiors. A typical manager would have between five and seven KRAs against which their performance is evaluated. This method of evaluation was introduced on the advice of external consultants in the mid-1980s as part of a performance-related reward system. The general idea behind the system is that the most senior managers first agree their KRAs with their director, and then agree KRAs with and for their subordinates so that, providing all subordinates actually achieve their KRAs, the senior managers will also achieve theirs. By this process, a senior manager's KRAs cascade down the organisational hierarchy, and in doing so become translated into more specific targets for each reporting subordinate manager. The type of KRAs that any manager has is largely influenced by the specific responsibilities associated with their job, although some may relate to the personal developments needs of the manager concerned. A typical set of KRAs might include projects to be completed by a fixed date, levels of operational efficiency to be achieved, customer service standards to be met, staff development objectives and so on. Within the ground rules of the system every manager's KRAs should include at least one 'financial' objective, which for many managers is simply to manage their department within their budgetary target. The weighting of each KRA in the overall assessment of the manager is a matter for discussion at the time when KRAs are set.

The formal assessment takes place in interviews between managers and their superiors and results in an overall grading of performance, which can range from less than satisfactory to excellent. This grading is used to determine the level of performance bonus earned, but in a rather indirect manner. The bonus earned is actually determined by reference to the average performance rating of a manager's peer group, so that a 'very good' performer in a 'very good' peer group could receive less than a 'good' performer in a 'satisfactory' peer group.

The total bonus pool available for distribution under the scheme is determined by the accounting results of the airline. The details of precisely how individual bonus payments are determined are not generally well understood by managers, who tend to see the bonus calculation exercise as a rather mysterious process which is performed by a computer programme. Thus the link between the degree of achievement of KRA targets and the amount of bonus received seems somewhat tenuous to many managers. A number of managers expressed the opinion that, whilst they did their best to meet their KRA targets, the money itself was not much of a motivating factor because the amount of bonus earned was difficult to reconcile with the quality of their achievement.

Apart from this aspect of the system, the use of KRAs was generally seen by managers as a useful control device. The system is flexible enough to incorporate a wide range of targets, and by careful choice of KRAs and their relative weightings, performance targets can be individually tailored to the responsibilities of any managerial position. For many managers, the inclusion of one or more financial KRAs was the only means by which they considered themselves to be held accountable for budget achievement. However, given that the performance review is a once-a-year exercise, that the penalties for not meeting a financial KRA are extremely difficult to quantify and that the accuracy of the cost-reporting system is open to question, it is unlikely that the KRA system in itself can provide an effective incentive to motivate budget achievement. This was not a major objective at the time when the KRA system was introduced.

The performance evaluation system appears to play an important role in integrating and communicating business objectives throughout ICA, and the review process provides some degree of accountability for managers' overall performance. The extent to which the prospect of financial rewards help to motivate performance is difficult to assess, but there seem to be reasons to doubt that they provide a major source of motivation, given the general lack of understanding of the way the system works. The inclusion of financial KRAs provides some degree of budget accountability, but does not compensate for the lack of a comprehensive budgetary control system in an organisation which is seeking to manage its costs more effectively.

Evaluation of the management accounting system

The earlier sections of this chapter have described the major components of ICA's management accounting system (MAS). The processes of planning and budgeting, cost reporting, cost management, and evaluation of product profitability and managerial performance contain nothing which is particularly unusual. They are standard control processes which will be familiar to almost any middle or senior manager in any reasonably large organisation. They are rooted in the concept of responsibility accounting wherein an organisation is divided into subunits which are accountable for the achievement of local operational and financial objectives.

ICA is a 'unitary' (as opposed to divisionalised) organisation; all its major activities are concerned with the maintenance of a complex network of operations which transports passengers and freight between hundreds of locations around the world. It is a classic functional bureaucracy (see Chapter 4) with a high degree of task specialisation within functions and a requirement for considerable integration between functions at the operational, control and decision-making levels. Most of the elements of ICA's MAS are operationalised within functions; for example, the planning and budgeting, cost-reporting and managerial evaluation components are all conducted within functional departments. These accounting practices and the accounting model on which they are based provide the technical rationality of the organisation within which management control is exercised. This particular rationality tends to promote and reinforce the primacy of functions to those who work within them, at the expense of the vision of the organisation as a system of interdependent parts.

Some components of the MAS do cut across functional divisions, as for example, with the budget review process which is conducted at executive board level and the evaluation of route performance. However these are quite remote from the vast majority of managers and the processes involved are not well understood, because they are simply not made visible to the majority. On one level everyone can appreciate the product as an amalgam of functional inputs which fuse together at the point of service delivery and that product quality is totally dependent upon successful integration between functions at this point. However the controls which have the most immediate impact upon the majority of managers are concerned with their own area of functional responsibility only, which creates a certain tension between what is perceived to be desirable from the organisation's viewpoint and what is required to satisfy more parochial functional objectives.

The existence of such tensions raises the fundamental question of how an organisation like ICA identifies appropriate units of accountability upon which to base its MAS. In many organisations the choice is fairly straightforward: accountability units may be divisions, operating sites or product groups, based upon the assumption of a reasonable degree of independence between units. This independence allows for autonomy in local decision making and optimisation at unit level. Such assumptions are not tenable with regard to the functional constituent parts of an airline which together form a complex operational system. The sheer complexity of the system and the bounded rationality of decision makers preclude the possibility of systemic optimisation coinciding with optimisation at the subunit level. There is no easy answer to this problem, but recognising its existence can at least sensitise managers to the limitations of accounting models as vehicles for optimisation across systems whose operational and economic logic is not well represented by the MAS. In ICA, it can be argued that the MAS tends to obscure the functional interdependencies which exist at the operational level, and tends to promote suboptimising behaviours by its concentrated focus upon within-function operations.

The evaluation of route performance can also be argued to be essentially reductionist in approach. Focusing on the performance of individual routes rather than functions is just another way of cutting the cake from an overall systems perspective, notwithstanding its usefulness as an aid to short-term demand management and seat capacity planning on existing services. The accounting method used is heavily dependent upon arbitrary cost and revenue allocation processes. It is therefore unlikely to provide a suitable basis for major decisions concerning the overall size and shape of the route network or the capacity of individual operational functions for overall system optimisation purposes. But it is exactly these issues which the management of ICA need to address when contemplating their response to the environmental challenges now facing them and their competitors.

Implications for management control systems design

In Chapter 1, management control was defined as 'the process of guiding organisations into viable patterns of activity in a changing environment'. This short definition encapsulates the fundamental control issue within ICA, that of how to encourage managers to adopt behaviours which are appropriate to the degree of environmental change to which the organisation is exposed. Environmental changes necessitate changes in priority amongst various dimensions of organisational performance, as well as the need to reconfigure the organisation to take advantage of new competitive opportunities that arise.

The picture which emerges from the description of its control procedures suggests that ICA now has a problem in finding a style of control which is appropriate to the demands of its present situation. The key issue for the company concerns how simultaneously to maintain its high quality image, increase its operational efficiency and compete effectively in new markets as they become open to it. This final section is an attempt to relate the issues of finding an appropriate style of control to the nature of the business and its environment.

In the classification of business types described by Goold and Campbell (1987a, 1987b), ICA is clearly a 'core business'. Its major activities are all concerned with the provision of air transport and there is no significant diversification outside this primary activity. Goold and Campbell suggest that under these circumstances, a strategic planning style of management control works best. By this they mean that top central management should be closely involved in setting the strategic direction of the company and creating an appropriate organisational culture of shared common values to support the strategy. Top management in ICA provided just such a style of leadership throughout the quality improvement initiative of the 1980s.

Goold and Campbell further note that there are potential weaknesses inherent in any core business. Firstly, lack of diversity across industries exposes a company to greater variability in earnings than would be expected of a diversified company, as industry fortunes wax and wane. International air transport is notoriously vulnerable to world economic conditions, so considerable variability in earnings is to be expected. Secondly, changes in the business environment can make a particular style of management less appropriate, eventually creating a need for difficult changes in style. Both of these points are clearly relevant in the ICA case. The recipe for success throughout the 1980s which was based on quality first and foremost was appropriate in a buoyant market, but required radical amendment to include cost and efficiency considerations as market conditions deteriorated. The process of introducing further changes in management style and control processes in response to the demands of a more competitive environment is unlikely to prove any easier.

McCosh (1990) draws the distinction between what he refers to as 'positive' controls and financial controls. Positive controls are those control system components which are aimed positively at the fulfilment of corporate goals, particularly goals concerning quality of output and market share. Financial controls, he argues, are aimed at avoiding corporate catastrophe and tend to be based on historic accounting measures. The nature of competition within the international airline industry indicates that ICA will in the future have to compete in terms of both quality of service and price. Quality controls are already well established, but need to be maintained and further developed as consumers become more demanding and competitors improve their own quality standards.

Increasing price competition indicates that ICA will have to become more efficient in order to satisfy the return requirement of investors. It has been argued that existing financial controls at operational levels in the company are distrusted by managers, are underutilised and have not been developed to meet the requirements of those managers who are in a position to control costs effectively. More fundamentally, as has been argued in the previous section, the accounting model of the organisation is more likely to encourage suboptimisation of operations than to promote informed debate about future resource allocation decisions.

This case illustrates the tension which exists in any business between the pressures for short-term financial results and the need to build long-term, sustainable competitive advantage. In the present recession this tension seems to be particularly acute in ICA because of their high fixed-cost base, which can be argued to be largely a consequence of their long-term competitive strategy. The precise form of ICA's strategy for obtaining sustainable competitive advantage has yet to emerge. Several possible strategic alliances with other airlines have been considered and rejected. Such alliances could lead to more efficient utilisation of the route network if a suitable partner with a complementary network could be found. Even if a suitable alliance was to emerge, the problem of long-term system optimisation would remain, and in a yet more complex organisational context.

ICA needs effective controls at the operational and strategic levels. This case study has identified some of the problems of control system design in a network organisation, where interdependence between constituent parts of the network needs to be recognised and co-ordination facilitated through the control system at both of these levels. The case should stimulate debate about the extent to which existing management accounting models and techniques are capable of satisfying such needs, or whether new approaches are necessary within the MAS and other parts of the management control system.

CHAPTER 16

Control and the National Health Service: some psychology of managing health care with budgets and cash limits

Derek Purdy

Introduction

As the opening chapters indicated, the issue of control is one which can be approached from a variety of perspectives. The approach taken in this chapter is through a psychological perspective. It is a psychological perspective because the focus is upon the way in which individual managers have responded to change in relation to the accounting system in their hospital, and the individual choices which these managers have made in relation to the financial management information with which they have been provided. In coming to this work, the author accepts the personal construct psychology of George Kelly which notes that it is possible for individuals to construe and respond to the same event in different ways, amongst other things (Kelly, 1955). The notions used to model this work are simplified because of the limited space available for this contribution, the limited time available to work with individuals, and the fact that it is not possible to detail all psychological issues.

The Otley and Berry (1980) model of control has been selected because the author considers this a simple but sound explanation of the basic psychological approach of individuals to control. The model suggests:

1. The need for an objective.
2. The fact that there is an objective simultaneously requires (an individual to produce) a predictive model about the objective.

3. In order to ascertain if the objective has been attained requires the objective to be measurable.
4. Finally, there must be an opportunity for any appropriate intervening action, in order to harmonise the objective and the actions being undertaken.

This last phase is important, because the mechanistic approach to control generally portrays the objective as something which is preset and unalterable, and consequently the actions concerned with control are directed towards producing conformity to the unalterable objective. In the Otley and Berry concept, it may be that the object remains unaltered and conformity is sought through amending actions; however the more dynamic aspect of the notion is that it also allows for the alteration of the objective to bring about conformity, so that it is possible (for an individual) to say that things are under control.

Examining the effect of something like budget information upon a manager is a potentially very complex undertaking. It will involve the background of the manager and his or her current state of knowledge as well as the organisation in which the manager works. To simplify the analysis of data from conversations with health service managers, eight psychological/ organisational issues were formulated (Purdy, 1993a, 1993b) and these are explained later.

The author wanted to conduct research work which would aid the understanding of the way individual health service managers deal with financial management accounting data, and explored the possibilities with some 13 hospitals and health authorities before gaining access to a teaching hospital. In the hospital in which the author eventually worked, a senior member of staff was appointed his liaison person. She ensured that the author did not conflict with any ethical issues, through discussing what he wanted to do, then arranging for a cross-section of managers with different approaches to handling accounting data, finally reading and commenting upon drafts of reports, both those given to staff and those for external publication. Although she had an overall control, nothing the author wanted to do, or wanted to write, was altered.

One of the reasons that the author wanted to examine accounting practices and effects within the NHS was because the NHS was changing. Previously it was considered that one of the most suitable ways of studying accounting practices and effects was at times of change (Wildavsky, 1975; Hopwood, 1983). The next section briefly outlines the context of these changes to the NHS.

A brief context

For a long time UK governments have been concerned about the increasing costs of NHS health care, so, to help control expenditure, the Labour government introduced cash limits in 1976. Simultaneously the report of the Resource Allocation Working Party (RAWP), which introduced the idea of a mechanistic formula for funding health districts, was implemented (Perrin, 1988). Since 1979, Conservative governments have reduced expenditure on the NHS and altered its structure so that central government has direct administrative control over resource allocation to Regional Health Authorities (McGuire *et al.*, 1991).

Until the early 1980s, the NHS had many functions devoted to the curing and care of patients, with hard-working and well-meaning doctors with ambiguous responsibilities. When new nursing management was introduced in 1974, a vast bureaucracy arose, with a wide range of responsibilities which people were not trained to assume. Some nurse managers lacked the technical grasp to handle complex nursing problems, and the budgetary grasp to accompany the financial responsibilities of nursing, training and deployment of staff (Strong and Robinson, 1988).

A study of the senior managers in a regional health authority in the mid-1980s found that they varied in their ability to understand financial management accounting data and this affected their ability to use such data. The most conspicuous example was the regional nurse manager, who initially had a limited ability to construe financial management accounting data, but improved this ability through natural learning while working with the accountants (Purdy, 1991).

In the early 1980s the government wanted information about both what had caused expenditure increases and what would be the costs of the anticipated patterns of health care. In general this information could not be provided because the NHS lacked the necessary management structure, control mechanisms and accounting systems. To promote change the government implemented the findings of its enquiry into NHS management which recommended general management at all levels. The report wanted responsibility pushed to the point of delivery of care, where effective action could be taken, and anticipated the development of budgeting at unit level (National Health Service, 1983). The concept of a 'unit' could vary from a hospital to a group of wards within a hospital. These changes were recommended to provide direction and personal responsibility for developing management plans, so that subsequent output could be measured against objectives, plans and budgets. Apart from each hospital being headed by a general manager, the organizational form was open to individual interpretation. This appeared to be a simplification of the control mechanism compared with the previous team management, operated since 1974 (Perrin, 1987), by the most senior managers from administration, estates, finance, medicine and nursing.

The government wanted to reduce total health expenditure, as well as increase the efficiency of the NHS. It wanted more accountability and more information for this and for planning. When the existing team management did not move to produce these changes, it instituted management changes which would. It replaced one hierarchical system with another and brought in better-paid general managers to install general management systems. These systems would encompass more objectives, more rules and more standardisation to provide more information which would demonstrate the accountability of the service. The government's gradual imposition of absolute cash limits can be considered to be a form of rule-based control. The Conservative government planned to move the hospital service to a form of market-influenced control with the notion of a split in the service between providers of health care, such as hospitals, and a new orientation of purchasers, for example general practitioners. One part of the new forms of information was to facilitate this market.

The way in which the government has viewed the issues in the NHS is in an autocratic top-down manner. This would appear to be no different to the rest of the public sector. It made policy to set the cash rules for general managers from the top. In turn successive levels of general managers were constrained with a cash limit by their superiors, throughout the hierarchy. In this way, the top-down objective for managers, at the lower levels, was to provide direct patient treatment and care within the cash constraint.

A framework for the study

Having considered the more overall and generalised context of the NHS, the focus now moves to the individual managers of ward nurses. This was the level of management which was reported to be of poor quality and weak with financial matters between 1974 and 1984 (Strong and Robinson, 1988).

The enquiry conducted with the ward unit managers (WUMs) was a longitudinal study. It comprised two conversations held with each individual manager during December 1988 and again in May 1990. The conversations dealt with financial management accounting data, the associated systems, how these were handled and any perceived changes. This was an approach based upon the individual WUM, so that differences between the WUMs were expected, even though it might be anticipated that the types of issue raised by them might be common. For example, the way in which an individual expressed their interest in budgets, and the ways in which the individual described them and used them, was considered to be directly related to the individual's personality and pattern of leadership (Argyris, 1952). Consequently there is a simple listing of eight psychological/organisational issues which were anticipated:

1. The budget is imposed without the manager's influence.
2. This budget is more related to cash limits than to the unit's work.
3. The financial management accounting data received are from a source hierarchically above the manager in the hospital, and are based upon a custodial accounting system for financial accounting.

4. The accounting data are inadequate and untimely for the manager. The accounting system does little to alter this situation and it is evolving to deal with cash-restricted budgets.
5. The manager has little appreciation of budgets and associated matters, and has not been trained in these areas.
6. The manager does not have financial awareness and does not understand the data, and consequently he or she has only a limited ability to use it.
7. The ability of a manager to control the expenditures from the cash-restricted budget will depend upon the extent to which he or she can control the activities of the area, and the extent to which the expenditures on these activities coincide with budget.
8. The manager considers that specific knowledge about the budget should not go any further, because, for example, the manager is responsible for the budget.

It is not desirable to classify these eight issues into other groupings, because of the manner in which some of the organisational and the psychological issues combine. For example, the notion that 'the budget is imposed without the manager's influence' is at the same time a notion about the organisational structure and about the nature of the manager within that structure.

In this context, a budget can be considered as a financial quantification of a plan, that is, a plan explained in monetary terms. A budget can also act as a control, where the financial components of the budget are an objective which can be measured and acted upon. The budget objective can form an unalterable quantity that has to be attained, or it can represent something quite flexible which moves with events. These issues are re-examined later.

Of course these are not the only issues which could arise, but, from the author's experience with others and from a position outside the NHS, these seemed to be the ones which might occur with 'naive' individuals. This framework was based upon the notion that, assuming that most of the managers were likely to come from within the NHS, the WUMs would be 'naive' in relation to financial management accounting data in general, and any new data in particular. Furthermore, it is impossible to know the situation in an organisation like the Hospital in advance of any study.

From this perspective, it was anticipated that a naive recipient of financial management accounting data would have difficulties in handling the data, and as a possible consequence of that naivety could choose to ignore the data. It was also possible that a naive recipient might improve his or her awareness of that data, and might learn through using the data, or through explanations about the data, or through formal training, or any combination of these actions.

The study: the ward unit managers

The ward unit managers worked in a teaching hospital which claimed to be one of the earliest to introduce

1. clinical budgets (budgeting based around the idea of a doctor as a centre of activity);
2. resource management (a concept of planning the deployment of funds in a hospital, rather than allowing them to go into the same areas that they had in perhaps previous years); and
3. unit budgets. The unit budget was the provision of funds for the structure which the hospital designated to be a unit. (During the course of the study, one of the original ward unit managers left and was replaced.)

In 1985/6 the hospital took the then rare decision to form clinical directorates. With this structure, doctors became responsible as clinical directors for the care and the costs of a unit of wards. Ward unit managers were appointed to help administer each unit and occupy the position of budget holder for the unit. They also took over some parts of the roles of the existing nursing officers. The majority of WUMs in this hospital had been nursing officers. In those instances where the WUM was not a nurse there was a senior clinical nurse to advise.

In the four units studied, the WUM was responsible for a group of between four to nine wards. They had the management responsibility for all of the staff on the wards from the registrar downwards. The WUMs were responsible for administering the unit's budget for all ward activities. The exceptions to this were the student nurses, and central services such as meals and cleaning. In the previous three years each WUM had received a cash-restricted budget for the whole unit. When the study started, the central accounting system provided each WUM with a monthly computer printout for the whole unit, but nothing about the individual wards.

The printout contained a summary of staff, an expenditure summary outlining staff, drugs, medical supplies and surgical equipment (ward supplies) and the amount of the annual budget. The expenditure summary also included the overall monthly total of cash paid out by the finance department for the unit, and the cumulative total of cash paid out during the financial year.

The conversations with the WUMs were approached in an open manner. They were told of the author's interest in financial management accounting data and asked to talk quite freely about their work in relation to any aspects of these. Notes of each conversation were taken, then written up and given to each manager for amendment or comment. (See Purdy, 1993a, for further details of the methodology and notes). These notes form the basis for the remainder of this section, which is a summary of the WUMs' position in relation to the framework of eight issues formulated earlier.

Imposition of the budget

The WUMs observed that the unit's budget had been imposed upon them. This was after all of them had in some way questioned, with the hospital's general manager, the way in which the budget had been set. Consequently the managers felt that they had no influence upon the budget and the amount of funds with which to operate the unit. The only way in which a budget might be increased was if a manager could identify and make a successful application for funds in an area which the government considered a priority.

The budget is a cash limit

The budget was imposed in the form of a cash limit, and it had been derived using the assumptions of the government and NHS systems, as well as the previous practices of the hospital towards allocating funds. The WUMs considered that there were problems with such a derivation: it was based upon outdated precedents which understated each unit's needs for staff; the government's cash limits calculated staff costs using the mid-point of the salary scale, but usually staff were above this point. Consequently WUMs recognised that the budget was faulty and would be immediately exceeded as soon as the financial year started. To deal with this, WUMs had reconsidered staffing in the context of maintaining safe nursing levels. Such was the pressure to reduce staff that one WUM produced a new nursing establishment to do so. In order to work sensibly, each WUM produced their own independent budget related to the unit, up to the cash limit.

The source of financial management accounting data

Each WUM received the budget from the general manager and the monthly printout of other data from the finance department. The WUMs felt these printouts were of little use, being expenditure summaries.

The adequacy of the data

This monthly printout was a problem for the WUMs, since it invariably contained inaccuracies, was always late and did not structure the data adequately.

By way of improvement some WUMS wanted less aggregation and more analysis, and some wanted separate ward data.

The appreciation of budgets and training

Initially, although the budgets did not make sense, the WUMs thought they had an appreciation of budgets. Over time they produced their own independent budgets yet each operated their own budget in a different manner. Two WUMs had been promoted from within the hospital and had received in-post training concerned with budgeting; the other WUMs had pre-hospital training which included budgeting, yet they still could not understand the unit budget. Each of the WUMs had fostered budget understanding on their own initiative.

Financial awareness and data use

The WUMs' ability to use the data was hampered initially by their lack of appreciation of the derivation of the budget. Those from outside the hospital were additionally hampered by a lack of understanding about the working of the unit. In contrast to the others, one manager had discussed the monthly unit printout with the ward sisters. This WUM went on to obtain similar monthly details for each ward which were passed on to the ward sisters, so that they could see the financial effects of their actions. This manager's idea was that the responsibility for certain expenditures fell to the ward sister, and she would be in a better position to control expenditures if she could construct a budget for her ward.

Expenditure control

Initially the WUMs found it difficult to control expenditures because they bore no relationship to the unit's activity. By way of reaction they produced their own independent budgets. The way in which these were controlled varied with the manager. One manager was keen to pursue budgeting with the ward sisters so that they became more involved with financial affairs and expenditure control. Another produced very precise budgets which were closely monitored against actual costs, and closed beds at times to remain within the budget. A third had prepared a budget, but the subsequent control was centred upon ensuring that any expense was currently necessary, irrespective of its inclusion in the budget. The fourth had controlled expenditure by changing the nursing system, budgeting on this basis, then monitoring events closely.

Financial data and responsibility

The WUM was responsible for the administration of the unit's budget, and was the recipient of the financial data about the unit, but the actual responsibility was with other people for the expenditures in some areas such as the ward sister in relation to direct patient care. It is in the areas of responsibility that the greatest diversity of practice occurs amongst the WUMs. This diversity occurs with the control of activity on the wards, the control of the budget for these activities, the manager's perception of the manager's responsibility for these activities, the manager's perception of the responsibility of ward sisters and the ward sisters' influence on the activities on the wards and the resulting costs.

Like many of the other seven issues, discussion about financial data and responsibility cannot be taken in isolation. These elements are also entwined with other issues. One WUM had discussed the unit's monthly financial data with the ward sisters in order to further the ward sisters' responsibility and involvement with the budget so that eventually they could create their own ward budgets. These would have defined the activities of the ward sisters and perhaps made these activities more visible to the ward sister, as well as providing her with the basis of a control mechanism. Ward budgets would also enable the manager to have some greater insights into ward activities and likewise provide the opportunity for the manager to exercise more specific control.

Initially a second WUM had involved the ward sisters with the financial management accounting data about ward supplies, and medical staff with drugs, because these were considered to be their areas of responsibility where they had the opportunities to keep expenditures within the budget. At the second conversation this involvement was considered to be greater than ever, and the ward sisters had profiles of staff levels for their own ward and were trying to minimise expenditures on ward supplies and drugs.

The third WUM, initially, was providing the ward sisters with monthly budget data about staff, and discussing these at monthly meetings, together with the costs of ward supplies and drugs, in order to get them to contain expenditures. The formal budgets were not discussed as they were considered to be irrelevant to the unit. The WUM did not want to pressurise the ward sisters into cash restriction, but rather to encourage them to minimise expenditure and keep within the budget.

The fourth WUM did not intend to pressurise the ward sisters as the WUM had been subject to enough pressure. Initially the WUM intended to obtain ward data and delegate the budget for ward supplies. Although the ward data were received, they were for the sole use of the WUM, and the delegation to the ward sisters did not occur. The WUM had tried to involve the doctors in minimising expenditure, but essentially the WUM was the person who had the responsibility to control the unit's expenditure.

Control at an individual level: cash limits, plans and budgets

There are a number of entwined notions relating to the individual and control which come out of these findings. It can be seen that the WUMs have been provided with a 'budget'. Previously a budget was defined as the financial quantification of a plan, but as far as the WUMs were concerned there was no plan relating to the unit. There was a plan by the general manager, since each WUM had been provided with a cash limit which had been imposed on each unit. The general manager's plan was to ensure these cash limits were not breached by any WUM. Although it took them several years, the WUMs eventually produced their own independent budget, which, from their perspective, was a financial quantification of a plan concerning the unit. Thus the cash limit was not really a budget for the WUMs until they each produced their own independent budget for potential expenditures. It would appear that the total cash limit of the individual units was a budget for the general manager, because it was the financial quantification of the planned allocation of the hospital's total cash limit. It would further appear that, in order for there to be control of the control mechanism of a budget, there needs to be some personal recognition of or identification with that mechanism. If this personal link does not exist, then the managers are left to manage a cash limit and not a budget.

The Otley and Berry (1980) control model has been cited as a simple but sound surrogate for an individual's psychological processes relating to control. It has also been observed that there are likely to be other factors, such as learning and training, which are associated with their control model, and which make it more representative of an individual's control processes. The ways in which these factors combine could make control either more or less effective at any point. The factors concerned will vary from the context of the organisation to the individuals involved.

The hospital's general manager had been given a cash limit, which was both a plan and a budget, and which had been imposed by the regional health authority. In terms of the Otley and Berry model, this was the objective which the general manager had to control. The operational objective for the general manager was to allocate the hospital's cash limit. This appeared to be relatively straightforward since it followed the ways in which the hospital's cash limit had been apportioned in previous years. Both the objective received by the general manager and the objective delegated by the general manager were cash limits. Both could be considered as plans and budgets, since they were identical in kind and they were identical in total. There were predicted objectives which could be measured and altered according to the amounts of money calculated to be spent and the amounts actually spent by the hospital in total.

When the general manager imposed the plan and the synonymous cash limit upon a WUM, a WUM only perceived the cash limit part, which was an objective received. The operational objective for a WUM was not the same as for the general manager, because the WUM had to allocate cash to the actual matters of patient treatment and care, and not merely produce another cash limit. Such a situation meant that, if a WUM ignored the planning perspective, there would be no objective, no prediction, no measurement and no alteration of these matters. At any point there would only be spent cash, and then unspent cash up to the extent of the cash limit. The underlying activities would not be specified or specifiable.

This meant that a WUM needed an objective, or even a series of objectives, that the WUM could relate to, such as a plan which indicated and represented the actual work of patient treatment and care. When there were predicted treatment and care operational objectives, it was possible to specify the underlying activities, then to attach financial quantities to form a budget, and then examine both the activities and the financial quantities. Another outcome of setting these operational objectives was that it was then possible for the WUM to investigate potential levels of treatment and care, the potential costs of these, and to vary these as the WUM wanted.

Some of these issues fall within the scope of the Otley and Berry model, whilst other issues are an elaboration of their model. The areas of elaboration include the ability of a WUM to learn or receive training about operational objectives, in order to predict these and the levels of finance attached to them.

Control at an individual level: influence, responsibility and accounting data

In order for an individual to be able to handle the financial management accounting data received and then to use the data for control, the individual needs to be in a position to influence the affairs within the context of the control issue. The ability to use both data and influence is associated with the individual's competence to understand the data and the context of the data.

The conversations with the WUMs showed that they were not in a position to influence the cash limit imposed upon their unit. They could manage the cash limit by producing a plan and a budget which they could then influence and control in various ways. The manner in which they chose to control the budget was bound up with the way they related to those concerned with the delivery of care, and where each manager considered the boundary of responsibility was positioned. These notions about responsibility revealed themselves in different ways.

All of the WUMs were concerned about the control of expenditure in their unit and to keep within the cash limit imposed. One of the largest areas of expenditure for a unit was for the provision of nursing care. All of the WUMs had examined this and made alterations. The most changed situation was in the unit where the WUM had considered providing the ward sisters with data about ward activities, with a view to getting the ward sisters to control their ward expenditures. This was not carried out because the WUM did not want to subject the ward sisters to the pressures felt by the WUM. Also the WUM felt strongly that the issue of controlling expenditure to keep within the cash limit was the WUM's responsibility. Having considered alternative objectives, in a manner consistent with the Otley and Berry control model as modified by the author, the WUM decided that the only way in which the unit could keep within the imposed cash limit was to change the work of nursing so that the system fitted the cash limit. In this way the WUM planned the system, set a precise budget and then personally monitored all nursing changes and all expenditures.

The other three WUMs had made alterations, but to the existing staff pattern, still in a manner consistent with the modified Otley and Berry model. These three WUMs also mentioned that they wanted the ward sisters to take a more active part in controlling expenditure, but in these units it was carried out. Each WUM had an individual approach to the issue of expenditure control and the methods through which the ward sisters could exercise their influence and control.

One WUM had provided the ward sisters with some data about the unit at the monthly meeting of the unit. At these meetings, the WUM had discussed these data with the ward sisters and the issue of cash restraints imposed upon the unit, and then urged the ward sisters to restrain activities to curtail expenditures. The second WUM had initially provided the ward sisters with the unit's financial management accounting data. These were discussed at staff meetings and at other times with the ward sisters, when they were asked to keep all spending to a minimum. In order to keep within the imposed cash limit, the WUM closed a ward for a period. At a later time, after experiencing difficulties with the financial management accounting data from the finance department, the WUM had produced plans for the unit and kept detailed costings and precise budgets of activities. The staffing profiles for each ward were agreed with each ward sister, then provided to each ward sister who was urged to minimise the ward expenditures. The WUM then personally monitored all budgets with actual activities and expenditures. Both of these WUMs acted in a manner consistent with the modified Otley and Berry model.

The third WUM wanted the ward sisters to acquire some understanding about how the decisions and the actions that they took on the ward became an expenditure for the ward and then the unit. The WUM wanted the finance department to provide the ward sisters with data about their wards, and anticipated that in time the ward sisters would be in a position to formulate plans and budgets for their ward. This WUM was seeking to establish a further tier of management and responsibility with budgets. The procedure would have been for each ward sister to have their own control mechanism, through which they established plans and budgets for their ward, with suitable assistance and agreement of the WUM, and which operated according to the Otley and Berry model, as modified earlier. When established, these plans and budgets would have formed a part of the WUM's Unit plans and budgets. It seems likely that such procedures would have provided the WUM with finer explications of control than currently existed. At the same time it might have led to closer financial control, and perhaps other controls, at the point of nursing care.

The exercise of control through influence and the use of data in context are also associated with the individual's ability to understand the data. Even if an individual can exercise influence and has received data, it may not be possible for the individual to act, and hence control, because the data are not understood. In this case the cash limits, in the form of budgets, were not understood by the WUMs or seen to be related to their own unit. Additionally, even though they had all received training about budgets, this apparently had done little to prevent their confusion and perhaps not helped them to exercise the most effective control. It seems as though control was not most effectively exercised until the WUMs had passed through a process of natural learning about budgeting, which also led them to produce their own budgets. Thus the Otley and Berry control model requires to be associated with learning to enable, for example, objectives to be established.

Also related to this issue is the timeliness of data provision, and the content of the finance department's data sheets. The WUMs considered that the unsuitably structured historic data sheets were of little use, and always too late. Sensible control can only be exercised when timely data are available and when the data are material which the users can understand and utilise.

Concluding observations

The earlier parts of this chapter have sought to demonstrate some of the issues faced by managers as they deliver health care and control cash budgets. The emphasis has been on a psychological perspective concerned with the way managers have responded to change with the provision of financial management accounting data and the imposition of cash limits. The chapter has been concerned to outline a general framework of psychological/organisational issues in which such managers can be individually located, and to summarise their common positions in relation to this. It has then moved on to detail and examine each individual's approach to the control of the workplace issues which each individual has perceived. This has been based upon conversations with the managers of four ward units.

For simplicity the issue of control has been explored using the four phases of the Otley and Berry control model, as a surrogate model of individual control. This model has been modified or elaborated to include a consideration of influence, information and training, but more particularly the learning associated with control. It has been found that the explanations of their actions by the ward unit managers can be encompassed by the elaborated model, even though this meant that the actual forms of control varied with each individual. The model also encompasses the actions of the general manager, although the evidence is based upon the WUMs' view of the general manager. These findings and analysis provide a method for explaining the sequential mechanism of the imposition of cash limits in the NHS by the government, which appears to be unproblematic until the delivery of treatment and care is required.

The government sets the overall cash limit for the NHS which is then allocated through the regional health authority to the general manager of a hospital unit. It would appear that all of the individuals who are concerned with these sub-allocations, up to and including the general manager, can act in a similar manner. Their immediate boss imposes a cash limit upon their area of responsibility and it is the individual's job to accept and to allocate the imposed cash limit. This seems to work in a straightforward manner because both the objective which is received and imposed and the objective which has to be operationalised are in the form of a cash limit. Also, in general, these allocations are simply based upon historical precedent and the previous year. After the hospital general manager has allocated the cash limit to the WUMs it is presented to them as a cash budget with which to finance the activities under their responsibility.

It was impossible for the WUMs to manage their cash budget by simple reallocation, as there was no management structure to allocate it to. This was because they were responsible for the health care activities in their units and needed to acquire some operational understanding of their unit's activities. The accounting systems were not set up to provide them with the types of data which they needed for both planning and control. The existing accounting systems concentrated upon stewardship control. In general the WUMs understood neither how the cash limit/cash budget related to their unit, nor what was the meaning or usefulness of the reporting data provided by the finance department.

In order to make the cash budget/cash limit meaningful, the WUMs had to create their own understanding of a budget and put it into their own perspectives, and so the WUMs created their own budgets. They did so in different ways which reflected the individual approach of the WUMs and local circumstances in the unit. Faced with a limit on the cash they could spend, the WUMs had to examine the alternative operational activities and prepare both an operational plan and a budget which did not exceed the cash limit. It was at this point that a plethora of issues confronted the WUMs. They had to plan for treatment and care which would match the cash limit, rather than plan wholly in a way which was consonant with the needs of patients, as perceived by medical and nursing staffs. This was because none of the WUMs considered that their cash limit would finance their unit's current level of activities. They had to find ways of immediately saving cash, or producing longer-term cash savings, or more effective treatment and care regimes which would allow an increase in the number of patients seen.

Over several years, the WUMs found ways of dealing with the cash limit, so that one WUM changed the nursing system, another closed beds, a third closed a ward and a fourth urged the ward sisters to restrain their expenditures. The project specifically sought neither complete details of the processes involved nor the views of the general manager about the performance of the WUMs. The WUMs indicated that their actions were accepted by the general manager and, in some cases, the gains which they had brought to the system were acknowledged. Confirmation of this would appear to be the continuation of the WUMs in their jobs.

The introduction of a general management structure into the NHS, along with the allocation of cash limits throughout the system, has had a variety of effects, and a few are considered here. There have been different types of controls introduced, in particular the control of a rigid unalterable cash limit at unit level. These in turn, and amongst other things, seem to have fostered the discussion of crucial issues, some of which perhaps went undiscussed previously, such as bed closures, or were not even considered, such as a changed nursing system. Although it is unlikely that the WUMs took any far-reaching decisions without discussions with others, the individual ways in which the problems were resolved may enable somewhat arbitrary and very localised decisions to be taken about treatment and care, which may resolve an issue in one location but have undesirable effects elsewhere.

There is a greater awareness of activities undertaken, a greater consciousness of the costs and expenditures of these, and a shift in the way in which financial matters are handled in the NHS. At the forefront of these reforms has been the introduction of cash limits and cash budgets at the operational level of the WUMs, together with their plans. One matter which seems to have caused a great deal of confusion, misunderstanding and misdirected anger at accountants is the fact that the notion of a budget was introduced into this operational level of management in the form of a cash limit. The general manager and the finance department provided the WUMs with an imposed cash limit, which all of the WUMs referred to as a budget. A budget was defined earlier as the financial quantification of a plan. This would seem to be a reasonable working definition because all of the WUMs initially thought that the imposed cash limit, called a cash budget, had a plan relating to their unit underpinning it. Of course this was not the situation: the general manager had a plan for allocating cash, and this did not resemble the operation of the unit. It was the limitation of the cash which had caused and was causing problems for the WUMs, not the notion of budgeting. Since the cash limit was presented to them as a cash budget, the notion of a budget took the blame for the notion of a limit. The notion of a budget was not introduced in a positive context; the budget was synonymous with the cash limit and, because of this synonymity, it seems likely to have prevented the useful aspects of budgeting from becoming apparent a lot sooner.

The positive aspects to the planning and budgeting practised by the WUMs are that now there are plans at the operational level of the patient which make available patterns of treatment and care; these plans can indicate where treatment and care are considered to be ideal and where this is not the situation; all of this can then be set into a financial context. A system such as this would facilitate planning from the level of the patient upwards, through the NHS to government. This seems to represent a more sensible approach than the uncertain results from cash limits. The government has sought to keep the amount of cash spent to its prescribed limits. This means that the basic issue which is being controlled is the cash limit. The overall cash limit for the NHS is centrally determined and this amount is apportioned throughout the NHS until it arrives at a manager, such as a WUM, who is to finance care and spend the cash.

It would appear that the method of allocating the cash does control the cash, but it does not take into consideration any consequences for care. It is left to those managers responsible for directly spending cash to arrange that this care is kept within the cash limit, as opposed to ensuring that the perceived care is available. It is not clear that this is the best way of managing health care, as opposed to managing cash limits.

CHAPTER 17

Management control in schools

Jane Broadbent

In this chapter we shall look at management control in schools, not only as an example of control in a specific situation but also as a vehicle by which to reflect upon the framework of control suggested by Ouchi (1979, 1980) which we referred to in Chapter 3. We shall use Ouchi's framework as a heuristic device giving 'ideal types' of different approaches to control and we show how these ideals of hierarchical (or bureaucratic), market and clan control can be used to understand the approaches to management and control in schools. The chapter will also illustrate the effect of organisational participants with deeply held values on political and legislative attempts to change control mechanisms in particular organisations. Before the introduction of legislation in 1988, schools in the UK had been involved with management control only in an educational sense. They are now having to grapple with broader management issues, following the introduction of local management of schools (LMS), the details of which we shall examine later in the chapter.

Introduction and historical background

The management structures of schools have been radically altered in recent years by a series of legislative acts which have been designed to change the accountabilities which exist in the educational sphere, as well as the location of decision making. Following the 1944 Education Act, which set up the postwar system of state education, a three-tier bureaucratic or hierarchical structure was developed. In this structure the levels of strategic, management and operational control described by Anthony and discussed in Chapter 2 may be identified. The control system was therefore hierarchical in nature. At the top of the hierarchy was the Department for Education[1] (the central government level), next was the local education authority (at local government level) and finally came the schools themselves. Strategic control in the guise of policy decisions was located at the Department of Education on a national basis, but the local education authority (LEA) as a subsection of the elected local authority (LA) had a great deal of power to set local policies and to influence the operation of schools in their control. The LAs were the legal owners of the schools and the equipment within them; they also were the direct employers of the staff. The LEA was the main focus of management control, controlling, for example, funding for the education services and deciding how to allocate the budget which had been set by the local authority and which was raised from local taxation and made available as block grants from central government. The LEA also had a role in the inspection of the educational standards of the school it controlled and could set educational policies. Advisory services acted to develop the educational aspects of the service and there were specialised departments looking, for example, to the maintenance of schools and the employment of teachers. Other departments of the local authority provided services such as cleaning, grounds maintenance and school meals. Whilst policy issues were decided both at central and local government levels by elected representatives, the headteacher dealt with the day-to-day conduct of the school, the operational control, and was responsible for the educational provision therein. The incumbent of that role had limited responsibility to commit resources, acting to channel requests to the LEA who could then determine priorities for the area as a whole. A board of governors existed for each school, and they had some input into discussions of local matters pertaining to the school and how the LEA policy was implemented at school level. There was no responsibility on this body to manage resources and the membership was limited, often biased towards LEA representatives. Control of teaching and learning processes within the classroom cannot easily be directly supervised and professional standards and values, which we might see as clan control, can be argued to have a large part to play in the operational control of the activity of teaching.

New control structures have now been introduced which can be argued to have changed the location of strategic and management controls and thus the relative influence of the different parties (particularly the LEA): some attempts to influence the professional control of the teaching process have also been made.

The new philosophy of control

Before turning to examine the nature of the new controls which have been imposed on schools it is useful to make quite explicit the philosophy which has underpinned many of the recent changes in control structures within the public sector in the UK (and in many other parts of the world: Hood, 1991; Broadbent and Guthrie, 1992). This changing philosophy has been referred to earlier (Chapter 3) and is characterised by a claim to move away from a system of hierarchical control to a system which lays claim to a reliance on a market-based one, but which still exists in the context of a hierarchy. Whether it achieves this market approach is debatable, but this does not undermine the extent to which the claims for the legitimacy of the approach rest in the context of 'the market' and reject the hierarchical or bureaucratic.

The roots of change in the public sector can be found in the Financial Management Initiative (FMI) the basic elements of which were laid out in Cmnd 8616, 'Efficiency and Effectiveness in the Civil Service'. The FMI implicitly uses a notion of private sector management to inform the approach to managing the public sector. It seeks to provide a framework within which individuals are made accountable and the use of financial resources is a central element of accountability. Hood (1991) lists seven characteristics of what he terms 'the new public management model':

1. The importance of financial devolution to service units.
2. Explicit standards and measures of performance for those units.
3. A clear relationship between inputs, outputs and performance measures.
4. Increased accountability requirements on the units.
5. A stress on private sector management styles.
6. A stress on competition and contracting between units.
7. A stress on efficiency and parsimony in resource usage.

As can be seen from the list, one element of FMI is the need to link input resources to outputs. This requires the ability to measure outputs, which is also a requirement of the market approach to control. The philosophy of market-based control is thus mixed into 'the new public management' model. It is perhaps clear that what is desired is control of the outputs of the system, but there is no real clarity as to whether this should be achieved through the direct (and perhaps hierarchical or bureaucratic) control of linking inputs and outputs (resources being given on the basis of the outputs actually achieved in a more bureaucratic way) or whether a market should be used as a means to mediate this relationship. The use of the market control has the advantage of the possibility of delegating blame for poor outcomes away from the controller (in this case the government) as any outcome is the responsibility of 'the market' or of the service to which the work has been delegated. We will demonstrate how a market-type logic has been used in designing the control systems for schools, without abandoning the possibility of the use of output controls through a hierarchical approach.

Changing processes of control

In summary we can argue that the imposition of FMI logic and a market approach in schools has led to operational and management control now being located at school level. The LEA's role in management control of the service is much reduced. Clan control of the activity of teaching has been put under some pressure by the requirements of the national curriculum and testing regimes (see below). Strategies are still controlled in a bureaucratic or hierarchical fashion by central government.

The Education Act 1986 started the process by which control of schools was to be taken away from the LEA and redistributed between the central government on the one hand and the schools and parents on the other.[2] This act set up the principle of parent representation on school governing bodies, a situation which some LEAs had already voluntarily adopted. This change signalled the perceived importance of parents in the process of educational management. However the most significant changes were started with the Education Reform Act 1988 (ERA). This Act introduced educational changes, the national curriculum with a programme of national testing and reporting of test and examination results, alongside LMS. It can be argued that the educational issues of the national curriculum and national testing form the basis for a challenge to the clan control of the teaching process. The central concern of this chapter will be with LMS and its implications for management control, rather than the educational changes, but it will be seen that LMS is closely related to education issues through the funding mechanisms.

LMS and formula funding

The practical implications of LMS are extensive. While responsibility for capital expenditure still lies with the LEA (who have a 'landlord' role) a school is now a responsibility centre with the task of preparing annual budgets and controlling the day to day expenditure of the organisation.

The issue of resourcing the school is rather more complex and to understand this we need to consider the manner in which resources are distributed to schools. The LEA still has some influence in this respect as it has to decide the overall amount which will be spent by all schools under its control. A small number of central services are still retained by them (home to school transport, for example) but 85 per cent of the overall educational budget must be distributed to schools (this proportion will increase to 90 per cent in April 1995). The LEA has the power to decide the distribution of the balance of the educational budget to the individual schools, but has to do this on the basis of a publicly stated formula (the aim being to give an objective basis on which schools can predict their budget share for planning purposes). An important element of the formula is that 75 per cent of the budget to be distributed to schools must be distributed on an 'age-weighted pupil numbers' basis.

The outcome of the implementation of formula funding is that the basis of provision of resources to schools is measured largely by pupil numbers; thus the ability of LEAs to give priority to other bases of need (for example, social deprivation) has been considerably reduced. The outcome has been that some schools have received relatively more, whilst others have received relatively less than they might otherwise have expected. In a time of tight control over the whole of local government spending the ability to protect the schools who were relative losers has been highly constrained and some painful readjustments have been inevitable. Given that the schools spend about 85 per cent of their budget on salaries, the outcome has been loss of jobs in some schools. Thus, not only have headteachers and governing bodies had to control their own budgets for the first time, they have often had to do so in the most difficult of situations, that of a declining resource base.

Local management of schools, delegated authority and standardisation

Local management of schools has also changed the location of decision making. In line with the philosophy of the new public management, the authority to run the school was delegated to the school level, to the governing body. Thus management control is delegated to schools and LEAs, as a consequence, have lost much of their role in this respect. The constitution of the governing body was defined to ensure representation from parents, local business people and teachers as well as the locally elected political parties. This was meant to increase the extent of accountability to different constituencies and to bring in experience from the private sector. Governing bodies have the right to hire and fire staff and to spend the resources allocated to them in whatever way they wish, provided the requirements of the national curriculum are met. The duties and responsibilities of the governing body are comprehensive but, de facto, the day-to-day operation of the school is now effectively in the control of the headteacher. Research has shown that the implementation of the LMS initiative has been soaked up by a small group of the school community seeking to 'protect' the rest of the school from these management changes, which they see as peripheral to the main educational aims of the school (Broadbent *et al.*, 1993; Laughlin *et al.*, 1994). One aim of the legislation was to try to ensure that a wider set of views were represented in the decision-making processes and it is unclear whether this has de facto been achieved. Empirical research also suggests that LMS has generated much stress for teachers who find themselves having to deal with financial and management issues for which they have had little training (Laughlin *et al.*, 1993; Broadbent, forthcoming).

By delegating responsibility to schools decision making was intended to be given to those who 'know best' – those who work at the operational level. The delegation of responsibility also provides the opportunity for the delegation of blame (Armstrong, 1989) for cuts to the local level and away from central government. This is a significant factor, given not only a downward pressure on LA spending from central government, but also a declining school population, leading to overprovision of school places and a need to close some schools. However it must be emphasised that the delegation downward to schools was accompanied by the centralised national curriculum. This ensured that, although schools can choose how best to use their resources to deliver the national curriculum, they have little choice of what to deliver. The delegation to local level is therefore countered by a strong centralising tendency which also emphasised a high level of standardisation. The process of standardisation is a familiar tactic for control and is illustrated in the scientific management approach of F. W. Taylor. It enables the comparison of actual performance against standard, any deviation can be highlighted and steps can be taken to 'control' that variation. Thus standards of achievement for pupils, albeit minimum standards, are set which will be checked through national testing regimes. In the case of schools the philosophy of LMS and the standardisation inherent in it further seems to imply that very similar resources can achieve the same educational outputs from different children. Finally we should note that the process of standardisation can also be seen as a strong challenge to the professional or clan control of the teaching process.

LMS and the philosophy of market-based control

Whilst the setting of standards provides a control mechanism through the comparison of actual performance against the standard set, it also provides the information which is deemed to be required in the attempt to implement a control strategy based on the 'market'. The attempt to introduce a 'market' has been facilitated by linking together financial and educational issues. This has been made possible because of the standardisation processes introduced as a consequence of the national curriculum which allows some measurement of 'output'. Added to this is the introduction of formula funding, which means that resources are closely linked to pupil numbers and a policy of open enrolment (see below). The market-based mode of control is premised on the existence of competition between different suppliers, and the possibility for those who require the service in question to have the ability to choose a supplier. It is assumed that schools will now compete to provide a service to pupils and that parents will choose more actively where to send their child to school. Popular schools will expand and unpopular ones will be forced to close (or improve).

Under the previous LEA bureaucratic system, schools received the children in their catchment area and the ability of parents to send their children to other schools was constrained. Now, under open enrolment, there is, de jure, much more opportunity for parents to exercise choice. De facto, this may not be the case; the physical capacity of schools still imposes some constraint on pupil numbers and geographical location or the socioeconomic status of the area may also play a part. In both urban and rural districts, travelling time to school will be a factor in constraining choice; for some parents with work commitments or with limited choices of transport there may be no choice at all.

The fact that much of the funding which a school receives is based on age-weighted school numbers means that a school has to be attractive enough to the pupils and their parents to enrol sufficient pupils to ensure enough funds to run a viable school. A viable school must be able to provide the national curriculum for its pupils and this means it must have sufficient numbers of staff to cover all aspects of the syllabi. It is assumed that schools will, therefore, compete for pupils to ensure they generate resources. It is also assumed that parents will exercise choice. In order to make a choice about the school which a child should attend it is assumed that information about the performance of the school will be required. The information which is assumed to be needed is not just the 'grapevine' information that exists in any community about the schools within it, but more 'objective' and public performance-related data. The data which are deemed to give an indication of the output of schools are statistics of examination performance – the national GCSE and A-level examinations are already reported in league table form and the testing which is planned to accompany the national curriculum is meant to supplement this – along with details of absenteeism. It is assumed that parents will make their choice of school on this basis and because schools need to retain sufficient pupil numbers they must take these indicators seriously.

This new approach to control in schools is a powerful one which uses ideas of delegation of responsibility, a philosophy of market-based competition at the operational level and a strong tendency to centralise and standardise. It gives an indication that in practice the dichotomy between hierarchical and market-based control is not clear-cut (see the critique offered in Chapter 16) and that control processes are often complex rather than tidy. The next question to be asked is the extent to which these controls produce the control required, to use Drucker's terminology (Drucker, 1964). Put another way, we may ask whether the controls produce the desired outcomes.

Approaches to the evaluation of controls in schools

The possibility that schools will 'raise standards' by placing greater emphasis on examination results based on a centrally controlled curriculum is, arguably, a focus which underlies the whole initiative. This interpretation is based on the assumption that government policy is geared towards a belief that better examination results will mean 'better' education. Accepting this argument allows us to evaluate LMS from two different perspectives. First is the issue of whether examination results do give an indication of the quality of the educational experience provided by a particular school. This leads us to consider whether a system based on this output control is appropriate for education. Second is the issue of whether the controls which are implemented achieve the control which is desired. The first issue might be argued to be a 'political' question of choice rather than a central control issue, but we will consider it here because it does impinge on the way in which the controls have an effect in a practical situation and because the need to define an output measure is central to the FMI approach to control. The second issue is important as it illustrates the dysfunctions associated with the practical working of the FMI as a control system.

Is there a linkage between examination results and school performance?

Perhaps one of the most contentious issues in the whole of the implementation of LMS and other elements of ERA is the issue of the testing of children's progress and the reporting of the test results. Results of both public examinations and the periodic tests associated with the national curriculum (standard attainment tests or SATS as they are called) are to be reported, and not just to individual pupils and their parents: but the overall results are to be collated and national league tables are to be drawn up. These results can, it is argued, provide the output measures which are necessary for a mode of control which is based on the philosophy of FMI and which wishes to see managers responsible for the outputs of their operational unit. The main issue of contention is whether the output measures selected do reasonably represent that which education sets out to achieve. It can be argued that the examination results are not a good proxy for the outputs of the educational process and that it is questionable whether the outputs measured bear any relation to the transformation of the inputs which occurs in the processes of teaching within the organisation. Teachers would argue that while examination results are important they are not the only outcome of education and may be more important for some children than others. The examination results tables only measure a limited range of a child's competence as a human being. Thus the 'value added' to a child by the school is not measured and the visibility attached to examination results emphasises one particular set of achievements (perhaps 'examination competences added') over the many other achievements a child may have.

In a critique of 'economic reason' Andre Gorz (1989) suggests that there are areas which should not be driven by economic reason because they do not create commodities. The caring professions such as teaching do not produce commodities because (using Gorz's definition) they are not activities geared towards providing items in a measurable amount of time at as high a level of productivity as possible. He argues that to follow this pattern might in fact be detrimental as the quality of care may well not be quantifiable in relation to output measures. He argues that service 'depends on a person to person relationship, not on the basis of quantifiable actions' (Gorz, 1989, p.143). Research (Broadbent *et al.*, 1993; Broadbent, 1992) has revealed much resistance to the idea that the outputs of the schools can be measured. This belief is justified by appeals to the value set of education. This value set is claimed by teachers to be rooted in relationships and based on a desire to help individual pupils achieve their own unique best.

It is important to highlight the fact that there is a lack of clarity in the linkages between inputs and outputs which are inherent in the way LMS is currently conceived. If we consider the way in which LMS and the market based system work, the implied relationship is between input resources (the amount of money which a school is allocated by the age-weighted formula) and output educational results (such as exam results or truancy rates). This relationship is mediated, as explained earlier, through the choice of the parent, the reported results providing the basis of a more informed choice. Thus a market-based approach is being applied. However the reported results establish no linkage between the status of the child which is put into the system to be educated and the eventual educational achievement of that child. This is seen as unfair to teachers, as the output results may well be the result of the status of a given intake of children rather than a 'better' educational process within the school. Put crudely, the ability, say, to recognise colours may be an incredible achievement for one child, but a matter of little consequence to another. Measuring both by the same scale does little justice to the achievements of either child – or the educators of either child.

This means that the information supplied to the 'market-place' can be irrelevant, misleading or biased in a technical sense. It should therefore lead to questions about whether the 'market' can really work in this area. However, if the 'market' fails to produce the results which the legislation requires, that is an increase in standards as measured by the outputs reported, there is the possibility of adopting a more hierarchical FMI approach based on the linking of input resources to outputs. This would result in schools being resourced, not on the numbers of pupils attending, but on the basis of the reported output measures. Because of the perceived crudity of the output measures, it is this possibility which schools most fear.

The control implications of the new system

In Chapter 6 we discussed research into the dysfunctions of budgeting and the unintended consequences of applying controls. Dysfunctions may arise for many reasons, but it is often noted that a successful control system will need to align individual objectives with those of the organisation (as in Hopwood's idea of self-control, discussed in Chapter 2). In commercial organisations some element of self-control is often seen as being best achieved through promoting the self-interest of managers who are offered salary bonuses for achieving objectives such as profit or sales targets. This type of linkage is not yet being applied in education, although the granting of some broad flexibility to governing bodies to set the salary point of individual teachers (subject to a national scale and some broad guidance) may be seeking to change this.

Even if these linkages were made, it is unclear whether teachers would respond in the desired way. A fundamental issue, perhaps, is whether the objectives of individual teachers, informed by a particular value set, can ever be seen to be in alignment with objectives imposed by the Education Reform Act in general and LMS in particular, for the professional work of teachers seems to be based on a very different value set (Broadbent, 1992). It has always to be remembered that a pathway of change is not one which can be unproblematically chosen. Laughlin (1987) emphasises the importance of changes in the life world (which includes the values) of the organisation in analysing the extent of organisational change. He notes that, without a fundamental shift in the life world, only first order change can be said to have taken place. By first order change we mean that an imposed change is either rejected outright or absorbed so that the organisation reorients itself to the change in a way which does not change the fundamental life world. The latter situation seems to describe schools at the moment, where the existence of a small 'absorbing group' of individuals who soak up the changes protects the rest of the school from their impingement (Laughlin *et al.*, 1994).

As well as leading to an absorption of change rather than fundamental changes in values or life worlds, the imposition of particular control systems can lead, not to control, but to manipulation of a system. Thus, it can be argued, as in any budgeting system, 'games' will take place in schools which will not particularly ensure that the system works as it is intended by those designing it, but will secure the required results for those operating it. For example, good examination results can be achieved by being selective about the intake of pupils rather than by giving higher standards of education. Further the possibility that the emphasis and corresponding visibility given to particular elements such as examination results will in turn make other elements invisible and less valued heightens the concern of teachers about the implementation of these new controls. Already there is public debate about whether more children with behavioural problems such as truancy are now being excluded from schools because of the likelihood that they will adversely affect the schools' scores on the league tables of measured outputs such as truancy rates. Thus selectivity of admissions and examination entries may ensue, as well as manipulation of results.

In summary we might conclude that an evaluation of LMS as a control system is problematic. Whilst it promotes a focus on certain outcomes, the desirability of those outcomes to teachers and pupils and what those outcomes actually 'measure' are open to question, because of both educational issues and the possibility of manipulating results.

Summary

This chapter illustrates a particular example of an attempt to change the control systems of an organisation. It illustrates how the previous systems of bureaucratic and clan controls have been challenged and how there has been an attempt to impose on schools a type of control based on markets in the context of a hierarchy. Thus the extent to which control systems in any organisation are often an amalgam of approaches is demonstrated. The issue of output controls in the context of schools is discussed. Problems associated with their use in this type of organisational context (in which agreement about the nature of outputs is not easily achieved and in which outputs are not easily quantified) have been highlighted. The example of LMS gives a useful illustration of the way in which the values of organisational members (or the organisational life world) can affect the extent of any change in that organisation.

It could be argued that LMS gives an example of an ideological approach to control and that the legislation which has imposed LMS has not taken account of the values of the teaching profession. Instead it has sought to impose the 'new public management' as a consequence of the ideological stance of the government. Thus we have a situation in which one set of deeply held values is in conflict with another. While government has the power to legislate we can also see that there is always a possibility of mobilising the resistance of those within the organisation which is the focus of the legislation.

We can also see the problems of control in a human service organisation where the essential inputs, children, are also the outputs. The task of learning has to be substantially achieved by the children themselves, under the guidance of teachers and the possible encouragement of parents. The fact that this transformation process is imprecise and that there is immense difficulty in measuring inputs and outputs makes the available control models very difficult to use. Because there is a great desire to achieve particular outcomes and there is a recognition of the limited extent to which control of the transformation process can be achieved, attempts to try to quantify and measure the desired outcomes have been made. The question with which we are left is whether we are attempting to measure the unmeasurable in an attempt to apply a control model which is inappropriate in the circumstances.

Notes

1. This is the current title of the department; it has had several different names throughout the period.
2. The desire to provide FMI and market-based control was perhaps one element which gave rise to changes. Another element might be argued to be a desire to eliminate the control of the LEAs over education. This might be seen as a response designed to neuter the power of the left-wing local authorities. Whilst this aspect of the changes is recognised it will not be discussed at length as the concern of the chapter is with the changing structures of control rather than the reasons for the changes.

CHAPTER 18

Management control in the financial services sector

Kim Soin

Introduction

The UK financial services industry is one of the largest sectors in the UK, employing around 400 000 people (more than any other industry except for the civil service and the health service). The productivity revolution that swept through the manufacturing industry a decade ago has now reached financial services. Because the industry is coming to restructuring late, the changes are being pushed through fairly fast. At Lloyds, the chief executive has predicted that up to 100 000 jobs will be cut from the industry this decade. The general consensus among the major UK banks is that there is enormous scope for rationalisation and a need to keep costs at an acceptable level in relation to income.

The development of management control systems in the UK banking industry has been inextricably linked to the changes that have taken place in the economic, political and regulatory environment over the last decade. This chapter outlines these changes and the way in which banks have responded, and explains how management control systems have changed and developed in relation to the new ethos in clearing banking. This new ethos is embodied in profitability, cost awareness and shareholder value. This is a marked shift from the past, when a banks' success was measured by the size of its assets. The marketing philosophy has moved from the mass marketing of the 1980s to market positioning and segmentation. There is now more interest in a profitable product line than in a full product line.

The detail of this chapter is based upon cost control systems, in particular activity-based costing (ABC). Traditional product-costing systems trace direct costs to products and allocate or apportion the remaining (indirect) costs to products, normally through a two-stage process. The indirect costs are first allocated into pools, and then allocated to products by methods such as direct labour costs or direct labour hours which are based on production volume. These traditional costing systems are being criticised for producing misleading product costs (Johnson and Kaplan, 1987; Cooper, 1987) which no longer reflect the resources consumed to produce them. ABC is the rejection of the conventional treatment of overhead in favour of identifying specific services (resources) being put into the process (activities) being costed. The concept underlying ABC systems rests on the premise that products utilise activities and activities consume resources. Emphasis is placed on the important role that activities play in 'causing' costs to be incurred. As in a conventional system, ABC is based on a two-stage procedure (Innes and Mitchell, 1991). The first stage is charging overhead cost to activity-based cost pools. The second stage is deriving and using a series of cost driver-based rates to attach the pooled costs to product lines. The design and operation of ABC is dependent upon three key factors: the choice of cost pools; the selection of means of distributing overhead cost to the cost pools; and the choice of cost driver for each cost pool.

This chapter will first examine the general nature of management control in the UK clearing banks from a managers' and consultants' point of view. Using contingency theory, the following section will identify the major classes of contingent factor which affect the organisations' control system. The chapter then moves to a consideration of the contingent factors influencing the UK banking environment, in particular the effect of the new capital adequacy requirements and the effect of deregulation on the financial services industry. A product of the environmental changes, activity-based costing is discussed in the fourth section, which is followed by case study evidence on the role of management control systems, and in particular ABC, in one of the UK clearing banks. The final section provides a critical evaluation of the role of management control systems in the UK clearing banks.

Management control

Banks are clearly facing considerable challenges and there is, and has been, a need for an 'appropriate response'. This response is manifested, in part, in the management control systems that are being introduced into the banks. Interviews with managers across the four UK clearing banks suggest that the principal types of control systems found in banks are budget control systems, cost control systems, risk control systems, security and staff control systems, premises control systems, personnel control systems and product control systems.

In practice the control systems listed above are operated separately but they also have an impact on each other. An example of these interrelationships is provided by the case of budgetary control. Product control affects the branch manager's budget; standard products are offered across the UK, and the interest rates and margins linked to those products are centrally controlled, with little scope for local deviation. Centralised personnel and premises functions mean that a large proportion of annual expenditure may be outside a branch manager's control. Risk control can restrict what a manager sees as potentially profitable business being taken on if those higher up the discretionary ladder disagree.

Management control systems, in banks as elsewhere, are complex. In one study Smith (1987) distinguishes between management controls and procedural and accounting controls. Management controls, he suggests, are designed to promote operational efficiency within the organisation and ensure adherence to management policies and minimise business risk. Management controls are 'essential in defining the environment in which the more detailed, procedural and accounting controls can operate'. They include:

1. formal allocation of responsibility and lines of reporting,
2. clearly defined and properly understood operating procedures,
3. approved authority levels,
4. permitted exposure limits,
5. budgetary control systems,
6. regular management reporting and
7. systems of internal check and internal audit.

Central to this understanding of control systems is the idea of a control environment. A control environment encompasses the attitudes, abilities, perceptions and actions of the institution's personnel, in particular management. A 'favourable' control environment requires the support and leadership of senior management and an acceptance of the need to ensure that the laid down procedures operate in practice.

The management and informational requirements for effective control and management in banks (Smith, 1987) should be:

1. accurate, consistent and reconcilable, where appropriate, with accounting records;
2. timely and sufficiently frequent for their purpose;
3. relevant to the recipient's decision-making requirements;
4. flexible and readily adaptable to changing needs;
5. inclusive of all group operation, risks and exposures;
6. forward-looking. as well as concerned with the past; and
7. capable of comparison to the main competitors.

Smith (1987) then goes on to develop a 'matrix of management information and control' which relates to planning, performance measurement and operational control. Appropriate key performance criteria are determined as a means of measuring the progress of the institution. Key variables here include inflation, interest rates and exchange rates. By reporting key finance indicators, management will not be swamped with information. Trend analysis is cited by Smith as a powerful control mechanism, as are control systems that monitor, identify and develop practical techniques to manage risk. This framework suggests the external environment will be of importance in looking at management control systems.

Contingency theory

As we have seen in earlier chapters of this book, management control can be looked at through many different lenses. Building on the suggestion in Smith's work that external issues are important, the definition of a management control system used in this chapter is that management control seeks to align the decision-making behaviour of individuals with the organisation's goals and strategies, which are in turn influenced by the internal and external environment (Middaugh, 1988). This is essentially a contingency approach to management control. As an organisation's structure and environment changes, so must its control systems.

The contingency approach to management accounting is based on the premise that there is no universal accounting system applicable to all organisations in all circumstances, (Emmanuel *et al.*, 1990). General all-purpose systems are unlikely to be uniformly successful: the management control system needs to fit the specific circumstances of the organisation for which it is intended. The major classes of contingent factor which have an impact on the organisation's control system have been identified as the environment, organisation structure, technology, strategy and culture.

The external environment will affect the nature of the control system. Accounting researchers have identified various environmental factors which will affect the type of management control system used. These include the degree of competition faced in the market-place (Khandawalla, 1972), the number of different products markets and the type of environment; that is, a 'tough' or 'liberal' environment (Otley, 1978). Gordon and Miller (1976) identify three main environmental characteristics hypothesised to affect control systems: dynamism, heterogeneity and hostility. A high rate of change will require frequent control reports. The number of different product markets served will lead to a decentralised control system with quasi-independent responsibility centres. In times of severe competition or market hostility, a more sophisticated control system is required. Other factors which may shape

an organisation's environment include government, customers and shareholders. Furthermore the existence of powerful groups in the organisation's
environment may increase the level of uncertainty it faces.

Technology as a contingent variable is characterised by its complexity and
degree of predictability in producing desired results. The technology the
organisation utilises is particularly important. Organisation structure is essentially concerned with matching task interdependence with the structure
imposed on it. Strategy is important for defining appropriate goals. Simons
(1987a) found that firms following different strategies employ (accounting)
control systems in different ways. Dent (1990) argues that, rather than taking
the objectives of the organisation as determined, the control systems are
influencing the formation of objectives. This suggests there may be a more
complex relationship between organisation and environment than contingency theory allows. However the importance of the environment is still
emphasised.

Contingency theory, therefore, allows for some explanation of the way particular control systems have been developed. The control systems in the UK
clearing banks have evolved in the context of the changes that have taken
place in the external environment. These changes will be considered by focusing on the environmental changes that have taken place over the last decade
and then illustrated in a UK clearing bank case study.

The UK banking environment

Banks play a central role in the UK economy by providing financial intermedi-
ation services. The big four commercial or clearing banks are Barclays, Lloyds,
Midland and the National Westminster Bank. These banks are service organisations which provide acceptance of deposits, a payments mechanism and
provision of credit. Their role has, however, changed over the last decade and
into the 1990s is continuing to change: the effects of deregulation, increased
competition and the introduction of new technology have introduced a
number of new entrants to the UK banking market: for example, building societies, major retailers and insurance firms. Banks, too, have been moving into
new lines of business. The focus of banking has moved towards sales and marketing (particularly in the branches) and towards a new cost awareness.

For a long time clearing banks in general paid almost no attention to the
development of pricing strategies or to the measurement and control of costs.
This is evidenced by conversations with bank managers who state that at the
beginning of the 1980s cost control had not even entered the decision maker's
conception. There was no emphasis on cost or cost awareness. The simple
reason was that they did not have to bother: competition as well as the banks'
possibilities of doing business were very restricted. This was because of the

oligopoly arising from the clearing banks' control of payment systems. In the 1980s however, the UK banking industry found itself facing problems associated with increasing competition from other sectors of the capital market.[1] Many activities previously conducted by banks could now be undertaken by others and it is not evident that banks have any permanent competitive advantage in these areas.

The 1980s was an important decade for the UK clearing banks: it was a time of overexpansion and neglect of prudence for the banking industry. Deregulation and 'Big Bang', which removed barriers to competition in the UK financial services industry, encouraged banks to purchase stockbroking firms, stock-jobbing firms and estate agencies. Barclays Bank, for example, combined its merchant banking arm, the brokers deZoete and Bevan, and the jobbers Wedd Durlacher Mordaunt. Lloyds Bank entered the estate agency market by acquiring a number of estate agencies and, at one stage, became the biggest estate agency in the country. Inevitably marketing was given a higher organisational priority in the 1980s, reflecting the intense competition in all segments of the market. Segmentation and branding of products were recognised as being applicable to banking and banks had felt it necessary to carry a whole range of products.

However the 1990s have added a new dimension to the UK clearing banks' strategy: they have lost some of their traditional informational, structural and reputational advantages. Now they are dediversifying because they have discovered that their diversity did not bring strength. It brought lack of control and severe losses. Diversification created overheads and placed an additional strain on the central management. Banks have pruned product lines and have become conscious of product profitability. Many of the banks' main products were, by 1989, in the mature or declining phases of their life-cycles (Morrison, 1989). In response to severe losses, the dominant financial ethos in UK clearing banking today is profitability, cost awareness and shareholder value.

The profound changes that have been taking place in the banking industry have been produced by a complex, interrelated series of components, including capital adequacy, the issue of costs and competition, risk and reward and intangibles such as quality of service.

Capital adequacy

The Basle Agreement (1988) on capital adequacy was implemented in the UK by means of the Banking Act 1987. This is essentially a form of control by government rules. Capital adequacy rules relate the amount of a bank's capital or 'own funds' to its risk exposure. The imposition of the capital adequacy requirements has had major implications for the required profitability of banking. This issue has proved to be of great importance because it is a restraint on banks' balance sheet growth and put pressure on banks to perform in line with stock market expectations in order to ease the raising of capital if it is necessary. Llewellyn (1991) emphasised that, as 'both internal and external sources of equity ultimately depend on the banks' profitability, the imposition of equity capital requirements has major implications for the required profitability of banking, the ability of banks to compete, and the type of business they are likely to conduct'. The effect of the capital adequacy rules was to increase the banks' cost of capital just at the time when the banks' had and still do have, an increased need for capital.

Lloyds Bank, for example, was determined to earn an adequate rate of return on capital that is invested in order to enhance shareholder value. Attracting capital at an adequate cost means that the bank has to create shareholder value by producing a rate of return on equity in excess of their cost of equity. Lloyds is also committed to the idea of creating shareholder value. This means increasing dividends from earning a return on capital in excess of others in the market, managing risk and trying to gain market price growth. The capital adequacy requirements have been a significant factor in the change to a performance-based culture in the UK clearing banks because of this new emphasis on market value.

Deregulation

Significant deregulation of the UK financial services industry which took place in the 1980s came through the Financial Services Act 1986 – 'Big Bang' and the Building Societies Act 1986. The Financial Services Act removed barriers to competition in the UK financial services industry and significantly increased the level of competition. Banks were, for the first time, allowed to participate on the UK securities market. The Building Societies Act gave UK building societies the opportunity to move away from their traditional mortgage lending business and into the personal finance arena, competing head-on with banks.

The effect of these two Acts was to increase competition for the personal customer account and hence reduce the profit margins that could be achieved on such businesses. A former Director of Retail Services in Barclays Bank believed that the most powerful catalyst for the changes in the banking industry was the deregulation of the building societies, the effect being, for the first time, to expose some of the clearers' core activities – such as across-the-counter personal services – to competitive pressure from new entrants. Deregulation and the 1990–93 recession has led to structural overcapacity in the financial services industry. This has led banks into programmes of rationalisation, for example, the pursuit of efficiency gains.

Clearing banks have faced more competition from non-traditional suppliers of financial services, such as Marks and Spencers Financial Services. Non-finance companies have a greater capacity to diversify into banking services than banks have to diversify out of finance. The effect of increased competition and declining profits meant that cost measurement and cost reduction have taken on great importance. The deregulated financial markets and the ensuing increase in competition has put pressure on cost structures which evolved during decades when competitive pressures were less intense. Additionally cost reduction is one component of attempts to raise operating profits to compensate for lending losses in the 1980s.

These changes in the banking environment have introduced an awareness of rationalisation, efficiency and cost control which in the past were not so important. The resurgence and recognition of control systems is largely a response to the need to embrace these concepts and ABC in particular is one control system which has gained great prominence in financial services. Awareness of ABC in financial institutions came from the financial/management accounting press and from management consultants. Additionally these developments in product costing, performance measurement and cost management systems in the retail financial services sector have lagged many years behind the development of similar techniques in manufacturing.

Activity-based costing

ABC as an approach to cost information was thought to provide accurate and relevant cost information as a guide for making profitable decisions about products and services, revenues and costs. It provided a way to organise the collection, processing and reporting of cost information that supports decision making and strategy formulation. Furthermore it was thought to yield accurate and relevant information for managers who may not be cost accountants, but who must utilise cost information to improve the competitive position of their financial institution. It is important to remember that costs are not just a threat to profitability; they can also be used as a competitive weapon by providing a barrier to entry (Bromwich, 1990).

Fitzgerald *et al.* (1991), from their empirical survey of service businesses, argue that there are five factors which occur in many, if not all, services:

1. the usual presence of the customer in the service delivery process;
2. the intangibility of many aspects of the service package;
3. the heterogeneity of service staff performance and customers' service expectations;
4. the usual simultaneity of service production and consumption, which means that services cannot be counted, measured, inspected, tested or verified in advance of sale;
5. the perishability of most services, which obviates the use of inventory as a buffer between peaks and troughs in demand

When they occur together, these five factors cause particularly difficult problems for service managers in scheduling operations, controlling quality, measuring performance and tracing and controlling costs.

The ABC approach is not, however, a panacea which will solve all management cost information needs per se. Its value is situationally dependent. ABC produces historic cost information which only has an indirect relevance to managerial decisions. Its role in decision making requires careful specification. Furthermore it does not overcome all of the procedural problems of conventional costing. Sephton and Ward (1990) believe that the introduction of ABC will provide the potential for retail financial services to be at the 'leading edge' of management accounting development and gain for themselves a competitive advantage. With its concentration on the relationship of overhead costs to products and customers, ABC is suitable for retail financial services with its complex product-to-process relationship and high fixed cost base. Sephton and Ward highlighted three areas in particular where retail financial services could gain considerable benefit from using ABC: (a) as part of the strategic management process, understanding cost behaviour and analysing profitability; (b) in the calculation of meaningful product costs; (c) in budgeting, forecasting and performance measurement in overhead departments.

There are two types of ABC systems, one with a strong strategic focus and one with a strong behavioural focus (Spicer, 1990). Strategic systems tend to be the most complex, involving many more activity-based cost pools and cost drivers than do behavioural systems. Accurate product costs seem to be of primary importance. Documented cases of firms experimenting with these systems reveal that all these firms are under severe competitive pressure, with diverse product mixes and facing a variety of pressing strategic decisions about the rationality of their product mix, pricing, make-or-buy and/or the disposition of their market resources (Spicer, 1990). Behavioural ABC systems tend to drive or reinforce behaviour which is consistent with the achievement of an existing, clearly defined strategy.

The next section discusses the reasons for the implementation of ABC in a UK clearing bank. The case outlines the changes that have taken place in the organisation and the changes ABC has brought to the organisation.

Management control: ABC in the context of a UK bank

The bank is a UK clearing bank which, since 1992, has undergone significant changes in its Payment Services Group.[2] These changes relate to reorganisation, restructuring and reworking. The person responsible for managing the change is the general manager, whose responsibility is to meet the strategic objectives agreed by the board. The strategy was to increase profitability in a competitive market and provide what is perceived by the bank to be an adequate return to shareholders: that means raising the share price and increasing dividends.

The tactical elements employed to build up to meeting the overall strategy included the development of costing control systems, personnel control systems, communication control systems and internal audit control systems. Control and measurement of cost were the key strategic elements. At present ABC and the resource engineering systems have been developed and are in use. The control system which is the focus of this case study is ABC, which was being used as a catalyst to induce fundamental cultural change in the organisation: that is, instilling a new cost awareness in the organisation. Organisation structures changed before the introduction of the new control systems and a number of new people had been brought into the organisation at very senior levels.

ABC was implemented across all parts of the bank. The bank perceived that in the current competitive environment there is a need for more information on costs, particularly when the bank is tendering for clearing contracts. When the project was initiated the bank was not in a position to break down these costs. This cost management approach has generated a great deal of interest from all the UK clearing banks. The aim of the ABC project in the bank was to be able to identify what exactly the costs and services in the clearing department were and to identify the cost drivers of the activities in the value chain. The foci of the ABC system are as follows:

- establishing what people did in terms of activities and analysing all jobs, departments and activities;
- establishing why the costing systems that were in place were very poor;
- establishing which activities were expensive and why were they being used;
- establishing what effect increased volumes being put through the system had on cost.

The practical reasons cited for the introduction of ABC included:

- understanding how costs increased and decreased with increased volumes of cheques being put through the clearing system;
- appreciating how resources were consumed and used in order to generate cost savings;
- establishing what is the process behind the cheque clearing process and how they changed;
- providing more accurate costing measures for the clearing process. Further advantages of using an ABC system were perceived to lie in its links to competitive advantage, market share and positioning.

Other reasons for the introduction of ABC are probably related to the personal ambitions of those promoting its introduction and seeing it as a means of developing a power base. Initiating new ideas is looked upon very favourably, particularly when they involve cost-saving identification devices. The ABC system implemented in bank operations was both a strategic and a behavioural system. From the behavioural perspective it enabled the bank to make better use of costs and resources. The strategic perspective allowed for reorganisation, for example with respect to marketing. This in turn has led to a greater awareness of costs and cost control which has influenced the pricing and marketing decisions of services.

The management control systems were all interlinked and to a large extent dependent on each other. The ABC systems were related to other management control systems. Between the resources engineering control system and the ABC system there was an information overlap. The communications systems enriched the control systems, and this synergy is related closely to technology. Note that technology has been an important element of the new control systems, for it has enhanced communication and made the flow of information more efficient. Technological change has meant that changes in procedures can be dealt with more efficiently. Information technology has provided the necessary software to make ABC a feasible control system.

ABC has, therefore, been introduced as a part of the management control systems in this particular bank. Its introduction was part of the attempt to change the culture of the bank (promoting cost awareness) which has arisen as the result of changes in the competitive environment and is enabled by technological changes. Whether there will be success in achieving the bank's aims remains to be seen. The system remains in its infancy at the time of writing.

Critical reflections on management control systems in banks

The contingency theory of management accounting suggests that the environment facing an organisation has an impact upon the organisation and its control systems. Environmental changes may therefore have implications for the control system in the case of banking. Financial services environmental changes have taken place. These are largely manifested in the deregulation and capital adequacy rules that have been invoked. The contingency approach to management accounting provides a useful framework for the case study for suggesting why these changes arise, but there are other critical issues which need to be addressed in relation to the nature of the MCS in this case study.

As Dent (1990) suggests, in addition to being affected by factors in the organisation's environment, management control is an interactive process. Contingency theory fails to take account of the two-way interaction between organisation and environment, seeing the pressure as only flowing from the environment to the organisation. It is a determinist model which ignores organisational choice. Contingency theory has also failed to consider the nature of the process of organisational control. Preston (1991), for example, argues that organisations are able to play a part in the creation of their environment, rather than simply responding to it. He proposes that environments may be contingent upon the actions of the organisation and, in turn, an organisation's structure and process may be contingent upon events in the environment. Where an environment begins and an organisation ends is not clear-cut and the relationship between organisations and their environments is more complex and interrelated than contingency theory would suggest. In the context of this complexity, strategy, culture and organisational change are important elements which relate to management control.

Strategy

Simons (1990) emphasises the potential power of management control in the process of strategy formulation as opposed to just strategy implementation. Control and strategy are linked in a dynamic process through language and discourse: strategy forms control systems and control systems form strategy. The link between strategy and control systems is not a simple one-way process but a highly interactive one (Dent, 1990; Simons, 1990). Dent suggests: 'New planning and control systems provide a means for re-orchestrating responsibilities and linkages into the environment, facilitating organisational change, not just in a passive way, but proactively' (1990, p. 20). Rather than taking the objectives of the organisation as determined, the management control system can actually influence the formation of objectives. Strategic change is portrayed by Dent (1990) as essentially an interpretive phenomenon involving the uncoupling of structures, systems and strategies from already existing paradigms and their recoupling to new ones. Uncoupling and recoupling is cast as an emergent process.

In the case of the bank discussed, ABC has been introduced as an element of overall strategy as a reaction to environmental change. Changes that have taken place in the environment are largely manifested in the deregulation and capital adequacy rules that have been invoked. Both have had an effect on strategy: in the 1980s, expansion and diversification; in the 1990s, contraction, with an emphasis on cost, efficiency and rationalisation. The change in strategy placed a new emphasis on the role of the management control systems. ABC was used as both a strategic and competitive weapon and as a means of instilling a fundamental cultural change in the organisation.

Culture

A new culture can be an important source of power and influence. Beliefs about being able to control costs, to rationalise and to create efficiency can often bestow privilege and status upon those who can achieve this through cultural change. The notions of efficiency, rationalisation and cost (which are embodied in ABC) are 'infiltrating the organisation settings, leading to the creation of particular agendas' (Dent, 1991, p. 707). ABC was being used to instil a fundamental cultural change in the organisation, one where the emphasis was on cost control.

The change in culture in the bank can be conceptualised as the 'uncoupling of organisational action from one culture and its recoupling to another' (Dent, 1991). The bank has gone from virtually no measurement and control of costs to a strict programme of cost control and rationalisation. It is an emergent process brought about by a change in the accounting system, one that is perceived to be a cost-saving identification device, namely ABC. The control system has therefore introduced a new concept of costs and resources. It has sought to change the whole banking culture from a process culture (a culture where only sufficient effort was devoted to getting through the work) to a business culture.

In the bank, a change in leadership, promoted by the demands placed on the organisation by its external environment, has been the impetus for the change in control systems and the ensuing cultural change. These particular MCS are 'facilitating organisational change, not just in a passive way, but proactively' (Dent, 1990). The following section will examine the extent of the change that has taken place in the bank, using a theoretical model developed by Laughlin (1991).

Organisational change

Laughlin (1991) in his model of organisational change puts forward the thesis that the processual dynamics of change in an organisation are conceptualised in relation to an environmental disturbance or 'jolt'. This disturbance triggers transitions and transformations along different tracks or pathways. The key assumption here is that organisations are naturally change-resistant, with a strong tendency to 'inertia', and will only change when 'forced' or 'kicked' into doing something. There is no single result for any disturbance, the degree of transformation will differ over time and across different organisations; there are a number of possibilities for the end result.

When viewed in terms of a theory of inertia (Starbuck and Hedberg ,1977; Jonsson and Lundin, 1977; Mintzberg, 1978; Miller and Friesen, 1984), attempts to introduce organisational and cultural change has been precipitated by a crisis: government regulation (capital adequacy) and government deregulation (Financial Services Act 1986 and Building Societies Act 1986). The real threats were only perceived when the financial services industry was deregulated and the capital adequacy rules were imposed.

The banking environment has itself become more unpredictable. The combined effects of deregulation, the capital adequacy requirements and the

harmonisation of the EC have made the banking environment very competitive and this in turn has led to uncertainty. Bank-wide there seems to be a con-
certed effort to work with these uncertainties. Many decisions are
'unprogrammed' and rely on the judgement of managers. ABC is being implemented bank-wide and resources engineering has been 'piloted' in other areas
of the organisation. This provides the 'kick' promoted by the environmental
change.

Central to Laughlin's framework is the way organisations are conceptualised: as being an amalgam of 'interpretive schemes', 'design archetypes' and
'sub-systems'.[3] The interpretive schemes, design archetypes and subsystems
are potentially, at some point in time, in some dynamic balance. This means
that at some level there will be certain characteristics that bind the organisation together and make it a coherent whole. It is only an environmental disturbance which will require the organisational participants, however reluctantly,
to shift the inert characteristics of organisational life.

Laughlin develops four models of organisational change: rebuttal, reorientation, colonisation and evolution. The first two are categorised as first order
change; things are made to look different while remaining basically as they
always have been. The interpretive schemes will not be affected. Second order
change will penetrate so deeply into the 'genetic code' that all future generations will acquire and reflect these changes. Second order change will affect
the interpretive schemes, design archetype and subsystems.

In the case of rebuttal, the disturbance is deflected, so that the organisation
is maintained exactly as it was before the disturbance. Reorientation changes
are assumed to affect not only the design archetype but the subsystems as
well. Change of a colonisation nature is not chosen but forced on the organisation and is change of a second order type. In the case of evolution, change is
chosen and accepted by all organisation participants freely and without coercion. These categories are not meant to describe all possibilities, but to provide
a framework upon which to develop understandings of the actual situation.

The nature of the change that is taking place in the bank is not as well
defined as the 'ideal types' of the model. Interviews with managers and senior
managers suggest that changes of different types have been taking place at
different levels of the organisation and it is too early to gauge whether cultural
change of a second order nature has actually taken place. A senior manager
interviewed sees the changes taking place at two levels: while senior managers, policy makers and the board see these changes as fundamental cultural
changes, at the lower levels of the organisation change remains of a first order
nature. Underneath the mantle of changes the old organisation still exists. In
some cases (where activities have not been changed drastically) people are
working in the same way as before and 'rebutting' the changes. In other situations the disturbance is accepted into the workings, but the heart of the
organisations remains unchanged. This senior manager believed that changes
that are decided at senior management level do not necessarily lead to change

of a second order nature. Different types of change will occur at different levels. Individuals at lower levels of the organisation will often refuse to accept management changes.

The second manager interviewed sees the change process happening in a way similar to that described in Laughlin's model: employees initially fought against the changes (rebuttal) and tried to ignore the benefits because a more competitive internal environment was being promoted. Eventually the changes were accepted into the organisation, but the heart of the organisation remained unchanged (reorientation). With the wave of redundancies and the level of uncertainty, it was a no choice situation'. Though the changes were forced upon the organisation and its participants, it seemed to be that the change had permeated into the very heart of the organisation (colonisation). The systems are now being used by organisational participants because they are experiencing the benefits for themselves.

There has been a definite attempt to change the culture of the organisation (by the new general manager). To enhance this cultural change, new managers have been imported at very senior levels and in placed key positions in the division, to ensure and support the changes that were taking place. The control systems were embedded into the wider organisational system, and were playing a key role in the organisation's development, formation of goals and strategic objectives and their subsequent achievement. Despite these attempts to colonise the organisation, it is clear that second order change is not universal.

Thus the formal control systems of ABC were supported by informal control mechanisms. Much of the behaviour observed in the bank seems to be shaped by emerging social standards and interaction, rather than by the formal control system (Hopper and Berry, 1983).

Conclusion

This chapter has provided a descriptive overview of change in management control in the financial services sector and has provided some case study evidence. The banking environment of the 1990s has served as a catalyst for the emergence of new control systems. These control systems are a direct result of the environmental changes and the mistakes made by banks in the 1980s.

Clearly management control in the financial services sector is being carried out in a wide variety of ways and it is evident that the process of management control cannot be separated from the process of organisational, operational or strategic control, and is therefore a complex and highly interactive process. The relationships between control systems and strategy, culture, organisational change and emerging social standards are highlighted as being particularly important when assessing the nature of management control systems in a bank. Management control in banking is a dynamic process where control systems are influencing the formation of objectives.

Notes

1. Institutions, other than banks, that canalize the supply and demand for long-term capital and claims on capital. For example, the Stock Exchange, insurance companies and other suppliers of core banking services.
2. The focus of this study was on the cleaning department in which an ABC system was being implemented.
3. Where the interpretive schemes are the underlying set of values and belief; design archetypes are the organisation structures and management systems; and the sub-systems are the tangible organisational elements (buildings, people, machines, finance).

CHAPTER 19

Manufacturing accountability

T. Colwyn Jones and David Dugdale

This chapter is concerned with roles of accounting in management control, especially in large-scale UK manufacturing enterprises. We focus on discussion of 'the new manufacturing environment' which many people have identified as emerging in the 1980s and claim constitutes a major reorganisation of production. Some argue this is a transformation as profound as the creation of 'the factory system' at the end of the eighteenth century, or the rise of 'the modern corporation' at the end of the nineteenth. If so, we would expect this change to have a strong impact on accounting and management control in the 1990s. We explore this through discussion of 'regimes of accountability' – sets of theories and practices aimed at ensuring that employees of the enterprise are held accountable for their activities and/or achievements. Accounting, as a distinctive discipline or occupation is not the only body of theory and practice relevant in this. However its contributions to the determination of ends (as objectives, targets or criteria) and the monitoring of means (through measurements, analyses and reports) have led to its gaining a central position in management control.

The title of the chapter was prompted by Burawoy's (1979) 'Manufacturing Consent', although our emphasis will be rather different. Burawoy was concerned with demonstrating how workers, by playing the game of 'making-out' within management control systems, came to accept their rules. This he referred to as 'consent'. He did not explore how managers had come to construct these systems or whether they had deliberately manufactured them to achieve consent. In our view, his workers might more accurately be seen as demonstrating lack of dissent rather than actively consenting to management regimes. Our focus is upon accountability and how managers have attempted to create it through management control systems in which there are different, and changing, balances between consent and dissent, in differing social contexts. We will examine ways in which accounting operates not just as *hard accountability* 'via financial results and numerically rendered information' but

299

also as *soft accountability* through its role in shaping 'contextual, subjective evaluation stressing human values and superordinate goals' (Hoskin and Macve, 1988, p. 68). We will argue that accounting is important not only in formal control systems as an external check on people's performances and achievements, but also in attempts to construct employees who are 'respons-ible' – or self-accountable. Both, to varying degrees, are present in regimes concerned with manufacturing accountability.

The nature of management control

Management control is inseparable from its organisational context. Ouchi (1980) classified economic organisation in terms of three mechanisms for mediating transactions between individuals associated through bureaucracies, markets and clans. We use a similar three-dimensional model but with funda-mental differences in interpretation and explanation.

Hierarchies and rules

Large-scale manufacturing enterprises are frequently vertically and horizon-tally integrated units of production administered by management hierarchies. Discussion of such organisations has been heavily influenced by Weber (1922) who characterised modern society as one where non-rational modes of thought (*traditional* and *affective*) were increasingly being replaced by *rational* forms based on calculation. These involved the conscious thinking through of cause and effect; of means and ends. The clearest demonstration of this was the capitalist enterprise where accounting was its purest expression. Enterprises had developed a specific form of rational administration – 'bureaucracy' – in which a hierarchy of offices, consisting of official duties, were regulated by a system of rules (see Box 19.1). These rules might take legal and/or technical forms and constituted the legitimate basis for authority to the extent that they were accepted as rational by members of the organisation. Officials acted, not on the basis of customary or habitual responses, or emotion, but by impersonally calculating the means and ends of action by applying the abstract body of rules to particular cases.

Weber predicted that this form of administration would become dominant in twentieth-century organisations and his concern was to analyse its structure and processes. Others were more actively involved in constructing such forms through their advocacy of management 'principles'. Taylor (1911) in the USA, Fayol (1949) in France and Urwick (1947) in the UK prescribed forms of administration which had much in common with Weber's model of bureau-cracy. Together with other writers and management consultants such as

Box 19.1 Weber's model of bureaucracy

Fixed jurisdictional areas where there are detailed official duties, whose conduct is limited by rules and which are methodically provided for each organisational activity.
A firmly ordered hierarchy of superior and subordinate offices.
Offices are both a centre of *written documentation* of activities and a post (or position) whose *public resources* are clearly separated from the *personal funds* of the office-holder.
A prescribed course of *expert training* (through formal education and/or experience) which prepares the individual to hold office.
The holding of office is the *primary activity* of the office-holder who is rewarded by salary.
The conduct of each office, and relations between them, are covered by *general rules* (which may also state how rules are to be changed).

Follett (1924), Gulick and Urwick (1937), and Barnard (1938), they produced what is now termed 'classical management theory'. Whilst their prescriptions differed in detail, they collectively advocated functionally separate departments, with specific duties for managers, to replace the wide-ranging activities in earlier forms of organisation. This, they claimed, would generate efficiency within enterprises.

There has been considerable controversy over bureaucratic organisation. Psychologists in the human relations traditions (for example, Mayo, 1933, 1945; McGregor, 1960; Argyris, 1964) objected to the mechanistic and impersonal nature of bureaucracy and saw it as stifling people's initiative, imagination and creativity, thus leading to inefficient use of human resources. Sociologists argued that bureaucratic forms were only efficient under certain conditions, such as large-batch assembly and mass production (Woodward, 1958a, 1958b) or in stable market and technological environments (Burns and Stalker, 1961) or where routine production resulted from the use of uniform raw materials transformed by well-understood processes (Perrow, 1970). Elsewhere they were inefficient. However, for economists adopting the 'transaction costs' approach, the rise of bureaucratic hierarchies in general had to be seen in terms of their economic advantages (Chandler, 1962, 1977; Williamson, 1975). If the 'invisible hand' of the market had been replaced by the 'visible hand' of management (Chandler, 1977) then this must be due to higher efficiency. In modern production raw materials are transformed into semi-finished goods and then into final products within multi-function enterprises without passing through markets. The reason must be that, for complex economic activities, the costs of market transactions rise to a point where they are unbearable and bureaucracies (despite their own inefficiencies) are preferred (Ouchi, 1980).

Whatever the explanation for the rise of bureaucratic hierarchies, the implication is that management control is to be achieved by specifying the actions required of enterprise members. Rules specify official duties, how they are to be carried out, the authority and resources available to managers and to whom (and for whom) they are responsible. Here the essential meaning of 'performance' is the conduct of duties in accordance with predetermined procedures; it is this which is to be monitored and reported. This emphasises *formal rationality* which is 'the extent of quantitative calculation or accounting which is technically possible and which is actually applied' (Weber, 1922, p. 85) and 'subordinate managers are ... evaluated on the basis of their conformity to organizational rules' (Hopwood, 1974, p. 19).

Markets and contracts

In recent years there has been increasing concern that large-scale enterprises have reached the limits of efficiency achievable under regimes of hierarchies and rules. One set of prescriptions for this involves the creation of market conditions within the enterprise. Organisations should be segmented into divisions and then departments which operate as mini-businesses 'buying' from internal suppliers and 'selling' to internal customers. This construction of sub-units of firms may be seen as an attempt to drive 'the discipline of the market' deep within enterprises, encouraging managers to see their interactions with each other as 'trading' relationships, and thus treating them as entrepreneurs whose objectives and activities are micro-level equivalents of traditional entrepreneurs. The problem, of course, is that departments are not independent businesses, and managers do not own them as personal property. Thus attempts to create market relations within enterprises can only be simulations – pseudo-markets with pseudo-entrepreneurial activity.

One influential approach to constructing management control which aims at constructing such pseudo-market conditions within the enterprise is agency theory (Hogler & Hunt, 1993). This begins with the assumption that remote owners (principals) have delegated decisions to managers (agents) whose interests are different and who must therefore be controlled. The organisation is seen as a network of contracts between individuals. Principals lack the time, expertise and detailed knowledge to specify exactly what their agents should do (Shapiro, 1987). Instead principals are concerned to set targets and monitor the outcomes of action. The theory assumes that agents are utility maximisers and, without control systems, will be inclined to be lazy and/or divert resources and efforts toward non-owner goals. Agency theorists have been concerned with payment systems as incentives for agents to pursue the goals of owners, and information systems which enable principals to monitor their achievements. The creation of such systems entails a cost to principals but is economically advantageous if this is less than the benefits of contractual control. However a central problem with this approach is that monitors are also agents and they in turn must be monitored (Armstrong, 1991). Thus the logical outcome of agency theory is an endless chain of regulatory relationships which eventually must become prohibitively expensive.

Emphasis on control through contracts and monitoring of outcomes focuses on Weber's concept of *substantive rationality*: 'the degree to which the provisioning of given groups of persons with goods is shaped by economically social action under some criterion of ultimate values ... [which are] bases from which to judge the outcomes of economic action' (1922, pp. 85–6). Unlike formal rationality, which is concerned with the means adopted by managers, substantive rationality focuses upon the relationship of means to ends. Unfortunately for those who wish to explain enterprises in terms of the pursuit of efficiency, these two forms of rationality can conflict. By following the letter of the law, decisions may go against the spirit of the law. Reliance on information about the outcome of managerial action may lead to managers attending only to those items which are reported, or diverting their efforts into constructing information which generates the preferred message.

Trust and values

There are limits to the extent to which enterprises can be controlled through formal application of either rules or contracts. Managerial jobs may be described as 'high discretion roles' (Fox, 1974) where 'if some crucial organizational roles are essentially complex, containing discretionary elements, and requiring skills and judgement, then the commitment and 'trustworthiness' of these members is most important' (Salaman, 1979, p. 98). Ouchi refers to organisations which exemplify such trust relationships as 'clans', where 'a variety of social mechanisms reduces differences between individual and organizational goals and produces a strong sense of community' (1980, p. 136). Central in this are shared values within the organisation supported by systems of shared meanings, language, symbols, myths and stories – the 'culture' of the organisation (Langfield-Smith, this volume). This might appear to circumvent the need for management control since organisation members share views on means and ends. Culture may be seen as 'a pervasive way of life, or set of norms' (Handy, 1985, p. 186) which preconditions relationships between organisational members. However culture is also viewed as an outcome of existing enterprise structures and processes (thus reflecting its rules and contracts) and as something which senior executives can design and implement in order to change organisations (Handy, 1985). Thus culture may be 'manipulated or cultivated to achieve better management control' (Langfield-Smith, this volume) if organisational members can be socialised with shared values.

If formal control can never be complete then an issue for management control is 'deciding who – not whether – to trust' (Armstrong, 1991, p. 13). What social mechanisms are available to identify or create trustworthy members? Salaman (1979) pointed to five features of the employment of managers which facilitate trust. First, managers often come from family backgrounds with strong business connections. Second, many have been educated on university courses, steeped in business ideology, and aimed at producing potential managers. Third, considerable care is taken in the recruitment of managerial personnel, selecting those who express empathy with the values of the organisation. Fourth, managers experience socialisation in corporate values through training courses and mission briefings. Fifth, managers are rewarded, not only for their adherence to rules and achievement of targets, but also for their commitment to 'appropriate' ways of thinking and acting. These rewards include their salaries, but also encompass the work itself (more intrinsically satisfying and less controlled than that of lower-level members) and their work conditions (which offer better surroundings and facilities, security, status, career prospects, pension rights, and so on). Overall, management control is directed at generating trust through the selection and socialisation of managers with a commitment to the values of the enterprise. As they explain and justify their decisions and actions – to superiors, subordinates and to themselves – they articulate these values which become internalised features of self-control. In this way management control is concerned with the social construction of trusted persons whose means and ends require less close direction and monitoring.

This is not confined to managerial levels. In the creation of Fordism – a dominant manufacturing paradigm of the twentieth century – Ford introduced not only a 'profit-sharing plan' (the $5 day of 1914) but also a sociology department to monitor the social life of employees and an English school to train immigrant workers in appropriate attitudes and habits. As one of the Ford educators put it, 'as we adapt the machinery in the shop to turning out the kind of automobile we have in mind, so we have constructed our education system with a view to producing the human product in mind' (Marquis, 1916, quoted in Meyer, 1980, p. 74). Thus, as Ford created a mass production system, he also attempted to construct the kind of worker to be employed within it. This is not to suggest that such attempts can be fully successful. Ford had 'labour problems' from the beginning and although Beynon's (1973) study of Fords in Liverpool some 50 years later found personnel managers still trying to recruit a 'responsible' workforce, production could hardly be described as demonstrating 'consent'.

More recently there has been considerable interest in the 'empowerment' of workers where instead of formal control 'everyone's work is guided by and aligned to a common vision that company leaders shape and project by their own example' (Johnson, quoted in Jayson, 1992, p. 31). Again the aim is to shape workers to enterprise interests and values (the common vision) as a precondition of self-control. We may be sceptical of the possibilities of completing this project – fully aligning worker interests with owner interests in a 'common vision' – but as Burawoy noted the everyday life of enterprises is characterised more by co-operation than by conflict.

Contradictions in management.   In identifying three aspects of management control – rules, contracts and values – we are not proposing a model of three types of organisation (such as bureaucracies, markets and clans). Instead we see manufacturing enterprises as characterised by various forms of hierarchical, market and trust relationships which co-exist (see Box 19.2). Bureaucratic organisation rests upon the legitimacy of rational rules (Weber, 1922) and hence is concerned with values. Market relationships exist within hierarchies of position and power. Trust alone cannot be relied upon since socialisation is never complete (Wrong, 1961) and because different hierarchical positions generate differing interests. Thus we would expect enterprises to display a balance of factors rather than a single 'style'. Nor do we argue that 'an efficiency criterion would make it possible to predict the form organisation will take under certain conditions' (Ouchi, 1980, p. 129). In order to explain how management control systems develop we need to explore issues which go beyond 'efficiency' and 'values' in enterprises and encompass the politics of management.

Marx (1868) distinguished two functions of management. Given any kind of division of labour – the separation of tasks and their allocation to different individuals or groups – then some form of organisation is required to relate and unify these discrete elements. Marx referred to this as *co-ordination and unity*. In capitalist enterprises there are also differences of interest between individuals and groups because they occupy different economic positions, and there are struggles over how resources are to be used and for whose ends. Here management is also concerned with *control and surveillance*. These twin functions of management are contradictory since enterprises are simultaneously collective, social organisations (in terms of production) aimed at

---

Box 19.2   The nature of management control

Social relations	Control mechanism	Focus of control
hierarchical	rules	activities
market	contracts	resources and outcomes
trust	values	persons

individual, private interests (increasing shareholder wealth). This creates tensions in any management control system since 'employers and managers are faced with the inescapable problem of achieving co-operative activity by antagonistic means' (Armstrong, 1991, p. 6). Owners must entrust their resources to people who do not share their interests and who therefore cannot be completely trusted. Attempts to resolve this by tighter control through rules or contracts may result in increased resistance from employees who thus become less trustworthy and require even greater control, thus increasing costs. Attempts to escape this by creating more 'high discretion roles' create more scope for employees to pursue their own interests. In this view enterprises are shaped not by some universal, abstract pursuit of efficiency but by the twin political processes of managers' control of workers, and owners' control of managers (Hopper *et al.*, 1987; Jones, forthcoming). In struggles over this two-sided management control, tensions and conflict imply that any balance between rules, contracts and trust will be unstable and changing.

Accounting and manufacturing enterprises

In UK (and US) manufacturing enterprises accounting has become an important, possibly the dominant, form of management control. Since this is not true of enterprises in Germany and Japan (Armstrong, 1985, 1987; Jones *et al.*, 1993) this cannot simply be seen as the logical and inevitable outcome of the need for financial information and usefulness of accounting. Hence it requires explanation.

The rise of accounting in management control.   Armstrong (1985, 1987, 1993) traced the rise of accounting in UK management, locating developments in historical social context. By the early years of this century the dispersal of shares among many owners, and active capital markets, had led to auditing becoming an important activity. From this base the accountancy profession extended its intervention in enterprises. Financial accountants gained importance in reporting the impact of economic slumps in the 1920s and the depression of the 1930s. They interpreted corporate crises in terms of problems of profitability and liquidity, and recommended tight financial controls. Typically this was through the adoption of 'holding company' forms of organisation where the information used to monitor subsidiaries paralleled that already familiar to accountants through annual reporting and auditing. Over the same period there was a development in costing. UK government policies during the First World War, aimed at restraining profiteering on cost-plus wartime contracts, led to the development of costing techniques in ministries and supplying enterprises. In 1919 the Institute of Cost and Works

Accountants (ICWA) was set up, recruiting members active in enterprises and stimulating the growth of budgeting and cost accounting systems. As financial and cost accounting became more important in enterprises career opportunities were opened up for accountants within management and on boards of directors. Accountancy was establishing an important position in UK manufacturing enterprises.

In the period of industrial reconstruction, following the Second World War, UK enterprises sent 'productivity teams' to the USA to study production organisation and methods. Accountants on these teams returned with a new set of accounting theories and techniques, and a new concept: 'management accounting'. They advocated 'divisional' rather than holding company organisational structures, and resource allocation and performance – reward payment systems to regulate activities. The ICWA became the Institute of Cost and Management Accountants (1972) and then the Chartered Institute of Management Accounting (1986). Increasingly it promoted its members as professionals concerned with 'executive' and 'strategic' issues. Management accountancy's role was defined far more broadly than cost accounting and its members became established at higher managerial levels, gaining ascendency over engineering, marketing and personnel occupational specialisms.

Thus Armstrong explained the rise of accounting in management control as the outcome of successful strategies by the accountancy profession to promote the services of its members to enterprises. Beginning with issues of resource allocation – regulating both external investment (financial accounting) and divisional investments (management accounting) – the role of accounting spread more generally in management control.

The fall of management accounting?   Management accounting in UK enterprises has been considerably influenced by ideas and techniques pioneered in the USA. However in recent years there has been a major debate over the role of this accounting in US enterprises. Johnson and Kaplan (1987) argued that as enterprises developed in the nineteenth century many stages of the process of converting materials into finished products were integrated within organisations. With the absence of market exchange between these stages there was a demand for measures to determine the price of 'output' from internal operations. It was from this that management accounting developed. Drawing on transaction cost theory, they explained the rise of large hierarchical organisations in terms of their efficiency advantages over markets. However the full benefits of organisation would not have been gained without an increase in the quantity and quality of management accounting information. In responding to this need, especially in companies such as Du Pont and General Motors, accountants created effective information systems so that: 'By 1925 virtually all management accounting practices used today had been developed: cost accounts for labor, material and overhead; budgets for cash, income and capital;

flexible budgets, sales forecasts, standard costs, variance analysis, transfer prices, and divisional performance measures' (Johnson and Kaplan, 1987, p. 12).

At this point innovation in management accounting appeared to stop. After 1925 financial accounting dominated, so that cost accounting became designed to meet the requirements of annual reporting and auditing rather than cost management. Cost information was increasingly less useful to managers since it ignored aspects of business (such as research and development, marketing, distribution) which were growing in importance, and because the attribution of overhead to products depended on bases such as labour hours or labour costs which were becoming inappropriate. The result was that 'today's management accounting is too late, too aggregated, and too distorted to be relevant for managers' planning and control decisions' (ibid., p. 1). Having explained the rise of management accounting in terms of its contribution to efficiency, Johnson and Kaplan now abandoned this theoretical framework and attributed its fall to the dominance of financial accounting and to outdated academic theories. The latter continued to assume one product/one process production, whereas manufacturing enterprises were now typically multidivisional, multi-product organisations. Management accounting had not responded to change after 1925 and had thus lost its relevance.

The new manufacturing environment

This critique by Johnson and Kaplan was given greater urgency by the view that the pace of change was quickening and precipitating a crisis in manufacturing enterprises. Changes in manufacturing in the 1980s were widely identified as a fundamental shift in the nature of modern production.

Flexible specialisation.   In an influential overview of this transformation, Piore and Sabel (1984) argued that changes in consumer taste were leading to the break-up of mass markets. The demand for products was becoming increasingly fragmented (with many market 'niches') and volatile (with more rapid 'fashion' changes). This produced strain in mass production systems designed to produce high-volume, long-run, low-cost, standardised products. In the new 'post-Fordist' environment there was a need to develop production systems capable of making a broad mix of products, moving between them as market conditions dictated, and changing rapidly to new ones. The need to respond to the new environment was made urgent by the increasing intensity of international competition – especially from Japan. Fortunately new technology (especially computer-based innovations) provided an opportunity to develop new production systems based on 'soft automation' (reprogrammable, flexible) to replace the 'hard automation' (dedicated, inflexible) of mass production. This could be linked to more flexible forms of work organisation using multiskilled workers, and decentralised management organisation which enabled rapid, local decision making responsive to particular markets. Together these would facilitate 'flexible specialisation', a new manufacturing strategy to replace mass production.

This view of a fundamental shift in manufacturing has been challenged both as to the scale and the nature of the changes identified, and the explanations advanced. Smith (1989) for example, noted that, while Sir Adrian Cadbury (Chairman of the Cadbury-Schweppes Group) stated in 1982 the need to adapt to more varied consumer tastes, his company actually reduced the number of its products by half in the 1980s. Shaiken *et al.* (1986) found that, as well as its potential for flexibility, computer-controlled technology offered new opportunities for integrated production so that batch production systems which had once been fragmented were becoming more like mass production. Hopper and Armstrong (1991) argued that the driving force behind change was not consumer taste. In the period after the Second World War the strength of organised labour had forced US giant corporations to come to terms with their workforces in a 'management – labour accord', the costs of which they were able to pass on to customers (in quasi-monopolistic US markets) and to smaller firms (with non-unionised labour). Increasing international competition in the 1980s put pressure on these enterprises to change their production systems, whilst the weaker position of workers (and their unions) in the new economic/political climate gave them the opportunity to change working practices.

These criticisms suggest that change in manufacturing has not been as widespread, unilinear or fundamental as much discussion of flexible specialisation implies. Nevertheless there is sufficient evidence of the development of new production practices for us to see the 1980s as period of significant change and to suggest that this has important implications for management control in the manufacturing of the 1990s.

Changes in manufacturing. Innovation in *production technology* – usually labelled advanced manufacturing technology (AMT) – has attracted considerable attention. Although developments are patchy, many enterprises have seen the arrival of computer numerical control machine tools (CNC), robots and computer-aided design – computer-aided manufacturing (CAD/CAM) systems. A few have adopted flexible manufacturing cells (FMC) or flexible assembly cells (FAC) and have aspired to flexible manufacturing systems (FMS) which link to management information systems (MIS). These technologies incorporate computer-based information and control systems and offer the long-term prospect of computer-integrated manufacturing (CIM).

Alongside these technological innovations there has been the adoption of new *production techniques*, particularly those associated with Japanese 'just-in-time' manufacturing (JIT). This, in Japan, is seen as a 'philosophy' aimed at reducing manufacturing costs by delivery of materials to production areas when they are required. It relies on materials being 'pulled' through the plant under the regulation of 'kanban' plates or cards which prompt workers to produce batches of the required materials, rather than the creation of stock which is then 'pushed' into the next stage of production. The system depends on smooth operation requiring 'zero defect' materials (since there are no just-in-case alternative stocks). In its most spectacular practice – 'jidoka' – production halts when faults are discovered and attention is focused on eliminating the error before production recommences. The 'kaizen' approach of continual improvement is aimed at achieving (or overachieving) levels of quality required to construct and maintain the JIT system, and quality circles of supervisors and workers monitor and improve the process. Although it is unlikely that many UK enterprises have implemented the full range of JIT activities (Jones *et al.*, 1993), techniques such as total quality control (TQC), total preventative maintenance (TPM) and statistical process control (SPC) have been introduced.

There have also been changes in *job design and work organisation* which may be seen as moves away from Taylorist and Fordist production. Kelly (1982) identified three widespread changes: first, reorganisation of flowlines where long chains of work roles are broken up either into several shorter chains or are replaced by individual workstations; second, the creation of flexible workgroups, where a number of work roles are amalgamated and distributed to groups where workers are allocated (or allocate themselves) to tasks as and when required; third, vertical role integration where a number of work roles once carried out by different workers are amalgamated in one job.

Employment relations have also changed. Atkinson (1984) identified three forms of flexibility pursued by UK enterprises in the 1980s: functional (involving the movement of 'multiskilled' workers between tasks); numerical (aimed at rapid increase and decrease in employment numbers depending on product market conditions); and financial (tying pay levels more closely to product output and labour market conditions). In his view, this represented a new employment model – 'the flexible firm' – where a core group of full-time, permanent employees was separated from a more marginal group of temporary, self-employed and subcontract workers, beyond which workers in other firms were increasingly being used for outsourcing of materials. His view that this amounted to a new managerial strategy has been criticised by Pollert (1988) on the grounds that it merely represents a redistribution of traditional practices, reflecting the growth in female employment and the decline in traditional male occupations. In terms of both work organisation and employment relations, the highly publicised activities of Edwardes (British Leyland), McGregor (British Steel and the National Coal Board), Shah (*Today* newspaper) and Murdoch (*Times* newspapers) may have been extreme cases not representative of management initiatives elsewhere. Nevertheless, under the encouragement of the Thatcher government, there does seem to have been some kind of 'employer offensive' (Hyman and Elger, 1981) in the 1980s where the weaker position of workers in labour markets and trade unions enabled management to make significant changes to working and employment practices.

There have also been signs of *managerial reorganisation* popularly labelled 'delayering'. This involves the stripping away of what are now seen as unnecessary layers of middle management and placing more responsibility in supervisory leaders of workgroups. Hopper and Armstrong argued that this is a consequence of the declining difficulty of controlling labour in the harsh economic climate of the 1980s and 1990s and thus 'the bureaucratic and costly apparatus of control in large core conglomerates, which had emerged in more benign economic conditions of the last fifteen years or so, is increasingly being questioned' (1991, p. 434). The achievement of this delayering is often accompanied by discussion of 'empowerment', where responsibility is delegated to lower-level employees – but only if they can be relied upon to pursue the goals set by senior management.

Overall there is evidence of significant change in production technologies and techniques, work and employment patterns, and managerial organisation in manufacturing enterprises in the UK. All of this implies a new environment for management control.

Accounting and formal management control

Most discussion of the contribution of accounting to management control focuses on its formal procedures – the way its measurements, techniques and criteria produce accounting information which contributes to setting targets, allocating resources, monitoring performance and rewarding achievement. Here accounting both reflects and shapes the rules and contracts of enterprise in the context of hierarchical organisation and attempts to create pseudo-market relations within the enterprise.

Controlling activities.   Traditional management accounting practices are built upon standard costing systems (originally developed in Taylorist and Fordist production) which employ a formula of standard labour cost plus standard material cost plus standard overhead to identify product costs. Control is then achieved through the monitoring of variances between these standards and actual costs. In the new manufacturing environment these standard costing systems have been criticised as outdated, misleading and irrelevant.

With increasing use of AMT direct labour is seen as a diminishing proportion of total costs. Yet it remains of central importance in standard costing both in itself and as a base for the recovery of overheads. In flexible low-volume production systems machine set-up and changeover times take on increased importance, but conventional accounting does not highlight these and they may become lost in an aggregate of indirect labour. TQM aims at zero-defect, but material standards may imply an acceptable level of scrap. JIT strives towards minimal stock based on small batches. However emphasis on material price variances may encourage bulk buying and measures of labour efficiency can lead to long production runs, both of which increase stock. In these and other specific ways traditional costing may be seen as out of step with new production systems, and overall the very notion of 'standard' has been seen as inappropriate in companies attempting to achieve flexible specialisation.

Alongside these criticisms of conventional accounting there was a stream of advice from academics and management consultants on more appropriate new approaches. The most influential of these has been activity-based costing (ABC). Shifting the emphasis from direct to indirect labour, Cooper and Kaplan argued that, 'Virtually all of a company's activities exist to support the production and delivery of today's goods and services. They should therefore be considered product costs' (1988, p. 96). The central aim of ABC is to trace costs from resources to activities to specific products by identifying cost drivers and measuring the costs which ensue. For example, the decision to produce a new part drawing triggers not only drafting, but also inspection, data processing, quality control, stock-keeping and parts-ordering activities (Johnson, 1992b). When the costs of all such activities are measured managers will be in a position to 'measure costs right: make the right decisions' (Cooper and Kaplan, 1988, title). The outcome of an ABC analysis typically shows that products made in small batches may consume a small number of direct labour hours but require almost as much indirect labour as large batches. Thus standard costing underrepresents their costs – they are not as profitable as traditional information suggests. This should not lead managers automatically to drop low-volume lines; instead the new information may highlight the need to develop flexibility and encourage investment in AMT which is capable of improving this.

As ABC developed, producing spin-offs of activity-based budgeting and activity-based management, it appeared to provide a powerful new means of management control more suited to the new manufacturing environment. However its critics argued that its 'solution' to the problems of standard costing was misleading or irrelevant. Its promise was that, by discovering the 'right' costs of products, managers would be able to produce more profitability. For some this was illogical, since 'Products are not profitable or unprofitable, businesses are' (Waldron, 1988, p. 1). Attention should be focused not on costs but on throughput.

The theoretical base for this view was supplied by Goldratt (1984) in developing the theory of constraints (TOC). In his view profit was simply revenue less costs. These costs have two elements: materials and operating expense.

Investment shows itself in the company in the form of inventory. Thus the measure for rate of return on investment (ROI) is:

$$\text{ROI} = \frac{(\text{revenue} - \text{materials}) - \text{operating expense}}{\text{investment/inventory}}$$

A company may increase its ROI by reducing operating expense, or invest-ment/inventory, but both are inherently limited since some minimal levels must be maintained. The alternative approach is to increase revenue-less-materials by achieving greater throughput from existing facilities. (Or to put this another way, revenue-less-materials is essentially a measure of the amount of throughput.) Since, in principle, throughput can be increased without limit, managerial attention should be focused on this, and not on minor issues of costing. In particular, managers should identify any factors which hinder the increase of throughput which are the system 'constraints'. In Goldratt's early work, these were identified as bottlenecks – often (but not necessarily) focal machines. The stripping of stocks (under JIT systems) from non-constraint locations in production would be beneficial since it should encourage reduction in lead times and increased customer responsiveness, thus promoting throughput. The bottlenecks, however, must be protected by a 'buffer' of stock to ensure that production never pauses. Management of con-straints was thus the key issue and here there was a fundamental disparity between views from 'the cost world' and from 'the throughput world'. The emphasis in management control should shift from reducing costs to increas-ing throughput.

In a break-away move, Galloway and Waldron (1988a, 1988b; 1989a, 1989b) advocated throughput accounting (TA) which would reform costing in line with an emphasis on bottlenecks and throughput. This return to a more tradi-tional emphasis was rejected by Goldratt and now there is considerable hos-tility not only between supporters of TOC and ABC, but between TOC and TA. So far, ABC seems to have made the largest impact in UK manufacturing, but even here many companies seem content to take the first step of analysing activities without moving to implement new costing systems (Lyne, 1993).

Controlling resources. Standard costing has also been the basis for traditional budgeting techniques. In large hierarchically organised enterprises, divisions and departments were defined as 'cost centres' and managers were held responsible for costs incurred within their boundaries. Budgeting processes can begin with complex and prolonged negotiations between higher and lower management concerning the distribution of resources. Once deter-mined, this is typically controlled through variance analysis, which has

FIGURE 19.1   Detailed Variance Analysis

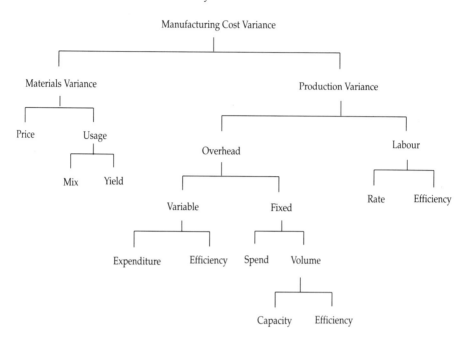

developed into a highly elaborate examination of divergencies of 'expected' (standard) from 'actual' costs (see Figure 19.1).

Whilst the logic of this approach may appear sound, its implementation can be problematic. Where it is applied rigorously in a 'budget constrained style' (Hopwood, 1974) management control outcomes may be viewed as dysfunctional. These problems are widely noted in textbooks. Effective negotiators may acquire a disproportionate share of resources; budget padding may be employed to provide slack; buck-passing may be rife. In order to stay within current budgets managers may delay or veto expenditure on items with longer-term benefit – for example, by failing to carry out regular machine maintenance.

In order to combat this, some companies have set up 'profit' or 'investment' centres instead. Here divisions or departments are monitored using profit or ROI figures in attempts to align subunits' contributions more closely with the overall profitability of the enterprise. Again many textbooks note the distortions which can creep in. Under ROI managers may retain assets which have little 'book value' and investment in new equipment may be delayed or avoided. Decisions may be directed at changes which improve local ROI but make little contribution to the overall goals of the enterprise. In some cases the companies have attempted to resolve this by relying instead on residual income (RI). However, as Emmanuel and Otley note, 'there are technical defects in any accounting measure, and to the extent that these are incorporated in controllable RI, the manager's commitment to it will be diminished' (1985, p. 175).

The development, first, of cost centres and then of profit and investment centres can be seen as attempts to create pseudo-market relations as divisions and departments are constructed as though they were mini-businesses within the enterprise. However these units are not autonomously operating in markets but exist within hierarchical relations. This generates contradictions and each solution generates new problems which have been addressed by refining ever more sophisticated formal accounting techniques. These contradictions become more intense when control of divisions and departments is closely linked to appraisal of their managers.

Controlling performance.   If enterprises are viewed as pseudo-markets with networks of contracts, crucial issues in management control are the setting of targets and the monitoring of their achievement by individual managers. Advocates of agency theory in accountancy (Jensen and Meckling, 1976; Fama, 1980; Watts and Zimmerman, 1986) argue that accounting offers principals (owners and executives) the potential for regulating their relationship with agents (managers) at minimum cost/maximum benefit. One key element here is the tying of managerial reward to performance – as measured by financial indicators. The payment of performance bonuses (averaging about a quarter of annual salary) to profit centre managers seems to have been a widespread practice in US enterprises for some time, and in the majority of cases these bonuses are decided solely or partially by a financial measurement formula (Vancil, 1979). This appears to have been far less common in the UK, but Ezzamel and Hilton (1980a, 1980b) found that profit measures were seen as a major factor in the promotion of managers in over half the companies they surveyed. Thus accounting frequently provides information which is concerned both with co-ordinating the activities of units and at the same time encouraging competition between managers (for pay and promotion).

The tension created by this contradiction is recognised in textbooks: 'Accountants often face a dilemma because they are supposed to fulfil two conflicting roles simultaneously. Firstly, they are seen as watchdogs for top management. Secondly, they are seen as helpers for all managers' (Horngren, 1977, p. 11). Practitioners recognise the problem this causes through the popular slogan, 'you get what you measure'. This implies either that managers concentrate their efforts on improving only those items which are highlighted in performance appraisal or that they manipulate information supplied to senior management to give the desired impression. As one financial controller told us, 'the minute you say that 'that' is what you are measuring, if you haven't got a balance and a check in the system 'it' will get better!' Providing such balances and checks leads to more elaborate accounting systems and increases costs, so that (eventually) proliferation of controls becomes prohibitively expensive.

Control and formal controls. Since the Second World War management accounting has undoubtedly been important in management control in UK manufacturing. It offered a means of measuring and reporting adherence to rules and fulfilment of contractual obligation through techniques of standard costing, budgeting, variance analysis and performance appraisal. In recent years, however, there has been increasing disquiet about accounting's role. This may be summarised as concern over the specific techniques employed, the focus of their attention and the way increasingly elaborate accounting, if rigorously applied, can produce ritualistic and/or antagonistic responses from managers. The last issue raises questions about whether the proliferation of formal 'controls' may generate greater difficulty in securing overall 'control' (Drucker, 1964) and ultimately become self-defeating (see Box 19.3).

Hopwood (1974) noted that some enterprises did not apply accounting in the rigorous manner of the 'budget-constrained' style. In some cases a looser, more flexible 'profit-conscious style' was adopted; in others a 'non-accounting style' was preferred. Assuming a rigorous application of accounting would be appropriate, Kaplan and others have sought to build new accounting systems in tune with the new manufacturing environment. An alternative prescription is that the emphasis in the 1990s should be to decrease reliance on any accounting system. The second view has been advanced by Johnson (a one-time close colleague of Kaplan) who not only attacked the development of activity-based

---

Box 19.3   Control and formal controls

It is increasingly … being realised that the distinction between controls and control is a crucial one. In many cases, for example, managers have actually achieved less overall control … as a result of using the ever-increasing number of individual controls. Subordinate(s) … have used their ingenuity to find ways of satisfying or even beating the controls, resulting in both intended and unintended consequences. The paradox often goes further. After recognising the reduction in real control many managers have quite naturally become even more concerned with regaining it. In order to do so they have called upon yet further controls with the result that the desired degree of control has become even more distant.

Source: (Hopwood, 1974), p. 18.

management but also questioned the value of all accounting information. He identified 'a new competitive environment – call it the global economy – in which accounting information is not capable of guiding companies toward competitiveness and long-term profitability' (Johnson, 1992b, p. 31). Responses in enterprises to this new environment were seen as constituting a broad trend from 'top-down control to bottom-up empowerment' (Johnson, 1992a, sub-title) in which accounting would have less importance.

Whilst we agree that there are limits to the effectiveness of accounting as formal controls, its importance is not confined to these. We argue that it is also important in other, less formal aspects of control. To explore this we must move away from an emphasis on rules and contracts, and become more concerned with accounting as an articulation of values contributing to the construction of trust relations.

Accounting and informal management control

Management accounting is more than a collection of specific measurements and techniques applied in particular ways. It constitutes a distinctive way of looking at, and talking about, enterprises. This has implications for management which go far beyond the formal control issues dealt with so far.

Manufacturing the worker.   To begin with standard costing, Miller and O'Leary (1987) note its roots in scientific management (Taylorism) which they argue was itself part of a broader movement of viewing, measuring and controlling people which was gaining momentum at the beginning of the twentieth century. Its origins may go back to the development of educational practices in the eighteenth century, when students became increasingly subject to regimes of writing, examination and grading (Hoskin, 1993). What these students learned was not only particular subjects – arts, sciences and social sciences – but ways of learning which they later reapplied in industry when they developed systems of measuring, reporting and rewarding workers and managers (Hoskin and Macve, 1988). Scientific management offered a means by which workers could not only be compared against each other and customary work effort, but also judged against a standard of abstract human effort. When the standard times for work were converted into standard labour costs managers created a new way to 'know' workers – in terms of their detailed contribution to production. Miller and O'Leary argue that, as workers came to be seen as objects measured against abstract standards, they themselves were altered in the process so that they became 'governable persons'. They were not totally docile, obedient employees but they were controllable through formal accounting systems. Even if standard costing systems were completely swept away in the 1990s (a highly unlikely prospect) the legacy of seeing people as aggregates of measurable activities and achievements will probably endure for many years.

An early indication of change in accounting systems resulting from a break with the scientific management tradition comes from Malmberg (1980). In a study of one Swedish company he found standard costing systems in place but their use had changed. The company had developed work groups which accountants treated as 'profit-centres' and workers were encouraged to improve on material and labour standards by the award of a symbolic 'profit'. This was reported to the group supervisors eight times a year and then discussed with workers. Malmberg, using the fashionable management language of the time, described this in terms of 'motivation' and claimed it increased workers' psychological satisfaction. The supervisors he quoted, however, saw it in terms of workers gaining a better understanding of 'financial realities' and the outcome was that 'many more workers become conscious of, and involved in, the ways in which their own work influenced the financial results' (Malmberg, 1980, p. 81).

Although there has been little research on such accounting change in the UK, we know of a number of companies which are currently developing accounting systems based on work groups, usually labelled 'cells'. Sometimes cells are merely a convenient accounting device for identifying and attributing costs, but often result from a physical reorganisation of workers and machines. In either case these cells are seen as receiving inputs from 'internal suppliers' and delivering output to 'internal customers'. Each cell 'owns' its costs, is supplied with financial information in order to 'understand' these and encouraged to work collectively to reduce them (as well as more generally improving production). In different economic and social conditions and with a differing managerial emphasis this is now not described in terms of 'motivation and satisfaction' but as 'responsibility and accountability'.

Here we detect a subtle, but perhaps significant, shift in management control. At the centre of this is a reconstruction of workers from producers of products to producers of profit. Under scientific management the amount of labour and materials required for production was predetermined and management control was directed at matching 'actual' to 'expected' performance. It was (in this sense) a fixed contract for a specified level of production. In cell accounting, standard costs are notional and workers are exhorted to continually improve levels of production, and control may be characterised as moving to 'responsible autonomy' (Friedman, 1977). Accountants are seen as advisors (helping cells to understand how to improve their profitability) and reporters (recording the financial outcomes of group efforts). This is accounting's version of 'empowerment' – the allocation of responsibility to workers and their supervisors to pursue corporate objectives defined in financial terms.

Managers talk of the need for a change of 'mind-set' for this to be successful. Broadly this involves the construction of self-conscious workgroups, and perceptions of managers as advisors rather than controllers. There are symbolic aspects to this: one company colour coded its cells as blue team, red team, and so on; another renamed its supervisors 'coaches'. Another element is changed practices. When presented with financial information on their performance and comparisons with other groups, cells can be called upon to explain current results and suggest improvements. In order to do this they need to investigate their performances through a financial perspective. In doing so they may come to reconceptualise their workplace as a world of profit rather than a world of production.

All of this may be exaggerated of course. In a general sense workers have always been aware that their employment is aimed at profit. The novelty we are suggesting is that managers may be deliberately constructing forms of accounting control in which workers and supervisors are encouraged to perceive their detailed activities in financial terms and are aware of themselves as financial actors. The empirical evidence for such change in management control is, at best, sketchy (but see Munro & Hatherly, 1993, for similar observations). The extent to which workers actually remodel themselves in line with this new conception of them is unclear. Some research suggests that this may be the case. Hopper *et al.* argued that UK coalminers had internalised 'the logic that profit and loss were absolute measures of performance – the bottom line' (1986, p. 126) and this had considerable impact on their campaign, and its public presentation, in the 1984–5 strike. Similarly Knights and Collinson (1987), in a study of a UK heavy vehicle manufacturer, identified accounting as a major element in workers' response to the closure of a division. Faced with a 'financial audit' which portrayed the division as loss-making, the workforce did not resist and accepted redundancy. In both cases the authors argued that alternative accounts could have been created, showing a different 'reality', but that workers (and their unions) did not challenge the managerial numbers. These studies are suggestive of the potential of accounting to influence workers' views of their workplaces.

Manufacturing the manager.   Accounting may be more powerful in shaping managerial perspectives. Here we may see it as a language of business shared by managers from many different occupational specialisms. More than this, it is embedded in managerial practices. The setting up of profit centres and investment centres is not only a technical means of creating pseudo-market relations through mini-enterprises within the enterprise. It is simultaneously an attempt to construct managers as mini-entrepreneurs (or 'intrapreneurs'). In one company a series of three-day finance schools was run for these managers. The course dealt with ABC, TA, target costing, marginal costing, and many other techniques. However the financial controller responsible for the course places more emphasis on the first morning where, in a series of case study exercises, managers are required 'to think like shareholders'. Only once they have adopted the appropriate orientation to finance (the perspective of owners) would financial knowledge be relevant. In his view, accounting techniques in themselves are of little importance; it is their purpose which crucial.

Such rather formal, one-off, approaches to constructing managers as financial actors are unlikely to be effective unless they are embedded in actual practices. In a detailed study of another company (Dugdale and Jones, 1993, 1994) we explored the way one such practice – investment decision making – incorporated accounting in the social construction of managers. Here there were no specific requirements for either the measurements or the techniques to be used for investment appraisal. Instead engineering staff proposing investment were expected to decide for themselves what financial information was appropriate. Nor was it believed that accounting numbers provided the 'right' answer to questions of costs and benefits of investment. Instead accounting information was used as the basis of probing proposals through the interrogation of proposers. The process was described as 'confidence building', gaining 'credence and credibility' and making sure people have 'thought about it'. Finance was not the only aspect of this interrogation. There would be questions on product and production technology, and markets. There would also be a general concern with corporate strategy. However accounting was a necessary element of the interrogation. The aim, as one manager put it, is that as proposer you must 'convince me that I should trust you'.

What is the basis of this trust? In our study it was concerned with shared perception and values within management. Proposers should see things from a business point of view. Managers are suspicious that engineers propose investments because they 'love to engineer things', 'build empires', 'do an interesting project', and so propose investment in 'singing, dancing, wonderful' machines. These are not 'business' reasons and so are not acceptable. What they must do is propose 'cost-effective, reliable solutions'. In this, the appropriate use of financial information is crucial: not because accounting produces right answers, but because it shows the proposer is thinking in appropriate ways. Here then we see accounting, not as an assembly of calculative techniques for formal control, but as a mode of thought, reflecting and expressing managerial perspectives and values, implicated in the construction of trust relations. Where these are established there need be less reliance on formal controls. But this does not imply their abandonment. Even trusted managers are encircled by financial controls. Indeed it is through the practices associated with these controls that trust is constructed.

Accounting and accountability

In this chapter we have discussed accounting's contribution to management control in terms of formal and informal practices. Accounting has been portrayed both as a collection of measurements and techniques, and as a mode of thought. We have related this portrayal to three mechanisms of control – rules, contracts and values – which are embedded in three patterns of social interaction – hierarchical, market and trust relationships. Such neat categories, whilst useful for the exposition of thoughts, carry the danger of becoming rigid frameworks for understanding enterprises. We do not intend them in this way. First, we are not suggesting that there are three 'types' of organisation. Instead we argue that enterprises can be analysed in terms of different patterns of social relations which co-exist and interact with each other. Second, we do not suggest that there are 'better' (or even 'best') forms of control, either from a moral viewpoint or in terms of the maximisation of some abstract achievement of efficiency. Rather we suggest that different patterns of control and surveillance and co-ordination and unity are the outcomes of particular social actions in specific social contexts. Third, we do not see these as universalistic rational responses to stimuli from objective external realities. While not wishing to dismiss notions of rationality and reality (see Jones, 1992) we recognise the importance of differing meanings in social action and how social contexts are differently interpreted in these meanings. Here ways of seeing and talking (such as accounting) both reflect and shape actions and contexts. Fourth, we do not regard the patterns we have described as clear-cut, self-contained or fixed. On the contrary, the contradictions of management control imply that social relations are ambiguous, interactive and unstable. Overall we view categories as a useful means of analysing enterprises, but not to be confused with representations of enterprises themselves.

Accounting and the new manufacturing environment.   To the extent that enterprises have been experiencing a period of transformation, we would expect this to be represented in changing regimes of accountability. We would not wish to draw direct causal connections between specific changes in the manufacturing environment and particular developments in accounting control. Instead we see the last few years as a period in which managers have become more intensely and urgently concerned with both the need and opportunity for change. This general concern has, in its various specific forms, been the product of their awareness of new technologies and production techniques, different forms of job design and work organisation, and changing managerial structures. These may be linked to wider identification of changing, and increasingly competitive, market conditions. Together they have produced a widespread feeling that existing organisational patterns are inappropriate to 'the new manufacturing environment'.

We would characterise this as a period of organisational 'unfreezing' – a time when existing patterns are no longer seen as capable of improvement by incremental change but must be transformed. Although traditional formal controls may remain in place they are seen as less relevant to current needs. However the outcome of this unfreezing cannot be predicted. On the one hand, the lack of certainty may hinder the construction of rules and contracts since managers are unable to specify exactly what is to be achieved and how this is to be done. Thus they may be forced to rely more heavily on trust relations, relying on people to do the 'right thing' – as suggested by the rise of interest in 'empowerment' and the need to develop 'a common vision'. Current changes may lead to less reliance on formal accounting control in the long term (Johnson, 1992a). On the other hand, uncertainty also offers a market-place for new forms of formal control claiming to be relevant to the new conditions. Hence the proliferation of new accounting systems (based on ABC, TOC, TA and many more). Thus management control may, after a short transition, refreeze around new accounting systems embodying formal controls.

However this is unlikely to be a stark alternative between increased reliance on informal control or the adoption of new formal controls. In such a period of change and uncertainty many enterprises appear to be considering, and experimenting with, several forms of change simultaneously. Thus companies claim to be 'using' many new accounting techniques (which their supporters consider incompatible) all at the same time. This is not so that managers can discover which one provides the 'right answer' to accounting issues, but because they offer a range of 'tools' to enable managers and supervisors to 'understand' their activities and achievements in financial terms – as part of an attempt to 'empower' them as financial actors pursuing an (as yet) ill-defined 'common vision'. If new patterns of formal and informal control are emerging from the unfreezing of manufacturing enterprises we anticipate that these will also prove contradictory and thus create new tensions, though in ways which cannot be predicted today.

Accountability.   At the centre of our discussion is the question of accountability (and its relation to accounting) as management control. Our analysis has suggested a number of ways in which accounting may operate as management control. Here the concept of 'accounting' has different meanings. At one level accounting is about *counting* – the conversion of activities and outcomes into numbers. At a deeper level these activities and outcomes are *accounted for* – they are reported upon (usually to superiors). At the same time the reporters may be required to *make an account* of their activities. This has the dual meaning of providing a narrative (how things happened) and an explanation (why they happened). Deeper again is the notion of being held *accountable* where the person who is counted, accounted for and makes the account is deemed responsible not just for the accounting but for the events and circumstances which have led to that accounting. Taken together these different facets of accounting may be seen as a regime of accountability. This hints at the deepest level of all – the construction of the *accountable person*. This would be someone who is so deeply enmeshed in practices of counting, accounting for, making accounts and being accountable that their view of the world, and of their own self, has become deeply permeated with accountability as a mode of thought – someone who, in a very precise sense, is self-accountable: who sees the world, interprets it, acts in it and evaluates his or her action in ways which mirror their external regimes of accountability.

But – and this is a very big 'but' – this is merely to explore the concept of accountability. It is most certainly not a description, let alone an explanation, of what is happening in manufacturing enterprises. There is no simplistic progression from counting to the accountable person, from hard accountability to soft accountability or even from formal controls to informal control. Nevertheless the delineation of the term 'accountability' may provide insights which prompt a different view of accounting from that provided by its equally absurd, but more usually discussed, counterpart. That absurdity is, of course, the view that accounting is an objective, neutral, factual statement of reality, entirely untouched by, and not touching, those persons who count and those who are counted.

To move away from absurdity, views of accounting as a technical practice and as a discursive discipline (when not extremist and doctrinaire positions) are both relevant to our understanding of management control. Accounting has more usually been recognised for its contribution to formal control through its array of techniques. We have pointed to some of its more neglected aspects in terms of constructing a vocabulary of action or language of business which carries a distinctive view of people as financial actors in financial contexts. Burawoy (1979) argued that when workers play the game of 'making out' in production they come to accept the rules of that game and that this implies that consent is manufactured–it is a product of the process. We would not be so bold. In 'playing the game' of formal accounting control, managers and workers construct practices which influence both the game and the players. This may be termed 'manufacturing accountability'. But the players are never fully constructed by the game, the game changes, and accountability is always an elusive and fragile phenomenon. It is never made, but always in the making – though no less real for that.

CHAPTER 20

Endpiece

Anthony J. Berry, Jane Broadbent and David Otley

In this chapter we will provide a brief overview of the three sections and explore some of the questions and issues that have arisen. In the language of Fayol, control appears as one of the universal activities of organisations and of managing. It had, for him, a central place in the list of planning, leading, organising, controlling and motivating. In this sense management control exists as an aspect of all domains of practical managing: marketing, production operations, personnel, purchasing, selling and so on. For we can discuss the control of the production process, control of personnel practices, control of the budgeting process and so on. Figure 20.1 illustrates this richness. The plane created by the axis of activities and the axis of domains is the plane of practice. From an inspection of this figure you can see how it is that Fayol and others could conceive of universal activities and of course in a straightforward practical sense they are right to do so.

In Figure 20.2 we add the third axis, that of academic disciplines. In so doing we create a plane which represents the multiple disciplines from which students may seek to understand the activities and their interactions; for example, we may examine planning through mathematical modelling. On closer inspection this plane might be found very abstract. We also create a plane which represents the likewise multiple disciplines from which students may understand the domains and their interrelationships; for example, we may explore marketing from the discipline of linguistics. The combination of the three axes of activities, domains and disciplines adds up to a three-dimensional space which shows, for example, that we can study control of production using social psychology or control of personnel using psychoanalytic theory.

So it is clear that management control as a plane of practice may be studied from the standpoint of any number of disciplines. To illustrate this point we note how economic theory led Williamson to explore control from the standpoint of markets as a counterpoint to hierarchies. The discourse of accounting

FIGURE 20.1   Activities and Domains: A plane of action

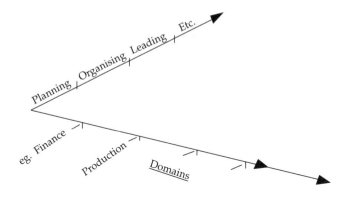

FIGURE 20.2   Activities, Domains and Disciplines

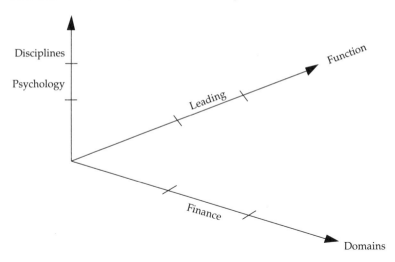

**Here, for example, we can see that the activity of
Leading in the Domain of finance may be studied
using the discipline of Psychology.**

has provided concepts such as cost absorption in activities to enable the flow
of resources to be traced through to products and shown how the budget
model may be used as a basis for understanding the relationship of inputs to
outputs of a system. In addition anthropology, the study of human societies,
has provided the concepts of culture from which Ouchi extended
Williamson's framework and aided Langfield-Smith in her chapter on culture
and control. And of course sociology and psychology have underpinned much

of the behavioural analysis of control processes. We would also note that these disciplines are not free from the sometimes vigorous epistemological debates taking place among scholars. While this is not primarily a research text, it is important to note that the research literature of these disciplines has informed our understanding of management control and shaped some of the contributions in this volume. For a wider discussion the reader is referred to Chua, Lowe and Puxty, *Critical Perspectives in Management Control*.

Parts I & II of this book were designed to explore control in a variety of ways which illustrate some of these different possibilities. In Part III, we presented examples of control in the context of various kinds of organisations. In this review of the volume it is not our intention to provide an integrating framework, but we do suggest that this simple framework of managerial activities, managerial domains and disciplines provides a very rich map of the field. It also provides a rationale for the inclusion of the types of issues covered which may seem, at first sight, to be somewhat diverse.

In Part I we reviewed how the subject of management control has been approached by different authors and theorists. In Chapter 1 we were concerned to establish our task as being to do with control in purposive organisations. From that standpoint we explored management control through the idea of domains in which control is encountered. This was followed by a discussion of the way control has been described and understood in some of the literature of organisation theory. Structures and procedures for control were examined prior to a discussion of the context for control.

We do not claim to have provided an overarching theory but we have sought to provide a reasonably coherent picture of some basic approaches to management control. The aim was to broaden the view of management control from that in the standard texts. The material is complex, mainly because the practical world of organisations is complex and we cannot give a normative answer to the question as to how we should control. Further we have endeavoured to indicate the limits of rational approaches as the problems of uncertainty, ambiguity and multiple and differentiated values are addressed. These are the reasons for both the multiple theoretical approaches put forward and for our unwillingness to offer clear prescriptive stances. We have sought, in Part I, to present our views in a manner that is complementary to those put forward in standard accounting and control texts. This text can be seen as an attempt to broaden the theoretical perspectives traditionally used to analyse the design and operation of management control systems.

In Part II, where the focus is on the examination of management control systems, we were concerned to present the variety of ways in which control has been understood in relation to particular issues. We have examined managerial issues of accounting, divisional management, strategy, operations management and performance measurement. While the varied styles and stances of the authors demonstrate some differences of approach, there is in these chapters an exploration in depth of some of the familiar problems of organisations. These managerial problems were complemented by discussions of control from the standpoint of the discipline of economics and the influence of culture. The latter was illustrated by studies of management accounting practices in Japanese companies in Japan and in the UK as a vehicle for exploring the differences in enacted culture and control between East and West.

In accordance with this approach, Part III contains some case studies of control in contemporary organisations, not as examples of perfect practice but to provide a practical complement to the more theoretical material of Part I and II. The examples were drawn from private and public, manufacturing and service organisations to provide some rich material for teaching and exploration.

Some final comments to students and managers

To students of management we would like to say that, in this book, we have been concerned to provide a counterpoint to the prescriptive and technical material found in the standard texts of management control which tend to equate control with management accounting. We do not, however, seek to dismiss these technical approaches for it is clear from the case material and from some of the chapters that of the ubiquity of accounting indicates its central importance. It is so because of its great virtue in giving a transorganisational language for describing some aspects of organisational activity. Moreover accounting provides a description in terms of some common notions of value expressed in monetary terms. It is a vehicle for control which can be argued to increase in importance as its logic is applied in more and more situations. What is clear from the considerations in this volume is that the social and cultural limits to the accounting discourse mean that great care must be taken in transferring the meanings attributed to accounting concepts when they are applied to organisations which are not predicated upon liberal market economics. In brief the notions of value which might exist in a wide range of organisations are not readily comparable and to assume they are because it is possible to record some interactions or transactions in accounting terms is a serious error. In any case accounting reduces the complexity in activity systems into a unidimensional depiction and, as such, oversimplifies many details essential to effective management control.

This notion of accounting as quantification of activity presupposes that all organisational matters of interest can be quantified and that that quantification is adequately meaningful. For example, it is possible to produce quantified management accounts for the process of control in schools, churches, professions and hospitals. However to assume that the activities and outputs of such organisations and their social significance are measured by such statements is to be misled as to the limitations of management accounting. Hence to base decisions about such organisations upon such management accounts would be a grave mistake.

The variety of the approaches to understanding control presented in this volume provides the possibility of reflecting upon them in the context of different organisational settings. Should you, the reader, generally see organisational analysis as a task of understanding the technical systems of acquisition of resources, production and distribution then it is likely that you will be out of sympathy with much of the material in this book, even though you might be able to make some progress with your problems. Should you see organisations as primarily social structures, you will also, surprising as it may seem, be out of sympathy with much of the material herein. For what we are setting out to encourage you to do is to make connections across the technical and social processes and to explore the significance of the issues raised, in order that you may develop a rich rather than an impoverished concept of managerial control in your organisation. So it is important that you explore the cases in Part III to broaden understanding through interpretation rather than analysis. They are not meant to be seen as essays in the simple application of ideas.

If you are currently managing in an organisation, we hope that you can build upon your own experience with the aid of the material in this book. Again we make no apologies for the discursive rather than prescriptive approach of the editors and authors. The literature of managing democratic organisations, empowered organisations, creative organisations and efficient and resourceful organisations has led scholars away from rather technical prescriptions. We set out with the premise that the underlying approach which essentially rejects simple technical prescriptions is necessary to effective management. The puzzle, as we see it, is that people in organisations which do have rather simple technical accounting systems for control have to locate them in the context of the markets and internal social structures and processes of their organisation, whether they recognise this or not. Hence we are encouraging the understanding of the significance and utility of processual approaches to management control.

This might seem to be a simple point but in practice it seems that managers do tend to a reductionist approach to information as the common use of targets and budgets as benchmarks for plans and action demonstrate (see, for example, Chapter 11). It seems that the perceived financial goals, because they are readily quantifiable, even if there is much slippage between what is known and what is represented, are commonly used as the ends which dictate present behaviour. It is unusual to find commercial organisations in the West which use process as the focus of management control, with goals as outcomes of the uncertainty.

Further there is in the privatisation movement a temptation to apply the technical process of management accounting to organisations which can in no sense be comprehended by such a curiously limited calculus. Yet the assumptions of the privateers is that such a calculus is not only universal but that it is somehow morally and politicoeconomically more effective and efficient than the more subtle, insightful processes which it replaces. Indeed there are always political processes in organisations and between organisations and their environments. Choosing not to recognise them cannot mean that they will be removed. The ideas in this volume provide at least a beginning for understanding from a widely drawn framework how management control may be developed in very varied organisations.

Of course you will have noticed that we have avoided much of the issue of power in organisations. Mostly we are concerned in this book with the issue of authority and its legitimacy, its explication in varied social and cultural contexts. Power presents some particular problems for the academic theorists and text writers. Central to these is the problem that control reduces to doing what one is ordered to do. There is no problem, other than the incompetence of the power holders. Of course such closed systems of power regress to warfare as a mode of control.

Conflict is, however, part of our concern. So a further problem with technical management accounting as a basis for management control is the assumption that all conflict is dealt with prior to the recording and measuring of transactions. This is an unlikely scenario. There is plenty of evidence and experience to show that the processes of management control carry within organisations some of the necessary conflict suppression and quasi-resolution or actual resolution of conflict.

In the material as we have presented it there is of course the problem of how any one individual relates to the ideas. Almost all accounting procedures have within them the risk of objectifying the experiencing self, as though the truth of human experience can be set aside by some such calculation. There is the risk then of reducing the very human concerns for our work, for each other, for our organisations and for the society in which we live to abstractions and then pretending that such abstractions are the stuff of intelligent management. This is to mistake the models for the substance, a common enough exercise when one group is seeking dominance over another.

Bibliography

Ackoff, R. (1974) *Redesigning the Future* (New York: John Wiley).

Ahmed, M.N. and Scapens, P.W. 'Cost Allocation Theory and Practice: The Continuing Debate', in Ashton, D., Happer, T. and Scapens, R.W. (eds), *Issues in Management Accounting* (Hemel Hempstead: Prentice-Hall pp. 39–60.)

Alchian, A. and H. Demsetz (1972) 'Production, Information Costs and Economic Organisation', *American Economic Review*, Vol. 62, pp. 777–95.

Aldrich, H.E. (1979) *Organisations and Environments* (London: Prentice-Hall).

Allaire, Y. and M.E. Firsirotu (1984) 'Theories of Organizational Culture', *Organization Studies*, Vol. 5, No. 3, pp. 193–226.

Allen, M. and D. Myddelton (1987) *Essential Management Accounting* (Hemel Hempstead: Prentice-Hall).

Alvesson, M. and L. Lindkvist (1993) 'Transaction Costs, Clans and Corporate Culture', *Journal of Management Studies*, Vol. 30, No. 3, pp. 427–52.

Amey, L.R. (1969) 'Divisional Performance Measurement and interest on Capital', *Journal of Business Finance*, Vol. 1, Spring pp. 1–7.

Amey, L.R. (1979) *Budget Planning and Control Systems* (London: Pitman).

Anderson, C. and F. Paine (1975) 'Managerial Perceptions and Strategic Behaviour', *Academy of Management Journal*, Vol. 18, pp. 811–23.

Andrews, K. (1971) *The Concept of Corporate Strategy* (Homewood, Ill.: Dow Jones/Irwin).

Ansoff, H.I. (1965) *Corporate Strategy* (New York: McGraw-Hill).

Ansoff, H.I. (1979) *Strategic Management* (London: Macmillan).

Anthony, R.N. (1965) *Planning and Control Systems: A Framework for Analysis* (Cambridge, Mass.: Harvard University Press).

Anthony, R.N. and D.W. Young (1984) *Management control in nonprofit organizations*, 3rd edn (Homewood, Ill.: Richard D. Irwin).

Anthony, R.N., J. Dearden and N.M. Bedford (1984) *Management Control Systems*, 5th Edn (Homewood, Ill.: Richard D. Irwin).

Anthony, R.N., J. Dearden and N. Bedford (1989) *Management Control Systems*, 6th edn (Homewood, Ill.: Richard D. Irwin).

Anthony, R.N., J. Dearden and. Govinjarajan (1992) *Management Control Systems*, 7th edn (Homewood, Ill.: Richard D. Irwin).

Aoki, M. (1984) *The Co-operative Game Theory of the Firm* (Oxford: Clarendon Press).

Aoki, M. (1986) 'Horizontal vs Vertical Information Structure of the Firm', *American Economic Review*, December, Vol. 76, No. 5, pp. 971–83.

Aoki, M. (1990a) 'The Participatory Generation of Information Rents and the Theory of the Firm', in M. Aoki, B. Gustaffson and O.E. Williamson (eds), *The Firm as a Nexus of Treaties* (London: Sage).

Aoki, M. (1990b) 'Towards a Theory of the Japanese Firm', *Journal of Economic Literature*, Vol. xxvii (March) pp. 1–27.

Argyris, C. (1952) *The Impact of Budgets on People* (Ithaca, New York: The Controllership Foundation).

Argyris, C. (1964) *Integrating the Individual and the Organisation* (New York: John Wiley).

Argyris, C. (1985) *Strategy, Change and Defensive Routines* (Cambridge, Mass.: Ballinger).

Argyris, C. (1990) *Overcoming Organisational Defences: Facilitating Organisational Learning* (Boston: Allyn & Bacon/Prentice-Hall).

Argyris, C. and D. Schon (1978) *Organisational Learning: A Theory of Action Perspective* (Reading, Mass.: Addison-Wesley).

Armstrong, P. (1985) 'Changing Managerial Control Strategies: the Role of Competition between Accounting and other Organisational Professions', *Accounting, Organizations and Society*, Vol. l0, No. 2, pp. 129–48.

Armstrong, P. (1987) 'The Rise of Accounting Controls in British Capitalist Enterprises', *Accounting, Organizations and Society*, Vol. l2, No. 5.

Armstrong, P. (1989) 'Variance Reporting and the Delegation of Blame: A Case Study', *Accounting, Auditing and Accountability Journal*, Vol. 2, No. 2, pp. 29–46.

Armstrong, P. (1991) 'Contradiction and Social Dynamics in the Capitalist Agency Relationships', *Accounting, Organizations and Society*, Vol. 16, No. 1, pp. 1–25.

Armstrong, P. (1993) 'Professional Knowledge and Social Mobility: Postwar Changes in the Knowledge-base of Management Accounting', *Work, Employment and Society*, Vol. 7, No. 1, pp. 1–21.

Arnold, J. and T. Hope (1990) *Accounting for Management Decisions*, 2nd edn, (Hemel Hempstead: Prentice-Hall).

Ashby, E. (1956) *An Introduction to Cybernetics* (London: Chapman and Hall).

Ashley Smith, D. and P. Smith (1987) 'Local authority annual reports', *Public Money*, Vol. 7, No. 3, pp. 52–6.

Ashton, D., T. Hopper and R. Scapens (eds) (1991) *Issues in Management Accounting* (Hemel Hempstead: Prentice-Hall).

Atkinson, J. (1984) 'Manpower Strategies for Flexible Organisations', *Personnel Management*, August, pp. 28–31.

Audit Commission (1992) *Citizen's Charter indicators: charting a course* (London: HMSO).

Baiman, S. (1982) 'Agency Research in Management Accounting: a survey', *Journal of Accounting Literature*, Spring, pp. 154–213.

Baiman, S. (1990) 'Agency research in managerial accounting: a second look', *Accounting, Organizations and Society*, Vol. 15, No. 4, pp. 341–371.

Baldamus, W. (1961) *Efficiency and Effort: An Analysis of Industrial Administration* (London: Tavistock).

Barnard, C. (1938) *The Functions of the Executive* (Cambridge, Mass.: Harvard University Press).

Bator, F.M. (1957) 'General Equilibrium, Welfare and Allocation', *American Economic Review* (March) pp. 22–59.

Beer, S. (1966) *Decision and Control* (New York: John Wiley).

Beer, S. (1979) *The Heart of the Enterprise* (New York: John Wiley).

Beer, S. (1972) *Brain of the Firm* (Harmondsworth: Allen Lane).

Benbassat, I. and A.S. Dexter (1979) 'Value and Events Approaches to Accounting: An Experimental Evaluation', *The Accounting Review*, Vol. LIV, No. 4, pp. 735–49.

Benefits Agency (1993) *Business plan, 1993/1994* (London: Department of Social Security).

Berry, A.J. (1983) 'Management Control and Methodology', in E.A. Lowe, and J.L. Machin (eds), *New Perspectives in Management Control* (London: Macmillan).

Berry, A.J. and D.T. Otley (1986) 'The Aggregation of Estimates in Hierarchical Organisations', *Journal of Management Studies*, Vol. 12, pp. 175–93.

Beyer, J.M. (1981) 'Ideologies, Values and Decision Making in Organisations', in P.C. Nystrom and W.H. Starbuck (eds), *Handbook of Organisational Design*, Vol. 2, (Oxford: Oxford University Press).

Beynon, H., (1973) *Working for Ford* (London: Penguin), reprint 1975 (Wakefield: EP Publishing).

Birnberg, J.G. and C. Snodgrass (1988) 'Culture and Control: A Field Study', *Accounting, Organizations and Society*, Vol. 13, No. 5, pp. 447–64.

Blau, P.M. (1955) *The Dynamics of Bureaucracy* (Chicago: University of Chicago Press).

Boulding, KE. (1956) 'General Systems Theory – the skeleton of a science', *Management Science*, Vol. 2, pp. 197–208.

Bourn, M. and M. Ezzamel (1986) 'Organisational Culture in Hospitals in the NHS', *Financial Accountability and Management*, Vol. 2, No. 3, pp. 203–25.

Bower, J.L. (1986) *Managing the Resource Allocation Process: A Study of Corporate Planning and Investment* (Boston: Harvard Business School Press).

Boyatzis, R. (1982) *The Competent Manager: A Model for Effective Managers* (New York: John Wiley).

Braverman, H. (1974) *Labor and Monopoly Capital* (New York: Monthly Review Press).

Braybrooke, D. and C.E. Lindblom (1963) *A Strategy for Decision* (London: Macmillan).

Broadbent, J. 'The Values of Accounting and Education: Some Implications of the Creation of Visibilities and Invisibilities in Schools', Sheffield University Management School Discussion Paper, 92/41; forthcoming in *Advances in Public Interest Accounting*, Vol. 6, No. 4.

Broadbent, J. and J. Guthrie (1992) 'Changes in the Public Sector: A Review of Some Recent "Alternative" accounting Research', *Accounting, Auditing and Accountability Journal*, Vol. 5, No. 2. pp. 3–31.

Broadbent, J., R.C. Laughlin, D. Shearn and N. Dandy (1992) 'It's a long way from teaching Susan to read', in G. Wallace, (ed.) *Local Management of Schools: Research and Experience*, Bera Dialogues, (Clevedon: Multilingual Matters).

Broadbent, J., R.C. Laughlin, D. Shearn and N. Dandy (1993) 'Implementing Local Management of Schools: A theoretical and empirical analysis', *Research Papers in Education*, Vol. 8, No. 2, pp. 149–76.

Bromwich, M. (1990) 'The Case for Strategic Management Accounting: The Role of Accounting Information for Strategy in Competitive Markets', *Accounting, Organizations and Society*, Vol. 15, No. 1/2, pp. 27–46.

Bromwich, M. and A. Bhimini (1989) *Management Accounting: Evolution not Revolution* (London: CIMA).

Bromwich, M. and S. Inoue (1992) 'Management Practices and Cost Management Problems in Japanese-Affiliated Companies in The United Kingdom', Working Paper, London School of Economics.

Brownell, P. (1981) 'Participation in Bugdgeting, Locus of Control and Organisational Effectiveness', *Accounting Review*, Vol. 56, pp. 844–860.

Bruns, W.J. and R.S. Kaplan (eds) (1987) *Accounting and Management – Field Study Perspectives* (Boston: Harvard Business School Press).

Bruns, W.J. and J.H. Waterhouse (1975) 'Budgetary Control and Organizational Structure', *Journal of Accounting Research*, Vol. 13, pp. 177–203.

Brunsson, N. (1985) *The Irrational Organisation* (Chichester: John Wiley).

Buckley, W. (1968) *Modern Systems Research for the Behavioural Scientist* (Chicago: Aldine).

Burawoy, M. (1979) *Manufacturing Consent: Changes in the Labor Process Under Monoploy Capitalism* (Chicago: Chicago University Press).

Burns, T. and G. Stalker (1961) *The Management of Innovation* (London: Tavistock).

Burrell, G. and G. Morgan (1979) *Sociological Paradigms and Organisational Analysis* (London: Heinemann).

Capps, T., T. Hopper, J. Mouritsen, D. Cooper and T. Lowe (1989) 'Accounting in the Production and Reproduction of Culture', in W.F. Chua, T. Lowe, and A.G. Puxty, (eds), *Critical Perspectives on Management Control* (London: Macmillan).

Carter, N. and P. Greer (1993) 'Evaluating agencies: Next steps and performance indicators', *Public Administration*, Vol. 71, pp. 407–16.

Chandler, A.D. (1962) *Strategy and Structure: Chapters in the History of the American Industrial Enterprise* (Cambridge, Mass.: MIT Press).

Chandler, A.D. (1977) *The Visible Hand: The Managerial Revolution in American Business* (Cambridge, Mass.: Harvard University Press).

Chandler, R. and P. Cook (1986) 'Compliance with disclosure standards in published reports and accounts of local authorities', *Financial Accountability and Management*, Vol. 2, pp. 75–8.

Chartered Institute of Public Finance and Accountancy (1982) *Local government comparative statistics 1982* (London: CIPFA).

Checkland, P. (1981) *Systems Thinking, Systems Practice* (Chichester: John Wiley).

Choi, F. and K. Hiramatsu (1987) *Accounting and Financial Reporting in Japan* (Wokingham: Van Nostrand Reinhold).

Chow, C.W., M.D. Shields and Y.K. Chan (1991) 'The Effects of Management Controls and National Culture on Manufacturing Performance: An Experimental Investigation', *Accounting, Organizations and Society*, Vol. 16, No. 3, pp. 209–26.

Christenson, C. (1983) 'The Methodology of Positive Accounting', *Accounting Review*, 58 (January) pp. 1–22.

Chua, W.F., T. Lowe and T. Puxty (1989) *Critical Perspectives in Management Control* (London: Macmillan).

Clark, B.R. (1972) 'The Organisational Saga in Higher Education', *Administrative Science Quarterly*, Vol. 17, pp. 178–183

Clark, K., R. Hayes and C. Lorenz (eds) (1985). *The Uneasy Alliance* (Boston: Harvard Business School).

Coase, R. (1937) 'The Nature of the Firm', *Economica*, Vol. 4, pp. 386–405.

Cohen, M., J. March and J. Olsen (1972) 'A garbage can model of Organisational Choice', *Administrative Science Quarterly*, Vol. 17, pp. 1–25.

Committee of Vice Chancellors and Principals and University Grants Committee (1987) *University management statistics and performance indicators* (London: CVCP).

Cooper, D. (1981) 'A Social and Organisational View of Management Accounting'. In M. Bromwich and A. Hopwood (eds), *Essays In British Accounting Research* (London: Pitman).

Cooper, D. (1983) 'Tidiness, Muddle and Things: Commonalties and Divergencies in Two Approaches to Management', *Accounting Organizations and Society*, pp. 269-86.

Cooper, R. (1987) 'The Two Stage Procedure in Cost Accounting, Part 1', *Journal of Cost Management*, Summer, pp. 43–51.

Cooper, R. and R.S. Kaplan (1988) 'Measure Costs Right: Make the Right Decisions', *Harvard Business Review*, September–October.

Covalesk, M.A., Dirsmith, M.W. and White, C.E. (1987) 'Economic Consequences: The Relationship between Financial Reporting and Strategic Planning, Management and Operating Control Decision', *Contemporary Accounting Research*, Vol. 3, No. 2, pp. 408–29.

Cyert, R.M. and J.G. March (1963) *A Behavioural Theory of the Firm* (Hemel Hempstead: Prentice-Hall).

Cyert, R.M., J.G. March and W.H. Starbuck (1961) 'Two Experiments on Risk and Conflict in Organizational Estimation', *Management Science*, Vol. 7, pp. 254–64.

Dalton, M. (1959) *Men Who Manage* (New York: John Wiley).

Daniel, S.J. and W.D. Reitsperger (1991) 'Linking Quality Strategy with Management Control Systems: Empirical Evidence From Japanese Industry', *Accounting, Organizations and Society*, Vol. 16, No. 7, pp. 601–18.

Deal, T.E. and A.A. Kennedy (1982) *Corporate Cultures: The Rites and Rituals of Corporate Life* (Reading, Mass.: Addison-Wesley).

Dearden, J. (1962) 'Limits on Decentralized Profit Responsibility', *Harvard Business Review*, July/August, pp. 89–90.

Dearden, J. (1968) 'Time span in management control', reprinted in *Readings in Cost Accounting, Budgeting and Control*, 4th edn Thomas, W. E. Cincinati: South Western Publishing, pp. 340–54.

Demirag, I.S. (1986) 'The treatment of exchange rates in internal performance evaluation', *Accounting and Business Research*, Spring, Vol. 16, pp. 157–64.

Demirag, I.S. (1988) 'Assessing foreign subsidiary performance: The currency choice of UK MNCs', *Journal of International Business Studies*, Vol. 19, No. 2, Summer, pp. 257–275.

Demirag, I.S. and A. Tylecote (1992a) 'The Effects of Organisational Culture, Structure and Market Expectations on Technological Innovation: A Hypothesis', *British Journal Of Management*, Vol. 3, No. 1, pp. 7–20.

Demirag, I.S. and A. Tylecote (1992b) 'Short-termism: culture and structures as factors in technological innovation', in R. Coombs, V. Walsh and P. Saviotti (eds), *Technological Change and Company Strategies* (New York: Academic Press).

Dent, J.F. (1987) 'Tension in the Design of Formal Control Systems: A Field Study in a Computer Company', in W.J. Bruns and R.S. Kaplan (eds), *Accounting and Management – Field Study Perspectives* (Boston: Harvard Business School Press), pp. 119–45.

Dent, J.F. (1990) 'Process model of relationship between business strategy and management control systems: Strategy, Organisation and Control: Some possibilities for accounting research', *Accounting, Organizations and Society*, Vol. 15, No. 1/2, pp. 3–25.

Dent, J.F. (1991) 'Accounting and Organisational Cultures: A Field Study of the Emergence of a New Organisational Reality', *Accounting, Organizations and Society*, Vol. 16, No. 8, pp. 705–32.

Department of Education and Science (1991) *The parent's charter* (London: DES).

Department of the Environment (1981) *Local authority annual reports* (London: HMSO).

Department of Health (1991) *The patient's charter* (London: HMSO).

Department of Health and Social Security (1983) *Performance indicators: national summary for 1981* (London: DHSS).

Department of Health and Social Security (1985) *Performance indicators for the National Health Service: guidance for users* (London: DHSS).

Department of Health and Social Security (1987) *The performance indicator analyst, version 1.0* (London: DHSS).

Department of Health and Social Security (1988) *Comparing health authorities* (London: DHSS).

Dermer, J. (1977) *Management Planning and Control Systems* (Homewood, Ill.: Richard D. Irwin).

Dermer, J. (1988) 'Control and Organisational Order', *Accounting Organizations and Society*, Vol. 13, No. 1, pp. 25–36.

Dermer, J. (1990) 'The Strategic Agenda: Accounting for Issues and Support', *Accounting, Organizations and Society*, Vol. 15, No. 1/2, pp. 67–76.

Dermer, J.D. and R.G. Lucas (1986) 'The Illusion of Managerial Control', *Accounting, Organizations and Society*, Vol. 11, No. 6, pp. 471–82.

Dess, G.G. and A. Miller (1993) *Strategic Management* (New York: McGraw-Hill).

Dow, G. (1987) 'The Function of Authority in Transaction Cost Economics', *Journal of Economic Behavior and Organization*, Vol. 8, pp. 13–38.

Drucker, P. (1964) 'Control, Controls and Management', In C.P. Bonini, R.K. Jaedicke and H.M. Wagner (eds) *Management Control: New Directions in Basic Research* (New York: John Wiley) pp. 286–96.

Drury, C. (1985) *Management and Cost Accounting* (London:.Van Nostrand Reinhold).

Drury, J. (1988). *Management and Cost Accounting*, 2nd edn (London: VNR International).

Drury, C. (1992) *Management and Cost Accounting*, 3rd Edn (London: Chapman and Hall).

Dugdale, D. and T.C. Jones (1993) 'Investment Decisions and the Social Construction of Trust', *Interdisciplinary Approaches to Accounting Workshop*, January Manchester Conference Centre.

Dugdale, D. and T.C. Jones (1994) 'Finance, Strategy and Trust in Investment Appraisal', *Management Accounting*, April, pp. 52–4, 56.

Emmanuel, C.R. and D.T. Otley (1985) *Accounting for Management Control* (London: Chapman and Hall).

Emmanuel, C.R., D.T. Otley and K. Merchant (1990) *Accounting for Management Control*, 2nd edn (London: Chapman and Hall).

Enthoven, A.C. (1985) *Reflections on the Management of the NHS: an American looks at incentives to efficiency in health services management in the UK* (London: Nuffield Provincial Hospitals Trust).

Etzioni, A. (1961) *A Comparative Analysis of Complex Organizations* (New York: Free Press).

European Commission (1991) *Directive on the adoption of standards for satellite broadcasting of television signals*, COM (91) 242, doc. C3-290/9 1, SYN3 50 (Brussels).

Ezzamel, M. (1992) *Business Unit and Divisional Performance Measurement* (London: Academic Press in association with CIMA).

Ezzamel, M. and H. Hart (1987) *Advanced Management Accounting: An Organisational Emphasis* (London: Cassell).

Ezzamel, M. and K. Hilton (1980a) 'Divisionalization in British Industry: A Preliminary Study', *Accounting and Business Research*, Spring, pp. 197–214.

Ezzamel, M. and K. Hilton (1980b) 'Can divisional discretion be measured?', *Journal of Business Finance and Accounting*, Summer, pp. 311–29.

Ezzamel, M., K. Hoskins and R. MacVe (1990) 'Managing it all by numbers: A review of Kaplan and Johnson's Relevance Lost', *Accounting and Business Research*, Vol. 20, No. 7, pp. 153–66.

Fama, E. (1980) 'Agency Problems and the Theory of the Firm', *Journal of Political Economy*, Vol. 88, No. 2, pp. 288–307.

Fayol, H. (1949) *General and Industrial Management* (London: Pitman).

Fiske, S.T. and S.E. Taylor (1991) *Social Cognition* (New York: McGraw-Hill).

Fitzgerald, L., R. Johnston, S. Brignall, R. Silvestro and C. Voss (1991) *Performance Measurement In Service Businesses* (London: CIMA).

Flamholtz, E.G., T.K. Das and A.S. Tsui (1985) 'Toward an Integrative Framework of Organisational Control', *Accounting, Organizations and Society*, Vol. 10, No. 1, pp. 35–50.

Follet, M.P. (1924) *Creative Experience* (London: Longman and Green).

Forester, J. (1961) *Industrial Dynamics* (Cambridge, Mass.: MIT Press).

Fox, A. (1974) *Beyond Contract: Work, Power and Trust Relations* (London: Faber and Faber).

Friedman, A. (1977) *Industry and Labour: Class Struggle at Work and Monopoly Capitalism* (London: Macmillan).

Gagliardi, P. (1986) 'The Creation and Change of Organisational Cultures: A Conceptual Framework', *Organization Studies*, Vol. 7, No. 2, pp. 117–34

Galloway, D. and D. Waldron (1988a) 'Throughput Accounting – 1: The need for a new language for manufacturing', *Management Accounting*, November, pp. 34–5.

Galloway, D. and D. Waldron (1988b) 'Throughput Accounting – 2: Ranking products profitably', *Management Accounting*, December, pp. 34–5.

Galloway, D. and D. Waldron (1989a) 'Throughput Accounting – 3: A better way to control labour costs', *Management Accounting*, January, pp. 32–3.

Galloway, D. and Waldron, D. (1989b) 'Throughput Accounting – 4: Moving on to complex products', *Management Accounting*, February pp. 40–1.

Ganley, J.A. and J.S. Cubbin (1992) *Public Sector Efficiency Measurement: Applications of Data Envelopment Analysis* (Amsterdam: North Holland).

Geertz, C. (1973) *The Interpretation of Cultures* (New York: Basic Books).

Glaister, K., and D. Thwaites (1993) 'Managerial Perception and Organisational Strategy', *Journal of General Management*, Vol. 18, No. 4, Summer, pp. 15–33.

Goffman, E. (1959) *The Presentation of Self in Everyday Life* (Garden City, New York: Doubleday Anchor).

Goldratt, E. (1984) *The Goal* (London: Gower).

Goold, M. (1991) 'Strategic Control in the Decentralised Firm', *Sloan Management Review*, Winter, pp. 69–81.

Goold, M. and A. Campbell (1987a) 'Managing diversity: Strategy and control in diversified British companies', *Long Range Planning*, Vol. 20, No. 5, pp. 42–52.

Goold, M. and A. Campbell (1987b) *Strategies and Styles: The Role of the Centre in Managing Diversified Corporations* (Oxford: Basil Blackwell).

Goold, M. and J.J. Quinn (1990a) *Strategic Control: Milestones for Long Term Performance* (London: Hutchinson).

Goold, M. and J.J. Quinn (1990b) 'The Paradox of Strategic Controls', *Strategic Management Journal*, Vol. 11, No. 1, pp. 43–57.

Goold, M., A, Campbell and K. Luchs (1993) 'Strategies and Styles Revisited: Strategic Planning and Financial Control', *Long Range Planning*, Vol. 26, No. 5, pp. 49–60.

Gordon, L.A. and D. Miller (1976) 'A Contingency Framework For The Design of Accounting Information Systems', *Accounting, Organisations and Society* Vol. 1, No. 1, pp. 59–70.

Gorz, A. (1989) *A Critique of Economic Reason* (London: Verso).

Govindarajan, V. (1984) 'Appropriateness of Accounting Data in Performance Evaluation: An Empirical Examination of Environmental Uncertainty as an Intervening Variable', *Accounting, Organizations and Society*, Vol. 9, No. 2, pp. 125–35.

Govindarajan, V. (1988) ' A Contingency approach to strategy implementation at the business-unit level: integrating administrative mechanisms with strategy', *Academy of Management Journal*, Vol. 31, pp. 828–853.

Govindarajan, V. and Gupta A.K. (1985) 'Linking Control Systems to Business Unit Strategy: Impact on Performance', *Accounting, Organizations and Society*, Vol. 10 No. 1, pp. 51–66.

Grabner, G. (1993) *The Embedded Firm* (London: Routledge).

Gray, J., D. Jesson and N. Sime (1990) 'Estimating differences in the exam performance of secondary schools in 6 LEAs – a multilevel approach to school effectiveness', *Oxford Review of Education*, Vol. 16, pp. 137–58.

Grinyer, J. (1986) 'An alternative to maximisation of shareholders' wealth in Capital Budgeting', *Accounting and Business Research*, Autumn, pp. 319–26.

Grinyer, P.H. and J.C. Spender (1979) 'Recipes, Crises and Adaptation in Mature Businesses', *International Studies of Management and Organisation*, Vol. 9, pp. 113–23.

Gulick, L.H. and L. Urwick (eds) (1937) *Papers on the Science of Administration* (Columbia: Columbia University Press).

Haka, S., L. Gordon and G. Pinches (1985) 'Sophisticated Capital Budgeting Selection Techniques and Firm Performance', *The Accounting Review*, Vol. lx, No. 4, pp. 651–69.

Hall, W.K. (1978) 'SBU's : Hot new topic in the Management of Diversification Business Horizons', February, reprinted in D.J. McCarthy, R.J. Minichiello, J.R. Curran(eds), *Business Policy Strategy*, rev. edn, (1979) (Homewood Ill.: Richard D. Irwin).

Hambrick, D.C. (1984) 'Taxonomic Approaches to Studying Strategy: Some Conceptual and Methodological Issues', *Journal of Management*, Vol. 10, No. 1, pp. 241–78.

Hammond, T. and A. Preston (1992) 'Culture, Gender and Corporate Control: Japan as "Other" ', *Accounting, Organizations and Society*, Vol. 17, No. 8, pp. 795–808.

Handy, C. (1985) *Understanding Organizations* (Harmondswoth: Penguin).

Hannan, M.T. and J.H. Freeman (1977) 'The Population Ecology of Organisations', *American Journal of Sociology*, Vol. 82, pp. 929–64.

Harrison, R. (1972) 'Understanding your organization's character', *Harvard Business Review*, May/June, pp. 119–28.

Hayes, R., S. Wheelwright and K. Clark (1988) *Dynamic Manufacturing: creating the learning organisation* (New York: The Free Press).

Hertz, D.B. (1964) 'Risk Analysis in Capital Investment', *Harvard Business Review*, Jan./Feb., pp. 175–86.

Hertzberg, F., B. Mausner and B.B. Snyderman (1959) *The Motivation to Work* (New York: John Wiley).

Hirst, M.K. (1981) 'Accounting Information and the Evaluation of Subordinate Performance', *The Accounting Review*, Vol. 56, pp. 771–84.

Hofer, C.W. and D. Schendel (1978) *Strategy Formulation: Analytical concepts* (St. Paul, Minn: West Publishing Co).

Hofstede, G. (1967) *The Game of Budget Control* (London: Tavistock).

Hofstede, G. (1985) 'The Interaction between National and Organizational Value Systems', *Journal of Management Studies*, Vol. 22, No. 4, pp. 347–57.

Hood, C. (1991) 'A Public Management for All Seasons?', *Public Administration*, Vol. 69, pp. 3–19.

Hopper, T. (1988) 'Social Transformation and Management Accounting', in *Proceedings of the Second Interdisciplinary Perspective in Accounting Conference*, Manchester.

Hopper, T. and P. Armstrong (1991) 'Cost Accounting, Controlling Labour and the Rise of the Conglomerates', *Accounting, Organizations and Society*, Vol. 16, No. 5/6, pp. 405–38.

Hopper, T.M. and A.J. Berry (1983) 'Organisational Design and Management Control'. In E.A. Lowe and J.L.J. Machin (eds), *New Perspectives In Management Control* (London: Macmillan).

Hopper, T., J. Storey and H.C. Willmott (1987) 'Accounting for Accounting: Towards the Development of a Dialectical View', *Accounting, Organizations and Society*, Vol. 12, No. 5, pp. 437–56.

Hopper, T., D. Cooper, A. Lowe, T. Capps and J. Mouritsen (1986) 'Management Control and Worker Resistance in the National Coal Board: Financial Controls in the Labour Process'. in D. Knights and H.C. Willmott (eds) (1986) *Managing the Labour Process* (London: Macmillan).

Hopwood, A. (1972) 'An Empirical Study of the Role of Accounting Data in Performance Evaluation', *Empirical Research in Accounting, Supplement to Journal of Accounting Research*, Vol. 10, pp. 156–82.

Hopwood, A.G. (1974) *Accounting and Human Behaviour* (Englewood Cliffs, NJ: Prentice-Hall).

Hopwood, A.G. (1983) 'On Trying to Study Accounting in the Contexts in which it Operates', *Accounting, Organizations and Society*, Vol. 8, No. 2/3, pp. 287–305.

Hopwood, A. G. (1985) 'The growth of "worrying about management accounting"', in K. Clark, R. Hayes and C. Lorenz (eds), *The Uneasy Alliance* (Boston: Harvard Business School).

Hopwood, A.G. (1987) 'The Archaeology of Accounting Systems', *Accounting, Organisations and Society*, Vol. 12, No. 3, pp. 207–34.

Hopwood, A.G. (1990) 'Accounting and Organisations Change', *Accounting, Auditing and Accountability*, Vol. 3, No. 1, pp. 7–17.

Horngren, C.T. (1962) *Cost Accounting: A Managerial Emphasis* (London: Prentice Hall).

Horngren, C.T. (1977) *Cost Accounting: A Managerial Emphasis*, new edn (London: Prentice-Hall).

Horngren, C.T. (1981) *Introduction to Management Accounting*, 5th edn (London: Prentice-Hall).

Horngren, C.T. (1984) *Introduction to Management Accounting*, 6th edn (Englewood Cliffs: Prentice-Hall).

Horngren, C. T. and G. Foster (1991) *Cost Accounting: a managerial emphasis*, 7th edn (Englewood Cliffs: Prentice-Hall)

Horngren, C.T. and G. Sundem (1991) *Introduction to Management Accounting*, 8th edn (Englewood Cliffs: Prentice-Hall).

Horovitz, J.H. (1979) 'Strategic Control: A New Task for Top Management', *Long Range Planning*, Vol. 12, pp. 2–7.

Hoskin, K.W. (1993) 'Education and the Genesis of Disciplinarity: The Unexpected Reversal', In E. Messer-Davidow, D.R. Shumway and D.J. Sylvan (eds), *Knowledges: Historical and Critical Studies in Disciplinarity* (London: University Press of Virginia).

Hoskin, K.W. and R.H. Macve (1988) 'The Genesis of Accountability: The West Point Connection', *Accounting, Organizations and Society*, Vol. 13, No. 1, pp. 37–73.

Hrebiniak, L.G. and W.F. Joyce (1986) 'The strategic importance of managing myopia', *Sloan Management Review*, Fall, pp. 5–14.

Hurst, E.G. (1982) 'Controlling strategic plans', in P. Lorange (ed.), *Implementation of Strategy Planning* (Englewood Cliffs, NJ: Prentice-Hall).

Hyman, R. and B. Anderson (1982) 'Solving Problems', in D.A. Kolb, I.M. Rubin and J.M. McIntyre (eds), *Organisational Psychology* (Englewood Cliffs, NJ: Prentice-Hall).

Hyman, R. and T. Elger (1981) 'Job Controls, the Employer Offensive and Alternative Strategies', *Capital and Class*, Vol. 15, Autumn, pp. 115–45.

Imai, K. and H. Itami (1984) 'Interpenetration of Organization and Market', *International Journal of Industrial Organisation*, Vol. 2, pp. 285–310.

Innes, J. and F. Mitchell (1991) *ABC: A Review With Case Studies* (London: CIMA).

Ivanevitch, J. (1976) 'Effects of Goal Setting on Performance and Job Satisfaction', *Journal of Applied Psychology*, Vol. 61, pp. 605–12.

Jackson, P. and B. Palmer (1989) *First steps in measuring performance in the public sector* (London: Public Finance Foundation).

Jalland, R.M. (1989) 'Plan-making in multi-divisional Companies' unpublished PhD thesis, University of Manchester.

Janis, I.L. (1972) *Victims of Groupthink* (Boston: Houghton Mifflin).

Janis, I.L. (1982) *Groupthink: Psychological Studies of Policy Decisions and Fiascos* (Boston: Houghton Mifflin).

Janis, I.L. and L. Mann (1977) *Decision-Making* (New York: Free Press).

Jaworski, B.J. and S.M. Young (1992) 'Dysfunctional behavior and management control: an empirical study of marketing managers', *Accounting, Organizations and Society*, Vol. 17, No. 1, pp. 17–35.

Jayson, S. (1922) 'Focus on People – Not Costs', *Management Accounting (US)*, September, pp. 28–33.

Jelinek, M.L. Smircich and P. Hirsch (1983) 'Introduction: A Code of Many Colors', *Administrative Science Quarterly*, Vol. 28, No. 2, pp. 331–8

Jensen, M. (1983) 'Organization Theory and Methodology', *Accounting Review*, Vol. 50, April, pp. 319–39.

Jensen, M. and W. Meckling (1976) 'Theory of the Firm: Managerial Behavior, Agency Costs and Ownership Structure'. *Journal of Financial Economics*, Vol. 3, pp. 305–60.

Jensen, M. and W. Meckling (1979) 'Rights and Production Functions: an Application to the Labor Managed Firm', *Journal of Business*, Vol. 52, pp. 469–506.

Johnson, G. (1987) *Strategic Change and the Management Process* (Oxford: Basil Blackwell).

Johnson, G. and K. Scholes (1993) *Exploring Corporate Strategy* (Hemel Hempstead: Prentice-Hall).

Johnson, H.T. (1992a) *Relevance Regained: From Top-down Control to Bottom-up Empowerment* (New York: Free Press).

Johnson, H.T. (1992b) 'It's Time to Stop Overselling Activity-Based Concepts: Start Focusing on Customer Satisfaction Instead', *Management Accounting (US)*, September, pp. 26–35.

Johnson, H.T. and R.S. Kaplan (1987) *Relevance Lost: The Rise and Fall of Management Accounting* (Cambridge, Mass.: Harvard Business School Press).

Jones, T.C. (1992) 'Understanding Management Accountants: The Rationality of Social Action', *Critical Perspectives on Accounting*, Vol. 3, No. 3, pp. 225-257.

Jones, T.C. (forthcoming) *Accounting and the Enterprise: A Social Analysis* (London: Routledge).

Jones, T.C., W.L. Currie and D. Dugdale (1993) 'Accounting and Technology in Britain and Japan: Learning From Field Research', *Management Accounting Research*, Vol. 4, No. 2, pp. 109–37.

Jonsson, S. and R.A. Lundin (1977) 'Myths and Wishful Thinking As Management Tools', in P.C. Nystrom and W.H. Starbuck (eds), *Prescriptive Models of Organisation* (Amsterdam: North Holland) pp. 157–70.

Kaplan, R.S. (1984) 'Yesterday's Accounting Undermines Production', *Harvard Business Review*, July/August, pp. 95–101.

Kaplan, R.S. (1985) 'The Obsolescence of Cost Accounting System' in K. Clark, R. Hayes, and C. Lorenz, (eds), *The Uneasy Alliance* (Boston: Harvard Business School).

Kaplan, R. S. and D.P. Norton (1992) 'The balanced scorecard – measures that drive performance', *Harvard Business Review*, Vol. 70, No. 1, pp. 71–9.

Kaplan, R.S. and D.P. Norton (1993) 'Putting the Balanced Scorecard to work', *Harvard Business Review*, September–October, pp. 134–47.

Katz, D. and R.L. Khan (1978) *The Social Psychology of Organisations* (New York: John Wiley).

Kelly, G.A. (1955) *The Psychology of Personal Constructs* (New York: W.W. Norton).

Kelly, J. (1982) *Scientific Management, Job Design and Work Performance* (London: Academic Press).

Kenis, I. (1979) 'Effects of Budgetary Goal Characteristics on Managerial Attitudes on Performance', *The Accounting Review*, Vol. liv, No. 4, pp. 707–21.

Kennedy, A. and R. Mills (1992) 'Post-completion auditing: a source of strategic direction?', *Management Accounting*, Vol. 70, No. 5, May, pp. 26–8.

Kerr, S. (1975) 'On the folly of rewarding A while hoping for B', *Academy of Management Journal*, pp. 769–83.

Khandawalla, P.N. (1972) 'The Effects of Different types of Competition on the Use of Management Control', *Journal of Accounting Research*, Vol. 10, pp. 275–85.

King, P. (1975) 'Is the Emphasis of Capital Budgeting Theory Misplaced?', *Journal of Business Finance and Accounting*, Spring, pp. 69–82.

Knights, D. and D. Collinson (1987) 'Disciplining the Shopfloor: A Comparison of the Disciplinary Effects of Managerial Psychology and Financial Accounting', *Accounting, Organizations and Society*, Vol. 12, No. 5, pp. 457–77.

Kornai, J. (1992) *The Socialist System: The Political Economy of Communism* (Oxford: Clarendon Press).

Kotter, J.P. and J.L. Heskett (1992) *Corporate Culture and Performance* (New York: The Free Press).

Kuhn, T.S. (1970) *The Structure of Scientific Revolutions* (Chicago: University of Chicago Press).

Langfield-Smith, K. (1993) 'Linking Management Control Systems And Strategy: An Examination of The Strategy Construct and Critical Review', paper presented at the European Accounting Association Conference, Turku, Finland, 28–30 April.

Langlois, A. (1986) *Economics as a Process* (Cambridge: Cambridge University Press).

Laughlin, R.C. (1987) 'Accounting Systems in Organisational Contexts: A Case for Critical Theory', *Accounting, Organizations and Society*, Vol. 12, No. 5, pp. 479–502.

Laughlin, R.C. (1991) 'Environmental Disturbances and Organisational Transitions and Transformations: Some Alternative Models', *Organisation Studies*, Vol. 12, No. 2.

Laughlin, R. and J. Broadbent (1993) 'Accounting and Law: Partners in the Juridification of the Public Sector in the UK?', *Critical Perspectives on Accounting*. Vol. 4, No. 4, pp. 337–68.

Laughlin, R. and R. Gray (1988) *Financial Accounting: Method and Meaning* (London, VNR).

Laughlin, R., J. Broadbent, D. Shearn and H. Willig-Atherton (1994) 'Absorbing LMS: The Coping Mechanism of a Small Group', *Accounting, Auditing and Accountability Journal*, Vol. 7, No. 1, pp. 59–85.

Lawler, E.E. (1973) *Motivation in Work Organisations* (Monterey (Caly): Brroks Cole Publishing Co.).

Leijonhufvud, A. (1968) *On Keynesian Economics and the Economics of Keynes* (Oxford: Oxford University Press).

Lévi-Strauss, C. (1967) *The Scope of Anthropology* (New York: Jonathan Cape).

Lilienfeld, R. (1978) *The Rise of Systems Theory* (New York, Chichester: John Wiley)

Lillis, A.M. (1992) 'Sources of influence on capital expenditure decisions: a contextual study of accounting measurement', *Management Accounting Research*, No. 3, pp. 213–27.

Lindblom, C.E. (1977) *Politics and Markets* (New York: Basic Books).

Llewellyn, D. (1991) 'Is There A Credit Crunch?', *Banking World*, May, pp. 23–6.

Locke, E.A. (1968) 'Towards a Theory of Risk Motivations and Incentives', *Organizational Behaviour and Human Performance*, Vol. 3, pp. 157–89.

Loft, A. (1991) 'The History of Management Accounting: Relevance Found', in D. Ashton, T. Hopper and R.W. Scapens (eds), *Issues in Management Accounting* (Englewood Cliffs, NJ: Prentice Hall) pp. 17–38.

Lorange, P. (ed) (1980) *Implementation of Strategic Planning* (Englewood Cliffs, NJ: Prentice-Hall).

Lorange, P. (1988) 'Monitoring strategic progress and ad hoc strategic modification', in J. Grant (ed), *Strategic Management Horizons* (Greenwich, Conn.: JAI Press).

Lorange, P. and D. Murphy (1984) 'Considerations in Implementing Strategic Control', *Journal of Business Strategy*, Vol. 5, pp. 27–35.

Lorange, P., M.F. Scott Morton and S. Goshal (1986) *Strategic Control* (St Paul, Minn.: West Publishing Co).

Lorsch, J.W. and S.A. Allen (1973) *Managing Diversity and Interdependence Division of Research*, Graduate School of Business Administration, Harvard University.

Lowe, E.A. (1971) 'Budgetary Control: An Evaluation in a Wider Managerial Perspective', *Accountancy*, November, pp. 764–9.

Lowe, E.A. and W.F. Chua (1983) 'Organisational Effectiveness and Management Control', in E.A. Lowe and J.L.F. Machin (eds), *New Perspectives in Management Control* (London: Macmillan).

Lowe, E.A. and J.L.F. Machin (1983) *New Perspectives in Management Control* (London: Macmillan).

Lowe, E.A. and R.W. Shaw (1968) 'An Analysis of Managerial Biasing: evidence from company's budgeting process', *Journal of Management Studies*, Vol. 5, pp. 304–15.

Lowe, E.A., A.G. Puxty and R.C. Laughlin (1983) 'Simple Theories for Complex Processes: Accounting Policy and the Market for Myopia', *Journal of Accounting and Public Policy*, Vol. 2, pp. 19–42.

Lowe, T. and T. Puxty (1989) 'The Problems of a Paradigm: A Critique of the Prevailing Orthodoxy in Management Control', in W.F. Chua, T. Lowe and T. Puxty (eds), *Critical Perspectives in Management Control* (London: MacMillan).

Lyne, S. (1993) 'An Evaluation of the Roles of Activity-Based Accounting Information', Management Accounting Research Group Conference, September, University of Aston.

Machin, J.L. (1983) 'Management Control Systems: Whence and Whither?', in E.A. Lowe and J.L.F. Machin (eds), *New Perspectives in Management Control* (London: MacMillan) pp. 22–42.

Maciariello, J.A. (1984) *Management Control Systems* (Englewood Cliffs, NJ, London: Prentice Hall).

Macintosh, N.B. (1985) *The Social Software of Accounting and Information Systems* (Chichester: John Wiley).

Mackey, J. (1991) 'MRP, JIT and Automated Manufacturing and the Role of Accounting in Production Management', in D. Ashton, T. Hopper and R. Scapens (eds), *Issues in Management Accounting* (Hemel Hempstead: Prentice-Hall).

Malinowski, B. (1922) *Argonauts of the Western Pacific* (London: Routledge and Kegan Paul).

Malmberg, A. (1980) 'The Impact of Job Reform on Accounting Systems'. in G. Kanawaty (ed.), *Managing and Developing New forms of Work Organisation*, Geneva: International labour organization, 2nd edn, pp. 79–94.

March, J. and J. Olsen (1976) *Ambiguity and Choice in Organisations* (Bergen: Universitetsforlaget).

March, J. and H. Simon (1958) *Organisations* (New York: John Wiley).

Marglin, S.A. (1974) 'What do Bosses do? The origins and functions of Hierarchy in Capitalist production', *Review of Radical Political Economics*, Vol. 6, pp. 33–60.

Martin, J. and C. Siehl (1983) 'Organisational Culture and Counterculture: An Uneasy Symbiosis', *Organisational Dynamics*, Vol. 12, pp. 52–64.

Marx, K. (1972) *Capital* (London: Lawrence and Wishart).

Marx, K. (1868, reprinted 1976) *Capital: Volume One* (Harmondsworth: Penguin).

Maslow, A.H. (1954) *Towards a Psychology of Being* (New York, London: Van Nostrand Rheinhold).

Mayo, E. (1933) *The Human Problems of an Industrial Civilization* (Cambridge, Mass.: Harvard University Press).

Mayo, E. (1945) *The Social Problems of an Industrial Civilization* (New York: Macmillan).

McCosh, A. (1990) 'Positive Control', *Economia Aziendale*, Vol. ix, No. 3, pp. 405–427.

McGregor, D. (1960) *The Human Side of Enteprises* (New York: McGraw-Hill).

McGuire, A. *et al.* (1991) 'The Economics of Health Care', in A. McGuire, P. Fenn and K. Mayhew (eds), *Providing Health Care* (Oxford: Oxford University Press).

Mead, M. (19 28) *Coming of Age in Samoa* (New York: Morrow).

Meek, V.L. (1988) 'Organisational Culture: Origins and Weaknesses', *Organization Studies*, Vol. 9, No. 4, pp. 454–73

Merchant, K. (1981) 'The Design of the Corporate Budgeting System: Influences on Managerial Behaviour and Performance', *The Accounting Review*, Vol. lvi, No. 4, pp. 813–29.

Merchant, K. (1985) *Control in Business Organizations* (London: Pitman).

Meyer, S. (1980) 'Adapting the Immigrant to the Line: Americanization in the Ford Factory, 1914–1921', *Journal of Social History*, Vol. 14, No. 1, pp. 67–81.

Michael, D. (1973) *On Learning to Plan and Planning to Learn* (San Francisco: Jossey-Bass).

Middaugh, J.K. (1988) 'Management Control In The Financial Services Industry', *Business Horizons*, May–June.

Milani, K. (1975) 'The Relationship of Participation in Budget Setting to Industrial Supervisor Performance and Attitudes: A Field Study', *The Accounting Review*, Vol. 1, No. 2, pp. 274–83.

Miles, R.E. and C.C. Snow (1978) *Organisational Strategy, Structure and Process* (New York: McGraw-Hill).

Miller, D. (1990) *The Icarus Paradox: How Excellent Organisations Can Bring About Their Own Downfall* (New York: Harper Business).

Miller, D. and P.H. Friesen (1980) 'Momentum and revolution in organisational adaptation', *Academy of Management Journal*, Vol. 23, pp. 591–614.

Miller, D. and P.H. Friesen (1984) *Organisations: A Quantum View* (Englewood Cliffs, NJ: Prentice-Hall).

Miller, E.J. (1976) 'Task, Territory and Technology', in E.J. Miller *Task and Organisation* (London: John Wiley).

Miller, P. and T. O'Leary (1987) 'Accounting and the Construction of the Governable Person', *Accounting, Organizations and Society*, Vol. 12, No. 3, pp. 235–65.

Mintzberg, H. (1973) *The Nature of Managerial Work*. Harper and Row.

Mintzberg, H. (1978) 'Patterns in Strategy Formation', *Management Science*, May, pp. 934–48.

Mintzberg, H. (1979) *The Structuring of Organisations* (Englewood Cliffs, NJ: Prentice-Hall).

Mintzberg, H. (1983) *Power In and Around Organisations* (Englewood Cliffs, NJ: Prentice-Hall).

Mintzberg, H. and J. Waters (1985) 'On Strategies Deliberate and Emergent', *Strategic Management Journal*, pp. 25–37.

Monden, Y. and M. Sakurai (eds) (1990) *Japanese Management Accounting* (New York: Productivity Press).

Morden, T. (1993) *Business Strategy and Planning* (London: McGraw-Hill).

Morgan, G. (1986) *Images of Organisation* (London: Sage, Beverly Hills).

Morgan, G. (1979) 'Internal Audit Role Conflict: A Pluralist View' *Managerial Finance*, Vol. 5, pp. 160–70.

Morrison, I. (1989) 'The Cultural Revolution In Banking: A 20-Year Perspective', Chartered Institute of Bankers' Cambridge Seminar.

Munro, R.J.B. and D.J. Halterly (1993) 'Accountability and the New Commercial Agenda', *Critical Perspectives on Accounting*, Vol. 4, No. 4, pp. 369–95.

National Health Service (1983) *Management Inquiry Report* (The Griffiths Report) (London: Department of Health and Social Security).

Nelson, R. and S. Winter (1982) *An Evolutionary Theory of Economic Change* (Cambridge, Mass.: Harvard University Press).

Newman, W.H. and J.P. Logan (1971) *Strategy, Policy and Central Management* (Cincinnati: South-Western Publishing).

Northcott, D. (1991) 'Rationality and Decision Making in Capital Budgeting', *British Accounting Review*, Vol. 23, No. 3, pp. 219–234.

Northcott, D. (1992) *Captial Investment Decision Making* (London: CIMA/Academic Press).

Otley, D. (1978) 'Budget Use and Managerial Performance', *Journal of Accounting Research* Vol. 1, No. 6, pp. 122–49.

Otley, D. (1990) 'Issues in Accountability and Control: some observations from a study of colliery accountability in the British coal corporation', *Management Accounting Research*, Vol. 1, pp. 101–23.

Otley, D. and A.J. Berry (1980) 'Control, Organization and Accounting', *Accounting, Organizations and Society*, Vol. 5, No. 2, pp. 231–46.

Ouchi, W.G. (1977) 'The Relationship between Organizational Structure and Organizational Control', *Administrative Science Quarterly*, Vol. 22, pp. 95–112.

Ouchi, W.G. (1979) 'A Conceptual Framework for the Design of Organisational Control Mechanisms', *Management Science*, Vol. 25, No. 9, pp. 833–49

Ouchi, W.G. (1980) 'Markets, Bureaucracies and Clans', *Administrative Science Quarterly*, Vol. 25, No. 1, pp. 129–41.

Ouchi, W.G. (1981) *Theory Z* (Reading, Mass.: Addison-Wesley).

Parker, L.D. (1979) 'Divisional Performance Measurement: Beyond an Exclusive Profit Test', *Accounting, and Business Research*, Autumn, pp. 309–19.

Parsons, T. (1964) *Social Systems* (New York: The Free Press).

Pascale, R.T. (1990) *Managing on the Edge: How Successful Companies Use Conflict to Stay Ahead* (London: Viking Penguin).

Pascale, R.T. and A.G. Athos (1981) *The Art of Japanese Management* (New York: Simon and Schuster).

Pask, G. (1961) *An Approach to Cybernetics* (London: Hutchinson).

Perrin, J. (1987) 'Resource Management and Clinical Budgeting', *Journal of Management in Medicine*, Vol.2, No. 2, pp. 99–106.

Perrin, J. (1988) *Resource Management in the N.H.S.* (Woringham: Van Nostrand Reinhold (UK), in Association with Health Services Management Centre).

Perrow, C. (1967) 'A Framework for the Comparative Analysis of Organisations', *American Sociological Review*, April, pp. 194–208.

Perrow, C. (1970) *Organisational Analysis: A Sociological View* (London: Tavistock).

Perrow, C. (1986) *Complex Organisations*, 3rd Edn (New York: Random House).

Peters, T.J. and R.H. Waterman (1982) *In Search of Excellence* (New York: Harper and Rowe, New York).

Pettigrew, A.M. (1979) 'On Studying Organisational Cultures', *Administrative Science Quarterly*, Vol. 24, pp. 570–81

Pettigrew, A.M. (1985) *The Awakening Giant: Continuity and Change in Imperial Chemical Industries* (Oxford: Basil Blackwell).

Pettigrew, A.M., L. McKee and E. Ferlie (1989) 'Hints on How to Ring the Changes', *Health Service Journal*, 16 February.

Pfeffer, J. (1981) 'Management as Symbolic Action: The Creation and Maintenance of Organisational Paradigms', in L.L. Cummings and B.M. Staw (eds), *Research in Organizational Behavior* (Greenwich, Conn: JAI Press) pp. 1–52.

Pfeffer, J. and C.R. Salanick (1977) *The External Control of Organisations: A Resource Dependent Perspective* (New York/London: Harper and Row).

Pike, R. (1983) 'The Capital Budgeting Behaviour and Corporate Characteristics of Capital-Constrained Firms', *Journal of Business Finance and Accounting*, Vol. 10, pp. 663–72.

Pike, R. (1988) 'An Empirical Study of the Adoption of Sophisticated Capital Budgeting Practices and Decision-Making Effectiveness', *Accounting and Business Research*, Vol. 18, pp. 341–51.

Piore, M.J. and C.F. Sabel (1984) *The Second Industrial Divide: Prospects For Prosperity* (New York: Basic Books).

Pollert, A. (1988) 'The "Flexible Firm": Fixation or Fact?', *Work, Employment and Society*, Vol. 2, No. 3, pp. 281–316.

Porter, M.E. (1985) *Competitive Advantage, Creating and Sustaining Superior Performance* (New York: The Free Press).

Preston, A.M. (1991) 'Budgeting, Creativity and Culture', in D. Ashton, T. Hopper and R.W. Scapens (eds), *Issues In Management Accounting* (Hemel Hempstead: Prentice Hall).

Purdy, D.E., (1991) 'Natural Learning in Committee B', *Management Education and Development*, Vol. 22, Part 1, pp. 60–70.

Purdy, D.E. (1993a) 'Accounting, Controls, Change and the Perceptions of Managers: A Longitudinal Study of Ward Units in a Teaching Hospital', *Financial Accountability and Management*, Vol. 9, No. 1, pp. 45–66

Purdy, D.E. (1993b) 'Ward Sisters and Financial Management Accounting', *Financial Accountability and Management*, Vol. 9, No. 4, pp. 279–96.

Putterman, L. (1986) *The Economic Nature of the Firm: a Reader* (Cambridge: Cambridge University Press).

Putterman, L. (1988) 'The Firm as Association versus the Firm as Commodity', *Economics and Philosophy*, Vol. 4, pp. 243–66.

Quinn, J.B. (1980) *Strategies for change: Logical Incrementalism* (Homewood, Ill.: Richard D. Irwin).

Radcliffe-Brown, A.R. (1952) *Structure and Function in Primitive Society* (Oxford: Oxford University Press).

Reece, J.S. and W.R. Cool (1978) 'Measuring investment centre performance', *Harvard Business Review*, May–June, pp. 29–49.

Ricketts, D. and J. Gray (1988) *Managerial Accounting* (Boston: Houghton Mifflin).

Roethlisberger, F.J. and W.J. Dickson (1964) *Management and the Worker* (New York: John Wiley).

Ronen, J. and J.L. Livingstone (1975) 'An Expectancy Theory Approach to the Motivational Impact of Budgets', *The Accounting Review*, Vol. 50, pp. 893–903.

Ronen, J. and S. Sadan (1981) *Smoothing Income Numbers* (Reading: Addison-Wesley)).

Rose, M. (1975) *Industrial Behaviour: Theoretical Development Since Taylor* (London: Allen Lane).

Roy, D.F. (1960) '"Banana Time" Job Satisfaction and Informal Interaction', *Human Organization*, pp. 158–68.

Roy, D.F. (1973) 'Banana Time, Job Satisfaction and Informal Interaction', in G. Salaman and K. Thompson (eds), *Control and Ideology in Organisations* (Milton Keynes: Open University Press).

Salaman, G. (1979) *Work Organization: Resistance and Control* (London; Longman).

Scapens, R.W. (1991) *Management Accounting: a review of contemporary developments*, 2nd edn (London: Macmillan).

Scapens, R.W. and J. Roberts (1993) 'Accounting and Control: a case study of resistance to accounting change', *Management Accounting Research*, No. 1, pp. 1–32.

Schein, E.H. (1984) 'Coming to a New Awareness of Organisational Culture', *Sloan Management Review*, Vol. 25, Winter, pp. 3–16

Schein, E.H. (1985) *Organisational Culture and Leadership* (San Francisco: Jossey-Bass).

Schiff, M. and A.Y. Lewin (1970) 'The Impact of People on Budgets', *The Accounting Review*, Vol. 45, pp. 259–268.

Schoderbeck, P.P., C.G. Schoderbeck and A.G. Kefalas (1975) *Management Systems: Conceptual Considerations* (Dallas: Business Publishers).

Schon, D.A. (1983) *The Reflective Practitioner* (New York: Basic Books).

Schonberger, R. (1986) *World Class Manufacturing* (New York: The Free Press).

Schreyogg, G. and Steinmann, H. (1987) 'Strategic Control: A New Perspective', *Academy of Management Review*, Vol. 12, No. 1, pp. 91–103.

Schwenk, C. (1984) 'Cognitive simplification processes in strategic decision-making', *Strategic Management Journal*, Vol. 5, pp. 111–28.

Schwenk, C. (1988) *The Essence of Strategic Decision Making* (Lexington, Mass.: Lexington Books).

Scott, B.R. (1971) 'Stages *Four of* Corporate Development – Part 1', Harvard Business School Case Services.

Seal, W.B. (1993) *Accounting, Management Control and Business Organisation: an institutionalist perspective* (Aldershot: Avebury).

Senge, P. (1993) *Fifth Discipline: Art and Practice of the Learning Organisation* (New Canon CT: Business Books).

Sephton, M. and Ward, T. (1990) 'ABC in Retrail Financial Services' *Management Accountant*, Vol. 13, pp. 29–33.

Shaiken, H., S. Herzenberg and S. Kuhn (1986) 'The Work Process Under More Flexible Production', *Industrial Relations (US)*, Vol. 23, No. 2, pp. 167–83.

Shapiro, S.P. (1987) 'The Social Control of Impersonal Trust', *American Journal of Sociology*, Vol. 93, No. 3, pp. 623–58.

Sheldon, A. (1980) 'Organisational Paradigms: A Theory of Organisational Change', *Organisational Dynamics*, Vol. 8, No. 3, pp. 61–71.

Shillinglaw, G.D. (1982) *Cost Accounting Analysis and Control* (Homewood, Ill.: Richard D. Irwin).

Simmonds, K. (1981) 'Strategic Management Accounting', *Management Accounting*, April, pp. 26–9.

Simon, H. (1957) *Administrative Behavior* (New York: Free Press).

Simon, Herbert, Guetzkow, H., Kozmetsky, G. and Tyndall, G. (1957) *Centralization versus Decentralization in the Controller's Department* (New York: Controllship Foundation).

Simons, R. (1987a) 'Accounting Control Systems and Business Strategy: An Empirical Analysis', *Accounting, Organisations and Society*, Vol. 12, No. 4, pp. 357–74.

Simons, R. (1987b) 'Planning, Control and Uncertainty: A Process View', in W.J. Bruns and R.S. Kaplan (eds), *Accounting and Management – Field Study Perspectives* (Boston, Mass.: Harvard Business School Press) pp. 339–62.

Simons, R. (1990) 'The Role of Management Control Systems in Creating Competitive Advantage: New Perspectives', *Accounting, Organizations and Society*, Vol. 15,

No. 1/2, pp. 127–43

Sims, H. and D. Gioia (1986) *The Thinking Organisation* (San Francisco: Jossey-Bass).

Skinner, R.C. (1990) 'The role of profitability in divisional decision making and performance evaluation', *Accounting and Business Research*, Spring, Vol. 20, pp. 135–41

Smircich, L. (1983) 'Concepts of Culture and Organizational Analysis', *Administrative Science Quarterly*, Vol. 28, No. 2, pp. 328–58.

Smith, P. (1987) 'Control In Banks', *Banking World*, Feb., pp. 21.

Smith, C. (1989) 'Flexible Specialization, Automation and Mass Production', *Work, Employment and Society*, Vol. 3, No. 2, pp. 203–20.

Smith, P. (1990) 'The use of performance indicators in the public sector', *Journal of the Royal Statistical Society*, Series A, No. 153, pp. 53–72.

Smith, P. (1993) 'Outcome-related performance indicators and organizational control in the public sector', *British Journal of Management*,Vol. 4, No. 3, pp. 135–52.

Smyth, P.S. and P.B. Checkland (1976) 'Using a Systems Approach: The Structure of Root Definitions', *Journal of Applied Systems Analysis*, Vol. 5, No. 1.

Solomons, D. (1965) *Divisional Performances: Measurement and Control* (Homewood, Ill.: Richard D. Irwin).

Spicer, B. (1990) 'New Directions In Management Accounting Practice and Research', *Management Accounting Research*, Vol. 1, pp. 139–54.

Spicer, B.H. and V. Ballew (1983) 'Management Accounting Systems and the Economics of Internal Organization', *Accounting, Organizations and Society*, Vol. 8, pp. 73–96.

Sproull, L.S. (1981) 'Beliefs in Organizations' in P.C. Nystrom and W.H. Starbuck (eds), *Handbook of Organisational Design*, Vol. 2 (Oxford: Oxford University Press).

Stacey, R.D. (1993) *Strategic Management and Organisational Dynamics* (London: Pitman Publishing).

Starbuck, W.H. and B. Hedberg (1977) 'Saving an Organisation from a stagnating Environment', in H.B. Thorelli (Ed.), *Strategy + Structure = Performance* (Bloomington: Indiana University Press) pp. 249–58.

Starkey, K., M. Wright and S. Thompson (1991) 'Flexibility, Hierarchy and Markets', *British Journal of Management*, Vol. 2, pp. 165–76.

Steers, R.M. (1975) 'Problems in the Measurement of Organisational Effectiveness', *Administrative Science Quarterly*, December, pp. 613–29.

Stewart, J.D. (1984) 'The role of information in public accountability', in A. Hopwood and C. Tomkins (eds), *Issues in Public Sector Accounting* (Oxford: Philip Allan).

Stewart, R. (1967) *The Reality of Management* (London: Macmillan).

Strong, P. and J. Robinson (1988) 'New Model Management: Griffiths and the N.H.S.', Nursing Policy Studies Centre, University of Warwick.

Swieringa, R.J. and Weick, K.E. (1987) 'Management Accounting and Action' *Accounting Organisations and Society*. Vol. 12 No. 3 pp. 293–308.

Taylor, F.W. (1911, reprinted 1947) *Scientific Management* (New York, Harper and Brothers).

Taylor, S. and J. Crocker (1983) 'Schematic Bases of Social Information Processing', In E.T. Higgens, C.P. Herman and M.P. Zamna Izanna (eds), *Social Cognition: The Ontario Symposium* (Hillsdale, NJ: Earlbaum).

Teubner, G. (1983) 'Substantive and Reflexive Elements in Modern Law', *Law and Society Review*, Vol. 18, no. 2, pp. 291–301.

Thode, S.F. (1986) 'The trouble with Divisional Hurdle Rates', *Business Horizons*, Jan–Feb., pp. 62–6.

Thompson, J.D. (1967) *Organizations in Action* (New York: McGraw-Hill).

Thompson, J.D. and A. Tuden (1959) 'Strategies, Structures and Processes' in J.D. Thompson (eds), *Comparative Studies in Administration* (Pittsburg: University of Pittsburg Press).

Thompson, S. and M. Wright (eds) (1988) *Internal Organisation, Efficiency and Profit* (Oxford: Philip Allan).

Tinker, T. (1988) 'Panglossian Accounting Theories: the Science of Apologising in Style', *Accounting, Organizations, and Society*, Vol. 13, No. 2, pp. 165–89.

Tocher, K. (1970) 'Control', *Operational Research Quarterly*, June, pp. 159–80.

Tocher, K. (1976) 'Notes for Discussion on Control', *Operational Research Quarterly*, June, pp. 231–9.

Tolman, E.C. (1949) 'There is More than One Kind of Learning', *Psychological Review*, Vol. 56, pp. 144–55.

Tomkins, C. (1973) *Financial Planning in Divisional Companies* (London: Haymarket Publishing).

Tosi, H. (1975) 'The Human Effects of Managerial Budgeting Systems', in J.H. Livingson (ed), *Management Accounting: The Behavioral Foundations* (Columbus, Ohio: Grid).

Trist, E. (1976) 'A Concept of Organizational Ecology', *Australian Journal of Management*, Vol. 2.

Trumpington, Baroness (1987) 'OR in government', *Journal of the Operational Research Society*, Vol. 38, pp. 907–12.

United Kingdom Government (1991) *The Citizen's Charter* (London: HMSO).

Urwick, L.F. (1947) *The Elements of Administration* (London: Pitman).

Van Gusteren, H.R. (1976) *The Quest for Control* (London: John Wiley)

Vancil, R.F. (1979) *Decentralisation: Ambiguity by Design* (Homewood, Ill.: Richard D. Wiley).

Veblen, T. (1953) *The Theory of the Leisure Class* (New York: Mentor Book, New American Library.

Vickers, G. (1965) *The Art of Judgement: A Study of Policy Making* (London: Methuen).

Vickers, G. (1967) *Towards a Sociology of Management* (London: Chapman and Hall).

Waldron, L. (1988) 'Accounting for CIM: The New Yardsticks', *EMAP Business and Computing Supplement*), February, pp. 1–2.

Watts, R.L. and J.L. Zimmerman (1979) 'The Demand and Supply of Accounting Theories: The Market for Excuses', *Accounting Review*, Vol. 54, April pp. 273–305.

Watts, R.L. and J.L. Zimmerman (1986) *Positive Accounting Theory* (New York: Prentice-Hall).

Watzlawick, P., P. Weakland and J.H. Fisch (1974) *Change: Principles of Problem Formation and Problem Resolution* (New York: W.W. Norton).

Weber, M. (1922 translated 1968) *Economy and Society* (New York: Bedminster Press).

Weber, M. (1948) 'The Social Psychology of the World Religions', in H.H. Gerth and C.W. Mills (eds) *From Max Weber* (London: Routledge and Keegan Paul) pp. 267–301.

Weick, K.E. (1976) 'Educational Organisations as Loosely Coupled Systems', *Administrative Science Quarterly*, Vol. 21, pp. 1–19.

Weick, K.E. (1979) *The Social Psychology of Organising*, 2nd Edn (New York: Random House).

Weick, K.E. (1983) 'Managerial Thought in the Context of Action', in S. Srivastva (ed.), *The Executive Mind* (San Francisco: Jossey-Bass).

Weiner, N. (1948) *Cybernetics* (Cambridge, Mass.: MIT Press).

Weitzman, M. (1976) 'The new Soviet incentive system', *Bell Journal of Economics and Management Science*, Vol. 7, pp. 251–7.

Welch, J.B. and Kainen T.L. (1983) 'Risk adjusted multiple hurdle rates: Better capital budgeting', *Financial Executive*, May.

Whyte W.F. (1948) *Human Relations in the Restaurant Industry* (New York: McGraw-Hill)

Wildavsky, A. (1975) *Budgeting: A Comparative Theory of Budgetary Processes* (Boston: Little, Brown).

Williams, K., J. Williams and C. Haslam (1989a) 'Do Labour Costs Really Matter?', *Work, Employment and Society*, Vol. 3, No. 3, pp. 281–305.

Williams, K., J. Williams and C. Haslam (1989b) 'Why take the stocks out? Britain v. Japan', *International Journal of Operations and Production Management*, Vol. 9, No. 8.

Williams, K. and C. Haslam (1991) 'How far from Japan?', *Critical Perspectives in Accounting*, Vol. 2, pp. 145–69.

Williams, K. J. Williams and C. Haslam (1992) 'Against Lean Production', *Economy and Society*, Vol. 21, No. 3, pp. 321–54.

Williamson, O.E. (1970) *Corporate Control and Business Behavior* (Englewood Cliffs, NJ: Prentice-Hall).

Williamson, O.E. (1973) 'Markets and Hierarchies: Some Elementary Considerations', *American Economic Association*, Vol. 63, No. 2.

Williamson, O.E. (1975) *Markets and Hierarchies: Analysis and Antitrust Implications* (New York: Free Press).

Williamson, O.E. (1985) *The Economic Institutions of Capitalism* (New York: The Free Press).

Wilson, R.M.S. and W.F. Chua (1992) *Managerial Accounting: Method and Meaning* (London: VNR).

Wolk, H., Q. Gerber and G. Porter (1988) *Management Accounting* (Boston: PWS-Kent).

Woodward, J. (1958a) *Management and Technology* (London, HMSO).

Woodward, J. (1958b) *Industrial Organisation: Theory and Practice,* reprinted 1965 (Oxford: Oxford University Press).

Wrong, D. (1961) 'The Oversocialized Concept of Man in Modern Sociology', *American Sociological Review*, Vol. 26, April, pp. 183–93.

Index